"A report from the front, the unconscionable front, which has brought an assault on our bodies, with its devastating price on individuals and families. Here is the work of clinicians who engage with the troubled bodies and eating of our times as they theorise their understandings and learning. There is much to learn here."

– Susie Orbach is a psychoanalyst and psychotherapist, co-founder of The Women's Therapy Centre. Her books include *Fat Is a Feminist Issue*, *Hunger Strike*, and the award-winning *Bodies*. Her most recent is *In Therapy*, annotated sessions from her BBC Radio series of the same name.

"Tom Wooldridge has assembled an impressive array of contributors to offer a rich and valuable survey of the contemporary psychodynamic approach to eating disorders. New therapeutic conceptualizations, including mentalization- and emotion regulation–based strategies, are applied to the special circumstances involved in eating disorders. At the same time, the deep traditional analytic insights are included and updated: Freudian, Kleinian, newer Object Relational, Developmental Psychoanalytic, and Self Psychology. All of this is coordinated with an interest in the effects of contemporary culture on how eating disorders develop and present, including attention to the 'pro-anorexia' groupings emerging on the internet and the occurrence of eating disorders in boys and men. This book will be invaluable to any practitioner working with such patients, and of significant interest to all."

– Stephen Seligman, DMH, Clinical Professor of Psychiatry, University of California, San Francisco; author of *Relationships in Development: Infancy, Intersubjectivity, and Attachment*; Joint Editor-in-Chief, *Psychoanalytic Dialogues*; Training and Supervising Analyst, Psychoanalytic Institute of Northern California & San Francisco Center for Psychoanalysis.

"*Psychoanalytic Treatment of Eating Disorders: When Words Fail and Bodies Speak* is an indispensable volume of psychoanalytically informed contributions to the literature on eating disorders. This irresistible recipe combines one part theory with two parts clinical wisdom. I was especially drawn to the treatment of the roles of specific emotions, like shame and anxiety. Equally useful for the seasoned clinician and those at earlier stages of their careers, this is a worthy addition to any clinician's library. These 15 authors represent the best in the field."

– Sandra Buechler, PhD, Author of *Understanding and Treating Patients in Clinical Psychoanalysis: Lessons from Literature*. Training and Supervising Analyst, the William A. White Institute, New York.

"Wooldridge provides us with a valuable collection of papers on the conceptualization and treatment of eating disorders. He also presents us with several chapters on contemporary cultural issues, including social media, which impact patients with eating disorders. Wooldridge and the contributing authors are keenly aware that eating-disordered patients are among the most difficult to treat. These patients present clinicians with potentially life-threatening crises and the possible need for substantial ancillary care. These assembled authors do not shy away from the thorny problem of combining psychoanalytic containment and understanding with the variations in frame needed to ensure safety, such as the potential necessity for a treatment team and hospitalization."

– Mary Brady, PhD, Author of *The Body in Adolescence: Psychic Isolation and Physical Symptoms.*

"For too long there has been a divide between psychoanalytic thinking and the treatment of eating disorders. This vital collection of essays is a key step in bridging that gap. Through vivid clinical examples, new theoretical advances are illuminated in ways that promise to deepen our understanding of eating disorders. With impressive clarity, this collection is a vital addition to the field that will extend what we understand as psychoanalytic. It will be of real value to both students and seasoned clinicians."

– Peter Carnochan, PhD, Author of *Looking for Ground: Countertransference and the Problem of Value in Psychoanalysis* (Relational Perspectives Book Series).

"This anthology of papers offers its readers what a skillful psychoanalytic treatment can offer an eating-disordered patient: it reintroduces meaning, metaphor, and substance into an otherwise concrete, impoverished, and symptom-dominated existence. As editor, Wooldridge has brought together an impressive anthology of papers that integrates multiple psychoanalytic perspectives. Without minimizing the need for symptom management with eating-disordered patients, Wooldridge's emphasis is on integrating classical psychoanalytic conceptualizations of eating disorders with contemporary psychoanalytic thinking, on development, phenomenology, affect regulation, dissociation, attachment, mentalization, and socio-cultural context. The individual chapters are theoretically and clinically rich, varied, thought provoking, and useful. They will nourish and hold both beginning and seasoned clinicians in their struggle to find words that can touch and transform those patients for whom words have perilously failed."

– Sarah Schoen, PhD, Supervising Analyst and Faculty at the William Alanson White Institute; Faculty at NYU Postdoctoral Program in Psychotherapy and Psychoanalysis, and Co-Editor of *Unknowable, Unspeakable, and Unsprung: Psychoanalytic Perspectives on Scandal, Truth, Secrets and Lies.*

PSYCHOANALYTIC TREATMENT OF EATING DISORDERS

Psychoanalytic Treatment of Eating Disorders: When Words Fail and Bodies Speak offers a compilation of some of the most innovative thinking on psychoanalytic approaches to the treatment of eating disorders available today. In its recognition of the multiple meanings of food, weight, and body shape, psychoanalytic thinking is uniquely positioned to illuminate the complexities of these often life-threatening conditions. And while clinicians regularly draw on psychoanalytic ideas in the treatment of eating disorders, many of the unique insights psychoanalysis provides have been neglected in the contemporary literature.

This volume brings together some of the most respected clinicians in the field and speaks to the psychoanalytic conceptualization and treatment of eating disorders as well as contemporary issues, including social media, pro-anorexia forums, and larger cultural issues such as advertising, fashion, and even agribusiness. Drawing on new theoretical developments, several chapters propose novel models of treatment, whereas others delve into the complex convergence of culture and psychology in this patient population.

Psychoanalytic Treatment of Eating Disorders will be of interest to all psychoanalysts and psychotherapists working with this complex and multi-faceted phenomenon.

Tom Wooldridge, PsyD, CEDS, is Chair in the Department of Psychology at Golden Gate University, San Francisco, CA, and an Executive Director at the National Association for Males with Eating Disorders. He has published numerous journal articles and book chapters on topics such as eating disorders, masculinity, technology, and psychoanalytic treatment. His first book, *Understanding Anorexia Nervosa in Males: An Integrative Approach*, was published by Routledge in 2016. He is an advanced candidate at the Psychoanalytic Institute of Northern California and has a private practice in Berkeley, CA.

Relational perspectives book series

LEWIS ARON & ADRIENNE HARRIS
Series Co-Editors
STEVEN KUCHUCK & EYAL ROZMARIN
Associate Editors

The Relational Perspectives Book Series (RPBS) publishes books that grow out of or contribute to the relational tradition in contemporary psychoanalysis. The term *relational psychoanalysis* was first used by Greenberg and Mitchell[1] to bridge the traditions of interpersonal relations, as developed within interpersonal psychoanalysis and object relations, as developed within contemporary British theory. But, under the seminal work of the late Stephen A. Mitchell, the term *relational psychoanalysis* grew and began to accrue to itself many other influences and developments. Various tributaries – interpersonal psychoanalysis, object relations theory, self-psychology, empirical infancy research, and elements of contemporary Freudian and Kleinian thought – flow into this tradition, which understands relational configurations between self and others, both real and fantasized, as the primary subject of psychoanalytic investigation.

We refer to the relational tradition, rather than to a relational school, to highlight that we are identifying a trend, a tendency within contemporary psychoanalysis, not a more formally organized or coherent school or system of beliefs. Our use of the term *relational* signifies a dimension of theory and practice that has become salient across the wide spectrum of contemporary psychoanalysis. Now under the editorial supervision of Lewis Aron and Adrienne Harris, with the assistance of Associate Editors Steven Kuchuck and Eyal Rozmarin, the Relational Perspectives Book Series originated in 1990 under the editorial eye of the late Stephen A. Mitchell. Mitchell was the most prolific and influential of the originators of the relational tradition. Committed to dialogue among psychoanalysts, he abhorred the authoritarianism that dictated adherence to a rigid set of beliefs or technical restrictions. He championed open discussion, comparative and integrative approaches, and promoted new voices across the generations.

Included in the Relational Perspectives Book Series are authors and works that come from within the relational tradition, and extend and develop that tradition, as well as works that critique relational approaches or compare and contrast it with alternative points of view. The series includes our most distinguished senior psychoanalysts, along with younger contributors who bring fresh vision. A full list of titles in this series is available at www.routledge.com/mentalhealth/series/LEARPBS.

Note

1 Greenberg, J., & Mitchell, S. (1983). *Object relations in psychoanalytic theory*. Cambridge, MA: Harvard University Press.

PSYCHOANALYTIC TREATMENT OF EATING DISORDERS

When Words Fail and Bodies Speak

Edited by Tom Wooldridge

Routledge
Taylor & Francis Group
LONDON AND NEW YORK

RBP

First published 2018
by Routledge
2 Park Square, Milton Park, Abingdon, Oxon OX14 4RN

and by Routledge
605 Third Avenue, New York, NY 10017

Routledge is an imprint of the Taylor & Francis Group, an informa business

British Library Cataloguing in Publication Data
A catalogue record for this book is available from the British Library

Library of Congress Cataloging in Publication Data
Names: Wooldridge, Tom, editor.
Title: Psychoanalytic treatment of eating disorders : when words fail and bodies speak / edited by Tom Wooldridge.
Description: Milton Park, Abingdon, Oxon ; New York, NY : Routledge, 2018.
Identifiers: LCCN 2017033101| ISBN 9781138702011 (hardback) | ISBN 9781138702042 (paperback) | ISBN 9781315203706 (master) | ISBN 9781351788816 (epub) | ISBN 9781351788809 (mobipocket)
Subjects: LCSH: Eating disorders—Treatment. | Psychoanalysis. | Psychotherapy.
Classification: LCC RC552.E18 P793 2018 | DDC 616.85/260651—dc23
LC record available at https://lccn.loc.gov/2017033101

ISBN: 978-1-138-70201-1 (hbk)
ISBN: 978-1-138-70204-2 (pbk)
ISBN: 978-1-315-20370-6 (ebk)

Typeset in Times New Roman
by Apex CoVantage, LLC

CONTENTS

ACKNOWLEDGMENTS

I am delighted to offer this book to the larger community, because it represents an aspiration I've had for a long time: to build bridges between the (often deeply divided) worlds of eating disorders treatment and psychoanalytic thinking. And writing the Acknowledgements section of this book is a particular pleasure, both because it offers me a chance to express my sincere gratitude to the many different individuals and groups who have been involved in this project and what it represents over the past few years and, equally important, because it signals my bringing this long gestation to a close.

My foremost appreciation goes to all the talented psychotherapists and writers who have submitted chapters to this book. I appreciate your confidence in what I envisioned. In addition, I'm thankful for Susan Warshaw's confidence in my proposal for a special issue of the *Journal of Infant, Child, and Adolescent Psychotherapy*; that project acquainted me with many of the authors whose chapters appear in the present volume.

My professional home at Golden Gate University provides a launching pad for my clinical work and research pursuits. I am especially fortunate to have such wonderful colleagues who support the Psychology Department. Molly Meksavan, Frances Sadaya, Cassandra Dilosa, and Nancy Lagomarsino have all helped to keep the department running during the months I was absorbed in writing and editing. I am also fortunate to be connected in my professional life to two wonderful organizations. My colleagues at the National Association for Males with Eating Disorders (NAMED) inspire me with their dedication of time, energy, and enthusiasm for this cause. And I am grateful to be a member of the Psychoanalytic Institute of Northern California. Finally, my deepest appreciation and love go to my family, especially my wife, Caroline Mok, PhD, who is also my colleague, and our son, Parker, who makes the larger world matter more than I had thought possible.

I wish to thank *The Journal of Child Psychotherapy*, which granted permissions for reproducing Chapter 2, and *The Journal of Infant, Child, and Adolescent Psychotherapy*, which allowed me to reproduce Chapters 1, 4, 6, 7, 8, 9, 10, 12, 13, and 15.

CONTRIBUTORS

About the Editor

Tom Wooldridge, PsyD, CEDS, is Department Chair and Assistant Professor in the Department of Psychology at Golden Gate University, San Francisco, CA. His book, *Understanding Anorexia Nervosa in Males*, was published by Routledge in 2016. He has also published numerous articles and book chapters on eating disorders, masculinity, technology, and psychoanalytic treatment and is on the editorial board of *Eating Disorders: The Journal of Treatment & Prevention.* In addition, Tom is an Executive Director of the National Association for Males with Eating Disorders, has a private practice in Berkeley, CA, and is an advanced candidate at the Psychoanalytic Institute of Northern California.

Contributors

F. Diane Barth, LCSW, is a psychotherapist in New York City. She graduated from the Psychoanalytic Institute of the Postgraduate Center in 1982 and has been working with and writing and teaching about eating disorders since 1984. Recent articles include "Alexithymia, Affect Regulation and Binge Drinking in College Students" published in the *Journal of College Student Psychotherapy*; "Social Media and Adolescent Development: Hazards, Pitfalls and Opportunities for Growth" published in the *Clinical Social Work Journal*; and "Listening to Words, Hearing Feelings: Links Between Eating Disorders and Alexithymia," published in the *Clinical Social Work Journal* special issue on Twenty-First Century Perspectives on Eating Disorders and Body Image in March 2016, which she also co-guest edited.

Mary Brady, PhD, is an adult, adolescent and child psychoanalyst. She is on the faculty at the San Francisco Center for Psychoanalysis. She is in private practice in San Francisco. Her paper, "Invisibility and Insubstantiality in an Anorexic Adolescent: Phenomenology and Dynamics," was published in the 2011 *Journal of Child Psychotherapy*, *37*(1), 3–15. Her book, *The Body in Adolescence: Psychic Isolation and Physical Symptoms*, was published by Routledge in 2015. She co-leads a consultation group on "The Treatment of Adolescents and Young Adults."

Judith Brisman, PhD, is Founding Director of the Eating Disorder Resource Center in Manhattan. She is co-author of *Surviving an Eating Disorder: Strategies for Family and Friends*, is an associate editor of *Contemporary Psychoanalysis*, and is on the editorial board of the journal *Eating Disorders* (Bruner Mazel). She is a member of the teaching faculty of the William Alanson White Institute, and she maintains a private practice in New York City. Dr. Brisman is known internationally as among the first in her field to develop a treatment program for bulimic patients. She has published and lectured extensively regarding the interpersonal treatment of eating disorders.

Lorraine Caputo, LCSW, is the Director of The Trauma Studies Program at the Manhattan Institute for Psychoanalysis in New York City and is a graduate of the Institute's psychoanalytic training program. There, she teaches a course in the Trauma Studies Program on the Transgenerational Transmission of Trauma and is a Training Analyst in the five-year program. Ms. Caputo is in private practice in Manhattan and in Maplewood, New Jersey.

Antonella Granieri, PsyD, is an Associate Professor in Clinical Psychology and past Director of the Post-Graduate School in Clinical Psychology at the Department of Psychology, University of Turin. She is a psychoanalyst, Full Member of the Società Psicoanalitica Italiana [Italian Psychoanalytic Society] (S.P.I) and the International Psychoanalytic Society (I.P.A), Individual Member of the International Federation of Psychoanalytical Societies (IFPS), and Full Member of the Sándor Ferenczi Association.

Kim L. Grynick, MA, LPC, has specialized in the treatment of eating disorders for the past 20 years. She served as clinical director of the Center for Discovery and Adolescent Change, a residential treatment center for girls and boys with eating disorders, and Rainrock Residential Treatment Center for women with eating disorders. She has presented at national eating disorder conferences and is a member of the Academy for Eating Disorders, the International Association of Eating Disorder Professionals, the Columbia River Eating Disorders Network, and the International Association for Jungian Studies. Kim is also certified in Interpersonal Neurobiology. She is a second-year PhD student at Pacifica Graduate Institute in the Jungian and Archetypal Studies Program. Kim maintains Siskiyou Therapy in Ashland, Oregon, a private practice focusing on recovery from disordered eating.

Susan Gutwill, MSW, LCSW, is a sociologist and psychoanalytic psychotherapist. She is on the faculty of The Women's Therapy Centre Institute (WTCI) in New York City and of the Center for Psychotherapy and Psychoanalysis of New Jersey (CPPNJ). She is co-author of *Eating Problems: A Feminist Psychoanalytic Treatment Model* by Carol Bloom, Andrea Gitter, Laura Kogel, and Lela Zaphiroupoulos. She is also a co-editor and contributor to *Psychoanalysis, Class and Politics*, with Lynne Layton and Nancy Hollander. She also teaches in many settings, most recently a case study series co-sponsored by The Rutgers Graduate School Continuing Education program with CPPNJ. Her private practice is in Highland Park, NJ.

Yael Kadish, PhD, is a lecturer and researcher at the University of Witwatersand, a clinical psychologist, psychotherapist, and candidate in psychoanalytic training. Her research interests include psychoanalysis, broadly conceived; the experience of motherhood; eating disorders; socio-cultural construction of the female body; gender-based violence and psychosis. She has published widely on eating disorders.

Starr Kelton-Locke, PhD, is a clinical psychologist and psychoanalyst in private practice in Marin County, California. She has 29 years of experience in the field of eating disorders conducting treatment, educational trainings, and prevention services. Dr. Kelton-Locke has presented at national and international conferences on embodied intersubjectivity, relational and biological neural systems involved in depression and anxiety, mentalization-based treatment (MBT), sub-symbolic forms of communication, and eating disorders. Her training in MBT was with its founders, Peter Fonagy and Anthony Bateman, at the UCLA Semel Institute.

Danielle Novack, PhD, is a clinical psychologist in private practice in New York City, and a candidate at the NYU Postdoctoral Program in Psychotherapy and Psychoanalysis. She completed a postdoctoral fellowship with a specialization in eating disorders at New York University's student counseling center, and has worked at the Renfrew Center of New York and as part of the eating disorder team at Barnard College's student counseling service. Dr. Novack is Adjunct Clinical Supervisor at Pace University.

Jean Petrucelli, PhD, is Director and Co-Founder of the Eating Disorders, Compulsions & Addictions Service (EDCAS) and Chair and Founding Director of the Eating Disorders, Compulsions & Addictions one-year educational certificate program at The William Alanson White Institute for Psychotherapy and Psychoanalysis. She is Adjunct Clinical Professor for New York University's Postdoctoral Program in Psychotherapy and Psychoanalysis, an Adjunct Clinical Professor at the Institute for Contemporary Psychoanalysis, and an Associate Editor for *Contemporary Psychoanalysis*. Dr. Petrucelli is the Editor of *Body-States:*

Interpersonal and Relational Perspectives on the Treatment of Eating Disorders (Routledge, 2015), which won the 2016 American Board & Academy of Psychoanalysis Edited Book Award; *Knowing, Not-Knowing & Sort-of- Knowing: Psychoanalysis and the Experience of Uncertainty* (Karnac Books, 2010); and *Longing: Psychoanalytic Musings on Desire* (Karnac Books, 2006); Co-Editor of the book *Hungers and Compulsions: The Psychodynamic Treatment of Eating Disorders and Addictions* (Rowen & Littlefield, 2009, 2001) and most recently, Co-Editor with S. Schoen of *Unknowable, Unspeakable and Unsprung: Psychoanalytic Perspectives on Truth, Scandal, Secrets & Lies* (Routledge, 2016). Dr. Petrucelli specializes in the interpersonal treatment of eating disorders and addictions and lectures nationally and internationally at conferences, analytic institutes and societies, universities, and treatment facilities. She is in private practice on the upper west side in New York City.

Timothy Rice, MD, is Assistant Professor of Psychiatry in the Division of Child and Adolescent Psychiatry at the Icahn School of Medicine at Mount Sinai, New York City. With Leon Hoffman, MD, he has written *Regulation-Focused Psychotherapy for Children*, a manualized psychodynamic approach for children with oppositional defiant disorder. This model was recently extended to adolescents with eating disorders in *Psychodynamic Psychiatry* through a case report of an adolescent with anorexia nervosa cared for through this modality.

Dana A. Satir, PhD, CEDS, is a clinical psychologist in private practice specializing in adolescents and adults with eating disorders, mood dysregulation, and relational difficulties. Dr. Satir is also an Adjunct Instructor at the University of Denver where she teaches graduate courses on eating disorders and psychodynamic psychotherapy. She has published numerous case studies and research papers on the topics of countertransference, therapeutic alliance ruptures, and treating complexities in personality and eating disorders. In 2013, Dr. Satir was awarded an early career fellowship from the American Psychoanalytic Association for the advanced study of psychoanalysis.

Anthony P. Winston, FRCPsych, is Consultant in Eating Disorders at the Aspen Centre, Coventry and Warwickshire Partnership Trust. He trained in psychiatry and psychotherapy in Leicester, where he was Lecturer in Psychiatry of Eating Disorders at the University of Leicester and an Honorary Senior Registrar in Psychiatry and Psychotherapy. He has carried out research into attachment style and eating disorders. His previous papers include "Reading and Playing in the 'Potential Space'", "Projection, Introjection and Identity in Anorexia Nervosa," "The Oedipus Complex in Anorexia Nervosa" and "Anorexia Nervosa and the Psychotherapy of Absence."

Kathryn J. Zerbe, MD, FAED, is a Training and Supervising Analyst at Oregon Psychoanalytic Institute, Clinical Professor of Psychiatry at Oregon Health and

Science University, and Faculty Member, Institute for Contemporary Psychoanalysis. She has authored numerous papers, chapters, and reviews and three books about eating disorders, including her landmark contributions *The Body Betrayed: Women, Eating Disorders, and Treatment* and *Integrated Treatment of Eating Disorders: Beyond the Body Betrayed*. Dr. Zerbe speaks nationally and internationally about the psychodynamic issues of eating problems across the lifespan and in 2011 won the National Eating Disorder Association's Lifetime Achievement Award for her clinical, teaching, and writing contributions to the field.

INTRODUCTION

Contextualizing psychoanalytic approaches to eating disorders

Tom Wooldridge

I am delighted to introduce this anthology, *Psychoanalytic Treatment of Eating Disorders: When Words Fail and Bodies Speak*, devoted entirely to the psychoanalytic conceptualization and treatment of eating disorders. It is my hope that this book joins recent publications – Petrucelli (2014), Petrucelli and Stuart (2011), Zerbe (2008), and Orbach (2009) to name an important few – in addressing a significant gap in the literature and serves as a meaningful contribution to a larger dialogue about the integration of psychoanalytic and symptom-focused approaches to the treatment of these often life-threatening illnesses. In this collection, we have gathered a number of important contributions from clinicians with a long history of thinking about and working with eating disorders. Before I discuss these, however, I wish to provide some comments about the value of psychoanalytic approaches to the treatment of eating disorders and to contextualize contemporary psychoanalytic approaches within a broader historical framework.

Despite the long history of psychoanalytic contributions to the treatment of eating disorders, contemporary endeavors have lost sight of the insights our field has provided. In my own work, I am repeatedly struck by how little of the psychoanalytic sensibility – that is, an emphasis on the depth and complexity of the patient's subjective experience and how that experience is shaped through a developmental process – infuses eating disorders advocacy, research, and evidence-based treatment (see Wooldridge, in press and Wooldridge, 2016, for my own efforts to counter this trend). Indeed, these endeavors emphasize and endorse evidence-based treatment focused on rapid symptom reduction. For example, the "gold standard" treatment for adolescents with anorexia nervosa is family-based therapy, which promotes an "agnostic" position with regard to etiological factors, particularly the family's role in the child's developing an eating disorder (Lock et al., 2001). And in fact there is evidence suggesting that no particular family style is implicated in the development of anorexia nervosa (Eisler, 1995). Furthermore, this position can be effective in mitigating shame and stigma, which may facilitate treatment engagement – an essential first step in all work with this difficult population.

Yet therapists who work with eating and body image problems often hear stories about the crushing impact of multigenerational criticism about weight, body type, and appearance (Zerbe, 2016). We hear, too, about the multiple meanings of food, weight, and body shape and how those meanings are embedded in complex familial and cultural systems. Throughout all of this, we attempt to understand and resonate with the deep anguish conveyed by bodily sufferings. Reflecting on this difficult work, I have often thought that our emphasis on rapid symptom reduction signifies not only our intent to help as quickly as possible but, also, our need to evade confrontation with our patients' profound emotional pain (and perhaps, at times, our own).

Several years ago, I met with a 16-year-old patient named Sara. The first time we met, I knew that something terrible had happened. Despite her youth, her skin was pale and her hair gossamer. As we walked toward my office, the painful hollows of her cheeks and the spindly insubstantiality of her legs left me uncertain about whether she was appropriate for outpatient treatment or, in fact, about whether I wanted to work with her at all. Before we'd exchanged a few words, I was scrambling to digest the impact of her physical presence. When working with anorexic patients, I've often thought, "Something terrible has happened." Their bodies are the canvas on which this catastrophe is rendered and, more often than I'd like to admit, I am tempted to evade a full emotional confrontation with this catastrophe.

Ultimately, an emphasis on rapid symptom-reduction may lead us to neglect less overt, and less easily measurable, aspects of the patient's experience. Patients with eating disorders contend with a difficult emotional landscape marked by isolation and loneliness as well as shame, guilt, and embarrassment, not to mention a profound hopelessness about the possibilities of emotional connection. Yet help with these struggles will never be found in a pill or a set of therapeutic exercises, despite the potential usefulness of both. It is, instead, only through a meaningful emotional connection that we can help patients begin to "bear the unbearable and to say the unsayable" (Atwood, 2012, p. 118). Psychoanalysts have a long history of striving to help our patients with this daunting task, and it is to the history of this endeavor that we now turn.

Psychoanalytic conceptualization and treatment of eating disorders

Beginning with Freud himself,[1] psychoanalysts have attempted to make sense of the tormented inner lives and the puzzling variety of behaviors of patients with eating disorders. For the sake of clarity, these explanations can be grouped into three categories, according to the theoretical schools from which they originate and the order in which they appear in the professional literature: drive-conflict, object relations, and self-psychology. As a fourth category, we also review contemporary ways of thinking about these phenomena that encompass relational psychoanalytic and integrative approaches. Of course, these divisions are highly artificial, and clinicians likely draw from a variety of theories in their work with this population.

Drive-conflict

While utilized less often in contemporary thinking about eating disorders, the drive-conflict model provides a way of thinking about the psychosexual meaning of eating-disordered symptoms as well as patients' ongoing efforts to negotiate a balance between these three aspects of the self – id, ego, and superego – which are often at cross purposes. A number of early theorists linked anorexia nervosa (the eating disorder that received the most attention, likely because of its visually striking symptomatology) and other eating disorders to problems in the oral phase of psychosexual development, highlighting the massively punitive superego and extreme self-denial that accompanied these patients' normal oral impulses. In addition, a number of early clinicians suggested that self-starvation was a defense against fantasies of oral impregnation (Moulton, 1942; Rowland, 1970; Waller, Kaufman, & Deutsch, 1940). Still others saw the patient's refusal of food as a defense against oral sadistic fantasies (Berlin, Boatman, Scheimo, & Szurek, 1951; Masserman, 1941).

Beginning with Anna Freud (1946), who saw disturbances in infantile feeding as a clear manifestation of ambivalence toward the mother, several authors have suggested that many of the functions tied to food and eating – incorporation and expulsion, frustration and gratification, love and hate – were manifestations of oral ambivalence and thus implicated in the dynamics of anorexia nervosa (Thomä, 1967; Ritvo, 1984). Others, such as Rose (1943), highlighted the associations between eating and growth and change, and the role of resistance to this process in the disorder. This observation is especially compelling given that the onset of the disorder begins shortly before or during puberty, a period of accelerated physical development.

More recently, the drive-conflict model has been applied to bulimia nervosa. Schwartz (1988), for example, argued that the disorder results from the mother's symbiotic unavailability during the child's early development, resulting from her ambivalence toward the child and her use of the child for her own narcissistic needs. In this scenario, the father is overly stimulating and seductive, and the child is frequently exposed to primal scene material. In this view, bulimia is defensive regression from unconscious Oedipal wishes, and the patient's devouring of the food and subsequent vomiting – often facilitated with a phallic finger – represents a defensive identification with both parents.

Object relations

Hilde Bruch's (1962, 1973, 1978) foundational work was the first to describe anorexia nervosa in the language of object relations. For her, self-starvation represents a struggle for autonomy, mastery, and self-esteem. Disturbances in the early mother-child relationship predispose the child to develop the disorder during adolescence, a time that demands an increased capacity for autonomous functioning. In her clinical work, she observed over-involved caretakers who were domineering, intrusive, and discouraging of separation and individuation. This, she argued, creates an internal confusion in children, expressed through body image disturbance (patients with anorexia nervosa tend to overestimate their body size), interoceptive disturbance (an inability to identify and respond to internal sensations, including hunger, fullness, and affective states), and all-pervasive feelings of ineffectiveness and loss of control.

Others theorists, including Selvini Palazzoli (1978) and Masterson (1978), also developed object relational descriptions of anorexia nervosa. The latter, for example, argued that these patients have an internal maternal object that becomes hostile and rejecting as she moves toward separation and individuation and another that becomes supportive and rewarding in response to dependent, clinging behavior. Each internal representation of the mother has its corresponding self-representation – the first as bad, empty, and guilty and the second as passive, compliant, and good. Working together, these internal objects undermine the patient's journey toward adulthood, which is incompatible with the symptoms and behaviors of the disorder.

Still others have emphasized the lack of transitional space and failures in symbolic function as central dynamics in patients with this disorder (Birksted-Breen, 1989; Boris, 1984; Sprince, 1984). Indeed, patients with anorexia nervosa are notable for their concrete, often alexithymic, descriptions of their experience and a stunted capacity to "play" in their self-explorations. For example, Lawrence (2001) expanded on failures in symbolization in patients with anorexia nervosa and argued that maternal function – which is seen as dangerously intrusive – is concretely equated with food (instead of symbolically represented) and, consequently, renounced. His formulation highlights the ways in which these patients tend to form transferences shaped by this fear of intrusion, leading them to avoidantly approach the therapeutic relationship. In fact, clinicians working with this population often report feeling relationally deprived by the patient, in the same way that the patient deprives himself.

Fewer investigations have been conducted of bulimia nervosa from an object relational perspective. Masterson (1995) described bulimia nervosa as a "closet narcissistic personality disorder." In his view, pathological grandiosity meets traumatic disappointment, and the resulting psychic pain is hidden behind a defensive idealization of the other and an accompanying neglect of the self. From a different point of view, Sugarman and Kurash (1982) proposed that patients with the disorder lack object constancy; when separated from the symbiotic mother, they are unable to evoke a mental representation of her for self-soothing. In this situation, bingeing is used to evoke a sensorimotor-based object representation of the mother, akin to the patient's early experiences of childhood feeding. Sugarman (1991), in contrast, highlighted the failure of patients with bulimia to communicate in symbolic form; the body, instead, is the vehicle for the expression of unconscious conflict.

Self-psychology

Self-psychologists have emphasized developmental failures in the processes of mirroring and idealization which, in turn, create difficulties in maintaining self-esteem and self-cohesion. In this context, eating-disorder symptoms serve restorative and regulatory functions for the personality. Goodsit (1997), for example, argued that patients with anorexia nervosa manifest a façade of pseudo-self-sufficiency when confronted with parents who are themselves self-absorbed, anxious, or otherwise unavailable. In this process, the maturation of the anorexic's self-object and self-regulatory capacities are unable to fully develop, leaving them painfully dependent upon others for their well-being. Bulimic patients, in contrast, are seen as more tension-ridden, impulsive, and conflicted about whether to pursue their own lives or to remain available to a parent who utilizes them to maintain his or her own psychic equilibrium. In this context, symptoms – whether self-starvation, bingeing, and/or purging – emerge as last-ditch efforts at self-soothing and tension regulation. Over time, eating disorders become chronic conditions that provide patients with a compensatory identity and sense of self.

With an eye toward the striking difference in prevalence of anorexia nervosa and bulimia nervosa between males and females, Sands (1989) suggested that young girls are presented with culturally shaped barriers to obtaining developmentally necessary mirroring and idealization. Whereas boys' needs for mirroring may be gratified through "showing off, being cocky, acting smart or aggressive" (p. 77), girls are expected to be "lady-like." It is only in the realm of physical appearance that girls are encouraged to seek mirroring and, thus, in later life women are more predisposed than men to manifest psychopathology through bodily symptoms such as eating disorders.

Contemporary contributions

Contemporary contributions bring together the insights of the past, including those provided by drive theory, object relations, and self-psychology, with an increased understanding of bio-social influences and the centrality of developmental thinking. The attempt to establish a single developmental pathway for eating disorders has been largely abandoned in favor of recognizing that eating disorders are shaped by the developmental period in which they emerge and, furthermore, are continually reshaped and repurposed throughout the life cycle. Katherine Zerbe (2008, 2015), in particular, has been an influential advocate of an integrative approach that situates each patient's struggles in a developmental context. In addition, eating disorders are now understood as influenced by the individual's biology and genetic predisposition, which shapes both that individual's resiliency and how they perceive, organize, and respond to experience (Maine & Bunnell, 2010).

Given the high level of concretization found in patients with eating disorders, as well as the often life-threatening nature of their symptoms, clinicians are increasingly integrating behavioral and systemic therapies, in addition to working with treatment teams that include physicians and nutritionists (see Wooldridge, 2016, for an overview of the role of treatment teams). Clinicians now regularly incorporate verbal contracts for substituting alternative behaviors for disordered eating behaviors or thinking, as well as food journaling and other behaviorally oriented coping mechanisms (see Petrucelli, 2015, for an overview). And given the insights of family therapists about the role of patients with eating disorders in their surrounding families (Selvini Palazzoli, 1978; Minuchin, Rosman, & Baker, 1978), clinicians regularly incorporate systemic approaches.

There has also been a surge of interest in the role of trauma and dissociation in the etiology and maintenance of eating disorders. An interpersonal and relational approach to understanding eating disorders understands as axiomatic that an eating disorder symptom holds dissociated parts of the patient's self and relational history (Petrucelli, 2015). In this view, symptoms such as starvation, bingeing, and purging are dissociative processes and, thus, attempts to maintain self-continuity and self-organization. In light of difficulties in appreciating emotional life, dramatic bodily actions are often used as a means of communication. The centrality of the body in this patient population broadens our conceptualization of self-states to include body-states (Petrucelli, 2014), that is, how one lives in the body at a given moment relative to felt experience, and the recognition that patients may need their therapists to feel, *viscerally*, what they do (Sands, 1997).

The present volume

Now let us return to the present volume. We have gathered 15 chapters. Some have been previously published, whereas others were prepared explicitly for this anthology. Ultimately, each was selected because it provides a valuable, psychoanalytically informed perspective on the theoretical conceptualization, clinical treatment, or contemporary issues related to eating disorders. This anthology is divided into three parts. As with many anthologies, you need not read these parts in order. Rather, each chapter stands on its own, while also providing a piece of a larger montage when read in conjunction with the other chapters included here.

Part I, "Conceptualization of Eating Disorders," includes five chapters. In the first, entitled, "Psychodynamic Improvement in Eating Disorders: Welcoming Ignored, Unspoken, and Neglected Concerns in the Patient to Foster Development and Resiliency," Kathryn J. Zerbe and Dana A. Satir use two case examples to elucidate six domains of intrapsychic and interpersonal functioning that demand attention, ranging from the bread and butter of our practice – the mitigation of shame and the integration of split-off affects and defenses, for example – to the less well-recognized, such as the tendency to spoil forward movement and the denial of death as a realistic possibility. With exquisite attention to developmental issues that arise at different points on the family and human life cycles and an acknowledgement of the importance of theoretical integration, the authors raise important considerations involved in the treatment of eating disorders that are uniquely elucidated by a psychoanalytic perspective.

In our second chapter, "Invisibility and Insubstantiality in an Anorexic Adolescent: Phenomenology and Dynamics," Mary Brady explores the clinical presentation and underlying dynamics of a certain class of patients with anorexia nervosa who present to us as invisible and insubstantial. This, she argues, is a separate, though at times overlapping, diagnostic category from other anorexic patients who have different aims, such as dominating the object (Quagliata, 2004), enacting grandiose wishes in relation to idealized men (Reich, 1973), or the maintenance of "no-entry" defenses (Williams, 1997). Brady locates the sense of visibility and substantiality to early experiences of being known and seen by mother (Bion, 1962) as well as to aspects of narcissistic object relations (Rosenfeld, 1964). The patient she has in mind has a persistent desire to locate herself within another, precluding the development of her own differentiated self. Paradoxically, however, the patient's symptoms "serve to make visible for the first time the terrible troubles a patient has heretofore been struggling with invisibly."

Antonella Granieri, in our third chapter entitled, "Primary Interactions and Eating Disorders: A Psychoanalytic Perspective," explores the relational exchanges linked to our childhood experiences of food and eating. These exchanges, when shaped by reciprocity and emotional attunement, contribute to our developing interoceptive awareness and somato-psychic integration, in addition to a constructive relational repertoire for the communication of emotional experience. Granieri provides a compelling clinical case to illustrate what may happen when these early relational exchanges are characterized by misattunement and intrusion, and how analysts must listen to the earliest layers of emotional experience for healing to be found.

Anthony P. Winston, in our fourth chapter, "An Island Entire of Itself: Narcissism in Anorexia Nervosa," charts one of the developmental pathways through which anorexia nervosa develops. In his view, the syndrome may emerge in tandem with a state of narcissism and its accompanying omnipotent defenses – an organization which the patient has not yet moved beyond or to which she has regressed. Early on, Bruch (1978) recognized that anorexia nervosa most often occurs as a developmental crisis, at a time when the adolescent is faced with the task of becoming increasingly self-reliant and moving beyond the confines of the immediate family. Winston frames this crisis as one of working through a narcissistic organization. The adolescent must both move beyond a state of relational isolation and develop the capacity to make use of potential space, which will facilitate more creative ways of navigating these developmental tasks.

Lorraine Caputo, in our fifth chapter, "The Dead Third in the Treatment of an Adolescent with Anorexia Nervosa," offers us a compelling case study of a young woman haunted by the ghosts of her parents' and grandparents' generations. Tracing the complex relationship between intergenerational trauma, bodily pain, and disordered eating, she draws on the theories of Fonagy (1999), who suggests that a breakdown in reflective function may be a vehicle for the intergenerational transmission of trauma, and Gerson (2009), from whom she draws the notion of *a dead third*, to understand the unfolding of this particularly complex case. Caputo's chapter highlights how disordered eating takes on meaning from its multiple contexts – developmental, relational, and cultural, each of which must be understood in the treatment process.

Part II, "Treatment of Eating Disorders," includes Chapters 6 through 10. In our sixth chapter, "From Knowing to Discovering: Some Suggestions for Work with an Anorexic Patient," Yael Kadish offers technical suggestions for work with patients with anorexia nervosa in the acute stages of the illness, when life and death often hang in the balance, and with whom therapists often experience intense countertransferential anxiety, which Kadish likens to "having a gun to one's head." Kadish considers a number of technical questions in light of the complex psychodynamics these patients present, including optimal session frequency, the need for an extended frame – which goes beyond the usual provisions of psychoanalytic treatment to include negotiating family involvement and medical monitoring – as well as managing an often fragile therapeutic relationship. With regard to the latter, Kadish follows Bruch (1973, 1978) in insisting the therapist maintain a more active, knowing stance toward the patient's difficulties.

Continuing to address issues of conceptualization and technique in patients with eating disorders, Judith Brisman offers our seventh chapter, "Heathen Talk: Psychoanalytic Considerations of Eating Disorders and the Dissociated Self." Here, she helps us to understand how essential it is for clinicians to deeply enter the world of eating-disordered thinking and behavior – the dissociated aspects of self that drive patients' most self-destructive endeavors. As therapists, we are always seeking an approach that attempts to integrate both the language of the patient and therapist while also searching for the parts of the patient who are yet to appear. Encouraging the integration of more action-oriented interventions, Brisman bridges the gap between psychoanalytic thinking and the modes of intervention that have become prevalent in the world of eating disorders treatment, such as the externalization of the eating-disordered behavior.

In our eighth chapter, "To Know Another Inside and Out: Linking Psychic and Somatic Experience in Eating Disorders," Danielle Novack develops a view of eating disorders in which the developmental process of mind-body differentiation has been interrupted. In this context, much of the communication that occurs between therapist and patient is nonverbal and in order to receive our patients' nonverbal communications, we must be able to use our own bodies as finely tuned therapeutic instruments that help us to connect to our patients' "unformulated experience" (Stern, 1983). With a compelling case illustration, Novack shows us how over time, the therapist identifies and contains bodily sensations, which can eventually make their way into language. This processes of de-somatization (Krystal, 1988) is linked with a complementary process of re-somatization, in which patients learn to re-inhabit their bodies in more personalized ways.

As previously mentioned, at present the field of eating disorders is dominated by symptom-focused treatments, the majority of which are grounded in systemic and behavioral approaches. With notable exceptions (e.g., Tasca & Balfour, 2014; Zerbe, 2008; Wooldridge, 2016), approaches grounded in psychoanalytic thinking have not been widely developed or researched. In this book we include two authors' attempts to right this imbalance. First, Timothy Rice, in our ninth chapter, "On Targeting Emotion Regulation Deficits in Eating Disorders Through Defense Analysis," offers us a compelling model for the treatment of eating disorders that attempts to address emotion regulation deficits observed in this patient population. This model elegantly dovetails with existing research on the psychodynamics of eating disorders – and in particular with recent findings highlighting the role of attachment insecurity (Tasca & Balfour, 2014) – as well as with the latest neurobiological research on the implicit emotion regulation system (Rice & Hoffman, 2014). Because this model can be operationalized and manualized, it offers a compelling alternative to the dominant behavioral and family-based treatment paradigms.

And in our tenth chapter, "Eating Disorders, Impaired Mentalization, and Attachment: Implications for Child and Adolescent Family Treatment," Starr Kelton-Locke draws on the foundational aspects of mentalization-based treatment (MBT) (Allen & Fonagy, 2006) to argue for an expanded model of MBT treatment that includes protocols for children, adolescents, and families affected by eating disorders. In this model, symptoms of eating disorders are understood to stem from deficits in emotional regulation, interoceptive awareness, self-cohesion, and self-esteem regulation. This approach is compelling given accumulating research that suggests that insecure attachment and associated deficits in the capacity of mentalization are risk factors for the development of eating pathology (e.g., Jewell, Collyer, Tchanturia, Simic, & Fonagy, 2015). Moreover, recent data from the neurosciences suggests that patients with anorexia nervosa, for example, show differences in the neural regions involved in self-knowledge and mentalization (McAdams & Krawcyzk, 2014, 2011).

Part III, "Contemporary Issues Related to Eating Disorders," includes Chapters 11 through 15. In our eleventh chapter, "The Low Spark of High-Heeled 'Girls': Hyperawareness and Hyperdeadness with Eating-Disordered Patients," Jean Petrucelli offers us a compelling meditation on the cultural pressures imposed upon women, especially those in celebrity and popular culture. With Amy Winehouse's death as a tragic example, Petrucelli shows us how the eating-disordered patient's 'hyperaware' fixation on her body and the accompanying starving, bingeing, or purging creates a 'hyperdeadness' – an anesthetization of (often painful) emotional aliveness that could not be tolerated absent a relational home.

In our twelfth chapter, "Psychodynamic Importance of 'Cyber' and 'in the Flesh' Friends in Psychotherapy with College-Aged Adolescents with Eating Disorders," F. Diane Barth examines the relationship among social media, friendship, and the development of eating disorders in adolescents. Eating disorders commonly develop in adolescence, a time of particular vulnerability to the influence of friends. And now, with the proliferation of technology in adolescents' lives, many friendships are carried out partly, and in some cases entirely, via social media. Arguing that friendships conducted through social media have both potential risks *and* benefits for adolescents navigating the attachment-individuation phase of development (Lyons-Ruth, 1991), Barth explores how we can open up conversation about the "cyber" world, leveraging its benefits while minimizing its risks. In some cases, she suggests, it may be necessary to join our patients in that world.

In our thirteenth chapter, "The Enigma of Ana: A Psychoanalytic Exploration of Pro-Anorexia Internet Forums," Tom Wooldridge offers a conceptualization of "pro-anorexia" (often abbreviated as "pro-ana") Internet forums grounded in qualitative research and a complex clinical case. Suggesting that these forums deserve our attention because of their increasing prevalence (Custers & Van den Bulck, 2009), Wooldridge argues that pro-ana forums are a double-edged sword, most often serving as a psychic retreat (Steiner, 1993), an escape from relatedness and other aspects of reality that are too difficult to bear, for their participations; yet, at other times, offering the possibility of meaningful connection and even access to potential space (Winnicott, 1971).In our fourteenth chapter, "Towards Social Justice: The Continuum of Eating and Body Image Problems: How Social and Psychological Realities Converge into an Embodied Epidemic," Susan Gutwill explores the convergence of psychological and social experience as it manifests inside and outside the consulting room for patients struggling with eating and body image difficulties. With a detailed attention to women's lived experience, she suggests that these difficulties emerge from a matrix of emotional experiences in the family, school, and larger culture, including the conditions of late consumer capitalism. In particular, she highlights the role of the advertising industry in selling diets, style, and beauty, as well as the role of agribusiness (i.e., the group of industries concerned with moving food from planting, to processing, to packaging and selling). Ultimately, analysis shows us that eating and body image problems are a form of social injustice.

In our fifteenth and final chapter, "Enduring Perfectionism: Seeing Through Eating Disorder Recovery and America's Cultural Complex," Kim L. Grynick brings a Jungian perspective to bear on our intrapsychic, interpersonal, and cultural ways of thinking about recovery from eating disorders. Her paper asks the question, "What does full and sustainable recovery from an eating disorder mean, and what does it require?" Looking to the roots of these rigid and often deeply entrenched symptoms, Grynick suggests that full recovery requires the presence of soul – that deeper, archetypal idea whose language is metaphor and image – as an integral aspect of the development of a full, and fully enlivening, personal identity. Yet, as she points out, this runs counter to our overarching cultural values, which presents a profound challenge to both therapists and patients.

Taken together, these 15 chapters provide an exciting overview of the state-of-the-art in the psychoanalytic treatment of eating disorders. It is my sincere hope that this book contributes to a creative dialogue among clinicians both inside and outside of the psychoanalytic community. I'd also like to note that for each of the cases discussed in the following chapters, consent was obtained from the patient or the patient's guardian; in other cases, the material has been heavily disguised or composite case material is utilized to protect confidentiality.

Note

1 While there is no evidence that Freud treated patients with eating disorders, there are numerous references to eating disturbances in his writings (see Caparotta and Ghaffari (2006) for an excellent historical overview of psychoanalytic contributions to the treatment of eating disorders that touches upon these references in more detail).

References

Allen, J. G., & Fonagy, P. (Eds.) (2006). *Handbook of mentalization-based treatment*. Chichester, England: Wiley & Sons.

Atwood, G. E. (2012). *The abyss of madness*. New York: Taylor and Francis.

Berlin, I. N., Boatman, M. J., Scheimo, S. L., & Szurek, S. A. (1951). Adolescent alternation of anorexia and obesity. American Journal of Orthopsychiatry, 21, 387–419.

Bion, W. R. (1962). *Learning from experience*. London: Karnac.

Birksted-Breen, D. (1989). Working with an anorexic patient. *International Journal of Psychoanalysis*, *70*, 29–39.

Boris, H. (1984). The problem of anorexia nervosa. *International Journal of Psychoanalysis*, *65*, 315–322.

Bruch, H. (1962). Perceptual and conceptual disturbances in anorexia nervosa. *Psychosomatic Medicine*, *24*, 187–194.

Bruch, H. (1973). *Eating disorders: Obesity, anorexia nervosa and the person within*. New York: Basic Books.

Bruch, H. (1978). *The golden cage*. Cambridge, MA: Harvard University Press.

Caparrotta, L., & Ghaffari, K. (2006). A historical overview of the psychodynamic contributions to the understanding of eating disorders. *Psychoanalytic Psychotherapy*, *20*(3), 175–196.

Custers, K., & Van den Bulck, J. (2009). Viewership of pro-anorexia websites in seventh, ninth and eleventh graders. *European Eating Disorders Review: The Journal of the Eating Disorders Association*, *17*(3), 214–219.

Eisler, I. (1995). Family models of eating disorders. In Szmukler, G., Dare, C., Treasure, J. (Eds.), *Handbook of eating disorders: Theory, treatment and research*. London: John Wiley & Sons.

Fonagy, P. (1999). The transgenerational transmission of holocaust trauma: Lessons learned from the analysis of an adolescent with obsessive-compulsive disorder. *Attachment and Human Development*, *1*(1), 92–114.

Freud, A. (1946). The psychoanalytic study of infantile feeding disturbances. *Psychoanalytic Study of the Child*, *2*, 119–132.

Gerson, S. (2009). When the third is dead: Memory, mourning and witnessing in the aftermath of the Holocaust. *International Journal of Psychoanalysis, 90*, 1341–1357.
Goodsit, A. (1997). Eating disorders: A self-psychological perspective. In D. M. Garner & P. E. Garfinkel (Eds.), *Handbook of treatment for eating disorders* (2nd ed.). New York: Guilford Press.
Jewell, T., Collyer, H., Gardner, T., Tchanturia, K., Simic, M., Fonagy, P., & Eisler, I. (2015). Attachment and mentalization and their association with child and adolescent eating pathology: A systematic review. *International Journal of Eating Disorders, 49*(4), 354–373.
Krystal, H. (1988). *Integration and self-healing*. Hillsdale, NJ: The Analytic Press.
Lawrence, M. (2001). Body, mother, mind: Anorexia, femininity and the intrusive object. *International Journal of Psychoanalysis, 83*, 837–850.
Lock, J., Le Grange, D., Agras, W.S., & Dare, C. (2001). *Treatment manual for anorexia nervosa: a family-based approach*. New York: Guilford Press.
Lyons-Ruth, K. (1991). Rapprochement or approchement: Mahler's theory reconsidered from the vantage point of recent research on early attachment relationships. *Psychoanalytic Psychology, 8*, 1–23.
Maine, M., & Bunnell, D. (2010). A perfect biopsychosocial storm: Gender, culture, and eating disorders. In M. Maine, B. Hartman, B. McGilley, & D. Bunnell (Eds.), *Treatment of eating disorders* (pp. 3–16). London: Academic Press/Elsevier.
Masserman, J. H. (1941). Psychodynamisms in anorexia nervosa and neurotic vomiting. *Psychoanalytic Quarterly, 10*, 211–242.
Masterson, J. F. (1978). The borderline adolescent: An object relations view. In S. C. Feinstein & P. L. Giovacchini (Eds.), *Adolescent psychiatry* (Vol 6, pp. 344–359). Chicago: University of Chicago Press.
Masterson, J. F. (1995). Paradise lost – bulimia, a closet narcissistic personality disorder: A developmental self and object relations approach. In R. C. Marohn & S. C. Feinstein (Eds.), *Adolescent psychiatry* (Vol 20, pp. 253–266). Hillsdale, NJ: Analytic Press.
McAdams, C., & Krawczyk, D. (2011). Impaired neural processing of social attribution in anorexia nervosa. *Psychiatry Research: Neuroimaging, 194*, 54–63.
Minuchin, L., Rosman, L., & Baker, L. (1978). *Psychosomatic families: Anorexia nervosa in Context*. Cambridge, MA: Harvard University Press.
Moulton, R. (1942). A psychosomatic study of anorexia nervosa including the use of vaginal smears. *Psychosomatic Medicine, 4*, 62–74.
Orbach, S. (2009). *Bodies (BIG IDEAS//small books)*. New York: Picador.
Petrucelli, J. (Ed.) (2014). *Body-states: Interpersonal and relational perspectives on the treatment of eating disorders (Psychoanalysis in a new key Book series)*. New York: Routledge.
Petrucelli, J. (2015). The relational montage of eating disorders. In J. Bresler & K. Starr (Eds.), *Relational psychoanalysis and psychotherapy integration: An evolving synergy*. New York: Routledge.
Quagliata, G. (2004). Some reflections on the processes of projection and introjection in eating disorders. In Williams, G. (Ed.), *Exploring eating disorders in adolescence: The generosity of acceptance*. London: Karnac.
Reich, A. (1973). A contribution to the psychoanalysis of extreme submissiveness in women. In *Annie Reich: Psychoanalytic contributions*. New York: International Universities Press, Inc.
Rice, T. R., & Hoffman, L. (2014). Defense mechanisms and implicit emotion regulation: A comparison of a psychodynamic construct with one from contemporary neuroscience. *Journal of the American Psychoanalytic Association, 62*(4), 693–708. doi:10.1177/0003065114546746

Ritvo, S. (1984). The images and uses of the body in the psychic conflict with special reference to eating disorders in adolescence. *Psychoanalytic Study of the Child, 39*, 446–469.
Rose, J. (1943). Eating inhibitions in children in relation to anorexia nervosa. *Psychosomatic Medicine, 5*, 117–124.
Rosenfeld, H. (1964). On the psychopathology of narcissism: A clinical approach. In *Psychotic states: A psychoanalytic approach*. New York: International Universities Press, Inc.
Rowland, C. V. (1970). Anorexia nervosa: A survey of the literature and review of 30 cases. *International Psychiatric Clinics, 7*, 37–137.
Sands, S. (1989). Eating disorders and female development: A self-psychological perspective. In A. I. Goldberg (Ed.), *Progress in self psychology* (Vol. 5, pp. 75–103). Hillsdale, NJ: Analytic Press.
Sands, S. (1997). Protein or foreign body? Reply to commentaries. *Psychoanalytic Dialogues, 7*, 691–706.
Schwartz, H. J. (1988). *Bulimia: Psychoanalytic treatment and theory*. Madison, CT: International Universities Press.
Selvini Palazzoli, M. (1978). *Self-starvation*. New York: Jason Aronson, Inc.
Sprince, M. (1984) Early psychic disturbances in anorexic and bulimic patients as reflected in the psychoanalytical process. *Journal of Child Psychotherapy, 10*, 199–215.
Steiner, J. (1993). *Psychic retreats: Pathological organizations in psychotic, neurotic, and borderline patients*. New York: Routledge.
Stern, D. B. (1983). Unformulated experience: From familiar chaos to creative disorder. *Contemporary Psychoanalysis, 19*, 71–99.
Sugarman, A. (1991). Bulimia: A displacement from psychological self to body self. In C. L. Johnson (Ed.), *Psychodynamic treatment of anorexia nervosa and bulimia* (pp. 3–33). New York: Guilford Press.
Sugarman, A., & Kurash, C. (1982). The body as a transitional object in bulimia. *International Journal of Eating Disorders, 1*, 57–67.
Tasca, G. A., & Balfour, L. (2014). Eating disorders and attachment: a contemporary psychodynamic perspective. *Psychodynamic Psychiatry, 42*(2), 257–276. doi:10.1521/pdps.2014.42.2.257
Thomä, H. (1967). *Anorexia nervosa*. New York: Int Press.
Waller, J. V., Kaufman, M. R., & Deutsch, F. (1940). Anorexia nervosa: Psychosomatic entity. *Psychosomatic Medicine, 2*, 3–16.
Williams, G. (1997). Reflections on some dynamics of eating disorders: 'No Entry' defences and foreign bodies. *International Journal of Psycho-Analysis, 78*, 927–941.
Winnicott, D. W. (1971). *Playing and reality*. New York: Basic Books.
Wooldridge, T. (2016). *Understanding anorexia nervosa in males: An integrative approach*. New York: Routledge.
Wooldridge, T. (in press). The entropic body: Primitive anxieties and secondary skin formation in anorexia nervosa. *Psychoanalytic Dialogues.*
Zerbe, K. (2008). *Integrated treatment of eating disorders: Beyond the body betrayed*. New York: W. W. Norton & Company.
Zerbe, K. (2015). Psychodynamic theory of eating disorders. In Smolak, L. & Levine, M. P. (Eds.), *The Wiley handbook of eating disorders* (pp. 253–268). Hoboken, NJ: Wiley.
Zerbe, K. (2016). Psychodynamic issues in the treatment of binge eating: Working with shame, secrets, no-entry, and false body defenses. *Clinical Social Work Journal, 44*(1), 8–17.

PART I

Conceptualization of eating disorders

1

PSYCHODYNAMIC IMPROVEMENT IN EATING DISORDERS

Welcoming ignored, unspoken, and neglected concerns in the patient to foster development and resiliency

Kathryn J. Zerbe and Dana A. Satir

> *I am in chains. Don't touch my chains.*
>
> (Franz Kafka, 1912)

Some of the most searing, unspoken questions that patients have when initiating any new treatment are, "Will this prescription you are offering really help me feel better and live longer? And if so, how can I know if I am getting well? Can I trust you to want, be able to, and bear finding the parts I keep concealed from others as well as myself? What side effects can I expect to have and are they worth the while if the anticipated benefit doesn't help me live my own life fully, as I see it and want it to be?"

We would like to believe that mental health practitioners working within a developmental perspective on the family and human life cycles tune in to these often hidden concerns in our practices, anticipate their unspoken presence and try to answer them specifically and concretely. Yet, we also know that we often fall below the mark we set for ourselves, in part because what the patient (and his/her family members) seek deepest reassurance about is unconscious and can only unfold over time as the defenses that maintained survival at such a high cost are worn away and new structures for living and 'meaning making' are put into their place. This quagmire is particularly true for those clinicians who treat the spectrum of eating disorders (EDs) because the manifest life-threatening symptoms are frequently denied or minimized and often are an indispensable cogwheel in the individual's quixotic survival mechanisms. We cannot know our patients with EDs fully unless we dwell in the experience of their symptoms; and yet with our good intentions, benevolent desires, and heroic efforts we aim to unearth all of the terror, yearning, and longing that will reveal a person who is prepared to face death in order to survive.

When these adaptations are sufficiently tinkered with, ED symptoms may almost miraculously diminish for a period only to return with abrupt force and fresh impedance that bewilder even the most experienced therapist. Eating-disordered patients, often described in case reports and in the literature as highly intelligent, fascinating, exquisitely sensitive, and strong willed, are difficult to treat. Many clinicians refuse to or are afraid to see even one in their practices (Thompson-Brenner, Satir, Franko, & Herzog, 2012). Even the most skilled experts experience themselves "betwixt and between" health/sickness, progress/regression, known/unknown, and ever changing landscapes of self and other (Bruch, 1978; Warren, Schafer, Crowley, & Olivardia, 2012). The epigram by Franz Kafka with which we begin this paper appositely captures this imbroglio for each member of the therapeutic dyad. Overtly, release from the chains of the illness is sought. But these same chains are rarely relinquished without struggle because they serve as the tether for a fragile sense of self. As this dilemma of the patient's is more fully comprehended, clinicians in our experience tend to have greater forbearance and fewer tendencies to act on their countertransference feelings. With better metabolized feelings, the clinician can then find a way to help the patient relinquish the chains that bind, protect, and suffocate while knowing full well he/she will get entangled with the chains him/herself.

We suspect that the major question for ED patients that can never be answered in the short term but must always be in the long term speaks to how one goes about creating a meaningful life and living in one's own skin. Our patients exist in a world, often reflected in microcosm in a particular family system, which exalts outward appearances and images and insufficiently endorses those factors that promote and strengthen the ongoing search for personal knowledge and ethical/moral decision-making. Slowing down, reflecting, sensing, feeling, being – these are universal needs and fundamental desires but overtime are eschewed, relinquished, and rejected by our patients in favor of the prevailing need to perform, accommodate, and succeed. We believe that a psychodynamic psychotherapy approach is fertile soil for ED patients to begin to till ground that eventuates in a fuller sense of one's unique selfhood because it welcomes the ignored, unspoken, and neglected concerns essential to living a vital life that have been split off, dissociated, or surreptitiously contained within the manifest symptoms of eating, self, and body image issues.

Although psychodynamic psychotherapy is time consuming and hence costly to provide, a significant literature that includes longitudinal, evidence-based, and qualitative studies is beginning to demonstrate its value in terms of quality of life, symptom remediation, re-established developmental trajectories, and improved resilience over the life cycle. These studies offer hope, guidance, and caution for both clinician and patient who undertake the hard work of bearing down on intransigent symptoms and jump starting a personal journey thrown off kilter by an unsavory and unwavering dance with death. Treatment of EDs is not for the faint of heart, in part because of the high medical morbidity and mortality rate associated with anorexia nervosa, bulimia nervosa, binge eating disorder, and other specified feeding or eating disorders (Crow et al., 2009; Fichter & Quadflieg, 2016; Steinhausen, 2002). It is not enough to be knowledgeable about EDs – the clinician must be attuned to the experience of being with these patients, which requires sensitivity to the visceral feelings in one's own body. Treatment requires clinicians to "buckle in" for a process that requires fortitude, pragmatism, and at times mutual vulnerability of unknown duration. The more insidious rationale for clinician burnout resides in the sadomasochistic relationships that are played out in the patient's relationship to self and others alluded to previously. These hefty chains – codified in the contemporary psychoanalytic literature as "Doer/Done To" enactments (Benjamin, 2004; Davies, 2003) – must be repeatedly confronted and worked through in the transference to become unyoked.

In the material that follows, we provide two extended case examples to descriptively ferret out six domains of intrapsychic and interpersonal functioning that we have found key in developing a fuller sense of self with ED patients in our psychodynamic practices. We chose to describe these longer-term treatments with some composite features to ensure strict confidentiality and abjure any identifying information of particular individuals. Our goal is to maintain accuracy in the types of storyline, themes, conflicts, and developmental deficits we have encountered throughout our clinical, supervisory, and teaching experiences. Four of the domains that we cull will quickly resonate with clinicians who work with and read about this population over the long term (e.g., mitigation of shame; recognition of split-off affects and defenses; achievement of greater intimacy and capacity to play; reduction in an overly harsh superego). Two of the areas are, however, less obvious and sparsely referenced in the psychodynamic literature on EDs. Confronting the tendency to spoil forward movement (i.e., addressing success anxiety) and denying the real possibility of death posed by the illness are so significantly consequential and ubiquitous in our experience as to warrant additional attunement to transference and countertransference issues that may interfere with recognition and working through. We speculate that these less referenced topics may mirror unformulated or dissociated experiences of our patients and require a willingness of clinicians to confront painful realities, limitations, and losses that are endemic in our work.

Before turning to the specific cases, we present a brief review of the psychodynamic evidence base and qualitative research studies that inform our practices, and are likely to be helpful to others in deciphering additional domains essential to self-development and sustained resiliency in the person who struggles with an ED.

Although this report grapples with some of the psychodynamic links that keep our patients bound, we believe that the psychodynamic method must, in the case of ED patients, be integrated with other forms of therapy (e.g., cognitive behavioral therapy [CBT], nutritional support, patient education modalities, art and experiential therapies, residential and wrap-around services). Initial reports indicate a robust effect when an integrative approach is taken, and many existing models of ED treatment recommend step-wise approaches that focus initially on stabilization and containment of symptoms before transitioning into more insight-oriented/depth psychotherapies. Research also confirms that experienced clinicians consciously and intuitively blend psychodynamic and cognitive behavioral methods regardless of the theoretical orientation that they consciously espouse in order to flexibly meet their patients' needs, personalities, and evolving presentations. We suspect that in "real world" clinical practice, clinicians who successfully assist patients in their recovery from a serious ED have a knack for and interest in exploring the existential concerns we describe while simultaneously serving as vehicles that champion growth, resilience, and freedom from the constraints imposed by a serious, long-standing eating disorder.

Research and literature review

Studies of the efficacy of psychodynamic psychotherapy for EDs are growing but limited. Qualitative and quantitative studies, naturalistic surveys, narrative and single-case designs, and consumer reports converge in their examination of the importance of psychotherapy in addressing concerns that patients have beyond symptom control, weight restoration, and improved body and self-image (for reviews see Zerbe, 2008, 2015, 2016). While there is a consensus among these reports in acknowledging the importance of support and empathic relationships when confronting concerns that lie beneath the manifest problem, there is little research that could guide what works for a particular patient based on developmental history, self-experience, and meaning/function of symptoms. As clinicians struggle to make sense of these enigmatic illnesses and how their patients are intertwined with them, there are even greater empirical gaps in training issues that might assist clinicians in questioning their assumptions and when changing course is necessary. Attachment to the therapist, reduction of a harsh superego, improved sense of security, willingness to engage in interpersonal relationships, enhanced ability to self-reflect (e.g., mentalize) and having fewer self-destructive relationships and behaviors are core areas addressed in psychodynamic psychotherapy. These domains of intrapsychic and interpersonal functioning are confirmed in some research reports which support improved outcome in ED treatment.

To date in the adolescent and adult literature there have been five controlled trials of psychodynamic psychotherapy for anorexia nervosa (AN) (Bachar, Latzer, Kreitler, & Berry, 1999; Dare, Eisler, Russell, Treasure, & Dodge, 2001; Lock et al., 2010; Treasure et al., 1995; Zipfel et al., 2014); two for bulimia nervosa (BN) (Bachar et al., 1999; Poulsen et al., 2014); and one for Binge Eating Disorder (BED) (Tasca et al., 2006; Tasca, Richie & Balfour, 2011). In Treasure et al.'s (1995) report comparing cognitive analytic therapy (a form of psychodynamic therapy) to educational behavior therapy, 63 per cent of patients had good to intermediate improvement overall. Although there were no significant differences in the endpoint body mass index (BMI) between the two groups, the cognitive analytic group improved on a number of self-assessment measures related to interpersonal functioning and sense of self-worth, suggesting important intrapsychic changes beyond manifest ED symptoms. Emphasizing the impact of the therapist-patient relationship as a positive force for change, interpreting unconscious meaning of symptoms, understanding core conflicts, and opening a door to new ways of thinking about the self, thus leading to an expansion of resiliency and symptom improvement, appeared central in other reports as well (Bachar et al., 1999; Dare et al., 2001; Tasca et al., 2006). These findings tend to support the importance of experiencing and maintaining a secure base of attachment for patients who have had insecure, disorganized, dismissive, and otherwise thwarted early caretaker relationships (Candelori & Cioca, 1998; Treasure, Corfield, & Cardi, 2012; Ward et al., 2001). In a recent randomized controlled trial comparing an integrative psychodynamic psychotherapy and cognitive behavioral therapy for adults with BN, reductions in binge eating were associated with improvements in attachment security in psychodynamic treatment (Daniel, Poulsen, & Lunn, 2016; Poulsen et al., 2014). While the causality of this relationship could not be determined, it does support the importance of a durable therapy relationship that helps patients repair early developmental traumas and develop capacities for benign introjects that foster capacities for self-soothing.

Treatment acceptance because of ambivalence about change is a major hurdle in treating EDs that can be attenuated when the therapeutic alliance is attended to in the treatment. Patients in a focal psychodynamic psychotherapy or enhanced cognitive behavioral therapy both substantially improved at a 12-month follow-up and reported positive feelings about their psychotherapists, likely contributing to a low drop-out rate (Zipfel et al., 2014). One in-depth qualitative analysis using a single-case study method, Alliance Focused Psychotherapy, based upon contemporary relational psychoanalytic principles such as repairing ruptures in the therapeutic dyad, attending to interpersonal conflicts, and confronting emotional avoidance and verbalizing and integrating feelings that had been silenced, demonstrated how a low-weight patient was able to engage in a process psychotherapy, gain weight, and address key issues of quality of life (Satir et al., 2011). Another published case study utilizing an integrative treatment for a patient with BN (four weeks of CBT, followed by 19 weeks of a psychodynamic psychotherapy), reported significant reductions in binge-purge behaviors as well as improvements in affect regulation, identity coherence, and an internalization of a sense of "good enoughness" as a response to harsh super ego functioning (Richards, Shingleton, Goldman, Siegel, & Thompson-Brenner, 2016). These changes were part of a process of exploration and insight that were borne out by the therapist's ability to reflect, experience, and survive treatment with the patient, her symptoms, and their interacting interpersonal worlds.

A significant number of patients actually undergo and benefit from treatment that ranges from "50 to 100 or more" visits (Tobin, 2012; Tobin, Banker, Weisberg, & Bowers, 2007). This longer duration dose of treatment and the positive dose-response effects have been studied in patients with histories of substance abuse, severe anxiety and depression, and trauma and early attachment problems (Leichsenring & Leibing, 2003; Shedler, 2010). Longer treatments tend to be psychodynamic in approach and may help patients achieve mastery over intense affects, gain a sense of effectiveness and self-awareness, understand the roots of self-loathing (Bers, Blatt, & Dolinsky, 2004), and promote new opportunities to learn about and sustain interpersonal relationships, including but not exclusively the one with the therapist (Thompson-Brenner & Westen, 2005a, b). Findings from a New Zealand study (Carter et al., 2011) indicated that a prolonged time frame of therapy is needed to show positive effects in patients' interpersonal functioning and produced better long-term results overall.

A notable outcome, across several different studies, is that while changes in ED symptoms in psychodynamic psychotherapies may be slower than those reported in behavioral treatments, at follow-up these differences are either no longer relevant or suggest psychodynamic treatments are superior in terms of ED symptom improvement. In one of the largest, multi-center clinical trials for AN comparing focal analytic therapy, enhanced cognitive behavioral therapy, and optimized treatment as usual (ANTOP study), patients' body mass index (BMI) at the end of treatment increased in all study groups, with more rapid improvements in weight gain in CBT (Zipfel et al., 2014). At 12-month follow-up, however, the data suggest greater improvements in BMI in focal analytic treatment. Similar results have been reported in trials for interpersonal psychotherapy, or IPT, for BN where patient improvement in ED symptoms at 20 sessions is delayed compared with CBT, but results at follow-up suggest treatments are equally effective in reducing binge-purge behaviors (e.g., Agras, Walsh, Fairburn, Wilson, & Kramer, 2000; Fairburn, 1997). It is noteworthy, however, that while IPT is based on analytic principles (Weismann, Markowitz, & Klerman, 2000), studies in EDs only consist of 20 sessions over 20 weeks, comparatively shorter to other analytic approaches.

One hypothesis for this timeline of change is that the psychodynamic psychotherapy process begins to shift the tectonic plates of self-other configurations through the use of the transference-countertransference matrix, re-enactment of relational patterns, and "sloppiness" or indeterminate qualities of exchanges in meaning (Stolorow & Atwood, 1996). By facilitating understanding and insight, learning to bear and work though intense affect states, and providing new relational experiences the protective mechanisms of ED symptoms are no longer needed and give way to healthy maturation. These gains are mutative both during and after treatment and ultimately become more integrated into patients' self-concepts, allowing for greater intimacy and expanded affective experiencing – all of which allow patients to feel more "alive."

Interestingly, qualitative reports (Adair et al., 2007; Beresin, Gordon, & Herzog, 1989; Fichter & Quadfling, 2004; Lamoureux & Bottorff, 2005; Miller, 1996) that emphasize the patients' experience of recovery are another resource of emerging data that infer how these tectonic plates may begin to shift and how the chains that bind the patient to his/her illness are gradually relinquished. Patients who are interviewed or complete questionnaires about how they feel they have improved over a course of treatment notice newfound abilities to access social support and invest in and work on their interpersonal relationships. In alignment with the factors we describe in the case examples, qualitative reports have also teased out that patients are able to reduce or to relinquish their identity as a person defined by their ED and are on their way to establishing a sense of having a true self that they describe as the "real me" or "knowing who I am." Less masochistic, they also report taking greater responsibility for self and facing down a victim mentality, all the while finding new capacities to enjoy the simple things in life and to self-soothe. One bottom line that also emerges from qualitative research and consumer surveys (Bell, 2003) is the patient's experience of having a person who wanted and could listen to them in depth, often for the first time, meeting a key developmental need. For many, the therapy relationship is one of the few times a patient can experience empathic attunement or being held in mind as if his/her own subjectivity is real, experienced, and mattered.

While the results we have described are promising, some methodological and systemic challenges have limited the scope of the existing research base. First, while definitions of recovery have somewhat varied across treatment outcome studies, most investigations are almost exclusively focused on the absence of ED symptoms as a means of evaluating treatment efficacy (i.e., Morgan & Hayward, 1988). While these changes are critical, our opinion is that they represent a piece of functioning that is necessary but not sufficient. In the absence of the internal structure provided by an ED, patients are especially vulnerable to relapsing because of uncontained feelings of emptiness and confusion; they are also overwhelmed by dissociative self-states that temporarily appear to multiply as the exoskeleton that the eating problem provided falls away but the nascent self-system has not yet solidified. Qualitative research also suggests that patients and therapists perceive recovery in related domains such as affect regulation, interpersonal relationships, and sexuality (e.g., Nordenbos, 2011) as essential as the remission of ED symptoms in finding a true self beyond illness.

While we have highlighted the psychodynamic empirical evidence, the ED field has been moving in a direction of greater treatment integration, in part, as this represents what clinicians in the community are already doing with our complex patients (Colli, Gentile, Tanzilli, Speranza, & Lingiardi, 2016; Thompson-Brenner, Weingeroff, & Westen, 2008). Many writers have described the importance of using behavioral techniques in the early stages of treatment and graduating to psychodynamic treatment during the middle and latter phases (Zerbe, 2008). This approach suggests maximizing the relative strengths of multiple treatments and accounts for the complexity of these illnesses that demand our best efforts, willingness to acknowledge mistakes, and ongoing commitment toward helping our patients actualize a better way of being in the world.

Clinical material

The adolescent and adult cases that follow illustrate six psychodynamic themes that we have found essential in finding and healing a whole person with an ED. Because the course of each treatment is of considerably longer duration than most research studies or single-case method reports (i.e., one is 15 years; the other two years, respectively), we have been witness to considerable periods of growth followed by plateaus or regressions in ED symptomatology and character development. We believe that each example shows how the benefit of psychodynamic psychotherapy is multifaceted, and that both patient and clinician learn from being with each other and evolve considerably over the treatment, making many course corrections along an often rocky road. Inclusion of other modalities (i.e., cognitive behavioral, educational) and countertransference reactions are omitted because they are described in a number of other contributions (see Satir, 2009; Woodridge, 2016; Zerbe, 2008), and in order to throw light on the psychodynamic formulation and interventions we found most pivotal. We recognize that these omissions may give the case summaries a feeling of being laundered, as if we are avoiding some of the more complex, messy, and often beguiling matters that confront clinicians who work with this population. By limiting the scope of our presentation, we attempt to highlight what a psychodynamic approach offers that is uniquely growth promoting and suggest how application of psychodynamic theory anchors, guides, and "holds" the therapist who desires to welcome and engage aspects of the patient that have been heretofore ignored, unspoken, and neglected.

Case 1: a doctor who needs caring and continuity

Dr. R. is currently a 44-year-old married physician and mother of one who has been in twice-weekly psychodynamic psychotherapy for 15 years.

Dr. R.'s entry into psychotherapeutic treatment began under extreme circumstances when she was 29 years old. Then in her fourth year of medical school, she collapsed during a delivery in her obstetrics/gynecology rotation; difficulties in rousing her led to immediate hospitalization and an extensive medical workup that revealed abnormalities in electrolytes, low BMI (17.0), and brief episodes of a benign arrhythmia that resolved under supportive hospital care. When queried by the attending physician about an underlying eating problem such as restrictive dieting, purging, or excessive exercise, she initially denied any difficulties until "outed" by her roommate. Mr. V., a fellow medical student, had worried about his peer's peculiar dietary habits, confronted her about the odor of vomitus in their apartment, and challenged her gaunt and bedraggled appearance for months, all to no avail. When Mr. V. talked with the medical team about his concerns, he naively but trenchantly observed, "I cannot understand how no one sees her problem here at the medical school and takes it up with her. It's been the same since day one. She is so skinny. She has all the telltale signs of starvation that we studied in biochemistry and physical exam classes. You never see her eating with anyone in the cafeteria. Yet she seems to keep going like the Energizer Bunny, living on air and working all the time, so she gets great grades in every subject and rotation."

Dr. R.'s story is not uncommon, the manifest eating disorder overtly denied but paradoxically a secret that is "hidden, but in plain view" (Zerbe, 2008). What is unique is the ease with which the patient began to shed her defenses quickly as the therapeutic alliance grew; over a considerable period, she has created a fuller life for herself that could not be imagined at the initiation of the psychotherapy process.

Mandated by the dean of her medical school to enter an outpatient, behavioral based program to gain weight and learn coping skills, this patient took several months off to focus on her illness and thereafter successfully graduated, achieving her first choice in a sought-after residency program. Despite improvement in manifest symptoms (e.g., her BMI hovered around 18.2–18.5) and attainment of important professional goals, she nonetheless felt, "At a loss about what's happening to me. I know I work way too much, much more than I have to, but it seems as if it is all I have in life." She now voluntarily sought psychotherapy to mollify existential concerns and to maintain a watchful eye on her eating disorder symptoms, which continued to linger despite substantial symptomatic improvement made in the behavioral program. This patient's manifest worries centered less upon the lethal eating disorder and more upon a dread that she would never have friends or a meaningful romantic relationship; she refused to say much about her family of origin in the psychodynamic diagnostic interviews and blamed herself for being "stubborn as a mule, a natural loner, in need of constant praise and attention when I am honest with myself."

Dr. R. arranged with her residency director to take time off work for psychotherapy appointments and was heartened when no one probed too deeply into her rationale because, "I would have to make up some story about trauma or rape. No way to begin by having the fact that you are 'one of those obsessed, self-absorbed body freaks' get around to the faculty and peers and have them joke about you behind closed doors, because they do and they will." There were grains of truth in her jeremiad; eating-disordered patients report feeling castigated and bullied in their social circles and hence seek out "others" with the same preoccupations, such as on pro-eating disorder websites and among peers. Dr. R.'s comments were also projections of her sense of internalized shame onto others. It was nearly a year into psychotherapy before she could acknowledge that she had only two short-term dating relationships in her teens, was still a virgin, and now, as she began to date a resident in another field, was overcome with fears about her sense of woeful inexperience and lack in the realm of men. In the transference, she viewed me as a critical parent who would get in the way of her establishing adult intimacy, a repetition of what had transpired during her high school and college years. She remembered her father repeatedly telling her that, "Your mother and I take care of your grandparents, and we see that loyalty as our number one responsibility after our children."

Dr. R. alleged that her father could not understand why she would want to go out on the weekends, prefer to be with her friends sometimes, or experiment with dating. "What's the matter with wanting to be with your parents at your age?" he scolded before she turned 19 and "escaped" by admission to a liberal arts college close to home. Moreover, nothing in Dr. R.'s family was an acceptable career choice except law, medicine, or academics. It took little prompting for this emotional waif to begin to wonder early in the therapy what might be different in her life had she been able to explore other career directions or intellectual interests. She personified Brandchaft's characterization of pathological accommodation wherein the process of self-definition is curtained to maintain "indispensable ties" and shuts down those "central affective strivings" that promote "development of individualized selfhood (Brandchaft, Doctors, & Sorter, 2010, p. 80)."

As Dr. R. trusted me more to speak her truth without revulsion and to encourage her desire to date and have friendships, I also risked the interpretation that her severe eating symptoms were in my mind ways she attempted to feel alive by vomiting out or perhaps killing off the punitive parent she had internalized (Zerbe, 1993b). She let me know that this understanding made no sense to her whatsoever and surmised that I was reading a "deep psychoanalytic text" or had attended a conference to learn something new but its application had nothing to do with her. Pleased that she could directly disagree while covertly acknowledging veiled interest in my life and ways I kept her mind, even if she felt those ideas misguided, I commended her directness. Her remarks signaled that I take a step back, slow down, and keep centering the work on the establishment of boundaries and experience of self. I then attempted to help her to face down fears of abandonment and establish more of a feeling of safety in her selfhood by concretizing her progress; as used as she was to achieving high marks for good behavior, I would signal a "thumbs up" when she let me know she was angry, afraid, or in disagreement and when she undertook a new (and implicitly verboten) activity.

Highly attuned to the expectations of others, Dr. R. studied and did research when off duty, was quick to volunteer for extra assignments if needed, and was mortified when an attending or senior peer criticized her. In the psychotherapy process, efforts were made to dampen down her punitive superego while encouraging her to consider how she alienated her peers with her competitive streak. She had almost no observing ego during her four years of residency when it came to understanding that her jumping the gun to know all the answers on ward rounds or to curry favor by showing up early or staying late made her appear obsequious and estranged from almost everyone. From Dr. R.'s point of view, she was simply doing her work, and there was always more work to be done. Despite the realistic rigors of residency, weight continued in the low normal range, overt bingeing and purging had by her accounts decreased, laboratory studies were within normal range, and weekly psychodynamic psychotherapy continued. In other words, the manifest eating disorder was still present but not alarmingly out of control, a solid therapeutic alliance was established, and there was slight forward movement when it came to talking about feelings and observing the relentless pattern of overwork and conscientiousness that got in the way of her deepening her relationships and having any fun outside of the hospital setting.

As she neared the completion of her formal training, Dr. R. and her boyfriend began to think about their future together. Both became anxious at the thought of what it would mean to be on their own as physicians and decided that it was best to take another year or so for fellowship positions together in town. This choice was an important one because it meant that Dr. R. had to finally tell her parents that she would not be moving back to her hometown, that she had a boyfriend who was important to her, too, and that there was more she "needed to learn that I can only get in a fellowship." The transference implications were again obvious, the patient having formed a healthier sense of dependency on the therapist from which she could gather strength to be clear with others, namely her parents, about her personal and professional decisions and to work through her annihilation anxiety of self-agency. When she and her boyfriend became sexual, she was sure that one of us would not survive her perceived destructive attack on her internalized parental objects; interpretation of guilt, clarification of central affects that ranged from a sense of being evil to overpowering and sensual, and pointing out developmental and historical antecedents of her fear of her success, in the context of "surviving" in the transference, ameliorated her tendency to attack herself out of fear of disloyalty. Dr. R. had formed an intimate attachment and reveled in the courage she knew it took to tell her parents about it. At this point in the treatment, progress had been made so that an expectable regression might be in the offing, theory being a usable guide in surmising when backsliding might occur based on unsolidified healthier defenses and the compulsion to repeat traumatic themes (Shabad, 1987). One could also likely surmise that a return to more restrictive and disordered eating would ensue and this was, in fact, the case. Two weeks after beginning fellowship, Dr. R.'s weight dropped and her potassium was low; she felt nauseated and hungry simultaneously; and her period had stopped. She seemed finally ready to accept the interpretation in the therapy that "progress is never linear" and that she was recreating her past by not putting her needs and desire first. Dr. R. asserted her fledgling sense of selfhood and curtailed starting her fellowship temporarily to work on getting her eating problems under control and to take a deeper look into why she might now be trying to self-sabotage by placing herself in physical jeopardy.

Now five years into a psychodynamic psychotherapy process, Dr. R. decided to increase her sessions to thrice weekly during this hiatus. She also showed that she had internalized self-care functions; she spontaneously structured her day with periods of reading fiction, began lessons in Cuban drumming, went for walks and took coffee breaks in order to "discover new parts of this town." While these positive shifts were empathically mirrored to the patient, it was also important to repeatedly query Dr. R. about her choices and how she understood her decisions given her tendency to tune in to the desire of others and the keen interest she had in being admired. Real fruit was born from this period because the interests she began have been sustained over time. The patient returned to her fellowship in six months and continued her therapy and her newfound activities, albeit at a reduced frequency because of career responsibilities. Capacities to love, to work, and to play were becoming slowly integrated into a new psychological structure, and the eating and body image symptoms, still a subject of sustained discourse between us, assumed a background beat in contrast to their initial cacophonic boom.

In the seventh year of treatment, Dr. R. and her boyfriend married after each joined a local practice in their subspecialties. New challenges emerged as she assumed a more adult developmental role as a physician and wife. Still experiencing herself some days as "a teenager all dressed up in a white coat," the respect and genuine affection she received from her patients and peers were not easily metabolized. When many might expect a natural termination process to ensue given substantial improvement, Dr. R. said that the twice-weekly sessions were "as important as ever, maybe even more" because "while doing the tasks isn't so hard anymore, I feel that being an adult and responsible for my husband and my patients bears down on me. It is a weight. Therapy is the only place I can talk about that load and not think that I am a fool who *should* be grateful."

Interpretations at this crucial stage centered on conflicts related to healthy dependence, autonomy, and owning and embodying success. A simple technical maneuver derived from the central formulation of ameliorating the punitive superego and allowing oneself to own one's success (e.g., confront one's tendency to self-sabotage resulting from hostile introjects) was the repetitious phrase of allowing herself to "aim for better, not for the best or the perfect." Elvin Semrad's (Rako & Mazer, 1980) admonition that "to get anywhere with patients you have to go the affective route" (p. 115) because "a necessary condition of human health (is) to be able to bear what has be borne, to be able to think what has to be thought" (p. 47) further anchored our work as Dr. R. permitted greater expression of feelings. She came further to grips with how her parents had consciously and lovingly wished her to achieve but how their own narcissistic demands kept them "raising the bar" because of their own projected and displaced need. This anlage of pre-Oedipal and Oedipal dynamics led to her lack of confidence, shame, and rage that were repeatedly played out in the transference (McDougall, 1989; Zerbe, 2016). Purging temporarily increased at these moments of intensely expressed feeling but did not signal a significant regression. Dr. R. quickly responded to tiny clarifications of her feeling states and how the tension that could be contained between us signaled a move toward greater sense of efficacy. Her sense that she was "finding the real me" is a characteristic found repeatedly among qualitative research subjects who discover "in the context of a human relationship . . . what it is like to be a real person with a cohesive sense of self, known and loved by others for herself" (Beresin et al., 1989, p. 127).

In the eleventh year of treatment a confrontation occurred that Dr. R. and I have subsequently come to view as a "defining moment" in her continuing development of selfhood. Dr. R. had mentored Dr. E., a charming, outgoing junior colleague, when she joined the group practice, and the two had become good friends and supports for each other for about three years. Seemingly out of thin air, Dr. E. became savagely verbally abusive to Dr. R. and precipitously quit her job, leaving Dr. R. befuddled, dismayed, and sad. In the psychotherapy the patient and I were both puzzled by this uncharacteristic, dramatic behavior of her friend. Dr. R. spoke clearly about her concerns for Dr. E. but also held on to her anger at what she experienced as personal betrayal and devaluation. Dr. R.'s eating and body image difficulties exacerbated as she now restricted her food, began to vomit daily, and exercised to the point of near exhaustion; she defended herself against psychic collapse and the full expression of her rage by the inexorable return of her former coping mechanism. At this juncture in the psychodynamic process I suspected the return of symptoms from her appearance and body habitus but Dr. R. denied a regression. After seeking out professional consultation about her case, I again risked the interpretation that she was attempting to "vomit out, get rid of, even murder" the bad object of Dr. E. who had, in fact, wounded her deeply but who was also a stand-in for earlier objects who had let her down. Although unreceptive initially to my push for her to take in this idea, my consultant urged perseverance as a way to work through the "traumatic theme" that had been warded off by the sense of helplessness (Shabad, 1987; McDougall, 1989) and active return to the "defensive armour" (Shabad, 1987, p. 190) of the eating disorder. In the fullness of time a forensic accounting investigation begun by the senior partners and business manager in the practice revealed that Dr. E. had brazenly embezzled funds and was close to being caught when she fled. In terms of the psychotherapy, my patient had no refuge but to confront this traumatic loss and to work on it, giving up bit by bit a sense of omnipotence that she could and should have foreseen and avoided Dr. E. in the first place.

Over the next several years, additional chains that bound this patient to her eating disorder became unlinked as life itself unfolded in the inexorable march of time. Dr. R. and I have witnessed and weathered the death of her father, the birth of a son, and a nasty brush with her own mortality unrelated to her eating disorder. Each biological event brought Dr. R. closer to the realization that life is both finite and precious. At the beginning of psychotherapy her eating disorder was life-threatening but totally split off and dissociated; even as a medical student and then physician she knew more than most individuals that her illness could be fatal, thereby exhibiting one more feature of the omnipotent defense. Existential death anxiety that resides within each individual (Becker, 1973; Farber, Jackson, & Tabin, 2007; Rank, 1936/1964) was held at bay by a belief system protesting that, as Dr. R. later put it, "My thinking that this could happen to someone else. Never to me."

Although medical and psychological management of eating disorders combined with patient education modalities such as classes and books assist patients in curtailing the dissociated and warded-off aspects of their own mortality, yet another feature of long-term psychotherapy of adults, is how clinician and patient must come to terms with our own aging and death. Bearing witness together of visible, verifiable changes in physical appearance (e.g., aging) and weathering personal loss and the most positive family transitions (i.e., marriage, birth of a child, graduation) is a non-negotiable transformational force in the work. Neither therapist nor patient can elude our basic "nature, fate, animal destiny" (Becker, p. 237) that is ultimately a bodily reality of "fate and the natural order of things (p. 238)." Traversing this important chapter, which can only come about within the fullness of time, enables further mitigation of shame and integration of painful affects within the intimate attachment of the psychotherapeutic relationship as the patient acquires the fortitude and courage to bear responsibility for one's own life. The limitations of self and bodily experience initially denied by the eating disorder are brought into better alignment when the ignored, unspoken, and neglected problems of one's singular, courageous, mortal existence are given open space to wander and to be more fully understood as the case of Dr. R. continues to exemplify.

Case 2: the teenager who must be heard

Before my first encounter with Ms. B., a 15-year-old female with AN, I had several anxious conversations with her mother, Mrs. L., on the phone. Mrs. L. expressed concerns about Ms. B's health, difficulties knowing what was "right" in terms of post-inpatient treatment, and a wish that she (the mother) might have someone to talk to who would provide the family with reassurance and calm. While these reactions are understandable and perhaps even warranted in the face of a lethal disorder like AN, the quality and intensity of Mrs. L.'s messages gave me pause. It was not until Ms. B. came into my office and her first instinct was to wrap her slender frame with a blanket I had on my couch that I began to think about what it might mean. Was Ms. B. trying to create a barrier to protect herself from outside intrusions such as her mother's inability to contain her own fears and worries? Was the blanket serving a second skin function for unintegrated affect states that threatened to overwhelm the continuity of experiencing (Bick, 1968); was Ms. B. hiding the shameful parts of herself under the covers, afraid to be seen? These initial moments with ED patients, their families, and our attunement to the body (theirs and ours) are the beginnings of a language we hope to help translate into words, as one's outer shell becomes safe to emerge from in the presence of another.

Ms. B. was the eldest of her parents' three biological children, living in an upper middle-class Northeast suburb. Ms. B.'s parents were nurturing, warm, and likeable, but they struggled with tolerating affects that were not confined to experiences of closeness, support, and positive achievement. These expectations were mostly implicit in terms of the family needing to be together often and get along, but the need to be loving and "on the same page" was experienced by Ms. B. as oppressive, with little room for other feelings or her own experience. To belong in this family, Ms. B. became a rule-abiding, straight-A, jazz band–conducting, camp counselor for disadvantaged youth and overall model daughter. She understood and allowed herself to be the little girl her parents enjoyed caring for, and as payment she subjugated some of her own desires for independence and exploration. Ms. B.'s parents did not cause her ED. However, the interaction of parent and child psychologies – Ms. B.'s perfectionistic and harm-avoidant temperament, her parents' fear of loss/separation and inability to contain negative affects, and Ms. B.'s resultant pathological structures of accommodation (Brandchaft et al., 2010) – created the vulnerabilities that in the presence of medical distress and weight loss formed fertile ground for a disease process.

Ms. B.'s illness could be traced back to 2013, two years before our first meeting, when she started experiencing gastrointestinal distress and excessive bloating. Eating food aggravated her condition and she began eating less in an effort to manage abdominal discomfort. Despite thorough medical workups, there was no identifiable physiological cause of her pain and Ms. B. was advised to take Prilosec and avoid dairy and acidic foods. Feeling discouraged, upset, and still suffering she decided to take matters in to her own hands (and body) and began severely restricting, hiding food, and rapidly losing weight. Ms. B. recalled thinking "actions speak louder than words" and in this case she wanted her actions to demonstrate that she needed help. Soon after, Ms. B. developed severe abdominal pain diagnosed as superior mesenteric artery syndrome (SMA), and was immediately hospitalized, put on a feeding tube to regain weight, and closely monitored. This was the attention she wished for and now people were forced to listen. But something had shifted in this process. Ms. B. had been polite, followed the rules, did what she was supposed to and, in her mind, no one had been there. The pain from the SMA paled to the rage of being abandoned in her own body. The once compliant, obedient, and polite girl became punishing, threatening, powerful, and terrified. This ED – first diagnosed as avoidant/restrictive food intake disorder (ARFID) and then as AN – deserved to be reckoned.

At the beginning of our outpatient treatment, sessions with Ms. B. were characterized by painstaking detail, as if every cell in her body needed to be accounted for but in a way that was split off from feelings and highly rigid. We started our work together by talking about the distension that was causing her so much distress. I understood this focus as having several important functions – learning more about the distension as an organizing principle (Stolorow & Atwood, 1996) and helping Ms. B. integrate split-off affects that were being concretized in the body (Zerbe, 1993a/b, 1998, 2001). I spent several months getting to know the inner and outer workings of Ms. B.'s gut and every related sensation.

It was already a year into psychodynamic treatment (and a considerable period of consistent weight maintenance), that Ms. B. revealed an important secret she kept "hidden but in plain view." Ms. B. informed me that she thought of her protruding belly as a "baby" whom she named Casper. This little boy persona had been a constant companion, growing inside of her for the past several years, and needed her thoughtfulness and care-taking. If Casper was ignored or rejected, Ms. B. explained, he would get angry and punish her by getting "bigger" and inflicting unbearable pain. Unlike early, classical psychoanalytic accounts of EDs, I did not understand Ms. B.'s self-starvation as a defense against sexual fantasies of oral impregnation (e.g., Abraham, 1920/1973). Instead, I came to think of Casper as a sadistic "other," who had been projected into her, perhaps by mother, and had become a foreign body or intrusive object (Bion, 1967). If Ms. B. attempted to distinguish herself from or live without Casper, this hostile introject threatened to hurt and punish her. Ms. B. learned quickly that, if she did not constantly pay attention to Casper, his screaming inside of her would threaten her ability to exist. This type of conflict characterizes introjective personality configurations (Blatt & Shichman, 1983), where internalized aggression is understood as a reaction to parental figures who are experienced as intrusive and thwart a sense of an independent, competent self.

Casper had wreaked havoc on the entire system, and everyone (treaters and parents) was trying to find a solution to make him go away. I told Ms. B. that while Casper was rejected by most everyone he was welcome in therapy and offered a place at the table, so to speak. In my mind, Casper represented an aspect of Ms. B.'s feeling and thinking that needed containment and metabolizing in an intersubjective context or else he would continue to punish and become more aggressive. At times, I would ask Ms. B. some questions to help him come out of the shadows of her psyche and to remind her that I knew he was an essential part of her being: How does Casper feel about what you are describing (being angry at your parents)? What does Casper say when you want to do this (get your driver's permit)? I believe that my willingness to come to know Casper over time and take him very seriously as a part of Ms. B. helped her bear the confusion of his and her needs. By not trying to "abort" or get "rid" of this baby, Ms. B.'s aggressive feelings were contained, experienced, and ultimately survived without damage, destruction, or forced re-introjection.

After a period of several months, Ms. B. spoke about Casper not "kicking as much inside of [me]" or "not being as angry," which I understood as significant progress and perhaps an internalization of more benign introjects (including this writer) who could offer soothing functions. It is worth noting that had I been practicing more behaviorally, I may have offered to challenge the way Ms. B. was perceiving her body shape as a distortion and offered some psycho-education around bloatedness after eating. This approach may have inadvertently re-enacted the subjugation that Ms. B. had known with her parents and their needs and caused increased dietary restriction to punish herself and get people to listen to the angry baby inside.

After working with Casper for a period of eight months and following Ms. B.'s significantly improved distension, the focus of our work shifted to symbolizing other aspects of emotional pain. Ms. B. was profoundly ashamed of having an ED and kept her diagnosis hidden outside of her immediate family. While EDs are stigmatized and perceived as illnesses associated with vanity and willfulness (Zerbe, 1992, 1993b, 1993/1995, 1998), the idea that Ms. B. had an ED implied she had created her pain and was at fault because there was no "pill" she could take to make it go away. I understood Ms. B.'s shame to be related to what Morrison (1983) describes as a sense of "core unworthiness," an experience of the self that is felt to be intolerable. It was one thing for Ms. B. to eat again, regain weight, and be in physical pain because of an ED. But to imagine that she could share these experiences with others and they could love and accept this aspect of herself was unfathomable. Ms. B. had some words to describe these painful states though they were not registered affectively and were mostly experienced as dissociated parts. My concordant countertransference was experienced in the form of fatigue and confusion/disorientation in sessions. Over the course of several weeks of mutual sleepiness, I realized we might gain traction by trying to understand the fragile self that was already forming before the ED developed. While some of Ms. B.'s friends were exploring their own nascent sexuality and experimenting with autonomy, Ms. B. had retreated into a world of sadness, frustration, Disney movies, and parental supervision. What had been so frightening and scary about development all along?

I invited Ms. B. to tell me more about her childhood, her relationships, and memories. We had grown closer over the last year of treatment, her confidence was growing, and she had come to know that I was someone able and wanting to listen to her most confusing, hated experiences kept at a distance from anyone's knowing, including her own. At the beginning of this middle phase, Ms. B. had difficulties finding words to describe her early experiences. She wanted me to "see what it was like," and so on her own initiative she decided to bring old photo albums into sessions. Through this sharing, Ms. B. and I found our way to the experiences of early adolescence when she encountered rejection and a profound sense of "othering" from a close peer. Ms. B. was mocked for her appearance and insulted for being "fat" and "awkward" from someone she had known and trusted.[1] Unsure and afraid, her response had been to avoid and retreat, but the damage had been done as these projections registered with Ms. B.'s deepest fears of her own appearance and sense of self-worth. Sharing this story was a bit of a gateway toward moving beyond the prevailing false-self dynamics, as Ms. B. started to tell me more secrets about what she most despised, from the yellowish tint of her skin, to the fullness of her face, and to the bony shape of her knees. As Ms. B. shed layers she continued to reveal parts of herself kept hidden – worries of being alone, desires to be loved, fears of not being "good enough," and frustrations with other people. She eventually brought in journal entries from before the hospital for us to begin exploring together – lists she had made of things she could not bear about herself but wanted to share. These developments signaled not only an important reduction in the shame around Ms. B.'s ED, but an unmasking of its life-preserving functions. This was a shift in treatment, marked less by a ferocious illness and more by the revealing of a scared, lonely, little girl striving to come forth and break free.

Uncovering these painful truths with Ms. B. required great caution, care and attunement – sometimes I made explicit the process that might be unfolding and wondered about the regulation experienced within it. I was careful to invite Ms. B. to move at her own pace and use whatever means to start revealing these hidden parts. In our encounters with emotional deadness, we were willing to move away from content in the here and now and locate affect where it could be felt more (the past). The process of our exploring demonstrated Ms. B.'s capacity to work and play with ideas, symbols, and another person in a relational context. While Ms. B. did not necessarily become more willing to discuss her ED symptoms with friends, at least initially, she felt increasing conflict with revealing herself to others, not wanting to lie about who she was or the pain she experienced. She was able to tolerate other less than perceived ideals of self in other facets of her life. When she uncharacteristically earned a 'C' on an English exam, she felt disappointed but also accepted imperfection, with humor; when she was worried about forgetting to return a library book and scared to tell her parents about a late fee, we processed the confusing feelings and her parents responded gently. These beginnings represent a desire to be understood as a separate being, emerging with feelings, signaling the formation of a true self that may come to be known.

While these steps suggest gradual and continued forward progress, inevitable ruptures and regressions have occurred, particularly in the context of impending separations or other significant life events marking developmental milestones or feared progression. For example, before her first extended trip away from home since the onset of the ED one and a half years prior, Ms. B. lost six pounds in two weeks (6% of her body weight). Ms. B.'s parents, while normally quite anxious about these sorts of developments, were more afraid of disappointing Ms. B. (and themselves) with this travel and opportunity to be "normal," like other kids her age. I questioned my own concerns internally – was I being the over-protective parent, preventing her from growing? Would I be willing to acknowledge the communication I thought Ms. B. was making despite the angry feelings it might inspire? Wouldn't it be easier to wait until Ms. B. returned from her trip to reflect on these developments together? Ultimately, I felt my being silent would be complicit, a re-enactment of the pain that had been minimized or rejected at various stages of illness and could not be tolerated by family.

I arranged for a call with Ms. B. and her parents in the final hours before her leaving, and described the reality as I understood it – Ms. B. was in a weight-loss phase, acting out a cry for help and returning to ED behaviors, and we needed to understand the underlying feelings. Ultimately, Ms. B.'s parents decided to let her go on the trip and Ms. B. returned without having lost additional weight. In our first in-person meeting after the phone conversation, Ms. B. told me she was upset that I had voiced concern and as a result she had to "remember and think about eating the entire trip." She also said I was the only one who was not threatened by her desires or afraid to stand up to her, which she found reassuring. Perhaps she was able to take the concern that was split off with her to stave off further weight loss; and perhaps in her testing out the negative transference we could continue working with the anger and frustration that could not be contained elsewhere. Mostly, I believe I offered Ms. B. a way to reflect on what was happening – how when faced with an inevitable step forward, she became worried, frightened, and retreated back to the comforts of her ED. When the second extended separation occurred several months later and Ms. B. lost a little weight in the weeks prior (again but less than the first occasion), we were able to talk in real time about her starvation as reliable coping, her fear of being rejected by other people, and her worries over losing precious attachments with parents and their dependence on her as the family's "glue."

Through all these phases and shifts in a treatment that continues to evolve and is ongoing, Ms. B. has realized that the risks of not growing, expanding, and maturing are greater than the risks of the chains of illness. Starting with the beginnings of our putting actions and feelings in to words, to the "birthing" of Casper after the first year of therapy, to a deepening alliance that facilitated the revealing of her most hated parts of self, and finally to her efforts at testing the therapy relationship and her own fears of forward progress well into the second year of therapy – we have traveled precious, treacherous, unforeseen ground. As we look ahead, the tasks of adolescence remain as crucial as ever and promise to test Ms. B.'s courage, sensitivity, and ongoing capacities for self-hood. Fortunately, she does not need to relinquish the safety and stability that our therapy has offered to continue finding herself before something more permanent can exist.

Discussion

Many of us have entered into the field of psychotherapy because our own psychologies are drawn to the helping professions – we hope to provide relief from pain, a balm for what aches, and a cure from disease. In this process we feel efficacious, as if our efforts can be welcomed, taken in by another and the ensuing changes seem, at moments, to transcend time, space, and person. Our work in EDs presents inherent paradoxes as our patients' pain is their relief, their balm, and their best attempt at a cure. Somehow in the quagmire of these illnesses we must remain invested in the idea of these symptoms as solutions to unbearable psychic pain; and we must also confront our own fears of approaching the chains, while recognizing that the weight of these shackles become a part of the self that can easily be forgotten, dismissed, or ignored because the alternative of living without their grip is more frightening. While we may want to champion hope and believe that our clients are among the 30 to 50 per cent who "fully recover," our task is much harder – we must wait, without knowing whether we can help; we must bear the terrifying affects and losses our patients know in their marrow; and we must realize our efforts are sometimes the gradual unraveling of a spool of thread that has never been revealed and may break many times in the process. Our goals as psychotherapists treating eating disorders are not always relief, balm, or cure – sometimes they are awakening, desiring, and depending. These are the tasks of finding a true self, one that can be experienced as cohesive, vigorous, harmonious, and alive (Kohut & Wolfe, 1978). It is an almost impossible feat for all involved at any given time, and yet we must endure for our patients and ourselves.

We have offered two in-depth case examples to highlight our six analytic themes as well as the treatment arcs we have come to know well in EDs, which are characterized by complexity, depth, questions, triumphant moments, confusion, and most of all, significant internal growth and change. On the surface, both Dr. R. and Ms. B. share a penchant for achievement, a drive to succeed, and a need to conform or accommodate to their parents' wishes, needs, and dreams. Not surprisingly, both women felt ashamed that they developed illnesses that are associated with what might be perceived as superficial desires or bodily gratifications, and yet it was likely the only way they could express the pain of feeling separate from their truest longings and being rejected and unknown (Kaufman, 1980/1992). One might propose that the chains of the EDs were compromises Dr. R. and Ms. B. had to make in order to find someone who might listen; life and death means may have been necessary to feel any degree of attunement on the parts of their environment.

What we find particularly striking, especially having written about these two patients' developmental trajectories independently from each other, pertains to our theme of spoiling forward progress and the necessity of assisting another human being in finding new meaning in life beyond the chains of the ED that had perniciously sustained them by serving multiple psychological functions (Satir et al., 2011; Zerbe, 2008, 2015). After mutual periods of relative symptom stability and at the cusp of new tasks of individuation and meaning making – for Dr. R. her emergence from residency and for Ms. B. her first independent trip from home – both patients seemingly faltered, regressed back to old ED behavioral patterns, and appeared ill-prepared to meet the next set of emotional and interpersonal challenges. Our position and experience allowed us to help our patients put into words what was being acted out and let them know explicitly and implicitly that we would not be destroyed or disappointed with their progress. While our patients may manifestly want these things – autonomy, intimacy, forward movement – the costs are great and they become identified with the punitive introjects of old who threaten to annihilate any efforts at differentiation. Our job, highlighted in the in-depth case material, was to help our patients relocate themselves, in their relationships with us, in order to find their own separate voice and try again.

In both therapies the emotional climates in the dyads were ones of attunement, empathic resonance, adaptation, and playfulness. There is a sense of a holding environment, shared in the therapeutic space, with an effort at reducing potential impingements so that the patients can have the experience of "going on being" (Winnicott, 1960). This is particularly evident during the year of working with Ms. B.'s internal baby Casper, where the needs of this child were attended to and not split off or aborted; a similar process could be observed with Dr. R. during her self-delayed fellowship and time away from professional pressures in order to pursue other needs and wants of her own. Through processes of identification, introjection, and projection over the course of many months and years, Dr. R. and Ms. B. were able to start internalizing the soothing functions of their therapists, who did not attempt to exert their will or influence but who also recognized the presence of two unique subjectivities, coexisting and mutually influencing each other. Notably, both therapists created the experience of new affective responses for their patients which appeared to resonate with internal struggles that allowed for the building blocks of a more flexible, resilient self (Brandchaft et al., 2010). For example, when Dr. R. rejected an interpretation (e.g., purging as eliminating a punitive introject), the therapist's response was one of positivity and adaptation. She incorporated the frustration Dr. R. felt and modified her interventions by concretizing progress (i.e., with the "thumbs up" signal) and created the boundaries needed to feel more safe and secure. Instead of asking Dr. R. to conform to the therapist's ideas, feelings, and needs, Dr. R. became the source of "tuning in" and was given space and freedom to push back, kick, or scream as needed without punishment or consequence. Later in the course of Dr. R.'s treatment she was able to make use of the previously rejected interpretation when her friend deeply disappointed her. Similar to the evolving research literature that demonstrates the importance of sequencing treatment interventions, psychodynamic hypotheses may resonate and be constructively metabolized at another point in treatment, supporting our view that growth in the self occurs over the long term and advances slowly, the therapeutic couple learning as they go from each other about what "fits" at any given moment.

This brings us to the central question for both patients and therapists: What does living life fully mean, especially beyond manifest ED symptoms, and how does therapy actually work to help our patients realize, confront, tolerate, and begin to experience these fundamental human questions and strivings? Clearly, establishing a sense of one's genuineness and revealing secrets once dissociated, split off, or believed to be unspeakable are key for those individuals whose family systems contributed to pathological accommodation. We believe that in this unfolding, just as in human development itself, there is no substitute for tincture of time. The psychotherapy process can be known and felt deeply only in long-term therapies, most often psychoanalytic treatments, spanning several years of intensive weekly and preferably more frequent sessions. As our cases have attempted to illustrate, therapeutic consistency, durability, and familiarity are the beginnings of the delicate underpinnings of those internal structures that needed to be formed, destroyed, re-formed and strengthened in a human relationship. To be part of the repetition of our patients' organizational systems and their patterned and reflexive ways, therapists must be drawn in, poked at, sensed, and experienced. This can only happen after a secure base has been established – an achievement that often takes months and years – where communication is understood as both manifest content and as internal felt experience that can be shared and reflected upon together. There is no substitute for the time it takes to disentangle from the shame of being, to begin feeling safe enough to explore oneself and the secrets one carries, and to start truly living and being in one's own skin. Even beyond these initial strivings, our patients' need for self-objects and new developmental experiences is a life-long process – one true accomplishment being the recognition of healthy dependency in the space of experiencing separateness. This becomes apparent for both Dr. R. and Ms. B. as their engagement in treatment shifts beyond the ED but they continue in intensive psychotherapy while they experience more of life and the demands and tasks needed to realize further who they are.

This work takes great effort and is rarely easy. The pernicious hold of the ED offers enormous promise for greater understanding of those chains that entangle human beings with other psychosomatic illnesses and has significant potential to assist clinicians in unearthing labyrinths of meaning and feeling that are part of the human condition. The chains that shackle can eventually give way to the ties that free – with the therapist, in the self, and within other significant relationships. In this way the ED becomes understood as a mechanism for survival that only threatens the new self, no longer needed to protect or guard what has already emerged. We seek for our patients their own freedom. What this means will be different and unique for each one, and we do not presume to know what this may be. Even more, what this means for each of us treaters is also unique – a life-long process and search of becoming more fully human. In our quest for answers our best training is the deeply personal search that allows ourselves the time to be the therapists our patients need in order for them to be and to become themselves. We may imagine what forms this "something more" might take that promotes the mysterious and ineluctable "coming into being and becoming." Psychotherapeutic improvement of EDs is not an endpoint in itself but an embarkation into self-discovery that we have the privilege to watch unfold daily in our consultation rooms.

Conclusion

Long-term psychodynamic psychotherapy affords patients with EDs new opportunities to develop a fuller, sturdier sense of self and to master symptoms simultaneously. Detailed case reports that support this approach augment extant and evolving research by examining case formulation, themes, and interventions that must be repeatedly worked on to foster development and resiliency. Only within the safe haven of a secure therapeutic relationship that evolves over time can the patient begin to experience those personal concerns that have been ignored, unspoken, and heretofore neglected that encase the manifest problem of the ED. Examples of extended treatments in the literature are a form of clinical research and support the evidence base of what treatments work for whom; they offer fresh perspectives in understanding our patients more deeply, framing new research questions, and encouraging practitioners to further dialogue among ourselves by expanding on what we glean as ameliorative factors in psychotherapy.

Note

1 There was also a resonance with the betrayal of trust she experienced with her distension by caregivers and doctors who she experienced as rejecting her pain.

References

Abraham, K. (1920/1973). Manifestations of the female castration complex. In H. A. Abraham (Ed.), *Selected papers on psychoanalysis*. London: Hogarth.

Adair, C., Marcoux, G. C., Cram, B. S., Ewashen, C. J., Chafe, J., Cassin, S. E., . . . Brown, K. E. (2007). Development and multi-site validation of a new condition-specific quality of life measure for eating disorders. *Health and Quality of Life Outcomes*, *5*, 23.

Agras, W. S., Walsh, B. T., Fairburn, C. G., Wilson, C. T., & Kramer, H. C. (2000). A multicentre comparison of cognitive – behavioural therapy and interpersonal psychotherapy for bulimia nervosa. *Archives of General Psychiatry*, *57*, 459–466.

Bachar, E., Latzer, Y., Kreitler, S., & Berry, E. M. (1999). Empirical comparison of two psychological therapies: Self psychology and cognitive orientation in the treatment for anorexia and bulimia. *Journal of Psychotherapy Practice and Research, 8*, 115–128.
Becker, E. (1973). *The denial of death*. New York: Palgrave Macmillan.
Bell, L. (2003). What can we learn from consumer studies and qualitative research in the treatment of eating disorders. *Eating and Weight Disorders, 8*, 181–187.
Benjamin, J. (2004). Beyond doer and done to: An intersubjective view of thirdness. *Psychoanalytical Quarterly, 73*, 5–46.
Beresin, E., Gordon, C., & Herzog, D. (1989). The process of recovering from anorexia nervosa. In J. R. Bemporad & D. B. Herzog (Eds.), *Psychoanalysis and eating disorders* (pp. 103–130). New York: Guilford.
Bers, S. A., Blatt, S. J., & Dolinsky, A. (2004). The sense of self in anorexia-nervosa patients: A psychoanalytically informed method for studying self-representation. *Psychoanalytic Study of the Child, 59*, 294–316.
Bick, E. (1968). The experience of the skin in early object-relations. *The International Journal of Psycho-Analysis, 49*, 484–486.
Bion, W. (1967). *Second thoughts: Selected papers on psychoanalysis*. London: Heinemann.
Blatt, S. J., & Shichman, S. (1983). Two primary configurations of psychopathology. *Psychoanalysis Contemporary Thought, 6*, 187–254.
Brandschaft, B., Doctors, S., & Sorter, D. (2010). *Toward an emancipatory psychoanalysis*. New York: Routledge.
Bruch, H. (1978). *The golden cage: The enigma of anorexia nervosa*. Boston: Harvard.
Candelori, C., & Ciocca, A. (1998). Attachment and eating disorders. In P. Bria, A. Ciocca, & S. DeRisio (Eds.), *Psychotherapeutic issues on eating disorders: Models, methods, and results* (pp. 139–154). Rome: Societa Editrice Universo.
Carter, F., Jordan, J., McIntosh, V., Luty, S., McKenzie, J., Frampton, C., . . . Joyce, P. (2011). The long-term efficacy of three psychotherapies for anorexia nervosa: A randomized, controlled trial. *International Journal of Eating: Disorders, 44*, 647–654.
Colli, A., Gentile, D., Tanzilli, A., Speranza, A. M., & Lingiardi, V. (2016). Therapeutic interventions in the treatment of eating disorders: A naturalistic study. *Psychotherapy, 53*, 152–162.
Crow, S., Peterson, C., Swanson, S., Raymond, N., Specker, S., Eckert, E., & Mitchell, J. (2009). Increased mortality in bulimia nervosa and other eating disorders. *The American Journal of Psychiatry, 166*, 1342–1346.
Daniel, S. I., Poulsen, S., & Lunn, S. (2016). Client attachment in a randomized clinical trial of psychoanalytic and cognitive-behavioral psychotherapy for bulimia nervosa: Outcome moderation and change. *Psychotherapy, 53*, 174–184.
Dare, C., Eisler, I., Russell, G., Treasure, J., & Dodge, L. (2001). Psychological therapies with adults with anorexia nervosa: Randomized controlled trial of outpatient treatments. *The British Journal of Psychiatry, 178*, 216–221.
Davies, J. (2003). Falling in love with love: Oedipal and postoedipal manifestations of idealization, mourning, and erotic masochism. *Psychoanalytic Dialogues, 13*, 1–28.
Fairburn, C. G. (1997). Interpersonal psychotherapy for bulimia nervosa. In D. M. Garner & P. E. Garfinkel (Eds.), *Handbook of treatment for eating disorders* (2nd ed.). (pp. 278–294). New York: Guilford Press.
Farber, S. K., Jackson, C. C., Tabin, J. K., & Bachar, E. (2007). Death and annihilation anxieties in anorexia nervosa, bulimia, and self-mutilation. *Psychoanalytic Psychology, 24*, 289–305.
Fichter, M. F., & Quadflieg, N. (2004). Twelve-year course and outcome of bulimia nervosa. *Psychological Medicine, 34*, 1395–1406.

Fichter, M., & Quadflieg, N. (2016). Mortality in eating disorders: Results of a large prospective clinical longitudinal study. *International Journal of Eating Disorders*, *49*, 391–401.

Kafka, F. (1968). *The trial*. New York: Schocken Books.

Kaufman, G. (1980/1992). *Shame: The power of caring* (3rd ed.). Rochester, VT: Schenkman.

Kohut, H., & Wolf, E. S. (1978). The disorders of the self and their treatment: An outline. *The International Journal of Psycho-Analysis*, *59*, 413–425.

Lamoureux, M., & Bottorff, J. (2005). "Becoming the real me:" Recovery from anorexia nervosa. *Health Care for Women International*, *26*, 170–188.

Leichsenring, F., & Leibing, E. (2003). The effectiveness of psychodynamic therapy and cognitive behavior therapy in the treatment of personality disorders: A meta-analysis. *The American Journal of Psychiatry*, *160*, 1223–1232.

Lock, J., Le Grange, D., Agras, W. S., Moye, A., Bryson, S. W., & Jo, B. (2010). Randomized clinical trial comparing family-based treatment to adolescent focused individual therapy for adolescents with anorexia nervosa. *Archives of General Psychiatry*, *67*, 1025–1032.

McDougall, J. (1989). *Theaters of the body: A psychoanalytic approach to psychosomatic illness*. New York: W.W. Norton.

Miller, P. (1996). Redefining success in eating disorders. *Addictive Behavior*, *21*, 745–754.

Morgan, H. G., & Hayward, A. E. (1988). Clinical assessment of anorexia nervosa: The Morgan-Russell outcome assessment schedule. *The British Journal of Psychiatry*, *152*, 367–371.

Morrison, A. P. (1983). Shame, ideal self, and narcissism. *Contemporary Psychoanalysis*, *19*, 295–318.

Noordenbos, G. (2011). Which criteria for recovery are relevant according to eating disorder patients and therapists? *Eating Disorders: The Journal of Treatment & Prevention*, *19*, 441–451.

Poulsen, S., Lunn, S., Daniel, S. I. F., Folke, S., Mathiesen, B. B., Katznelson, H., & Fairburn, C. G. (2014). A randomized controlled trial of psychoanalytic psychotherapy or cognitive-behavioral therapy for bulimia nervosa. *The American Journal of Psychiatry*, *171*, 109–116.

Rako, S., & Mazer, H. (Eds.) (1980). *Semrad: The heart of a therapist*. New York: Jason Aronson, Inc.

Rank, O. (1936/1986). *Will therapy*. New York: Alfred Knopf.

Richards, L. K., Shingleton, R. M., Goldman, R., Siegel, D., & Thompson-Brenner, H. (2016). Integrative dynamic therapy for bulimia nervosa: An evidence-based case study. *Psychotherapy*, *53*, 195–205.

Satir, D., Goodman, D., Shingleton, R., Porcerelli, J., Gorman, B., Pratt, E., . . . Thompson-Brenner, H. (2011). Alliance-focused therapy for anorexia nervosa: Integrative relational and behavioral change treatments in a single case experimental design. *Psychotherapy*, *48*, 401–420.

Satir, D. A., Thompson-Brenner, H., Boisseau, C. L., & Crisafulli, M. (2009). Countertransference reactions to adolescent eating disorder patients: Relationships to symptoms and personality. *International Journal of Eating Disorders*, *42*, 511–521.

Shabad, P. (1987). Fixation and the road not taken. *Psychoanalytic Psychology*, *4*, 187–205.

Shedler, J. (2010). The efficacy of psychodynamic psychotherapy. *American Psychologist*, *65*, 98–109.

Steinhausen, H. (2002). The outcome of anorexia nervosa in the 20th century. *The American Journal of Psychiatry*, *159*, 1284–1293.

Stolorow, R. D., & Atwood, G. E. (1996). The intersubjective perspective. *Psychoanalytic Review, 83*, 181–194.
Tasca, G., Ritchie, K., & Balfour, L. (2011). Practice review: Implications of attachment theory and research for the assessment and treatment of eating disorders. *Psychotherapy, 48*, 249–259.
Tasca, G., Ritchie, K., Conrad, G., Balfour, L., Gayton, J., Lybanon, V., & Bissada, H. (2006). Attachment scales predict outcome in a randomized controlled trial for binge eating disorder: An aptitude by treatment interaction. *Psychotherapy Research, 16*, 106–121.
Thompson-Brenner, H., Satir, D. A., Franko, D., & Herzog, D. B. (2012). Clinician reactions to patients with eating disorders: A review. *Psychiatric Services, 63*, 73–78.
Thompson-Brenner, H., Weingeroff, J., & Westen, D. (2008). Empirical support for psychodynamic psychotherapy for eating disorders. In R. Levy & S. Ablon (Eds.), *Evidence-based psychodynamic practice* (pp. 67–92). New York: Humana.
Thompson-Brenner, H., & Westen, D. (2005a). A naturalistic study for bulimia nervosa, Part 1: Comorbidity and therapeutic outcome. *The Journal of Nervous and Mental Diseases, 193*, 573–584.
Thompson-Brenner, H., & Westen, D. (2005b). A naturalistic study for bulimia nervosa, Part 2: Therapeutic interventions in the community. *The Journal of Nervous and Mental Diseases, 193*, 585–595.
Tobin, D. (2012). The rationale for psychodynamic psychotherapy of eating disorders: An empirically constructed approach. In P. Bria, A. Ciocca, & S. DeRisio (Eds.), *Treatment and recovery of eating disorders* (pp. 97–108). New York: Nova Science.
Tobin, D., Banker, J., Weisberg, L., & Bowers, W. (2007). I know what you did last summer (and it was not CBT): A factor analytic model of international psychotherapeutic practice in eating disorders. *International Journal of Eating Disorders, 40*, 754–757.
Treasure, J., Corfield, F., & Cardi, V. (2012). A three-phase model of the social emotional functioning in eating disorders. *European Eating Disorders Review, 20*, 431–438.
Treasure, J., Todd, G., Brolly, M., Tiller, J., Nehmed, A., & Denman, F. (1995). A pilot study of a randomized trial of cognitive analytical therapy vs. educational behavioral therapy for adult anorexia nervosa. *Behavioral Research and Therapy, 33*, 363–367.
Ward, A., Ramsay, R., Turnbull, S., Steele, M., Steele, H., & Treasure, J. (2001). Attachment in anorexia nervosa: A transgenerational perspective. *British Journal of Medical Psychology, 74*, 497–505.
Warren, C. S., Schafer, K. J., Crowley, M. E., & Olivardia, R. (2012). A qualitative analysis of job burnout in eating disorder treatment providers. *Journal of Eating Disorders, 20*, 175–195.
Weissman, M. M., Markowitz, J. C., & Klerman, G. L. (2000). *Comprehensive guide to interpersonal psychotherapy*. New York: Basic.
Winnicott, D. W. (1960). The theory of the parent-infant relationship. *The International Journal of Psychoanalysis, 41*, 585–595.
Wooldridge, T. (2016). *Understanding anorexia nervosa in males: An integrative approach*. New York: Routledge.
Zerbe, K. (1992). Eating disorders in the 1990s: Clinical challenges and treatment implications. *Bulletin of the Menninger Clinic, 52*, 167–187.
Zerbe, K. (1993a). *The body betrayed: Women, eating disorders, and treatment*. Washington, DC: American Psychiatric Press. (Published in paperback, Carlsbad, CA: Gurze Books, 1995.)
Zerbe, K. (1993b). Whose body is it anyway? Understanding and treating psychosomatic aspects of eating disorders. *Bulletin of the Menninger Clinic, 57*, 161–177.

Zerbe, K. (1993/1995). *The body betrayed: Women, eating disorders, and treatment*. Washington, DC: American Psychiatric Press: Carlsbad, CA: Gurze Books.
Zerbe, K. (1998). Knowable secrets: Transference and countertransference manifestations in eating disorder patients. In W. Vandereyken & P. J. Beaumont (Eds.), *Treating eating disorders*. (pp. 30–55). London: Athlone Press.
Zerbe, K. (2001). When the self starves: Alliance and outcome in the treatment of eating disorders. In J. Petrucelli & C. Stuart (Eds.), *Hungers and compulsions: Contemporary perspectives in the psychoanalytic treatment of eating disorders and addictions* (pp. 183–208). New York: Jason Aronson, Inc.
Zerbe, K. (2008). *Integrated treatment of eating disorders: Beyond the body betrayed*. New York: W.W. Norton.
Zerbe, K. (2015). Psychodynamic theory of eating disorders. In L. Smolak & M. Levine (Eds.), *Handbook of eating disorders* (pp. 253–268). Oxford: Wiley-Blackwell.
Zerbe, K. (2016). Psychodynamic issues in the treatment of Binge eating disorder: Working with shame, secrets, no-entry, and false body defenses. *Clinical Social Work Journal*, *44*, 8–17.
Zipfel, S., Wild, B., Groß, G., Friederich, H., Teufel, M., Schellberg, K. E., . . . Herzog, W. (2014). Focal psychodynamic therapy, cognitive behaviour therapy, and optimised treatment as usual in outpatients with anorexia nervosa (ANTOP study): Randomised controlled trial. *Lancet*, *383*, 127–137.

2

INVISIBILITY AND INSUBSTANTIALITY IN AN ANOREXIC ADOLESCENT

Phenomenology and dynamics

Mary Brady

Introduction

Certain anorexic patients experience themselves, and present to us, as 'invisible' and 'insubstantial'. I intend to discuss this clinical presentation and its dynamic roots. I offer the case of 'Clare', an adolescent in analysis, in order to describe her sense of invisibility and insubstantiality, and my efforts to understand and interpret these problems. My purpose is to describe particular clinical issues and link them with the perplexing psychological forces underneath.

I am considering 'invisibility' and 'insubstantiality' as two phenomenologically related ideas with different emphases. Webster's first definition of 'invisible' is 'incapable by nature of being seen'. The first definition of 'insubstantial' is 'lacking substance or reality', and the second is 'lacking firmness or solidity'. If one feels that one is substantial, then one can expect to be seen. Clare frequently described herself as feeling invisible, and occasionally as feeling insubstantial – for instance, she felt literally insubstantial when her male friends would pick her up and toss her around. Her slight body concretely expressed her insubstantiality.

I suggest that the experience of visibility, rooted in infantile experience of being seen and known by mother, is further developed or hindered by processes related to separation and differentiation. 'I' cannot feel like an 'I' who can be seen, unless I develop a sense of self, differentiated from others. Clare felt a dire need to maintain a sense of indivisibility from her object. The proclivity to defend herself against anxiety through phantasied merger prevented Clare from developing a sense of a separate and substantial self. She saw her own needs as irrelevant (except for the urgent need to feel merged with her object) and experienced herself as 'for other people'.

As referred to previously, I consider the sense of visibility and substantiality to be related to early experiences of being seen and known by mother

(Bion, 1962) and also to aspects of narcissistic object relations well described by Rosenfeld (1964):

> [I]n narcissistic object relations . . . the self becomes so identified with the incorporated object that all separate identity or any boundary between self and objects is denied. . . . In narcissistic object relations the defences against any recognition of separateness between self and object play a predominant part. Awareness of separation would lead to feelings of dependence on an object and therefore to anxiety.
>
> *(Rosenfeld, 1964, pp. 170–171)*

Differentiation requires a slowly increasing capacity to tolerate anxiety and conflict.

Underlying the sense of invisibility described here is a lack of separation and differentiation from mother, and an effort to live inside her skin. This is not primarily with the aim of dominating the object (as in another group of eating-disordered patients described by Quagliata, 2004) nor from grandiose wishes (as described from an ego psychological point of view by Reich (1973) in submissive women who organise themselves in narcissistic object relations to idealised men).[1] As opposed to a primary wish for omnipotent control or grandiosity, 'invisible' (and I would add 'impotent') patients cannot conceive of the right to or a wish for a self, and desperately seek the experience of merger with another to prevent terrifying experiences of separation.

Such excessive reliance on phantasied merger impedes the development of a healthy sense of identity, including a capacity to tolerate pain and boundaries. The excessive reliance on projective identification (in the service of merging) depletes the sense of self and can lead to experiences of depersonalisation, especially when separations loom.

Klein, in her 1955 paper 'On identification' discusses projective identification utilizing J. Green's (1950) novel, *If I Were You*. Fabian, the main character of the novel, makes a pact with the devil to become someone else. Grotstein (1981) in a discussion of Klein's paper describes invisibility as a part of projective identification:

> Though Klein did not emphasize it in her interpretations, my own re-reading of *If I Were You* compels me to mention the first stage in projective identification. Klein laid stress on the second stage, that of fusion with another, but it is important to note the earlier step, that is, the basic quest for invisibility. Projective identification involves the desire of the infant – or the suffering adult – to become invisible, to disappear, or generally speaking, to negate one's own existence. Such phantasies of disappearing usually come at a high cost to self-esteem, the sense of authenticity, and self-connectedness. Patients who describe this phenomenon believe

> that the body or soul that they have denied is no longer available to them for reparation.
>
> *(Grotstein, 1981, p. 130)*

With Clare, both aspects of projective identification contributed to her invisibility and insubstantiality. Firstly, the wish to be invisible – not to have to consider her own wishes and fears – left her denuded of her own experiences of herself. Secondly, the phantasied merger – played out in her relationships, including in the transference – left her bereft of developing her own reflections and resources. Her anorexic erasing of her body specifically expressed disinterest in her own bodily needs as well as her own self and life.

Merging can also involve a wish to find a warm place inside another, which could create the potential for containing good aspects of the self. Clare, instead, would give herself over to another stronger personality, without any discrimination between strength and an actual emotional capacity to help her develop. This overly persistent desire to locate herself within another precluded the effort to gain her own voice and to make herself heard in relation to another. As Grotstein (2000) describes, 'If the infantile aspect of the personality seeks to invade the object or become the object, the projective reidentification that takes place involves a dedifferentiation of self and object (we are identical)' (p. 73).

Experiences of agency and efficacy are aspects of the capacity to have a sense of a visible self. Broucek (1979) reviewed experiments conducted with infants and concluded that 'the sense of efficacy and the pleasure associated with it are . . . the foundation of self feeling' (p. 312). This emphasis is different from, but not in contradiction with, Bion's (1962) view of the infant's sense of self as developing in conjunction with maternal containment and reverie. Had Clare's mother been able to be more assertive in her maternal containment (not abruptly leaving and weaning Clare at six months), Clare would not have suffered the loss of a sense of efficacy that maternal containment allows. Such helplessness likely led Clare to over-rely on a wish to merge with her object, further depleting her interest in her own capacities. 'The mothering person sustains the infant's sense of efficacy by predictability and reliability in her behavior' (Broucek, 1979, p. 314). In a later paper, Broucek (1982) discusses shame as the result of helpless loss of the object. Substantial shame 'with abandonment and isolation anxieties may lead to clinging attachment behavior, under-mining the separation-individuation processes and promoting regressive efforts to re-establish a symbiotic type of relationship' (Broucek, 1982, p. 371). Although Broucek worked within an ego psychological framework that did not contain the concept of internal object relations relied on by Rosenfeld, both theorists are describing the phenomena of invisibility and defensive attempts to merge with another that Clare exhibited.

Paradoxically, an eating disorder can also serve to make visible for the first time the terrible troubles a patient has heretofore been struggling with invisibly. The starvation can be an unconscious attempt to bring to light a problem the patient hasn't been able to solve. Clare's anorexia caused her parents to bring her to treatment where her sense of self could begin to be known. That which was too frightening to say she made visible through bodily distress and starvation.

Anorexia

Lawrence (2001, p. 52) comments that one of the difficulties in treating eating-disordered patients is that while the symptoms are relatively consistent, 'the motives behind the symptoms are not always the same'. Indeed, the anorexic patients she describes bear similarities to and dissimilarities from my patient. In her thinking about anorexia, Lawrence emphasises an unconscious attack on the oedipal couple. Clare's need to maintain a sense of indivisibility from her object could be seen through this lens. However, as clinicians we are always trying to listen for our patients' most compelling desires and anxieties, and, for Clare, an attack on the couple seemed much less visceral than her desire to live within her mother's skin, resulting in a diminishment of the development of a self. It may be that Clare represents a sub-group of anorexics in whom aggression is less marked, although, of course, present. Clare could feel her willingness to starve herself out of existence, but also seemed relieved to be able to locate parts of her that were opposed to this wish. This is in contrast to anorexic patients I have seen who gloat at the image of people suffering at their funerals.

Lawrence (2001, p. 44) describes one 'atypical anorexic patient' who related a 'white out' situation in her mind, 'in which snow had suddenly and heavily fallen, obscuring all sense of differentiation and at the same time annihilating all life'. Lawrence relates this phantasy to 'a state of mind in which the parents as a couple in particular no longer exist'. She saw her patient as endlessly involved in efforts to deny recognition of the parental union. Clare was similar in her desire to be one with her mother (and with me in the transference), but Lawrence experienced her patient as more controlling and attacking than I did mine. Indeed, my patient's aggression was quite subsumed by her desire for psychic oneness.

My thinking in this paper does not refute various considerations of the bases for anorexia described by others. Birksted-Breen (1989) summarises these multiple foci: the defence against greed and the wish for oral impregnation (Berlin, Boatman, Sheimo, Szurek, 1951); the disturbance of body image as related to puberty (Crisp, 1973); and the Kleinian emphases on paranoid fears of being poisoned, or envy and the fear of endangering the good object (Klein, 1957). Additionally, Williams (1997) emphasises that young people who develop eating disorders have been the recipients of parental projections. Lawrence (2002, pp. 837–838) adds that the presence of the intrusive object 'so prevalent in anorexia is often linked to intrusive aspects of the patient's psychopathology'. She describes, '(Anorexia) . . . as a disorder in which a failure to differentiate adequately from the mother leads to difficulties in mastering sexual anxieties of intrusion, which become concretely enacted in the refusal of food' (Lawrence, 2002, p. 838).

Birksted-Breen (1989) also notes that many theoreticians have been 'impressed . . . by the anorexic's wish for, and fear of fusion with her mother (Bene, 1973; Spillius, 1973; Bruch, 1974; Boris, 1984; Sprince, 1984; Hughes, Furgiuele, & Bianco, 1985)' (Birksted-Breen, 1989, p. 30). These observations are in concert with my own, but I am emphasising in this paper the narcissistic object relations and the consequent effect of invisibility and insubstantiality related to the avoidance of experiences that would render a more substantial sense of self.

Clinical material

History

Slender, artistic and waif-like, Clare began treatment with me when she was 15, at the start of her sophomore year of high school. We met three times a week, using the couch during most of her treatment. During the summer before her freshman year, Clare developed anorexia. Her weight declined to 100 pounds at 5 feet 6 inches. That year she started group therapy for eating-disordered girls and was also closely followed by her paediatrician, who told Clare she would be hospitalised if she lost any more weight. She did not make a connection with the group, and, after a summer break, she and her family decided to seek treatment with me.

Clare is the youngest of three children in an affluent, educated, creative family. Clare's mother described her as a difficult, clingy baby who 'cried all the time – some of the time if with me, all of the time if not with me'. Clare's mother described feeling 'terrible' about weaning Clare abruptly and then leaving for three weeks when Clare was six months old in order to travel with her husband for a movie he was producing. Thus Clare, and mother's own need to be with Clare, were made invisible and subordinated to father, rather than being contained and supported by him. Despite mother having other good qualities, her inability to assert herself on her own or Clare's behalf led to a difficulty for Clare to be able to internalise a vigorous maternal object.

Clare has two brothers, one a year and a half and another two and a half years older than she. The three siblings are close, but Clare sees males as able to participate in the world in a manner females cannot. She shares with her mother a central emotional role in the family, but with little sense of how she can be visible outside the family. She envies her brothers their seeming ease in this area, as they excel at prestigious schools and in sports.

Clare's father is a highly successful movie producer who grew up in a frigid, status-obsessed family. He travels intermittently for his work now, but was gone for extended periods when the children were younger. Clare's mother is a sensitive, talented woman who in some ways is a warm and involved mother. She turned to Clare in her husband's absences and Clare often slept with her while father was away, until well into adolescence. Clare is highly identified with and idealising of her mother and, although chronologically adolescent, has made little differentiation from her.

Clare had not begun menstruating when she began treatment. Neither she nor her parents expressed any concern about this, and they were in no hurry for her sexual development to become visible in this way. During an early meeting with Clare's parents, her mother told me of having been molested as a child by a parish priest, whom her parents were unwilling to question or to oppose. Her story was of an extreme abuse and lack of protection as a child, to the extent that I literally felt sick to my stomach as I listened. This terrible background affected Clare in terms of very fearful fantasies regarding sexuality as well as an identification with a powerless victim. Clare said, 'I don't understand it that he had so much power and people were so afraid of him.' Mother's need for protection from sexual predation had been radically unseen in the prior generation, and Clare likewise could not imagine any visibility in relation to her own boundaries. Mother's horror at the sexual predation she had suffered made me wonder whether any sort of sexual initiative would be particularly abhorred in herself or her daughter. Although both mother and daughter are attractive, and appeared to take a quiet pleasure in their femininity, it seemed likely to me that the vigorous, healthy erotic joy observed in mothers' and babies' enjoyment of each other's bodies (Reddy, 2008) was inhibited, hindering the origins of sexual self-worth for Clare.

In both their families, Clare's parents as children had experienced being treated as narcissistic objects. In reaction, they had created a protective, idealised environment for Clare and her brothers, insulating them from traditional authority. However, this created a situation in which everyone's feelings were consulted and the children were never told to do something. If Clare felt overwhelmed and didn't want to go to school, no one made her go, leaving Clare with inadequate preparation to go forward and stick with something difficult. Although adolescents complain about parental authority, the reasonable exercise of parental authority acknowledges a difference between parents and adolescents, and thus of specific adolescent needs. This distinction between the generations is one place where a sense of differentiation occurs, which contributes to a felt experience of visibility.

Later, this issue also emerged in the transference when Clare might not feel like coming to a session. I said that it might be the most important time to come when she didn't feel like it, and that it could make it harder for her if our sessions always seemed in question. I thought that she needed to experience that we could have differences and to internalise an important object who was strong enough to take a stand with her. She settled into attending her sessions regularly. She still struggled with eating too much or too little, and spent a lot of time ruminating about these issues.

In addition to Clare's disturbance in eating (anorectic symptoms at times, overeating at others), her parents also described her as overwhelmed with emotions – frequently sobbing, wailing or scratching herself in emotional fits. She also had great trouble sleeping. Before treatment Clare experienced academic work as pointless.

Beginning treatment

Clare took easily to our work – it seemed a relief for her to put her feelings into words and her emotional fits subsided within the first months of treatment.

From the beginning of treatment, Clare desired to emulate as well as to be better than her mother. Competition and projective identification with her mother were elements of the eating disorder. Just before Clare became anorexic, mother had been preparing for a triathlon and had become quite fit. Mother felt this had contributed to Clare's obsession with not eating and mentioned Clare's envy that mother had made herself skinny. Clare described only being able to eat when she could see her mother eating. She was preoccupied with her mother's body and felt she had no idea what was alright for her to eat unless she could see what her mother ate. She told me that it was easier to eat when she was on a trip with her mother, 'because I could see that she does eat, I thought she hardly ate anything, but I could see she ate whatever she wanted, like cookies'. I commented that Clare thought she should eat in the same manner her mother did, and that her body should be like her mother's body. Thus, we can see both a lack of differentiation from mother, and if a difference is observed (mother's weight loss), the effort is to abolish the difference and remove the source of painful envy in order to return to an undifferentiated state.

After a few months of treatment, Clare and her family began to consider her going away to a residential ballet programme. While I understood that the family was relieved that Clare's symptoms had diminished, I also thought that they were avoiding recognition of the seriousness of her problems. I spoke with her parents about how it is typical of eating-disordered girls to be able to look good, but often at the expense of a real consideration of their inner lives. I suggested that what was going on inside Clare was not that solid yet and while a part of Clare was eager to get on with her life, another part of her was just beginning to settle down inside. I think that ultimately Clare understood this point of view and dropped her considerations of going away.

I think my intervention was a necessary balance to her parents' loving but permissive style with her. Such an intervention (here necessitated by the possibility of a premature ending of the treatment) raises the issue of the relative benefits of active, directive interventions versus interpretation. Both are potential contributors to a sense of visibility. An insightful interpretation could make an adolescent feel seen and known in a way that they have not felt before. Making a suggestion that an adolescent is not ready for something yet seems to me to have a different quality. If it is accurate, it could lead an adolescent to feel understood. Actively thinking and interacting differently than the family may lead an adolescent to have a sense of limits and containment, as well as to differentiate familial objects from others. It may also interest an adolescent in a different quality of mind. I am reminded of Alvarez's (1995) idea that some patients may need to respect their analyst before they love them. While there is warmth in Clare's family, difference and limits are avoided. They are drawn to action, but instead of stemming from thought, it is in the direction of avoiding it. Indeed, there is a manic quality to this family – constantly going off on exciting vacations and travelling to their various homes, but with a sense that basic emotional needs are not tracked and visible.

Merging vs. weaning

Clare next began to discuss strange experiences of her body, both past and present. She experienced herself as looking different every time she saw herself in the mirror. She began to recount memories of the worst period of her anorexia, and described strange states she had experienced – dizzy, altered states. Torturously preoccupied with her mother's eating and weight, Clare was unable to sort out her right to or desire for an identity different from her mother's. Just being around her mother and noticing how thin she was made Clare feel bad about her own body. Retrospectively, I thought that the impulse to interrupt treatment prematurely had been a recapitulation of Clare's abrupt weaning and loss of mother at six months. When this traumatic sequence was averted, I believe that Clare felt more secure and wanted by me, and the treatment deepened through her recollection of these highly disturbed experiences of her body.

Clare's experience of her father was coloured by a dazzled admiration for his functioning in the world. However, this awe seemed to make it difficult for Clare to have a father she could talk to and use to help her with her problems. He occupied a different orbit that Clare could not inhabit and it often seemed difficult for him to enter into her struggles.

Mother's history of sexual abuse continued to emerge as the priest was finally prosecuted for other cases of abuse. These were horrifying stories for Clare to internalise, contributing to both an image of sexuality as something horrible and to preoccupation with her mother – not just as an object of admiration and competition but also as an object damaged by this horrible history. This made the separation necessary for Clare's own development a fearful undertaking. This history was a 'ghost' (Fraiberg, Adelson, & Shapiro, 1975) haunting Clare. Clare feared sexuality becoming visible in her body. Her physical invisibility was a defence against the fear of being abused, as well as against her own sexual fantasies.

Clare continued to make progress in her external world – during her first year of treatment, her symptoms were minimal and she became more engaged with school and friends. But, when the summer break came, Clare became somewhat destabilised.

Eating issues emerged again. Her family was preoccupied with setting up a new resort home. When Clare experienced her mother or me as unavailable, her functioning would decline. I had regular phone sessions with Clare during this period, but her fragility when separate from familial or transference objects was obvious.

Meanwhile, though almost 16, Clare still had not started her period. I recommended this be reviewed with her doctor. After some time Clare had a check-up and the doctor recommended tests to evaluate her hormonal functioning. Clare and her family seemed to keep putting off the blood tests. Clare experienced my investigating this issue as taking her to task. In this period, she identified me with her medical doctor with whom she was angry for pushing her to eat. She had felt frightened by her doctor's concern about her anorexia, as she had been denying the problem. Similarly, I was left to feel concern regarding her menstruation, while she disowned the issue. Although Clare could see that she feared boys and sexual relations, she did not seem to link this with her reluctance to have her period. She told me of frequent fears that a man would grab her on the street. She described feeling confused that her mother's family could not have known about the sexual abuse when it was so nearby. I interpreted that she might be trying to see if I would ignore her health and eating problems, or be clear that it's not good for her to starve herself nor for people to molest children. I described her feeling that my and her doctor's attention to her body somehow did not seem like attention to her self. There was a split in what she identified as her – she was her emotional life, but not her body. Her unconscious effort to project these concerns into me left them temporarily invisible to her. She related stories to me about her parents' early efforts to get her to eat during her worst anorectic period and how it scared her to see her parents frightened.

Around this time, an incident at home occurred during which Clare's father yelled at her and was physically rough with her. Clare felt frightened of his anger. Her mother was present and, though she did not like his anger, she said nothing. I felt that this sort of incident was a recapitulation of mother's family dynamics in a milder form – a man in authority got away with things and was not challenged. With Clare, I explored the meaning of male power in her family and the role for women of being admirable but with little control over anything but their own bodies. Clare could see that her feeling of helplessness with her father and brothers (she had close relationships with them but they also teased her mercilessly) contributed to her fears of being able to hold her own with a male.

Developing a sense of self

Clare's progress in her external life continued. Largely symptom-free for her junior and the beginning of her senior year, she became passionate about her academic work. When the director of her ballet troupe encouraged her to audition for the lead role in a performance, she did so and was chosen. While this was an accomplishment, it was suggested by someone else and did not include her own ability to conceive of an ambition and to pursue it visibly. Her friendships seemed of real depth, but she often struggled with what people wanted from her. The following vignette is typical of her pull to conform to other people's wishes. I had run into her outside my office before a session; she was walking arm in arm with a friend. She did not mention this, so a few minutes into the session I remarked:

A: You didn't say how it felt seeing me outside, when you were with your friend.

P: That's Y – she's a junior. I don't know if I've talked about her. She knows I come to therapy; she goes to therapy too. We usually go the same days but she wasn't going today. But it felt awkward, like I wasn't sure whether I should follow you in or stay with her.

A: Someone would know what you were supposed to do – but you're unsure if it's me, your mother, or Y.

P: You or Y in this situation. I had a feeling that I should make you both comfortable. It doesn't matter how I feel, I can take it – but I can't – like having to stay home from school yesterday. I felt like I was the connecting person between you and Y.

Her own thoughts or experience seem of little interest to Clare, compared with getting me, or someone else to tell her how to think.

Current treatment

Until recently, Clare had limited involvement with boys although many boys asked her out. She tended to be interested in somewhat unavailable boys, which seemed like a communication that her underlying fears needed further resolution and that she just was not ready yet.

Clare applied to university in Europe and was accepted. Both Clare and her family were destabilised by this development. She began to talk of her father seeming depressed in relation to her impending departure. Mother took a role in a television show that necessitated frequent travel and seemed linked to finding new avenues for herself as her daughter prepared to leave home. Clare came to sessions feeling overwhelmed, deserted and with a resurgence of her anorectic symptoms. I suggested we increase our meetings (she had dropped the third session the prior year, feeling she didn't need it). Clare had lost about 10 pounds and she was slender, but her weight was not alarming. However, she identified the return of familiar feelings from her anorexic period such as wanting to skip meals and to eat as little as possible. Though concerning, this resurgence of symptoms in a transitional period led to an intensified use of our work. She began dating boys and she talked to me extensively about anxiety about her genitals being damaged in intercourse and her fears of being exploited by males.

Current work has centred upon the unavailability of Clare's family just at this juncture when Clare is going abroad to college. While Clare is close to her mother, I think she is afraid she won't be able to find her emotionally as she becomes a young woman (just as she lost her during the abrupt weaning process). In this context, Clare told me the following dream:

> *I was somewhere – the atmosphere was of the Moulin Rouge, dark with neon lights on the building. I was trying to find someone but I didn't. Then I have Madeleines and then the dream jumps to I'm in bed at home and eating the Madeleines and I wake up and feel full, then I feel hungry – sad. The image is like in the movie 'Moulin Rouge', dark, back-lit, in the past.*

A: Your search for someone makes me think of your missing your mother now.
P: (In a small voice) She's so far away. We had Madeleines at home when I was little.
A: Madeleines remind you of your mother.
P: That I'm hungry and longing for her.
A: You miss her very much right now and perhaps especially fear you won't be able to find her or me in the Moulin Rouge atmosphere of sexuality.

In this period of upheaval, as Clare faced major separations from her family, friends and me, she had difficulty regulating physical contact with boys, social contact and eating. Her inability to limit boys' physical approaches to her was similar to her problem with food. Rey's (1994) concept of anorexia being a defence against bulimia is relevant here. Because Clare feels she cannot regulate food entering her body, she has to remove herself from it. Her expectation that boys cannot be told 'no' is also a projection of her own inability to say 'no'. The eating disorder both mirrors her larger difficulties with saying 'no', and allows her to say 'no' in other areas (e.g. avoidance of school). The following segment of a session illustrates these issues:

P: I stayed home from school yesterday. I feel weak when I do that. I was feeling tired socially after the party Sunday night. I remember telling you Monday that I already felt I had eaten a lot that day, then I had dinner. That full feeling makes me eat more instead of stopping eating.
A: Why?
P: I feel bad when I feel full and then I just keep eating and go into it and then I can't go out the next day until all the food settles. I didn't want to go to school, so the over-eating allows me not to go, but then I can never enjoy it.
A: You comfort yourself by over-eating when you are under strain and miss me, but then handle the emotional pain by hiding yourself – yet the hiding makes you feel weaker.

During Clare's final summer before leaving for university, we had a five-week break, because of a combination of both of our vacations. While such breaks were worrisome before, this time Clare had an especially difficult time hanging on to a sense of continuity with me. She began to miss sessions. She described going from one guy to another in an effort to get a hold of someone in a concrete way in the face of the changes ahead. However, she made minimal discrimination between good and bad experiences – leaving her invisible again. Clare made little effort to stand up for her sessions when any other event or person interceded, although she seemed to want to come. When I pointed out her passivity in this regard, she said it felt as though I was one more person telling her what to do. My countertransference experience of her missing sessions in this period was of feeling ignored, angry, forgotten and disregarded. The hours themselves had become invisible. I realised that in the face of her passivity I was often thinking for her, which contributed to her not expecting to think for herself.

When I interpreted these issues, I found that she rather quickly became engaged in thinking for herself. She was demonstrating that she wasn't incapable of thinking, but instead characteristically representing herself as someone who couldn't think without me. I believe this plea of incapacity was a way to bind me to her as well as a projective identification – I am left with all the worries she has disowned. This incapacitating of herself attached her to others and to me in a dependent manner but left her own capacities invisible and undeveloped. For instance, one day she told me, 'I feel like I'd fall apart without your help.' When I asked what she meant she replied, 'I don't think I would fall apart as I did in freshman year because I can observe myself so much more.' When I did not immediately accept her engaging me in her helplessness, she was more able to reflect on her developing capacities. At this point, she seemed capable of more thinking than she sometimes had shown.

Painful anxiety led Clare to rely on projective identification – including of good aspects of herself, such as her capacity to think. Projective identification temporarily renders invisible something that she cannot tolerate (Berman-Oelsner, 2008).

Conversely, the ability to bear pain gradually leads to a sense that one can face knowing oneself – 'learning from experience' (Bion, 1962).

As I interpreted her defensive uses of invisibility, Clare began to speak more of her real qualities, including her capacity to observe herself. Meanwhile, her parents had been away for a month at their island home and her brothers had been racing sailboats off the Australian coast. I felt that her family was being compulsively active in the face of their internal difficulties with separation. Immediately after her parents returned Clare and I had the following exchange:

P: My father told me at dinner that he already missed our island house, that it's hard to be back in the city and back to work. I understand but it's hard to hear. And my mother is saying she is going to miss the island house too. My father was saying he can't wait to see my brothers; I felt like what am I – invisible? I had a dream last night; in the dream I was with my family and my extended family. Everyone else was in couples, like everyone was getting married; it was like in a musical, everybody getting out of cabs to get married and singing. I had a lonely feeling, and then everyone else who was not getting married was getting high. And I wasn't doing that either. The dream was taking place at my grandparents' home in Newport, which emphasises the lonely feeling because I always feel disconnected there.

A: The dream seems to echo the feelings you were just talking about, your parents being together, your brothers being together, and you're watching and feeling alone.

P: Yeah, and thinking about everyone getting high at college. My friend A. is at Stanford for a summer programme. It's funny because she's the friend who's the most cynical about everything and she's at Stanford. She's having phone sessions with her therapist and living in a dorm. I was asking her what it was like.

A: Perhaps you're thinking about what our relationship will be like with the changes ahead.

P: What I want to keep about here is that it's where I get in touch with myself. I try to do that in other places, but it's most here, that's a good thing. I don't know what's going on with my parents; they've been gone so long. I guess it makes it easier to leave here.

A: I'm thinking of what you were saying yesterday about feeling you're supposed to have done something exciting to keep your father interested, I wonder if it could feel that way here – that I might not like you as well if your developments are quiet.

P: When I have sad thoughts is when I need you the most, so I don't think I feel you won't be interested. But with my parents – my father is never still . . . (the session continues with a description of her parents' action orientation and her feeling it is hard to be seen next to her brothers' adventures.)

The following day she told me she'd had another dream:

> *I was at the gym on the basketball court, so there's that out of place feeling again. That feeling is there, but then there are a lot of people around, definitely guys, and I'm the centre of attention, feeling well liked, powerful, but I'm not choosing amongst them, so I'm leaving myself alone again. I woke up with the sense of their voices around me and the feeling of being wanted.*

Clare is becoming more aware of her own powers of attraction and of her inability to use her powers. This piece of work is under way but remains incomplete as we face her impending departure for college. She is becoming more conscious of her fear of choice and power, which will hopefully help her to resist her inclination to defensively retreat into invisibility and anorexia. We have agreed to phone sessions in order to continue this work.

Conclusion

In the foregoing description of an analysis of an adolescent, I have tried to depict the multiple determinants involved in an anorexic girl's presentation of herself as invisible and insubstantial. First, she had internalised her mother's frightening sexual history and this affected her fears and fantasies regarding her sexual development. Consequently, she attempted to make her sexuality invisible, literally making herself small, weak and insubstantial – an expression through her body and body ego (Anderson, 2005) of her terror at entering the sexual realm. Second, she internalised her family's use of manic activity. This manic defence seemed related to her parents' fears of their own inner lives and over-reliance on their substantial and impressive achievements in the world. This led to my patient's emotional needs being largely invisible to her parents and herself. Moreover, emotion was seen as female in the family and of secondary importance to adventure and accomplishment. Third, my patient's phantasised merger with her mother and subsequently with me in the transference (e.g. I would think for her instead of with her) left her own developing self unexamined and uncontained. This impoverished the adolescent process of psychological separation and interfered with the painful but potentially exciting development of her own identity. Fourth, my patient could feel a part of herself that was willing to kill herself through starvation, but also experienced other aspects of herself that wanted to live. This frightfully destructive part was expressed in the effort to starve herself out of existence. Finally, as Clare has grown stronger, it has become clear that she presents herself as invisible and helpless as a plea to engage others. This defensive invisibility also serves to fend off experiences of her power, desire and greed, which are just emerging in a visible way for her. She is beginning to notice her powers to attract, but is still unsteady in her confidence in finding any real enjoyment or pleasure in being visible, especially with men.

My hope is to help Clare to bear the mental pain that will finally allow her to be visible to herself, and to experience herself as substantial. Becoming visible and substantial means that anxiety must be contained long enough to become available for emotional experience, thought and symbolisation (Berman-Oelsner, 2008) instead of immediately discharged into eating disorder symptoms. Over time, Clare may be able to experience the pleasures of being distinct more fully, and loosen her hold on merging as the only bearable solution.

Note

1 My patient was also less ill than the 'no-entry' anorexic patients described so well by Williams (1997).

References

Alvarez, A. (1995). Motiveless malignity: Problems in the psychotherapy of psychopathic patients. *Journal of Child Psychotherapy*, *21*, 2167–2182.

Anderson, R. (2005). *Adolescence and the body ego: The re-encountering of primitive mental functioning in adolescent development*, Unpublished paper presented at The Sixteenth Annual Melanie Klein Memorial Lectureship, January 8, Los Angeles.

Bene, A. (1973). *Transference patterns in a case of anorexia nervosa*, Unpublished paper.

Berlin, S. A., Boatman, S. A., Sheimo, S. A., & Szurek, S. A. (1951). Adolescent alternation of anorexia and obesity. *American Journal of Orthopsychiatry*, *21*, 2387–2419.

Berman-Oelsner, M. (2008). *Discussion of Mary Brady's paper 'Invisibility of the self in an anorexic adolescent*, Unpublished paper presented at The Eating Disorder Conference, San Francisco Center for Psychoanalysis, December 6.

Bion, W. R. (1962). *Learning from experience*. London: Karnac.

Birksted-Breen, D. (1989). Working with an anorexic patient. *International Journal of Psycho-Analysis*, *70*, 30–40.

Boris, H. (1984). The problem of anorexia nervosa. *International Journal of Psycho-Analysis*, *65*, 315–322.
Broucek, F. (1979). Efficacy in infancy: A review of some experimental studies and their possible implications for clinical theory. *International Journal of Psycho-Analysis*, *60*, 311–316.
Broucek, F. (1982). Shame and its relationship to early narcissistic developments. *International Journal of Psycho-Analysis*, *63*, 369–378.
Bruch, H. (1974). *Eating disorders, obesity, anorexia nervosa and the person within*. London: Routledge & Kegan Paul.
Crisp, A. (1973). *Primary anorexia nervosa or adolescent weight phobia*, Unpublished paper.
Fraiberg, V., Adelson, V., & Shapiro, V. (1975). Ghosts in the nursery: A psychoanalytic approach to the problems of impaired infant – mother relationships. *Journal of the American Academy of Psychiatry*, *14*, 387–421.
Green, J. H. F. (1950). *If I were you*, ed. J. H. F. McEwen. London: Eyre and Spottiswoode.
Grotstein, J. (1981). *Splitting and projective identification*. New York: Jason Aronson, Inc.
Grotstein, J. (2000). *Who is the dreamer who dreams the dream?* Hillsdale, NJ: The Analytic Press.
Hughes, M., Furgiuele, M., & Bianco, M. (1985). Aspects of anorexia nervosa in the therapy of two adolescents. *Journal of Child Psychotherapy*, *11*, 117–132.
Klein, M. (1955). On identification. In R. Money-Kyrle (Ed.), *Envy and gratitude and other works: 1946–1963*. New York: The Free Press.
Klein, M. (1957). Envy and gratitude. In R. Money-Kyrle (Ed.), *Envy and gratitude and other works: 1946–1963*. New York: The Free Press.
Lawrence, M. (2001). Loving them to death: The anorexic and her objects. *International Journal of Psycho-Analysis*, *82*, 43–55.
Lawrence, M. (2002). Body, mother, mind: Anorexia, femininity and the intrusive object. *International Journal of Psycho-Analysis*, *83*, 837–850.
Quagliata, G. (2004). Some reflections on the processes of projection and introjection in eating disorders. In G. Williams (Ed.), *Exploring eating disorders in adolescence: The generosity of acceptance*. London: Karnac.
Reddy, V. (2008). *How infants know minds*. Cambridge, MA: Harvard University Press.
Reich, A. (1973). *Annie Reich: Psychoanalytic contributions*. New York: International Universities Press, Inc.
Rey, J. (1994). Anorexia nervosa. In J. Magagna (Ed.), *Universals of psychoanalysis in the treatment of psychotic and borderline states*. London: Free Association Books.
Rosenfeld, H. (1964). *Psychotic states: A psychoanalytic approach*. New York: International Universities Press, Inc.
Spillius, E. (1973). *Anorexia in analysis*, Unpublished paper.
Sprince, M. (1984). Early psychic disturbances in anorexic and bulimic patients as reflected in the psychoanalytical process. *Journal of Child Psychotherapy*, *10*: 199–215.
Williams, G. (1997). Reflections on some dynamics of eating disorders: 'No Entry' defences and foreign bodies. *International Journal of Psycho-Analysis*, *78*: 927–941.

3

PRIMARY INTERACTIONS AND EATING DISORDERS

A psychoanalytic perspective

Antonella Granieri

In a newborn's primary interactions with his or her caretaker, food signifies more than the satisfaction of a biological need. It is also intimately linked to relational exchanges (Caccia, 2006; Escosteguy Carneiro, 2008). Thus, it is not that children only enjoy food itself. Rather, they enjoy being fed by an individual who cares for them and who is attuned to their emotional lives (Winnicott, 1957; Stern, 1977, 1985). As part of the experience of contact with caretakers at feeding times, children progressively learn to associate feelings with objects and to build thoughts and representations (Freud, 1946). Subsequently, the relational exchanges that occur during feeding become the core of the development of self-awareness and knowledge systems. For children, then, nourishment means not only the concrete act of eating food but also a progressive introjection of their parental relationships and of the emotional contents linked to them. As stated by Bion (1962):

> There is reason to believe that the emotional experiences associated with alimentation are those from which individuals have abstracted and then integrated elements to form theoretical deductive systems that are used as representations of realization of thought. There is reason for using [the] alimentary system as a model for demonstrating and comprehending the processes involved in thought.
>
> *(Bion, 1962, p. 62)*

Thus, feeding is deeply involved in the building of thought processes and in the development of the inner world. As highlighted by Stern (1985), the initial dimensions of the newborn's self are mainly physiological, and his or her emotional responses have to be interpreted by caregivers to allow for the development of more complex psychological states. From a psychoanalytic perspective, this assumption plays a fundamental role, to the extent that the capacity for an object relation to provide "emotional nourishment" often represents a key to interpreting clinical data. According to Taylor (1987), the food-object (that is, the internal object which represents the child's experience with food) contributes to shaping the experiences of reciprocity and attunement that constitute the basis for a comfortable interoceptive awareness, which is a foundation for the processes involved in somato-psychic integration. Additionally, the food-object contributes to the generation of the interpersonal patterns involved in the intentional communication of affective states.

From a developmental perspective, the exchanges that take place during breast-feeding or bottle-feeding play a key role in the child's emotional, cognitive, and social growth. A parent's ability to maintain emotional responsiveness during feeding will nurture the child's physical well-being and psychic balance. On one hand, sensitive nurturing provides the necessary support for the child's development of adequate systems of homeostatic self-regulation, thereby increasing positive emotions. On the other hand, it facilitates the child's discovery and confident exploration of his or her mental states by means of attunement and mirroring with the caregiver (Gergely & Watson, 1996). In contrast, as widely shown by infant observation and research (Chatoor, Schaefer, Dickson, & Eagan, 1984; Cicchetti, Rogosh, & Toth, 1998; Chatoor, Ganiban, Hirsch, Borman-Spurrell, & Mrazek, 2000), if parents are insufficiently accessible on an emotional level, food may lose its function as a form of a psychological nurturing. Instead, according to Eigen (1999), it can become "toxic nourishment," and act as a vehicle that introjects negative relational experiences. In this way, parts of the mother's "toxic" unconscious enters the child's growing psychic organization (Aulagnier, 1975) and encysts into the child's mind, which brings about feelings of estrangement and anxiety.

Winnicott (1936) had already clinically foreseen that the early childhood eating disorders (EDs) are symptomatic displays of emotional pain that children experience because of the lack of attuned mutuality with their caretakers during breast- or bottle-feeding. Some years later, Bruch (1962, 1979, 1978) highlighted the connection between EDs and difficulties in the separation-individuation process. Specifically, the mother is unable to perceive her child as a separate other and projects her feelings and needs onto the baby. Consequently, the child's capacity to differentiate between interoceptive perceptions is compromised and he or she is deprived of the basic awareness needed to build an individual sense of identity.

Thus, from a psychoanalytic perspective, EDs may be understood as related to deficits in self-regulation as well as the interactive regulation of emotional states connected to childhood family configurations that were characterized by entanglement and emotional neglect (Jenkins & O'Connor, 2012; Granieri & Schimmenti, 2014; Schimmenti & Caretti, 2016).

Primary cares and affect dysregulation

The caregiver's effectiveness in correctly identifying the child's physiologic and behavioral activations and associating them with specific states of mind is fundamental for the growth of a child's ability to transform his or her emotions into psychologically more complex phenomena (e.g., feelings). Subsequently, this influences children's ability to integrate emotional processes with cognitive processes (Fonagy & Target, 1997; Bouchard et al., 2008). Of course, affective regulation is not a one-time occurrence or only related to cognitive skills. Instead, naming and defining the nature of an emotion as well as understanding and modulating it means being able to constantly heed the variability of the emotional experience.

If a mother is attuned and responsive, in most cases the dyad is able to establish reparative processes during important relational exchanges (especially during breast-feeding), which can mend the interactional "mistakes" that could bring about unsynchronized states (Tronick & Weinberg, 1997). For children in these "good enough" dyads, positive emotional states will prevail in both incidence and duration as the result of the affective attunement that is typical in these relationships (Beebe & Lachmann, 2002; Lachmann, 2008; Likierman, 2008).

In fact, caregivers' behaviors and reactions to children's emotional expressions help children to focus their attention on their own experiences. Then, children will be able to shape and form connections between those experiences. Therefore, growth seems to move from a sensory experience of reality toward increasingly complex representations of the inner and outer worlds. The distinctive feature of this progression seems to be the result of developing mentalization skills (Fonagy & Target, 1997). This process requires the ability to conceive the existence of thoughts and feelings in both the self and in others as well as perception of the link between mental states and outer reality.

In the context of secure attachment, caregivers give meanings to the affective signs produced by children and think about their mental states. Because of children's immaturity in psychic organization, each child will need to be helped by his or her caretakers to interpret reality; it is the caretaker's task to translate and introduce reality step by step, as a means of making it easier to "digest" (Bion, 1962).

Conversely, parents who are unable to understand their children's mental experience may deprive them of a foundation for the development of a real, coherent, and cohesive self. In fact, emotionally neglected children who are not provided a chance to experience their own "intentional being" in their caregivers' minds will likely develop curtailed skills in shaping mental images of themselves and those of others. This state is often expressed by disorders during growth and by painful pathologic states in adulthood (Barbasio & Granieri, 2013; Barbasio et al., 2015; Giovannelli et al., 2016; Schimmenti et al., 2017).

The interactive regulation mechanisms in the ongoing communication between parents and children are complex, and there is no existing simplification of this system. Furthermore, the psychological and behavioral relational vectors that could control the interaction quality and outcomes associated with children's emotional development remain unclear. However, it should be acknowledged that adults' emotional, cognitive, and behavioral spectrums are much wider than that of children. As a result, the centrality of the parents' capacity to hold their child in mind and to be attuned to their needs as related to healthy affective growth is clear (Winnicott, 1969).

Primary caretakers act as useful and essential leaders for their children's scouting of reality during feeding times because they place their mirroring function at their children's disposal (Fonagy & Target, 1997). Therefore, affective regulation deficits may arise from the failure of the primary parental holding system, making the subjective experience of the child unbearable and overwhelming and creating "indigestible" affective states. These difficulties with emotional regulation may be related to the arising of eating disorders, which are paradoxical expressions of overwhelming emotional pain in circumstances where the ability to think about painful mind states is missing.

Developmental trauma and eating behaviors

Damaged bonds with primary caregivers, which are often linked to early interpersonal trauma, cause serious deficits in children. These deficits are not only related to their ability for affective self-regulation but also to processing and relationally negotiating their wishes. Subsequently, the traumatic elements that spring from these negative relational experiences are split off, creating a situation in which emotional and relational needs are negotiated concretely, via food, and linked to deep feelings of shame. How these individuals relate to food may be an implicit portrayal of their earlier object relationships, which were marked by a lack of reliability and regularity. In other words, the reactualization of symptoms linked to food intake becomes a response to overwhelming emotions that are unthinkable in terms of the psychic functioning these persons have attained.

Relationships with highly intrusive caregivers invade the child's own psychic space, leaving little room for the elaboration of his or her own emotional experience (Aulagnier, 2001). This, in turn, affects the connection between emotional experience and symbolic processes. Based on a relational psychoanalytic perspective, Gentile (2007) asserts that relationships with intrusive caregivers play a key role in the severe forms of EDs that are often associated with other psychic disorders. In these cases, a crumbling of the patient's inner boundaries can be observed and the physical presence of relational objects is perceived as utterly essential for survival.

Such primary contexts may impair the child's developing sense of ownership in relation to his or her own bodily and mental life. Therefore, patients with EDs are entrenched in their dysfunctional eating behaviors because those behaviors seem to, somehow, preserve a small degree of ownership in relation to body and mind. In other words, when there is a lack of emotional safety, autonomy, and self-sufficiency, the aim of dysfunctional eating behaviors is, in part, to foster a sense of personal agency.[1] However, these behaviors reinforce a sense of the self as damaged and, at times, represent an identification with neglectful caretakers, ultimately leading the individual into escalating feelings of shame and helplessness. Then, the primary interpersonal wound created is often reactualized through reveries, daydreams, and behaviors that aim to erase the need for others and relationships. Moreover, because the body is the projection screen for deadly objects stemming from primary, traumatic links with caretakers, compulsory binges and food rejection may amount to an angry response aimed at denying and attacking the body.

Additionally, dysfunctional eating behaviors are often attempts to regulate extremely painful emotions, especially those that may influence an individual's narcissistic balance. This condition is shared with different forms of psychic distress, whereby an object or a behavior plays the role of regulating the "outer" emotions in response to a lack of adequate internal resources to contend with traumatic stressors. From this perspective, EDs can be conceptualized as dysfunctional strategies of affect regulation that are connected to an impaired capability to recognize, metabolize, and mentalize affects (Lunn & Poulsen, 2012).

Clinical case: Claudio

Claudio was 16 years old when I first met him. His mother expressed concern about her son's frequent self-induced vomiting, which had brought about considerable weight loss, jeopardized the young man's school attendance, and appeared to have the potential to influence negatively his long-term academic performance.

Claudio is the only son to a separated couple and lives with his mother, who immediately struck me as controlling and, at times, evasive. She justified her considerable anxiety about every decision that involved her son by invoking her deep sense of responsibility, which she described as significantly exceeding the average mother's. In addition, this sense of responsibility keeps her from pursuing employment. In contrast, Claudio's father is often away because of important and dangerous missions abroad: he is a high-ranking army officer who is enthusiastic about his job, which, as he says, he shares with "motivated and brave" young men.

The presence of an absent father (Pace, Cacioppo, & Schimmenti, 2012) and an anxious and intrusive mother came to light during introductory conversations with Claudio. The mother's intrusion manifests, for example, in the way she checks her son's intimate hygiene in a step-by-step manner. Refraining from any critical comments, Claudio informed me he is never left alone while showering: his mother stays with him, helps him dry himself off, and cleans the bathroom afterward.

Claudio's mother has always been intensely anxious about his physical condition and, in fact, Claudio was often treated for physical ailments in his early life. For instance, he reported that he was hospitalized five times during his first year of life because of bowel cramping, vomiting, and lack of appetite. Furthermore, Claudio's mother's anxieties persisted throughout his development. For example, when he was attending primary school, she did not directly prevent him from taking part in birthday parties or field trips. Instead, she simply asked him to think about the possible risks involved in these types of experiences and to consider whether his "state of health" would allow him to participate.

In most cases, in agreement with his mother's assessment of his fragility, he decided that it did not.

Thus, as Claudio developed, each inner and outer stimulus he experienced was filtered through his mother's anxious and phobic image of the world. Ultimately, this deeply interfered with his process of separation and individuation. His mother's concerns about his health turned into an internal operational model, and throughout our sessions, I witnessed a compulsory repetition of this way of thinking for all events in the young man's life. For example, he informed me that he checks his state of health the moment he wakes up: every morning he wonders whether his bowels are functioning well, whether his stomach is aching, and whether his heart is beating properly. Frequently, he decides that it would be best to set a particular diet for the day and to return home immediately after school. However, if he chooses to eat breakfast, he often vomits afterward, which leaves him with barely enough strength remaining to attend school and engage in learning. Both he and his mother always want him to return home immediately after school.

During the working-through process I was able to develop the following understanding of Claudio's psychic development: At the beginning of his psychic life, Claudio's mind developed in relationship to a primary sadistic object, which he has internalized and with which he adhesively identified. A hypertrophic and inaccessible ego ideal was created, giving rise to feelings of shame and worthlessness as well as impotence and guilt before this internal persecutory object, which wields enormous unconscious destructiveness (Chasseguet-Smirgel, 2003, 2005; Kestemberg, Decobert, & Kesyemberg, 1972; Reilly, 2004). Moreover, the lack of appropriate and consistent responses to his needs deprived Claudio of a basic awareness of separateness on which to build his own sense of identity. Thus, a disavowal of his ego boundaries took place and deeply impacted Claudio's developing body image and impaired his capacity to reasonably distinguish among interoceptive perceptions such as hunger, fullness, cold, arousal, or strain.

In these circumstances, Claudio's eating disorder developed as an attempt to regain a degree of autonomy and a sense of subjectivity and interpersonal efficacy, although, of course, delimited to the realm of eating. His body – a body that cannot experience pleasure and desire, but only the need for impulsive and compulsive eating behaviors – became a psychic retreat in which Claudio could protect himself from intrusive attacks by a sadistic internal object (Schimmenti & Caretti, 2010; Steiner, 1993), without giving up the relationship with such object.

During his first year of psychotherapeutic treatment, both Claudio's relationship with his mother and his inability to live independently were not directly addressed and manifested as ego syntonic. For Claudio, the exclusive and fused relationship with his mother worked like a drug that could anaesthetize his states of excruciating psychic pain. These states were only evident in his self-induced vomiting and self-exclusion from his peer group. Indeed, at the age of 16, he was not involved in any sports and had no friends. Instead, his relationships were based on his schoolmates' perception of him as an eccentric but intelligent and kind individual. For example, he had a top grade point average. While he behaved kindly toward his schoolmates, if they invited him to eat lunch together, he would typically decline, unless he had exact knowledge of where they were going to eat.

In addition, Claudio sought ways to maintain the illusion that all emotions and relational events can be controlled. In large part, this illusion was sustained because Claudio remained at home as much as possible. In fact, his home became an alternative space where Claudio could conceal his emotional difficulties, which would be revealed were he to enter the social world. In addition, by staying at home Claudio was able to sustain the illusion of being able to keep even the most minor relational events under control (e.g., when to answer his mobile, when to accept an invitation). He exercised his limited relational capacities through involvement with Facebook and other indirect methods as surrogates for face-to-face communication. As part of these technologically mediated relationships, he communicated via text messages on his phone, SMS, and Facebook, which he could conveniently do from his room. Indeed, Claudio was unable to contend with the emotional demands of face-to-face relations (Schimmenti, Guglielmucci, Barbasio, & Granieri, 2012).

During this period, our sessions were tedious. Claudio spent most of our time reporting his physical preoccupations, and the only emotional experience I could discern was a nameless dread that appeared whenever anything related to the mother-son dyad arose. My experience, in contrast, was marked by an impotent hatred, feelings that I took to be unmentalizable by Claudio. Moreover, even the most basic interpretations referring to disturbing behaviors such as sleeping with his mother were "thrown up" by Claudio. He perceived them as extraneous and intrusive objects, or as if they were a sort of food, too excessive for a newborn to digest.

Although an 18-year-old young man, Claudio still needed something different than the interpretation of verbal associations. Rather, his need was closer to a mirroring function of the feelings we exchanged during our sessions – feelings that were being shared "in small bites." Indeed, whenever a traumatic event has taken place at a young age, the verbal level alone cannot elicit any insight that will be useful for working through pre-verbally rooted emotional configurations. Over time, Claudio developed the skill needed to bear his most painful emotions; this process, in turn, gave reality a meaning that took the place of his previous generalized turmoil. In this way, he has become able to begin experiencing our therapeutic relationship as increasingly free from persecutory distresses. Consequently, he has become able to accept the feelings he shared with me and to "digest" them instead of somatizing them.

As time passed, Claudio also became able to experience and express new emotions in the therapeutic relationship. In one session, Claudio became angry with me because I had to change a session to a different time of day that did not match our established frame. Claudio's forthright expression of his anger was something thoroughly new for him. That day, interestingly, he refrained from vomiting after his meal. Moreover, he seemed relieved that we were both still "alive" after this event and that neither of us had experienced the feeling of being forsaken or denied.

After two years, Claudio's eating-disordered symptomatology was in remission. He had gained weight, did not vomit regularly, and no longer only ate only bland food. However, his capacity to engage in the larger social world remained underdeveloped. Indeed, he was beginning, with some effort, to emerge from his symbiotic relationship with his mother and to work against his tendency to isolate himself at home. His schoolmates supported him in this endeavor, as they began to appreciate him for more than his cognitive performances. That said, in the occurrence of any hitch or hindrance, the maternal imago returned and said, "Was it really worthwhile to expose yourself to such risks and frights?"

Longer therapeutic work allowed Claudio to partake in some outdoor activities with his peer group, albeit with a "parachute," or a means of finding a way out of his discomfort, if necessary, in place. For example, he can now stay away for a ski holiday with his companions and hold back the impact of his mother's paralyzing anxiety if he knows that his father, although far away, will provide him with taxi fare to return home if needed. Such arrangements provided enough security for Claudio to risk new forms of relational engagement and, in addition, for his mother to tolerate his absence.

Claudio's analytic work is still in progress for, as previously stated, any unpredicted difficulties are enough to paralyze his developing capacities. For example, recently he went to a concert that he had wished to attend for some time. At first, he was happy to be there, but he soon became frightened because of the chaotic crowds and loud noises. Amidst the bustling crowd of youngsters, Claudio found that the chance to watch his companions sing and dance had no more meaning for him and, afterward, briefly regressed to his self-induced vomiting behavior.

Several meetings with Claudio's parents during the treatment have shed additional light on the emotional functioning of the family. Indeed, the father's extended absences (first job-related and then because of the separation) were experienced by Claudio's mother as deeply traumatic. As an anxious, phobic, and helpless person, she was forced through this experience to take up an autonomous role she was not equipped to fill. She made use of her son to fill her inner vacuum, and this link had to be created in such a way that she would not risk losing her last remaining love object. Because of this, the link was not aimed at building Claudio's healthy narcissistic grounding; rather, it provided a means for her to ward off her terror of loss.

Only at the end of his second year of treatment has Claudio become able to definitively ascertain that the "frail stomach" belongs to his mother. Her stomach could not contain all the anxieties that a young man would typically use as experiences along his path toward individuation. For his part, since he was away for his missions or overwhelmed by his own guilt, Claudio's father could not significantly influence the mother-son link. On the contrary, he seems to have attempted to rid himself of the inhibiting and stifling relationship with Claudio's mother through a relationship with a new woman who also travels around the world for her job but also values their close and intimate moments. In our sessions, the father confronted the fact that his freedom could only become real after leaving his son as a hostage and crutch for his ex-wife.

Our work together has allowed Claudio to understand how, beginning in childhood, food and relationships (and their accompanying feelings) are deeply intertwined. Now a little older and significantly healthier, he is able to appreciate the lightness he experiences when he can eat calmly, savoring tastes and pleasant conversation, for example, with his paternal grandmother, leading him to feel more positive about life. Together with his paternal grandmother and father, the latter who has just returned from a mission, he is now cooking the kinds of pizzas and cakes he enjoys most. Moreover, he feels free to use the wrong measurements as well to rejoice when the outcome satisfies him: this is now a virtuous cycle consisting of positive emotions. In a metaphorical sense, he is moving from eating food that must be sterilized before swallowing to eating a pizza, although perhaps not a perfect one since it is too salty, yet it is a food he likes regardless.

While Claudio has shown significant gains in our work together, in his future analytic work he still has to undergo several trials related to his self-image, self-esteem, and potential. Furthermore, he continues to struggle with the integration of his sexual identity. Thus, Claudio's ego remains vulnerable, although it is already organized enough that he is conscious of his recent gains and improved independence. However, help is still required because adversity continues to have the potential to paralyze, sink, or overwhelm him in the future.

Clinical implications

In clinical work with patients with eating disorders, work on personifications will be unavoidable (Gaburri, 1992).[2] The working through of early relational experiences does not take the form of a free verbal association interpretation. On the contrary, we now know that the experiences contributing to both the normal and the traumatic object relationships that develop during this period take place too soon in life to be consciously recollected. These early experiences are kept in parts of the brain that are separated from those where memories, as we understand them, are codified, stored, and reused. By itself, the verbal level is not enough to work through pre-verbal emotional configurations. Similar to Claudio's case, sometimes interpretations alone may be harmful because they are far from, or even alien to, the patient's emotional reality (Granieri & Schimmenti, 2014).

It is only a psychoanalyst's genuine willingness for deep listening and sharing that may reach the patient and his or her psychic experiences that are beyond words (Granieri, 2003; Seganti, Albasi, & Granieri, 2003). We must allow the therapeutic relationship to organically unfold and give patients with eating disorders a chance to gather their strengths as well as to find the emotional holding necessary to oppose the self-destructive drives of a helpless and frightened self.

Notes

1 For a psychoanalytic perspective on agency, see Borgogno (2011). According to Borgogno, analysts that lend their bodies and minds genuinely and courageously can help patients restore a sense of personal agency as well as vitality.
2 With *personification* Gaburri refers to the relational dynamic in which one member of the dyad (such as the analytic couple) unifies and collects upon himself/herself the projective identifications circulating in the emotional field.

References

Aulagnier, P. (1975). *The violence of interpretation: From pictogram to statement* (A. Sheridan, Trans.). London: Routledge, 2001.
Barbasio, C. P., & Granieri, A. (2013). Emotion regulation and mental representation of attachment in patients with Systemic Lupus Erythematosus: A study using the adult attachment interview. *The Journal of Nervous and Mental Disease*, *201*(4), 304–310.
Barbasio, C. P., Vagelli, R., Marengo, D., Querci, F., Settanni, M., Tani, C., Mosca, M., & Granieri, A. (2015). Illness perception in Systemic Lupus Erythematosus patients: The roles of alexithymia and depression. *Comprehensive Psychiatry*, *63*, 88–95.
Beebe, B., & Lachmann, F. M. (2002). *Infant research and adult treatment: Co-constructing interactions*. New York: The Analytic Press.
Bion, W. R. (1962). *Learning from experience*. London: Karnac, 1984.
Borgogno, F. (2011). *The girl who committed Hara-Kiri and other clinical and historical essays* (A. Spencer, Trans.). London: Karnak Books, 2013.
Bouchard, M., Target, M., Lecours, S., Fonagy, P., Tremblay, L., Schachter, A., & Stein, H. (2008). Mentalization in adult attachment narratives: Reflective functioning, mental states, and affect elaboration compared. *Psychoanalytic Psychology*, *25*, 47–66. doi:10.1037/0736–9735.25.1.47
Bruch, H. (1962). Perceptual and conceptual disturbances in anorexia nervosa. *Psychosomatic Medicine*, *24*, 187–194.
Bruch, H. (1978). *The golden cage: The enigma of anorexia nervosa*. Cambridge, MA: Harvard University Press.
Bruch, H. (1979). *Eating disorders: Obesity, anorexia nervosa, and the person within*. New York: Basic Books.
Caccia, O. (2006). Eating difficulties in early infancy and experience of the combined object. *Infant Observation*, *9*, 295–303. doi:10.1080/13698030601070649
Chasseguet-Smirgel, J. (2003/2005). *The body as mirror of the world*. London: Free Association.
Chatoor, I., Ganiban, J., Hirsh, R., Borman-Spurrell, E., & Mrazek, D. A. (2000). Maternal characteristics and toddler temperament in infantile anorexia. *Journal of the American Academy of Child and Adolescent Psychiatry*, *39*, 743–751. doi:10.1097/00004583–200006000–00013
Chatoor, I., Schaefer, S., Dickson, L., & Eagan, J. (1984). Non-organic failure-to-thrive: A developmental perspective. *Pediatric Annals*, *13*, 829–843.
Cicchetti, D., Rogosch, F. A., & Toth, S. L. (1998). Maternal depressive disorder and contextual risk: Contributions to the development of attachment insecurity and behavior problems in toddlerhood. *Development and Psychopathology*, *10*, 283–300. doi:10.1017/S0954579498001618
Eigen, M. (1999). *Toxic nourishment*. London: Karnac.

Escosteguy Carneiro, M. I. (2008). Three boys and their stories: Atypical eating and primitive relations. *International Journal of Psychoanalysis, 89*, 1145–1163.

Fonagy, P., & Target, M. (1997). Attachment and reflective function: Their role in self-organization. *Development and Psychopathology, 9*, 679–700. doi:10.1017/S0954579497001399

Freud, A. (1946). The psychoanalytic study of infantile feeding disturbances. *The Psychoanalytic Study of the Child, 2*, 119–132.

Gaburri, E. (1992). Emotions, affects, personification. *Rivista di psicoanalisi, 38*, 324–350.

Gentile, K. (2007). Resisting to survive or self-destructing to resist? The ongoing paradox of transformation. In M. Suchet, A. Harris, & L. Aron (Eds.), *Relational psychoanalysis* (Vol. 3). Mahawa, NJ: The Analytic Press.

Gergely, G., & Watson, J. S. (1996). The social biofeedback theory of parental affect-mirroring. The development of self-awareness and self-control in infancy. *International Journal of Psychoanalysis, 77*, 1191–1212.

Giovannelli, L., Barbasio, C. P., Burroni, A. G., Fassino, M., Parodi, A., & Granieri, A. (2016). Alexithymia, dissociation, and trauma in patients with chronic skin conditions. *Giornale Italiano di Dermatologia e Venereologia, 151*(4), 347–352.

Granieri, A. (2003). *La comunicazione "al di là delle parole": l'orso bianco*. ["Beyond words" communication: The white bear]. *Abilitazione e Riabilitazione, 12*, 93–98.

Granieri, A., & Schimmenti, A. (2014). Mind – body splitting and eating disorders: A psychoanalytic perspective. *Psychoanalytic Psychotherapy, 28*, 52–70. doi:10.1080/02668734.2013.872172

Jenkins, P. E., & O'Connor, H. (2012). Discerning thoughts from feelings: The cognitive-affective division in eating disorders. *Eating Disorders, 20*, 144–158. doi:10.1080/10640266.2012.654058

Kestemberg, E., Decobert, S., & Kesyemberg, J. (1972). *La faim et le corps: Une e'tude psychanalytique de l'anorexie mentale* [Hunger and the body: A psychoanalytic study of mental anorexia]. Paris: PUF 2005.

Lachmann, F. M. (2008). The process of transforming. *International Journal of Psychoanalytic Self Psychology, 3*, 1–15. doi:10.1080/15551020701721937

Likierman, M. (2008). A meeting of minds: Crucial moments in the mother-infant interactions. *Journal of Infant, Child & Adolescent Psychotherapy, 7*, 199–204. doi:10.1080/15289160802515579

Lunn, S., & Poulsen, S. (2012). Psychoanalytic psychotherapy for bulimia nervosa: A manualized approach. *Psychoanalytic Psychotherapy, 26*, 48–64. doi:10.1080/02668734.2011.652977

Pace, U., Cacioppo, M., & Schimmenti, A. (2012). The moderating role of father's care on the onset of binge eating symptoms among female late adolescents with insecure attachment. *Child Psychiatry and Human Development, 43*, 282–292. doi:10.1007/s10578-011-0269-7

Reilly, E. A. (2004). The case of the bulimic mafia and the tools of their trade. *Psychoanalytic Psychotherapy, 18*, 374–389.

Schimmenti, A. & Caretti, V. (2010). Psychic retreats or psychic pits? Unbearable states of mind and technological addiction. *Psychoanalytic Psychology, 27*(2):115–132.

Schimmenti, A., & Caretti, V. (2016). Linking the overwhelming with the unbearable: Developmental trauma, dissociation, and the disconnected self. *Psychoanalytic Psychology, 33*(1), 106–128. doi:10.1037/a0038019

Schimmenti, A., Guglielmucci, F., Barbasio, C. P., & Granieri, A. (2012). Attachment disorganization and dissociation in virtual worlds: A study on problematic Internet use among players of online role playing games. *Clinical Neuropsychiatry, 9*(5), 187–195.

Schimmenti, A., Passanisi, A., Caretti, V., La Marca, L., Granieri, A., Iacolino, C., Gervasi, A. M., Maganuco, N. R., & Billieux, J. (2017). Traumatic experiences, alexithymia, and Internet addiction symptoms among late adolescents: A moderated mediation analysis. *Addictive Behaviors*, *64*, 314–320. doi:10.1016/j.addbeh.2015.11.002

Seganti, A., Albasi, C., & Granieri, A. (2003). *Linguaggio e sensazioni: "Tra il dire e il fare." Strategie di costruzione dialogica della salute* [Language and feelings: "Between saying and doing." Strategies in dialogical construction of health]. *Ricerca in Psicoterapia*, *6*(1–2), 3–28.

Steiner, J. (1993). *Psychic retreats: Pathological organizations of the personality in psychotic, neurotic and borderline patients*. London: Routledge.

Stern, D. N. (1977). *The first relationship: Infant and mother*. Cambridge, MA: Harvard University Press, 2002.

Stern, D. N. (1977). *The interpersonal world of the infant: A view from psychoanalysis and developmental psychology*. New York: Basic Books, 1985.

Taylor, G. J. (1987). *Psychosomatic medicine and contemporary psychoanalysis*. Madison, CT: International Universities Press.

Tronick, E., & Weinberg, M. (1997). Depressed mothers and infants: The failure to form dyadic states of consciousness. In L. Murray & P. Cooper (Eds.), *Post-partum depression and child development* (pp. 54–85). New York: Guilford Press.

Winnicott, D. W. (1936). *Through paediatrics to psychoanalysis: Collected papers*. London: Karnac, 1984.

Winnicott, D. W. (1957). *The child and the family: First relationships*. London: Tavistock.

Winnicott, D. W. (1969). *Psycho-analytic explorations*. Cambridge, MA: Harvard University Press, 1989.

4

AN ISLAND ENTIRE OF ITSELF

Narcissism in anorexia nervosa

Anthony P. Winston

Introduction

The origins of anorexia nervosa continue to be debated: it is unlikely that there is a single cause and there are probably a number of developmental pathways that can lead to its emergence. It seems possible that anorexia nervosa, like depression or obsessive-compulsive disorder, represents one of a number of biologically predetermined behavioural responses which are activated under conditions of psychological stress. Psychoanalytic theories of its aetiology have tended to concentrate on themes such as sexuality, emotional control, psychic intrusion and the development of a sense of self (see Winston, 2012, for a review). Rather than a single psychodynamic process, however, there may be a number of different processes that can result in the clinical syndrome of anorexia nervosa. The nature of the process (or processes) at work in each patient will have a significant influence on the meaning of food, weight and shape for her[1] and on how the "illness" is thought about in therapy. This paper attempts to describe one of those processes, in which anorexia nervosa develops out of a state of narcissism and omnipotence that has persisted beyond the time when it is developmentally appropriate or to which the patient has regressed.

Anorexia nervosa provides a highly congruent cognitive and behavioural framework for the expression and maintenance of the narcissistic position. The anorexic world is one of isolation, in which one of the most primitive and powerful connections with the outside world – that of eating – is denied. It is also an omnipotent world, in which the patient makes all the rules and triumphs over one of her most elemental needs. Her preoccupation with food and weight becomes all-consuming and external object relations shrink into irrelevance. In her denial of the need for food, the anorexic can symbolically deny her need for a dependent relationship with the outside world and assert omnipotently that she can survive without it. Some cases of anorexia nervosa, which might be termed "narcissistic anorexia," seem to arise when early object relations have made it impossible for the infant to achieve an adequate degree of separation from her mother or when the relationship has been excessively anxiety-provoking; in the latter situation narcissism develops as a defense against relatedeness. In these cases, therapy needs to help the patient to make peace with both her psychological need for relationship and her physical need for food and to allow both to find their natural place within her.

The concept of narcissism

Narcissism, like many psychoanalytic terms, has been used in different ways by different authors and at different times. Freud (1914) introduced the concept of narcissism within the context of his libido theory. He described narcissism as a state in which libido is withdrawn from the external world and redirected towards the ego; he believed that this investment of the ego with an excess of psychic energy resulted in megalomania. He distinguished between primary narcissism, in which the infant directs his libido towards the ego and there is no object relatedness, and secondary narcissism, in which the ego withdraws from object relations in order to recreate the state of primary narcissism; in this state, external objects are experienced as aspects of the self (Freud, 1914; Grotstein, 1993).

In this paper, the term "narcissism" is used to refer to a state in which self and object are not differentiated. Consequently, there can be no experience of relatedness and external objects are felt to be completely within the individual's control; it is for this reason that narcissism and omnipotence are so intimately related. There is an absence of emotional investment in external objects, which are not considered to be real in a psychological sense. In this state, the patient is unable to "use" the object, in the sense described by Winnicott (1969), because the object remains within her omnipotent control. The patient is unable to experience the object "as an external phenomenon, not as a projective entity . . . as an entity in its own right" (Winnicott, 1969, p. 713).

Primary narcissism is conceptualised as an early developmental state before the differentiation of self and object. It is therefore an objectless state, in which the infant has no experience of being separate from those around her. Secondary narcissism, by contrast, is a regressive state in which the patient withdraws from the outside world and rejects the idea of an object outside herself. The patient retreats into an omnipotent state in which she convinces herself that her external objects are completely within her control. Secondary narcissism develops when object relations become too painful or anxiety-provoking and are thus felt to be overwhelming. This may occur when the patient has had a traumatic experience of being in contact with a disturbed or non-attuned mind in childhood or when disappointment and a sense of helplessness are experienced as intolerable. Secondary narcissism may function as a defence against the fear of loss, the pain of dependence or the frustration of not being able to control the object.

Rosenfeld (1964, 1971) has described how secondary narcissism (which he refers to as "narcissistic organisation") serves as a defence against the anxiety, envy and aggression which are generated by the patient's awareness that she is dependent on her objects and that they are both separate from her and outside her control. The patient's envious wish to devalue or destroy any object on whom she might come to depend makes it difficult for her to value the analyst or the analysis and is a powerful impediment to progress. In Rosenfeld's view, "the strength and persistence of omnipotent narcissistic object relations is closely related to the strength of the envious destructive impulses" (Rosenfeld, 1971, p. 172) and emergence from a narcissistic state is inevitably accompanied by the appearance of aggression towards the analyst. It is noteworthy in this context that, in my experience, aggression and envy are emotions which anorexics often find particularly difficult to acknowledge.

Both primary and secondary narcissism can be observed in anorexia nervosa. Narcissism is incompatible with relatedness and narcissistic anorexics therefore struggle to form meaningful relationships. This may be one reason why adolescence, in which the formation of new relationships is central, is the period in which anorexia nervosa typically develops. It is important to emphasise that narcissism is rarely, if ever, an absolute state. In both primary and secondary narcissism, the important question is not whether the patient is narcissistic but to what extent. Secondary narcissism, like the paranoid-schizoid and depressive positions, is probably best thought of as a relatively fluid state, a "psychic retreat" (Steiner, 1993), which the patient can move in and out of.

The Oedipal dimension

I have argued elsewhere (Winston, 2006) that one of the roots of anorexia nervosa may be a failure to work through the frustrations of the negative Oedipus complex (Lampl de Groot, 1927), so that the child remains in a state of fusion with her mother and believes she can have whatever she wants; this is primary narcissism. This situation can arise when the mother cannot allow herself to fail the child and give her an experience of "optimal frustration" (Kohut, 1971), which would enable her to discover the limits of her power and to distinguish what is her from what is not. In this case, the mother is not "good enough" (Winnicott, 1953) but too good.

The other factor that may contribute to such a situation is a father who is unable to interpose himself between mother and child. He is therefore unable to introduce an awareness of external reality, which would enable both mother and daughter to recognise that there is a world outside their relationship and that the state of primary maternal preoccupation (Winnicott, 1956) cannot continue forever. An exclusive relationship with the mother is developmentally appropriate in the early weeks but, as time goes on, the role of the father is to help the child and her mother to realise there is an outside world that also needs to be taken into account. The father may be unable to do this because he is constitutionally ineffective or because he has been actively excluded by a mother who, because of her own needs, wishes to perpetuate the fused relationship longer than is developmentally appropriate (Winston, 2006).

The tragedy of the anorexic in this situation is to have fulfilled her Oedipal desire for union with her mother. This leads to a persistent sense of omnipotence, which is both enormously gratifying and terrifying to her. In this narcissistic world, there is no external object to frustrate her desires and no reality to challenge her belief that she can have whatever she wants. Thus, she comes to believe that she has created everything she experiences and the entire world is a "hallucination" (Winnicott, 1953).

Narcissism and the potential space

The narcissist exists in a world of isolation, without relationship. When there is no relationship, as Winnicott (2005) has pointed out, there can be no potential space and without a potential space there can be no creativity. The potential space is a psychological space that develops within the framework of a secure attachment. It is inhabited by both mother and infant, jointly created by them but not owned or controlled by either. It is the area within which communication, connection, attunement and reciprocity take place. These characteristics enable the potential space to be an arena where play takes place and where patient and therapist play together to create new meaning. If there is no such space between mother and infant, or patient and therapist, the development of a sense of self is profoundly inhibited (Winston, 2009).

When there is no potential space, the child cannot emerge from the narcissistic state. In primary narcissism, the potential space has never developed. In secondary narcissism, the child retreats from it because the experience of connectedness with the other is too anxiety-provoking, for example, because the space is full of unprocessed and uncontained maternal emotion. She withdraws from the potential space into narcissistic omnipotence, convincing herself that the world outside does not exist or, if it does, that she can control it completely. Not surprisingly, anxiety-provoking connectedness in adult relationships or therapy can reactivate such traumatic experiences and trigger regression to a narcissistic state.

The inability to relate to another in a playful, exploratory way can be seen, in contemporary terms, as a failure of mentalization (Bateman & Fonagy, 2011). Mentalization might be seen as one aspect of play, in particular that aspect which recognises the mind of the other; it is no accident that mentalization-based therapy emphasizes the importance of playfulness. Narcissism, which denies both reciprocity and the reality of the other's mind, is thus the antithesis of mentalization. In the context of anorexia nervosa, the potential space may also be seen as the area in which feeding takes place. For mother and infant, feeding is also a shared activity in which both are emotionally invested. Like play, feeding requires attunement, communication and reciprocity. If it is to go well, the mother has to be able to respond empathically to the infant's feelings, while recognising that they are distinct from her own.

Case 1: primary narcissism

Joanna was an only child and her mother was a single parent. Her father had left home when she was six weeks old and she had had no contact with him since. Her mother was a successful writer who had high ambitions for her daughter ("my golden girl") to follow in her footsteps; she frequently told Joanna that they did not need anyone else in their lives and together they would take on the world. Joanna's mother described her as "the perfect baby," who was easy to feed. Her mother continued to breast-feed well into Joanna's second year and needed a great deal of encouragement to wean her. Throughout her childhood, her mother had been very controlling of Joanna's diet, insisting that she should only eat food that she had prepared herself. When Joanna developed anorexia nervosa at the age of thirteen, her mother found it very difficult to accept any advice that health professionals gave about her daughter's diet.

Joanna was eighteen years old when she was referred to the eating disorders clinic. By this stage, she had also started self-harming by cutting and had taken several small overdoses. She had had two previous experiences of therapy, both of which had ended after only a few weeks with Joanna complaining that the therapists did not understand her. Her new therapist felt some trepidation about starting to work with Joanna in view of her dismissive comments about her predecessors.

To begin with, Joanna was prickly and difficult to engage and it was evident from the beginning that she had a deeply enmeshed relationship with her mother. Her mother insisted, with Joanna's agreement, on attending the first consultation with the therapist and answered many of the therapist's questions on Joanna's behalf. When the therapist commented on this, Joanna looked surprised and replied that her mother knew her better than she did, so it was quite natural for her to answer the questions. Joanna's mother seemed to be a dominant and oppressive presence in the therapy sessions, to the extent that the therapist felt largely irrelevant. Her interpretations were often met with responses such as "That's what my mother says" or "I don't think my mother would agree with that." The therapist felt unable to be of any use to Joanna and started to experience disturbing fantasies of Joanna committing a violently self-destructive act, for which she would be held responsible.

After about a year, things seemed to improve. Joanna had become somewhat less critical and warmer in sessions and the therapist congratulated herself that Joanna had stayed in therapy longer with her than with previous therapists. She felt that their relationship had become more collaborative and started to look forward to sessions rather than feeling anxious about them. Her supervisor commented on the fact that the therapist now seemed to be much more positive about Joanna and wondered what had happened to her fantasies of Joanna doing something violent and self-destructive. The therapist replied that she felt that Joanna was now well engaged in therapy and was able to be kinder to herself and more flexible. She went on to explain that Joanna's mother had arranged for her to see a nutritionist, under whose guidance she had started to relax some of her dietary rigidity and to try new foods. However, it emerged that the nutritionist was not simply advising on diet but was also teaching Joanna relaxation techniques and giving her encouraging motivational cards. The therapist regarded this as a positive development, which indicated Joanna's increased psychological flexibility.

The supervisor pointed out that it was unusual for the therapist to be so unconcerned about a patient who was receiving therapeutic input elsewhere. The supervisor wondered whether the unconscious aggression which had previously stimulated the therapist's violent fantasies was now being acted out in an attack on therapy, with the patient seeking most of her help elsewhere. Over time, the therapist came to realise that she had in fact been drawn in to the patient's narcissistic world to the extent that she was unable to recognise her aggression and had come to accept the patient's view of her sessions with the nutritionist as entirely healthy. She had in effect lost her ability to think independently and become a player in a drama of the patient's construction.

Joanna failed to gain weight and had to be hospitalised. In hospital, she was angry and argumentative. What she told the nurses was often untrue, for example, saying that the dietitian had agreed to change her menu and that the psychiatrist had told her mother she would be discharged soon. Staff became increasingly frustrated and hostile towards Joanna and described her as manipulative and dishonest. Splits began to appear in the clinical team. The psychotherapist was able to help the team to see that, in her profoundly narcissistic state, Joanna found it very difficult to distinguish between what she wanted to be true and what actually was the case and that it might be more helpful to see her statements as examples of "symbolic equation" (Segal, 1957) rather than deliberate and conscious lies. She also pointed out that her aggression was a response to the challenge to her omnipotence which hospital treatment represented. Joanna's time in hospital continued to be difficult, but she did gain weight and the danger of staff acting out their negative feelings towards her in a punitive way was averted.

Case 2: secondary narcissism

Elaine was just under three years old when her younger brother was born. She found it very difficult to tolerate this intrusion into her exclusive relationship with her mother. She changed from being a confident, friendly and outgoing child to one who was oppositional and difficult to feed. She started to refuse many of the foods she had previously eaten, and her mother had to make special meals for her, which were different from what the rest of the family ate. At the age of twelve, she decided to become a vegetarian. She also suffered a series of illnesses and problems – asthma, school refusal, social anxiety and, finally, anorexia nervosa – which required her mother to spend a great deal of time with her, to the exclusion of her brother. Her mother, as a result of childhood experiences with her own mother, was highly anxious about her ability to be a good mother to Elaine and consequently found it impossible to ignore Elaine's demands. Elaine's father spent long periods away from home on business and seemed to find it very difficult to support her mother in dividing her time more equally between the two children. Elaine's mother devoted herself to caring for Elaine, and her brother spent much of his time being looked after by his grandparents.

When she eventually came into therapy at the age of sixteen, by now suffering from anorexia nervosa, Elaine presented as both childlike and superior. The therapist was struck by her need to control the session. She was always brought to the session by her mother but often arrived late because her mother had some other commitment beforehand. Elaine did not see this as a problem and refused to contemplate making her own way to the sessions. Although she dressed in the style of someone younger than her years, she sat upright and rigid in the chair in a way that reminded the therapist of a schoolmistress; this seemed to fit with her air of condescension towards him. Elaine frequently announced at the beginning of the session what she intended to talk about, as though setting the agenda, and there seemed little room for spontaneity.

If the therapist pursued an interpretation that Elaine had rejected, she became enraged, insisting that she knew what she felt and the therapist had no right to suggest otherwise. The therapist felt that, in Elaine's mind, his role was merely to reflect and reinforce her beliefs rather than to challenge them. Elaine found it very difficult to understand that there was a distinction between what she wished for and what might actually happen. During the course of therapy she decided to apply to study art at college, an ambition her mother encouraged. One day, Elaine came to the session and reported angrily that her school art teacher had tried to persuade her to choose a different course. Elaine reported this as evidence of the teacher's stupidity and seemed totally unable to appreciate that the teacher might not feel she had an aptitude for art. When the therapist asked how she would feel if she did not get a place on her chosen course, Elaine looked puzzled and said she had never thought about it. The therapist asked if Elaine had an alternative course in mind in case she was not accepted to study art. "Why would I have another course in mind?" she asked, "it's what I want to do." She seemed genuinely not to understand that there might be a difference between what she wanted and what was realistic.

The therapist felt that it was essential to assert his ability to think the thoughts that Elaine could not entertain and thereby assert that there was a reality that lay outside her omnipotent control. He suggested that perhaps the art teacher felt that art was not the right course for her. Elaine retorted that the therapist had never seen her artwork and clearly did not know what he was talking about. When she arrived half an hour late for the next session, the therapist suggested that this was her way of trying to reassert her omnipotent control over him and punish him for having expressed a thought she did not want to acknowledge.

For many months, Elaine and her therapist fought for control of his mind. Elaine questioned the therapist's qualifications and experience and pointed out that her mother had wanted her to see a different therapist. The therapist felt overwhelmed by rage and unable to think clearly about her. He came to see this as an attack on his ability to think and a projection of Elaine's own anger at him for daring to challenge her omnipotence. Gradually, however, he found himself able to think more calmly and clearly about Elaine. She started coming to the sessions on time, and a significant point seemed to have been reached when she asked him what he thought she should do about a problem she had with a friend. This seemed to indicate the beginning of a more collaborative relationship, in which Elaine was able to acknowledge the fact that the therapist had an independent mind. The sessions became less confrontational and more playful, and it seemed that she was beginning to emerge from a state of narcissistic isolation into one of interpersonal relatedness.

Therapeutic processes in narcissistic anorexia

The two foregoing cases illustrate how narcissistic anorexia may develop. In Joanna's case, it seems that mother and daughter had never separated and there was confusion in the mother's mind between her needs and her daughter's. Her insistence on them taking on the world together implied a belief in a state of persistent fusion that allowed little space for Joanna to develop a sense of her own identity. This was reflected in Joanna's prolonged breast-feeding and her mother's over-involvement in her diet. Rather than use therapy to help her to separate from her mother and begin to develop a sense of self, Joanna replaced her indulgent mother with the nutritionist who was endlessly supportive and nurturing but rarely, if ever, challenging. The experience of being treated in hospital was particularly difficult for her because she was unable to recreate the omnipotent relationship that she had had with her mother and the nutritionist and which she had tried to perpetuate with her therapist.

Elaine, by contrast, seems to have been able to emerge from a state of primary narcissism and achieve a degree of separation, as evidenced by the early description of her as confident and outgoing. However, the arrival of her younger brother, complicated by her mother's difficulty in sharing her care between the two siblings and managing Elaine's envy of her brother, seems to have resulted in a regression back to a narcissistic state, in which she could remain psychologically fused with her mother. Later, anorexia nervosa became the means by which she could maintain this state of fusion and exclude from her world anyone who might threaten it.

The essential task of therapy with a narcissistic patient is to help her to realize that there is an external world, which is outside her control. As Rosenfeld (1971, p. 175) puts it, "It is essential to help the patient to find and rescue the dependent sane part of the self from its trapped position inside the psychotic narcissistic structure as it is this part which is the essential link with the positive object relationship to the analyst and the world." In Winnicott's terms, the therapist has to help the patient to "place the analyst outside the area of subjective phenomena" so that he or she can become an object to be used (Winnicott, 1969, p. 1). In narcissistic anorexia, the need to eat comes to symbolise those aspects of life that are potentially outside her control and therefore need to be ruthlessly subjugated by her omnipotence.

The shift out of narcissistic isolation is achieved largely by the therapist's implicit insistence that he or she exists independently of the patient and that there is an external reality, including the reality of the need to eat, which needs to be acknowledged. One way this can be demonstrated is by the therapist continuing to remind the patient of the importance of eating and gaining weight. Another is by adherence to the therapeutic frame and a refusal to modify it despite the patient's demands. More subtly, it is shown by the therapist continuing to be able to think his or her own thoughts and not just those projected by the patient.

Of course, the patient will be enraged by this and will attempt to exert omnipotent control of the therapist. She may refuse to adhere to therapeutic boundaries, for example, about appointment times or the therapist's availability outside sessions. She may also attack the therapist's ability to think and to make connections (Bion, 1959) and generate in him or her a sense of confusion, impotence and incompetence. She will often resist the therapist's attempts to "feed" her by rejecting interpretations, because to take them in would imply dependence and need. When the patient begins to accept and make use of the therapist's interpretations, it is a sign that she is emerging from the narcissistic position and allowing herself to be fed.

Some entirely non-psychodynamic interventions may be unexpectedly helpful in this context. Compulsory treatment for anorexia nervosa is commonly thought of as psychologically damaging and therefore to be avoided if at all possible. Under some circumstances, this may well be true. For some patients, however, it may demonstrate that there is a limit to their self-destructive omnipotence and reaffirm that there is a reality (including the reality of the need to eat) which they cannot control. This may explain the relief that some patients show when a decision is made to begin feeding them without their consent. Similarly, family therapy approaches, which aim to empower the parents to take control of their child's eating, may also be beneficial in limiting her omnipotence. By encouraging the parents to function in a unified way, family therapy can help the parents to give the child a belated experience of being unable to dominate and split a united parental couple.

By helping the patient to emerge from narcissistic isolation, the therapist enables her to develop a sense of herself as a separate entity. This requires the painstaking creation of a potential space between them, in which they both share and in which neither is dominant. This is by no means an easy task, as the patient will try hard to recreate a situation of omnipotence and obliterate the potential space. This may take the form of inviting the therapist into a battle in which one has to be the winner and the other the loser. The most obvious arena for this kind of battle is over weight and eating, where the therapist becomes increasingly insistent that the patient must eat and the patient becomes equally insistent that she will not.

One of the major difficulties in working with a narcissistic anorexic is that therapy can only be effective if the patient is willing to allow the therapist to help her. This means that she has to give up the safety of the narcissistic position, in which she believes she has no need of others, and acknowledge her need for the therapist. Rosenfeld (1971) has pointed out that, to receive help, the narcissistic patient has to acknowledge her weakness and relinquish her sense of superiority. It is something of a paradox that the patient needs to have – or develop – enough capacity for relationship to allow the therapist to help her emerge from her narcissistic state. This is one of the reasons why the early stages of therapy with a narcissistic patient are so difficult and demand such perseverance form the therapist.

It is essential to work through some of the anxieties against which narcissism is a defence before expecting the patient to be able to move on from the narcissistic position. Attempts to interpret the patient's narcissism before this has happened, and before the healthier parts of her personality have formed a trusting attachment to the therapist, are likely to be experienced as intensely threatening and will only intensify the patient's resistance. Interpretations of this sort at an early stage in therapy are also likely to be experienced by the patient as an intolerable, retaliatory return of her own repressed aggression. Instead, the therapist has to help the patient to develop some capacity for dependence and external object relations, so that she can begin to establish a relationship with the therapist and the rest of the world. The restricted object relations of the narcissistic anorexic patient result in a very limited development of the transference, and this is one reason why lack of transference is often such a striking feature of work with anorexics. The development of transference can therefore be seen as evidence of maturation and a move away from narcissistic isolation.

Case 3: therapy with a narcissistic anorexic

Gemma was referred to the eating disorders clinic at the age of seventeen. She began the first consultation by explaining that she had already researched available treatments for anorexia nervosa and had concluded that the most appropriate treatment for her would be cognitive-behavioural therapy. When the therapist suggested that perhaps it would be a good idea to hear a bit about the problem before deciding on the treatment, Gemma became agitated and angry, saying that she knew what she wanted and her family agreed with her.

The therapist offered to see Gemma for six exploratory sessions so that he could form a fuller picture of Gemma's difficulties before they decided what sort of treatment might be most useful. Gemma agreed reluctantly, while continuing to insist that it was a straightforward issue and she did not understand why the therapist was not prepared to respect "patient choice" and offer her "evidence-based treatment." The therapist managed to suppress his feelings of irritation and wondered why Gemma needed to be so insistent. It seemed to him that she was terrified of the possibility of a discussion between them and of a potential space developing. Gemma's dogmatic insistence seemed to be a defence against the enormous anxiety generated by any uncertainty and by the possibility of allowing the therapist to enter into her world as a separate person.

Exploring her history, the therapist discovered that Gemma's parents were both professional people, who set great store by academic and material success. Gemma had been sent away to boarding school at the age of eleven and remembered her parents telling her that this would give her the best academic opportunities because she would not be distracted by trivial activities. At school she had been very successful academically but was unable to make friends.

Gemma talked readily and fluently about her problems with eating, often using technical psychological and nutritional terms, which made it clear that she knew a great deal about anorexia. Although she appeared to be insightful, her insights seemed to be presented to the therapist fully formed, in a way that left the therapist with nothing to do. The unconscious message from Gemma seemed to be that she had already done the therapeutic work and did not really need the therapist. The therapist felt disconnected and uninvolved during the sessions and his mind began to wander. In one session he found himself recalling a patient he had met as a medical student, who had suffered a stroke and developed "fluent aphasia," a condition in which the patient speaks fluently and confidently but without any meaning.

At times, the therapist tried to interrupt Gemma to make an interpretation. Her response was usually either to dismiss the interpretation as clearly wrong or to indicate that she had already considered what the therapist had suggested and then to dilate on her own thoughts about it. If the therapist persisted in pursuing his interpretation, Gemma would point out with hostility that the therapist was just like her father, who always had to be right. Not surprisingly, nothing the therapist said seemed to be of any help to Gemma and she seemed to be unable to take in anything nourishing from him, in the same way that she was unable to take in more literal nourishment.

The therapist's initial irritation gave way to a pervasive sense of deadness and emptiness. He stopped trying to compete with Gemma to say something that she would value. Instead, he commented on how sad it was that Gemma had been unable to let him help her. Gemma looked confused and taken aback, and the therapist became anxious that he had made a serious error. However, the tone of the session shifted slightly and Gemma began to talk about how she felt that she had to be the best at everything and always in control. The therapist wondered whether Gemma's strong preference for cognitive-behavioural therapy might reflect her wish for a therapy that would enhance her sense of control and at which she could excel. Somewhat to the therapist's surprise, Gemma said that she thought there "might be something in that." There was a noticeable softening of her demeanour and she agreed to continue the exploratory work for a few more sessions. Over the next few months, she was able to explore the way in which she had dealt with her feelings of emptiness and of being unwanted by her parents by retreating into a narcissistic state of isolation and a relentless focus on achievement, in which she was able to retain a sense of being in control of her world.

Gemma's relationship with the therapist began to feel more real. She became less anxious about eating "forbidden foods" and her weight started to increase slowly. She revealed a dry sense of humour and they were occasionally able to share a joke. As time went on, however, Gemma started to become depressed. She became preoccupied with the ending of therapy but was able to think about this in relation to her feelings of abandonment by her parents. Gradually, her rigid dietary control started to loosen and she was able to admit to enjoying food. An important moment came when Gemma came to a session with a cake that she had baked for the therapist. The therapist was able to see beyond the fact that Gemma had brought him something to eat and recognised that the cake symbolised both the emergence of Gemma's creativity and the reality of the relationship that had made this possible.

Conclusion

For a proportion of patients, anorexia nervosa may be thought of as a narcissistic disorder. Narcissistic anorexia may arise as a developmental failure or as a regression from the anxiety and pain of relatedness. Therapy needs to provide the patient with an opportunity to emerge from this state and develop the capacity for object relations. To do so, the therapist has to provide an experience of attunement and attachment, while resisting the pressure to be absorbed into the patient's omnipotent control and preserving the capacity to think independently. This leads to the development of a potential space, in which the patient can begin to "use" the therapist and explore a world outside herself. This in turn makes it possible for her to allow herself to be fed and, eventually, to feed herself. It is the central experience of relatedness in therapy that enables the patient to move from being "an island entire of itself" to being "involved in mankind" and "a part of the main" (Donne, 1624).

Note

1 I have used the female pronoun to refer to patients because most anorexics are female, and the themes described in this paper are explored in the context of mother-daughter relationships. The significance of primary narcissism and its relationship to the Oedipus complex in male anorexics is beyond the scope of this paper.

References

Bateman, A. W., & Fonagy, P. (2011). *Handbook of mentalizing in mental health practice*. Arlington, VA: American Psychiatric Publishing.

Bion, W. R. (1959). Attacks on linking. *International Journal of Psycho-Analysis, 40*, 308–315.

Donne, J. (1624). *Meditation 17, devotions upon emergent occasions*. London: Printed by AM for Thomas Jones.

Freud, S. (1914). *On narcissism: An introduction*. S.E. 14 (pp. 67–104). London: Hogarth Press and the Institute of Psycho- Analysis.

Grotstein, J. S. (1993). Foreword in Symington N *Narcissism: A New Theory*. London: Karnac.
Kohut, H. (1971). *The analysis of the self.* New York: International Universities Press.
Lampl de Groot, J. (1927). The evolution of the Oedipus complex in women. *International Journal of Psycho-Analysis*, *9*, 332–345.
Rosenfeld, H. (1964). On the psychopathology of narcissism: A clinical approach. *International Journal of Psycho-Analysis*, *45*, 332–337.
Rosenfeld, H. (1971). A clinical approach to the psycho-analytical theory of the life and death instincts: an investigation into the aggressive aspects of narcissism. *International Journal of Psycho-Analysis*, *52*, 169–178.
Segal, H. (1957). Notes on symbol formation. *International Journal of Psycho-Analysis*, *38*, 391–397.
Steiner, J. (1993). *Psychic retreats: Pathological organizations in psychotic, neurotic and borderline patients*. London: Routledge.
Winnicott, D. W. (1953). Transitional objects and transitional phenomena: A study of the first not-me possession. *International Journal of Psycho-Analysis*, *34*(2), 89–97.
Winnicott, D. W. (1956). *Through paediatrics to psycho-analysis* (pp. 300–305). London: Karnac.
Winnicott, D. W. (1969). The use of an object. *International Journal of Psycho-Analysis*, *50*, 711–716.
Winnicott, D. W. (2005). *Playing and reality*. London: Routledge.
Winston, A. P. (2006). The oedipus complex in anorexia nervosa. *Psychoanalytic Psychotherapy*, *20*(1), 1–15.
Winston, A. P. (2009). Anorexia nervosa and the psychotherapy of absence. *British Journal of Psychotherapy*, *25*(1), 77–90.
Winston, A. P. (2012). Psychodynamic approaches to eating disorders. In J. R. E. Fox & K. Goss (Eds.), *Eating and its disorders* (pp. 244–259). Chichester: Wiley-Blackwell.

5

THE DEAD THIRD IN THE TREATMENT OF AN ADOLESCENT WITH ANOREXIA NERVOSA

Lorraine Caputo

Introduction

In this paper I examine my work with a young teenager, whom I will call Sophie, who suffered a brief episode of anorexia from which she recovered, in part, because the therapy made room for the ghosts which haunted her from her parents' and grandparents' generations. While the ghosts of family traumas were acknowledged by Sophie, it became clear that she had not fully integrated these family narratives in her psyche. In adolescence, these buried traumas led to an emotional and medical crisis for Sophie. The ghosts were there because Sophie, a loyal young woman, carried the pain of those who came before her, but also because the ghosts had not yet been metabolized, perhaps by her parents, perhaps by her mother, and perhaps for the reason that in most circumstances trauma does not move through generations in a clean and cauterized way. Her great-grandparents had escaped Europe during the Holocaust to settle in Chile. Her grandparents and her parents were forced to flee Chile because of similar anti-Semitic circumstances and a politically repressive regime. Sophie was very aware of her family's history and felt haunted by the memories of her family's past.

Many analysts have wondered how the ghosts of trauma past can be transmitted through generations. Abraham and Torok (1994) refer to the "phantom": "The phantom is a formation of the unconscious that has never been conscious – for good reason. It passes – in a way yet to be determined – from the parent's unconscious into the child's. . . . The presence of the phantom indicates the effects on the descendants of something that had inflicted narcissistic injury or even catastrophe on the parents . . . the phantom which returns to haunt bears witness to the existence of the dead buried within the other" (pp. 173–174).

Fonagy (1999), in his work with an adolescent with obsessive-compulsive disorder (OCD) whose mother was a second-generation survivor of the Holocaust, began an attachment-theory formulation of transgenerational vulnerabilities associated with severe trauma. He speculated that a disruption in mentalization and reflective functioning in parents were possible vehicles for the transmission of trauma to the next generation. Fonagy's research showed that "high reflective capacity in the caregiver in narratives of childhood attachment relationships predicts attachment security in infants, particularly if the caregiver reports a significant history of trauma or deprivation" (p. 102). His patient's mother was reported to carry "the persistent shadow of the Holocaust" (Moses, 1993). Drawing on Kestenberg (1982), he suggests that, if a parent has a "dissociative core," it permits the direct transmission of unconscious traumatic fantasy from mother or father to child" (p. 105). In contrast to transmissions that are grounded in the child's identification with his or her parent, in these cases the child is *immersed* in another reality (the parent's).

In the teenage case presented in this paper, Sophie's anorexia and moments of dissociation and derealization seemed to connect back to her family's history of trauma in the Holocaust. While Fonagy (1999) had direct access to the mother's treatment in his case, I was left to track the shadow of the Holocaust through the somatization that occurred in Sophie's life through her anorexia, as well as a complex pain syndrome, and through her evolving ability to discuss her family's traumatic history and its impact on her. As Adrienne Harris states in her introduction to *Ghosts in the Consulting Room*, the somatic carries so much of the "ghostly, spectral, and ambiguous" which can be unlocked when "the narrative enters treatment, when fragments and chaos are ordered through naming and genealogy . . . in the permanent tasks of mourning, both triumph and despair and this must be parsed and held by analyst for the patient and for him/herself" (p. 6–7). At times, this task can be endless and, ultimately, exhausting; Harris quotes Margaret Little as having said, "Mourning is for life" (Little, 1985, p. 6).

Clinical history and treatment

Sophie was a high school freshman when she was referred to me by her school guidance counselor and by a neurologist who was treating her for complex regional pain syndrome (CRPS), also known as reflexive sympathetic dystrophy (RSD). RSD is a chronic pain syndrome that can develop after an injury. Sophie's began after a lacrosse injury where she sprained her ankle. The pain level in patients with RSD is often out of proportion to the injury. The pain can become chronic and can cause extreme sensitivity to touch and a burning sensation at the site, leading some to wear loose-fitting clothing. There is controversy over the exact cause of RSD, and psychosomatic and prior mental health concerns have been identified as possible correlates. In the *Psychiatric Times* about RSD or CRPS, King (2006) writes: ". . . it has been proposed that there may be changes in the brain, most notably in the primary sensory cortex, secondary to CRPS, and that these can lead to a distorted body image. What role these changes may play in the pain and other symptoms of CRPS is still the subject of speculation" (p. 9). But King (2006) states, ". . . the diagnosis of pain disorder associated with both psychological factors and a general medical condition identified as CRPS would be appropriate. Furthermore, by applying both diagnoses, health care professionals would ensure that psychological issues are not overlooked" (p. 9). Sophie had seen many specialists for this mysterious pain disorder, and the family was continuing to pursue more appointments with pain specialists. There was no mention, at the time of the referral, that Sophie might have an eating disorder. The family and the doctors all seemed to be speaking a different language about her pain disorder. Her neurologist thought it was a psychosomatic illness connected to an underlying depression. The family thought her symptoms were purely medical. Yet Sophie had suffered episodes, characterized by moments of dissociation and derealization since middle school, which were accompanied by thoughts of killing herself by jumping out of a window. She also shared with me that she had a "council" of warring voices inside of her, with the more sadistic and angry voice being the scariest and the most powerful. I came to feel fragmented as I tried to integrate the somatic and the psychological, looking for the pattern to help make sense of all of this to the patient and to myself.

Despite this complicated weave of problems, Sophie was a very likeable, reflective, and energetic young teenager who wanted to understand her problems. She began our work together with openness and curiosity. She was the first person to mention having purposely lost 20 pounds in a month's time the past summer, primarily by restricting caloric intake and because of extensive exercise related to a lacrosse summer camp. She had not menstruated for the six months before her first appointment with me in the early winter. She put her weight loss into context. As a ten-year-old, "I was adorable, but chubby." According to Sophie, "puberty happened overnight" and "I shot up; I lost all of my baby fat. I was suddenly getting more attention for my looks and feedback that I was attractive. I felt shame over enjoying this attention." She felt she had become a vain person and was fearful she could not be smart, ambitious, and also attractive, and interested in boys. These qualities did not mix in her mind. She also became uncomfortable with how men responded to her on the street. Right before she had lost the 20 pounds, her father had taken her to a soccer match in New York. While her father went to use the men's room, Sophie was approached by men sitting around her, who asked for her number and made comments about her appearance. She felt frightened and objectified and claimed that these experiences of men objectifying her body led her to objectify her own body. "I came to feel my body was a thing and that my mind and body were two separate things; I figured if my body was an object, it couldn't feel pain."

As I became aware of what looked like anorexia I began to wonder if some of the medical issues had been precipitated by the loss of weight over that past summer or if both the anorexia and RSD were manifestations of psychological conflicts, particularly related to her anxiety about becoming a young adult. I also began to wonder about the importance and influence of the family history of the maternal and paternal grandparents' generation, who had to escape the Holocaust, leaving relatives behind who had perished, which was followed by the need to flee their second country, because of anti-Semitism and oppression, for the United States. Sophie brought her family history up regularly as our sessions progressed. There were horrific stories about family members who had starved in Europe and died in the camps. There were stories of the brutal treatment of an uncle who was forced to jump from a plane into the ocean by the dictatorship in their South American country. And at one point, Sophie began to discuss how thin one set of grandparents were, calling them 75-year-old anorexics who worked very hard to be thin. She felt oppressed by their focus on thinness when she visited them or when they visited her.

Not eating had complicated meanings for Sophie. Paradoxically, being thinner made her more attractive, and also less attractive as she lost her curves in order to deflect male attention. The rapid loss of weight was accompanied by the RSD, which began after a sports injury in her foot. She now feels that developing the RSD after the anorexia had helped her to see her "body, mind, and soul as unified, as I began to feel pain." As destructive as the weight loss had been, it also seemed to be a way to bring attention to her internal pain. She began to realize how disconnected from her body she felt; she also began to recognize there were times when she experienced moments of depersonalization and derealization, not just when dieting, but also in relation to her place in the world in general.

Sophie was very attached to her family. As the oldest of four children she felt like she was carrying the legacy of her grandparents' suffering. As time went on, it became clear she had been listening very carefully to her family's stories and had become a receptacle of the family narratives of trauma, repression, and escape from possible annihilation. Because of her deep sense of loyalty and connection to her extended family, she was clearly passionately attached to this narrative and as a result, her sense of where their history ended and hers began had blurred.

She also lived under the shadow of the accomplishments of both sides of her family. Her paternal grandparents were accomplished journalists who had escaped the totalitarian regime of their last homeland before fleeing to the United States. Both maternal grandparents were psychiatrists who had fled the same country, leaving behind practices and a disappeared relative. Her parents, both born in the family's second homeland, had immigrated to the United States as young children, later attending Ivy League colleges and graduate schools at prestigious universities. Had they remained in their home countries, they could not have had these successes. Sophie felt obligated to be accomplished and perfect. The anorexia had begun before her freshman year of high school, when she felt the pressure to perform as a student who could be accepted into Ivy League universities. Yet, she was terrified that she could not get into those colleges. She also admitted how much she wanted to just spend her time watching her favorite Netflix movies and television shows. She also just wanted to spend time with her many close friends, laughing and sharing secrets. She felt very conflicted about having to achieve so much, especially since she felt this was her destiny, an unavoidable requirement of her family and her extended family.

The developmental, cultural, and relational third

Gerson's (2009) writing about *the dead third* resonated in this case for me. In Gerson's discussion of the third, he elaborates the concept of the "live third," whether "person, relationship, or institution – which serves the elemental function of solidifying an individual's sense of person, place, and purpose" (Gerson, 2009, p. 1343). I utilize his operational way of thinking about the concept of the third in three domains: the developmental, relational, and cultural. All three domains operated in my work with Sophie.

In the developmental domain, we can see her anorexia as a symptom of the re-emergence of the Oedipal issues of childhood as she began to feel the conflicts around attractiveness and her own sexual desire. Marsha Levy Warren (2000) has looked at the importance and impact of Oedipal issues on the family of young adolescents:

> Puberty is not an experience that young adolescents experience on their own; puberty is a family event. The hormonal changes that usher in the secondary sex characteristics that engender adolescence move children into a new phase of life characterized by having bodies that more resemble those of adults than those of children, both in terms of physical appearance and inner sensation. Sexual feeling is introduced into the family at this time in a new way. Once in the realm of the parents' private relationship and the child's autoerotic life, sexuality is now in the arena of the parent-child relationship: parents become aware, often acutely, of their adolescent children's budding sexuality, adolescents become more aware of their parents' sexuality, and both become aware of growing feelings of unease related to their prior modes of being affectionate with each other.
>
> *(p. 125)*

She and her father often watched early episodes of "Game of Thrones" together, and she would describe her discomfort when sex scenes came on the screen and how she would try not to look at or talk to him while the scenes unfolded. She was particularly enthralled with the first sexual experience of the character of Daenerys, who had been married at age 12 to a man much older than she. It is a particularly erotic scene and one which some, including this therapist, would have seen as a child rape, as Daenerys is clearly resistant to the relationship. Sophie describes her father as an "ugly" man to whom she could never be attracted; she could not choose a man like him. She said she might not be able to find a Jewish man if he were as unattractive as her father. Given that her father, in reality, was not an ugly man and was pleasant looking, I read in this a defense against the incest taboo.

In my initial meeting with her parents, Sophie's father seemed to be worried about her emerging sexuality, with a specific worry that I found perplexing. He was concerned that she would be a young woman who could easily be pressured into having sex at an early age. In fact, she was far from being sexually active and expressed no desire to have sex before she was at least an older teen. His anxiety seems clearly related to how puberty had come to feel like a runaway car to him, one which he felt he could not have control over. Clearly, Sophie was worried about becoming sexual and what it would mean. Her preference to have no period may have been provoked by concern that, once she began to menstruate, she would be free to become sexual and lose something in her relationship with her father and her mother. In both a professorial and childlike way, she observed to me: "A girl got her period in the shtetl and was married to a 40-year-old butcher; now, one has a long period of time between the beginning of one's menstruation before becoming an adult. I prefer to be a child as I can still always become an adult, whereas, if I see myself as an adult, then I cannot be a child anymore." This period of work opened up the loss of innocence she was experiencing about entering adolescence and young adulthood. Some of our work was to help her see that she could still be playful in her family, with friends, and in our sessions while moving towards young adulthood.

The desire to remain a child played itself out in the early weeks of treatment when Sophie told her parents she felt suicidal when her mother would not let her sleep in her bed one evening. She had felt "angry" at her mother for not letting her be "her baby" that night. Afterwards, she went out to the roof outside of her bedroom, but denied an intention to act on her thoughts of jumping. Paradoxically, she claimed being on the roof gave her a sense of freedom, which she "desperately" wanted. This incident led to our work around regulating her responses to her mother's perceived rejections, and the anger she felt towards her mother, but often denied or buried and, in many cases, directed towards herself. The freedom she felt on the roof that night was a complicated feeling because it could lead to a self-destructive act. We began to unpack what she needed to be free from and whether that would lead to her harming herself as a way to escape her complicated feelings of anger and loss, particularly in relation to her mother. She was able to identify other moments during which she felt rejected, criticized or attacked by her mother and how both angry and confused this made her.

Extending Gerson's (2009) "live third" as someone or something which serves the "function of solidifying a sense of purpose, place, and person," Sophie's extended family – their accomplishments and their difficult history – were part of solidifying Sophie's identity. But that role was threatened by a schism in the family between her mother and her father's parents and sister. Despite their shared history, there was a mysterious animosity between the women, which led to a tortuous and painful disruption of Sophie's identifications and disidentifications with these women, in how she saw her body and emerging womanhood. Sophie had been witness to many of their arguments. One such argument between her mother and Sophie's paternal grandmother and aunt during a holiday celebration led to an angry exchange between her parents on the ride home. "The other children cried," Sophie reported, "but I didn't feel anything."

Sophie was very forthcoming about how conflicted she was by how differently the women on both sides of the family expressed their womanhood. We explored these differences, especially as Sophie had expressed her worries about becoming a vain woman who cared only about her looks and being attractive. In another session she had made reference to both grandmothers and a paternal aunt as "vain," as they valued looking good, styling their hair, going for manicures and pedicures, and also valued being thin. She also felt her heaviness as a child was judged by both sets of grandparents. Her maternal grandmother was thin. She would make comments about Sophie's weight as a younger child. A few years into treatment, Sophie was planning to visit the family's second homeland with her maternal grandparents. Her biggest worry was that in the culture of that country, she would be seen as "fat," because she had gained weight and begun to enjoy eating and food. She worried her grandmother would be critical of her eating or pressure her to exercise. This visit precipitated more anxiety about her weight and, in particular, her thighs. We began discussing ways for her to shield herself from being triggered on this trip into not eating and becoming once again overly preoccupied with weight loss.

While Sophie's mother saw her own mother and her in-laws as superficial, Sophie was trying to find a middle ground between the two styles of womanhood in her family. She wanted to be comfortable with being beautiful, but was also worried she would become superficial. She thought her mother to be "the most beautiful woman in the world," but saw that she was not as concerned with her weight or with wearing makeup, and was focused on her work and her mothering responsibilities. However, she was also aware of how unhappy her mother felt juggling work and family issues, and was able to discuss feeling worried about being as unhappy as her mother seemed to be with her life. She felt that the one way her mother showed her love was through preparing food and going out to eat. The therapist's intuition about this was that Sophie's explicit conflict between her mother and the other women of the family was actually about who would "own" Sophie's identity as woman. We worked to find ways for her to see that she did not have to make a choice, but she could be both serious and pretty, interested in boys and her attractiveness. She could construct her own balance between being interested in her body and being a serious student, without seeing it as black and white.

A dream about identity, dependence, and separation

Early in the treatment, Sophie brought a dream that expressed her confusion and conflict over creating her own unique female identity, her fear of disloyalty to her mother, her fear of her emergent sexual desires, and the pull to become ill and passive rather than an agent of her own sexual and adult identity and desires. The dream delineated her fear of becoming independent, wishing to stay childlike and connected to those she loves. This was particularly evident as she described herself in the dream as being an "albino teletubby connected to multi-colored wires":

> I had a dream that took place at the high school, but it was also a dormitory, hotel, and hospital setting. Everyone in my family was staying there.
>
> I dreamt that my mom cheated on my dad. But this woman wasn't my mother! The woman was vain and deceitful, unlike my mother. The woman (who was my mother, but not my mother) denied having an affair. My mother is very honest, would never do this. I kept wondering, why are you cheating?
>
> At first I went to the hospital floor and was embarrassed because I was attached to the EEG and in a hospital robe. My hair was in a sock. I looked like an albino Teletubby with two gauze socks over my head attached to multicolored wires. My maternal grandmother took me to a room where my mother was having an affair with this man.

The dream opened up one of our initial discussions about these conflicts. As the oldest of four children, it now appeared to me that Sophie's astonishment and anguish over her mother's cheating may have referred back to the way she felt as each child was born to her parents and her parents became more preoccupied with the newer babies and with maintaining both of their academic careers, making the Oedipal triangle more diffuse and less embracing of her. This led us to look at her feelings about being the oldest child, including the rivalry she felt for her younger sister and disdain for that sister, who was more "superficial" and not as "serious" as Sophie.

But Sophie agreed that the mother in the dream expressed her own self and what she was working on psychically. The dream deals with the mother's perfidy but also Sophie's fear of her own perfidy. Would she cheat on her mother by not being serious enough, accomplished enough? Was it okay to enjoy being attractive, and happy with being both a serious and intelligent woman with comfort in her attractiveness? Would she stop being the adorable, chubby 10-year-old attached to her family, or would she remain frozen in childhood, like a mutant tele-tubby connected to an EEG, attached to her mother by illness? By protracting her illnesses and the family's frantic visit to multiple doctors before her treatment began, her illness began to become a metaphor for her strong wish to be taken care of, a fear of growing up, and a strong need for more from her relationship with her mother. When she had begun counting calories and obsessively restricting her food intake, she attempted to hide this behavior from her mother who would be "busy feeding the other kids"; yet it did seem Sophie needed her mother to notice her and find her. In feminist literature on eating problems we are reminded that, "satiety . . . like hunger and food . . . can encode separation, differentiation, autonomy, entitlement, limits, and boundaries. When food represents one's earliest attachments, the difficulties in those relationships shape one's relationship to satiety as well as food and hunger" (Bloom, Gitter, Gutwill, Kogel, & Zaphiropoulos, 1994, p. 110). Sophie became afraid to feed herself, to feel satiated. She wasn't ready to be the child at the table who could feed and satiate herself.

Next, I examine Sophie's issues in light of the cultural third described by Gerson and particularly his concept of the "dead third." I wait to examine the relational third of the therapeutic relationship afterwards because the third of our relationship encompasses my ability to witness the cultural third, to recognize the "dead third" in this family, and in her psyche.

Gerson's (2009) focus on what distinguishes the trauma of survivors of genocide gives us a metaphor for how that trauma might move forward to other generations:

> My focus . . . is on trauma occasioned by intentional acts of violence committed by social and political entities that are aimed at the annihilation of a class of people for racial, ethnic, or political purposes. Survivors of genocidal acts have each been subjected to a specific form of violence that has left an enduring residue based on the moments and form of the horrors experienced, the personality of the victimized and the presence or absence of a mediating "live third."
>
> *(p. 1344)*

Gerson (2009) goes on to state that the absence of a mediating live third precipitates a "loss of faith in a protective world" (p. 1345) that victims of genocides experience. It is this kind of "loss of faith in a protective world," however hard to decipher, that brought Sophie to treatment, albeit encapsulated in her anorexia and RSD. As treatment progressed she would often discuss the terror her grandparents and great-grandparents experienced, uncovering a residue she had been managing for some time in her psyche. She remembered having a thought in middle school that perhaps nothing around her was real or that perhaps she and other students were really lizards. This unreal feeling that the world around her was reptilian in nature speaks to a world in which the third is dead and indifferent.

In this context, we began to see her food restriction as a way to avoid the loss of innocence and childhood. In the back of my mind while treating her, I began to think that for Sophie, amenorrhea could symbolize a wish not to grow up, to avoid becoming an adult who would have to face the possibility of a dead third, of a world indifferent to human suffering. The absence of her periods meant life would not move forward in a world that was clearly dangerous and potentially murderous. By dieting, losing weight, and objectifying her body, she may have been excavating the absent object, the lost object of her extended family's traumas. That lost object was endangered by the conflicts that had arisen between her mother and the female members of her father's family. Sophie was carrying around this legacy and wanted the "freedom" she had described after going to her terrace. Was this a freedom from the knowledge of the losses her family had experienced? Or from the denial of those losses?

Haydee Faimberg's (2005) thoughts are relevant to this story:

> [I]dentity was determined by what was excluded from the history of the parents; identity remained, therefore, in solid connection with this history, and since it was organized under the aegis of negation, it can be labeled a negative identity . . . the threatening absent object, not symbolized yet as a lost object, is a present non-object.
>
> *(pp. 17–18)*

Sophie's body became a "present non-object" when she lost weight and her menstruation. Referral to a medical doctor who specialized in adolescence and adolescent eating disorders was a way to help Sophie and her family begin to identify her as an emerging adolescent and to help her to pay attention to her body in a positive way. The emphasis on re-establishing menarche helped her to be cognizant of the rhythms of her body again and to engage in a project of moving forward with growth and sexual development. It was also a way to make connections between healthy eating and overall medical health. In time, Sophie began gaining weight and six months into treatment she began to menstruate again.

It seems salient to mention here that I am overweight, do not always wear makeup, and was struggling with similar issues to those of my mother's around career and raising a family and self-care. I had also grown up with an angry mother who was bitter and dissatisfied that she had not achieved more in her life. My mother was never confident in her appearance and had two sisters who were very confident in their beauty, in many ways glamorous, and successful in the world of beauty. I understood only too well the conflict about identifications with women within one family expressing their gender expressions in very different ways. I was also very loyal to the grandparent immigrant generation of my family and expressed that loyalty through food, finding it hard to find my way culturally as I assimilated more into a mainstream, non-immigrant world. I think Sophie may have sensed I had also struggled with integrating the conflicting messages from family, culture, and society about weight and body image and may have felt comforted that I understood how complicated this could be.

Disney and the alive and animated third

The family had participated in a complicated but creative denial of the history and pain in their past, which contributed to Sophie's reluctance to grow up. It was played out in their multiple and extended trips to Disney World and a fascination with the Disney stories. When discussing their trips we had lively and exciting sessions. Sophie would bring books on animation to our sessions, full of a great passion for the genre. As defined by Merriam Webster dictionary, *animate* can mean the following: "to give life to" or "to make or design in such a way as to create apparently spontaneous *lifelike* movement" (emphasis mine) (Merriam Webster's Collegiate Dictionary, 1993).

Her obsession with animation and with film in general seems to be an effort to revive a "dead third," resuscitating the near deadness in her family and in herself. Disney may itself have become an alive third for this family. The Disney princesses and animated characters gave Sophie a reprieve from having to deal with the adult issues of competition, envy, and aggression. Her favorite character had been Belle because she was a girl interested in books, but in later sessions she reported feeling less connected to Belle and other female characters, seeing their strength as dubious in the context of the world of Disney. She did identify Mulan, who dresses as a boy to enter the Army and bring pride to her family, as one character that she continued to love and admire.

A pause and a disruption

After two years of treatment, Sophie was doing well. In particular, she had traveled to a foreign country with a youth group, was doing well in school, and had gained weight and was menstruating. No medical issues had interfered with going to school. Finally, she decided she wanted to stop therapy. While I had some hesitation about ending treatment with her, all of the facts pointed to a successful outcome. After meeting with her family, we decided to go ahead with termination, with the knowledge she could come back at any time.

That time came about four months later, after Sophie had relapsed not to anorexia but to the multiple somatic issues that had plagued her for some time. Because of the medical issues, she had stopped going to school and would most likely have to repeat her junior year of high school. Her mother called me to see if she could come back to have "support" and "someone to talk to." I was, of course, available to see her again. We met briefly until she, her family, and medical doctors decided she would go away to a specialized day program, a very good program for adolescents to address psychosomatic and pain-related conditions. She and her mother came back from this program with a behavioral and family skills approach to tolerating pain and illness in her body, with the goal of remaining functional, in addition to more insights into the personality issues she brought to her problems and an openness to addressing the points of "dissociation" and "derealization" that had occurred for her since middle school. When she checked those words off on a form at the program she realized how much she felt she dissociated.

Sophie began to look at how easily she became elated and "grandiose" about her abilities as a student, which would then lead to a somatic collapse from the pressure to be perfect and to avoid disappointing her entire extended family. Her inability to complete homework assignments since beginning high school evolved into a bigger problem; she had been lying to her parents and her teachers about her homework, saying it was finished or had been turned in. Because she was so smart and capable, her teachers believed her when they could not find her homework and she adamantly stated she had turned it in. I was the person she had initially admitted this to in the first phase of her treatment with me. However, in retrospect, her decision to leave treatment also reflected a grandiose flight into health. She was fleeing something in the treatment that we would not have a chance to examine. Perhaps she was also lying to me and herself about her ability to complete this work together, just as she had lied to her teachers about completing her work for them.

Sophie's personality style could be manic, yet it never convinced me, or the psycho-pharmacologist who saw her, that she was diagnosable with bipolar disorder. The moments of elation and grandiosity were difficult to avoid in the therapeutic relationship, where I would join in admiring her brilliance and her effusive stories that revealed an ebullience that could be contagious. The enactment in the therapeutic relationship seemed to mirror what might go on with her parents. I received some narcissistic gratification in having and admiring this very bright and creative young patient, and yet I was uncomfortable with how gratifying it was. I had my own teenager at home struggling with separating and becoming her own person, and was struggling not to project my own goals for her life onto her. I found myself wanting Sophie to achieve more, even though I knew how much the academic pressure and expectations she had internalized were taking a toll on her.

Faimberg (2005) writes that "alienated identifications (which are alienated because they partially depend on conflicts of a generation that is not the patient's) respond to the mechanisms of appropriation and intrusion" . . . [where a parent] "cannot love the child without appropriating his identity for themselves and they cannot acknowledge his independence without hating him and subjecting him to their own history of hatred" (p. 11). I thought my response to Sophie in sessions was replicating something about her relationship with her mother, her grandmothers, and her wish to entertain, charm, and hide what was really going on in her mind. And perhaps it was a way of enlivening them and me. When I could extricate myself from the narcissistic identification I was having with her, and allow myself and her to feel depressed and sad in the session, the psychological quietness felt more authentic and grew to be less frightening for her and me. It was during those sessions that she could discuss her frustration with her mother's anger, resentment, and disappointment in her life. She was also frustrated by her father's use of her as a confidant to discuss the mother's issues and its impact on parenting, and while he had no power, he seemed to advocate for his daughter with the mother. (In recent family meetings he has become more of a voice of balance in advocating for less academic pressure and to decrease their high expectations of performance for her and for a decrease in angry reactive interactions between them and her.)

When Sophie could feel the sadness she felt in those sessions with me, she could decrease the manic activity and become more centered and could even be more accomplished in a centered and focused way. When I could bear her sadness, hopelessness, and anger, she finally said, "You know, I think I don't do my school work because of the Holocaust."

I said, "The Holocaust?"

"Yes, I feel like what's the use? That could happen to me, so why bother? That's what I think sometimes. Everyone is accomplished in my family, but it didn't matter. They were either killed, disappeared, or were forced to flee from their countries."

I wanted to say, "That won't happen here. I won't let it happen; your parents won't let it happen," but I didn't. I knew that in our post 9/11 world, many young people live with an anxiety about a potentially destructive world and that it was important to listen and acknowledge that fear. I listened and let her talk about her fears of being Jewish, and how the need for increased security at her synagogue triggered those fears; about her paternal grandparents, journalists, who had to flee their second homeland after they were targeted for their writings about the repressive regimes – material she had hinted at, but which now had new meaning for her.

Sophie was living with the internal traumas of her family's external traumas; she existed in a "nest of dead thirds" (Gerson, 2009). She needed help acknowledging and mourning the loss of those dead thirds through her link to those generations, inside of herself. In the relational third of the therapeutic relationship, Sophie and I had to acknowledge the meaninglessness her family had experienced with the dead thirds who had betrayed them or, worse, annihilated them before she could move on to experience meaning in her life as an emerging young adult. The treatment allowed for her fears to be acknowledged, for loss to be metabolized, and for her to express herself as a young teen with joys and passions. She is now about to transfer to a school where she will be able to "start over" and be able to focus on her academic and social growth while still nesting in her family. She plans to play a sport again in a more relaxed way and wants to focus on her interest in art and sculpture.

References

Abraham, N. (1975). Notes on the phantom: A complement to Freud's metapsychology. In N. Abraham & M. Torok (Eds.), *The shell and the kernel: Renewals of psychoanalysis*. Chicago: University of Chicago Press.

Abraham, N. & Torok, M. (1994). Secrets and posterity: The theory of the transgenerational phantom. In N. Rand (ed.), *The shell and the kernel* (pp. 165–171). London: University of Chicago Press.

Bloom, C., Gitter, A., Gutwill, S., Kogel, L., & Zaphiropoulos, L. (1994). *Eating problems: A feminist psychoanalytic treatment model*. New York: Basic Books.

Faimberg, H. (2005). *The telescoping of generations: Listening to the narcissistic links between generations*. New York: Routledge.

Fonagy, P. (1999). The transgenerational transmission of holocaust trauma: Lessons learned from the analysis of an adolescent with obsessive-compulsive disorder. *Attachment and Human Development*, *1*(1), 92–114.

Gerson, S. (2009). When the third is dead: Memory, mourning and witnessing in the aftermath of the Holocaust. *International Journal of Psychoanalysis*, *90*, 1341–1357.

Kestenberg, J. S. (1982). A metapsychological assessment based on an analysis of a survivor's child. In M. S. Bergmann & M. E. Jucovy (Eds.), *Generations of the holocaust* (pp. 137–158). New York: Columbia University Press.

King, S. A. (2006). Complex regional pain syndrome. *Psychiatric Times, 23*(7), 9.

Levy-Warren, M. H. (2000). A contemporary look: Adolescents and the incest Taboo. *Journal of Infant, Child & Adolescent Psychotherapy, 1*(4), 123–140.

Little, M. (1985). Working with Winnicott where psychotic anxieties prevail. *Free Association, 5*, 1–19.

Merriam-Webster's collegiate dictionary (10th ed.). (1993). Springfield, MA: Merriam-Webster, Incorporated.

Moses, R. (Ed.) (1993). *The persistent shadows of the Holocaust: The meaning to those not directly affected.* Madison, CT: International Universities Press.

PART II

Treatment of eating disorders

6

FROM KNOWING TO DISCOVERING

Some suggestions for work with an anorexic patient

Yael Kadish

Introduction

Outpatient clinicians are sometimes asked to treat anorexic patients in the acute phase of the disorder. By acute I mean the stage at which the symptoms of starvation are prevalent and there is an appreciable health risk. These patients are in the throes of the illness; however, they may not be at a weight low enough to warrant hospitalisation, as yet. In this situation the therapist treats a patient whose life is at risk, and this pressure can feel like one is working with a *gun to one's head.* This paper is offered in the hope that it will assist psychoanalytically informed clinicians grappling with the technical challenges presented by anorexic patients on a *razor's edge*. The paper is written with a focus on adolescent patients; however, most of the content has application for anorexic patients of any age.[1]

Many writers have described the challenging nature of clinical work with anorexic patients[2] (Birksted-Breen, 1989; Bruch, 1973, 1978; Lawrence, 2002, 2008; Risen, 1982; Sours, 1974; Tierney & Fox, 2010; Zerbe, 2008). Anorexia is understood to be a disorder with heterogeneous underpinnings, including Oedipal, and often also pre-Oedipal difficulties (Lane & Chazan, 1289; Plaut & Hutchinson, 1986; Swift & Stern, 1982). In the cases of anorexic patients with pre-Oedipal difficulties, a pathological mother-daughter relationship is suggested to be at the heart of it. Taipale, Tuomi, and Aukee (1971) have called it an illness of two generations. Many authors describe a frustrated mother who is hostile towards her daughter's strivings for personal differentiation (Bruch, 1973; Spignesi, 1983). There is a fundamental misattunement between mother and infant, which comes to be inscribed on the psyche of the baby during development. She is experienced as intruding upon her daughter's mind, overwhelming her and impairing internal boundary formation (Birksted-Breen, 1989; Lane, 2002; Likierman, 1997; Williams, 1997b). An enmeshed mother-daughter relationship ensues where the daughter's wish for fusion with her mother fluctuates with her terror of being intruded upon and annihilated (Lawrence, 2002; Farber, 2000). The fraught mother-daughter relationship impairs the daughter's ability to separate and individuate; however, a good enough father, or third, is just as vital for the healthy developmental navigation of the pre-Oedipal and Oedipal phases (Kavaler-Adler, 1992; Magagna & Goldsmith, 2009). Unfortunately, the fathers of anorexics have not helped their daughters to achieve healthy separation. In the literature, fathers of anorexics are characterised as having been emotionally detached, feeble, and/or seductive (Brody, 2002; Bruch, 1973, 1978; Risen, 1982; Williams, Williams, Desmarais, & Ravenscroft, 2004). The lack of true self-other differentiation can be seen to manifest in the anorexic symptom, for example, where the individual experiences the maltreatment of her[3] body as being at the same time an attack on her mother and the maternal body (Ritvo, 1984), and on the Oedipal level, an attack on the creative parental couple (Magagna & Goldsmith, 2009).

Many writers note the anorexic's wish to avoid intrusion (Birksted-Breen, 1989; Bruch, 1973, 1978; Lane, 2002) which can follow from any sort of trauma (including sexual abuse trauma), experienced at any developmental stage; of course, the nature of the trauma and the stage of development will have a specific effect on the unique individual's psychology. In relation to this last point, I have discussed two sub-types of anorexia I have encountered in my work, elsewhere (Kadish, 2011, 2012a, 2012b, 2013, 2015); however, this is not the direct focus of this paper.

The anorexic seeks thinness at all costs and is terrified by the idea of being fat. She is driven by the need for total control of her body, which represents, in a symbolic equation, her wish to disavow her instinctual needs and to control her inner life (Lawrence, 2008; Sours, 1974). Furthermore, her separation-individuation failure means that the anorexic experiences her body as being dangerously penetrable. Part of her struggle is thus an attempt to defend herself against intrusions into her very being. Williams (1997b) regards anorexia as being essentially a no-entry defense.

The foregoing discussion helps to throw light on an aspect of the illness noted from the earliest writing on it. Anorexic patients have great difficulty in relation to sexual maturation with all of its implications, that is, sexuality, pregnancy and childbirth (Likierman, 1997; Magagna & Goldsmith, 2009; Plaut & Hutchinson, 1986). In health, these bodily transformations and accomplishments are preceded by a holistic intrapsychic progression based on a foundational sense of psyche-somal goodness and intactness; this progression continues throughout life's stages and transitions. The anorexic has either not managed wholesome bodily cathexis because of early difficulties, or cannot access this accomplishment because of later trauma, including unprocessed traumatic loss. Psychosexual maturity challenges the anorexic's fear of intrusion and has various frightening fantasies associated with it.

Chronic mother-infant misattunement and/or developmental traumata impair the foundation of the distinction between inside and outside, me and not-me, as well as a sense of unconscious confusion about one's own and other's bodily organs, zones and functions (Winnicott, 1960a; Bick, 1968). In such cases, bodily transformations and the inherent psychological demands of puberty and adulthood are especially frightening. For example, menstruation can have unconscious meanings such as bodily damage, messiness and inadequate sphincter control (Magagna & Goldsmith, 2009; Plaut & Hutchinson, 1986). In another example of these unconscious somatic confusions, Likierman (1997) describes an anorexic patient who dreamt of a *raping breast*. The patient's anorexia functioned to prevent the development of a womanly, potentially maternal body in an attempt to remain insensitive to her own infantile states, and as a safeguard against the possibility of pregnancy.

Many writers have noted that although not the norm, a significant percentage of anorexics have experienced traumatic sexual intrusion and that this bodily violation is an important component of these patients' anorexic illness (Magagna & Goldsmith, 2009). Such patients may have also experienced pre-Oedipal disruptions, or may have had a relatively healthy early developmental period. Ivy had been anorexic since she was 15; there was attachment trauma in her history, as well as an experience of sexual violation in latency. After two years of twice-weekly therapy, which followed five months in hospital, 19-year-old Ivy had made quite a good physical recovery and was working in therapy. One of the issues that bothered her now was that she had a boyfriend, but she was utterly terrified and repulsed by the idea of sexual intercourse. She was certain that she would lose Nathan if she didn't have sex with him. The ego-syntonic layer of her repetition compulsion came in the form of the conviction that she needed to confront her fears aggressively because she was the one who *had issues*. This decision could not be softened in therapy, and she pushed herself to go through with sex during our December break. No doubt my absence during this time was an important part in the traumatic enactment.

In her first session back she told me about what had happened over the break. Describing their first few sexual encounters she said she had experienced initial feelings of desire and arousal, but that once intercourse began, things changed. She immediately felt utterly repulsed and had fantasies of his penis being fecal, causing her body to freeze in horror. Nathan had felt disturbed by this, seeming to have an intuitive understanding that he was being used as a sort of prop in some kind of awful private drama in Ivy's mind. He refused to have sex with her on this basis, and his alarm and distress allowed Ivy to become aware and to begin to understand the multiple strands of this repetition compulsion.

Treatment considerations

Because of the life and death urgency of anorexic symptoms, some have questioned whether psychoanalysis or psychoanalytic psychotherapy is optimally appropriate, in that the pace of such work is typically slow and deep (Shipton, 2004). There are clinicians who work with patients in full analyses (Birksted-Breen, 1989;

Lawrence, 2008; Rolland, 2006), while others favour a once-weekly approach, believing this to be the more suitable frequency for this particular disturbance, where there is a driving need for self-sufficiency and there can be great difficulty with the idea of taking from another. On the whole, frequent weekly sessions seem preferable (Magagna & Goldsmith, 2009); however, the anorexic sensitivity to the idea of intrusion must be kept in mind and processed when it emerges.

Another complication for the work is the nature of the patient's motivation for seeking the treatment and the fact that insistent parents often bring in younger patients, which is not an ideal therapeutic foundation. I have generally found that as long as there is some personal motivation on the patient's part, it is enough to make a start. Because of the *solution* offered by anorexia, it is less usual for patients to begin treatment with robust motivation for real change through a mutative relational process; instead, their motivation often comes from a fervent wish to eliminate painful feeling states.

Indeed, the typical anorexic patient has a well-developed intellect and functions well academically but experiences tremendous difficulties tolerating her emotional life and inner world (Magagna & Goldsmith, 2009). For this reason the latter should be the focus of interventions; however, this is no easy matter. In anorexia the psychological *stance* is of hypervigilance; mental alertness and a drive for total control comprise a formidable barrier against treatment efforts. The clinician needs to find a way, over and over, to forge moments of alive connection with a person who exists, intricately suspended between life and death, because she believes she cannot endure any other way of being.

Starting out: setting up an *extended frame*

The clinician must be aware of the dangerous synthesis of fierce mental control, combined with something akin to a delusion of immortality in the anorexic mindset. This places her at risk of death through her own actions but is not something that can be managed in the same way frank suicidality would be. As a consequence there are treatment demands that need immediate attention; however, in managing these one is faced with a call for almost diametrically opposed technical responses: activity vs. receptivity. On the level of concrete reality and ethical practice, careful, active case management is required. On the level of unconscious communication, the deathliness must be *sat with* and slowly worked through in the realm of the transference-countertransference. These conflicting demands also require practical measures such as the setting up of a more extensive frame than we would normally need to make therapeutic work possible.

At the start of the work it is essential to set up what can be thought about as an *extended frame*, a working alliance structure that incorporates the usual psychoanalytic frame (the matters of time, place and remuneration), but of necessity goes much further. The clinician who undertakes to work with a patient whose symptom implies she has not accepted the basic working alliance condition to keep herself safe in the world, must grapple with a thorny ethical dilemma. Anorexic patients are often able to engage in a rational manner with almost all other matters, and might be performing especially well in intellectual endeavours. Paradoxically, there is often complete denial of the mortal danger she is in, which has a jarring, delusional quality (Andersen, 2008). She might starve herself to death, or die from the physical complications of her condition, yet anorexic patients typically respond to concerns about their physical health in a dismissive, denialist and/or highly defensive manner.

I offer the example of 17-year-old Gretchen; in the first weeks of treatment, she would tell me in a breezy tone that her body was able to function perfectly well on coffee and two apples a day. She said she was aware that other people weren't able to, but she knew her body to be ". . . different in that way; it just carries on." This is not an unusual interaction in work with an anorexic patient. During this early phase (and sometimes more enduringly) it seems that the body is experienced and related to, more like an abstract representation, an image in the mirror, or in the mind – rather than a concrete biological reality. Associated with this are great difficulties with the idea of having a body, of bodily-ness and linked to this, bodily processes, products and needs. Gretchen described her body as ". . . a vehicle to carry my head around from place to place." Like many anorexics she was highly invested in her mind and intellect, which she saw as being utterly separate from her body, with its potential for greed and mess. I have discussed this aspect in detail in an earlier paper (Kadish, 2011). This complicated situation will obviously be a focal point for the therapeutic work, but must first be managed by setting up the appropriate extended frame to protect the patient's physical health as best as possible.

Family meetings and support structures

The average age of onset of anorexia is between 15 and 19 years, although a relatively significant number of patients present at between 10 and 14 years of age (Micali, Hagberg, Petersen, & Treasure, 2013). The fact that the majority of individuals seek help while they are minors makes family participation more easily managed than with later onset or later-presenting anorexic patients. It is often the case that anorexia occurs in a family economy in which certain things are "not seen" and there is collusion with the illness in various subterranean ways (Shipton, 2004). Family therapy seems to be a promising intervention with anorexia (in addition to individual work or even on its own) but is not always an option for various reasons.

I suggest that in individual treatments, patients should be seen with parents and/or caretakers for at least one session to set up supportive structures to augment the treatment; these are described subsequently. It is highly preferable to see the patient alone for one or two sessions before the family meeting. This time should be used to assess whether individual work seems viable. It also allows for the inchoate beginnings of the therapeutic relationship before the family meeting; the latter can feel very psychically taxing for the patient. It cannot be overstated that in performing these initial more active, less classically analytic interventions, one's tone and manner should always be thoughtful, careful and as analytic as possible.

The purposes of the preliminary sessions should be shared with the potential patient so that the initial seeds of trust can be sown through candid communication. The clinician might say something like: "You need to be well enough for us to do this work; otherwise, we may need to consider hospitalisation until you are well enough." The patient's feelings and concerns about the meeting and the extended frame can then be worked with somewhat before the meeting. The therapist should also ask if there's anything she would like to raise in the family meeting forum.

Medical monitoring

As already mentioned, it is vital that at least one medical professional, either a general practitioner (GP) or a psychiatrist, is enlisted to regularly monitor the patient's weight and vital signs as well as electrolytes. The physician also needs to be mindful of, and responsive to, signs of the organ damage that can accompany eating disorders. When symptoms are very prevalent and weight is low, it is advisable that the physician is seen at least twice a month, but weekly visits are best. The physician and therapist should be free to contact each other when necessary.

At the family meeting the serious and potentially deadly nature of anorexia should be mentioned, in a frank (non-alarmist) manner, as the rationale for the medical monitoring. This is important because all involved need to be aware of the full clinical syndrome; it is an aspect of ethical practise and reality testing that will continue into the therapeutic work. Understandably, family members sometimes become very distressed when this is mentioned and often ask what they can do. It is best to suggest a caring and sensitive but non-intrusive approach. It should be communicated that the patient needs help with the medical monitoring (being taken to appointments with her physician, etc.) but that she also needs the 'mental space' (or some such phrase) to begin to understand more about her difficulties in living her life. At this point in the session it can be helpful to ask the patient how she would like to be supported by her family, that is, what would be helpful and what would not be.

I always recommend that the parents/caregivers consult their own therapist for support. This can be very valuable, especially if it is ongoing. Besides the provision of support for the parents, the therapeutic work can modify some of the family dynamics that have contributed to their daughter's illness.

Returning to the matter of medical monitoring, in the case of an adult patient the clinician should contract for psychotherapy only on the basis that a physician is managing the medical side of the illness regularly. If there is an actively engaged family member/s or partner in the picture, it can sometimes be helpful to see them (once-off) with the patient early on, with the idea of enlisting support to oversee the patient's basic health.

Ultimately, the therapist needs to be able to hand the medical management over to the physician, in order to focus on the therapeutic work.

Therapeutic work and the challenging topography of the anorexic complex

Difficulties with relationship

For psychoanalysis, relationship is both the vehicle of healing and the method. This provides a significant challenge for a great number of anorexic patients as they struggle tremendously with triangular post-Oedipal relations, experiencing difficulties forming and maintaining bounded, intimate relationships (Birksted-Breen, 1989; Bruch, 1973, Lawrence, 2002, 2008; Williams, 1997a). Dependency is felt to be very dangerous because of serious, vacillating conflicts around fusion and intrusion. Indeed, just tolerating the therapeutic relationship is often the biggest stumbling block for the work, especially initially. No aspects of the therapeutic relationship can be taken for granted, including the working alliance, as mentioned previously. Working in the transference-countertransference needs to be managed carefully because it can be extremely trying and can bring about a buttressing of resistance.

As previously discussed, the anorexic girl is engaged in a resolute attempt to control her internal world and all of its terrifying turmoil (Lawrence, 2001). To orchestrate this she turns inwards, taking her body as her primary object, ruling it with tyrannical control. This feeling of omnipotence, a sense that she is without needs, gives her extreme pleasure (Bruch, 1973, 1978; Williams, 1997b). In his summary of the anorexic's presentation, Boris (1984, p. 435) comments on the anorexic's: ". . . utter conviction that her anorexia is her last, best achievement [that this] leave[s] little for either the transference or the therapeutic alliance." Anorexia is felt by the patient to be a way of fending off mental breakdown or even insanity and occurs at a time of real psychological crisis (Shipton, 2004). If the work progresses and the acute symptoms subside, the clinician will continue to work with what emerges from underneath the symptom complex, that is, the deeper wounds, anxieties, conflicts and defenses.

A knowing stance

As already mentioned, the underlying psychic structure of a patient who develops anorexia might be situated anywhere across the spectrum, from more neurotic functioning individuals, all the way through to more psychotic functioning persons (Zerbe, 2008). Although no two anorexic patients are the same in terms of their more deeply underlying psychology, there are commonalities in the symptomatic presentation of the illness, as noted by most writers. Accordingly, I suggest that technique must be constantly attenuating to the patient's presentation, but moreover, that during the acute period where deathliness is the overwhelming force, it is beneficial to work with what could be called *knowing stance*. This phrase appears immediately to imply a theoretical paradox, a seeming diametrical opposition in relation to the characteristic psychoanalytic attitude of evenly suspended attention and of being without memory or desire (Bion, 1967). Ultimately, the needs of the patient must drive technique and I suggest that this knowing stance, entailing more active technique, is not unlike Bruch's suggestion to use psycho-education in the acute stages (Bruch, 1973, 1978). It seems to me that with many anorexic patients, if one relies solely on what might be regarded as a more classical technique, this can run the risk of collusion with the death-drive–imbued symptom. I explain here why I say this.

At the very start of the illness an anorexic patient often receives positive comments from others on her weight loss and self-discipline. At a certain point, however, people see that it has *gone too far*. At that point they will try to reason with or even threaten her, insisting she eat more. The anorexic rebuffs these attempts with powerful defensiveness, denial, and often with duplicity – for example assuring people she has already eaten, hiding food in napkins at mealtimes, secretly feeding her meal to pets under the table, etc. When attempts to stop or reverse her worrying weight loss and rigid dietary habits have been repelled often enough, loved ones start to feel exceedingly helpless. They *tiptoe* around the individual, fearing anything they say might exacerbate the precarious situation, and the anorexic is usually treated with kid gloves to a large extent. The therapist must not fall into this pattern.

In treatment it becomes clear that the anorexic patient has ego strength enough to appeal to; this is evidenced in the characteristic control essential to anorexia. The fastidiously maintained status quo is proof of an ego able to maintain life lived on a razor's edge. This is partly the reason for attempting to reach her via a knowing stance: her ego is being used against her by self-destructive parts of her and this must be confronted. A classically abstinent stance can thus be felt to be inadvertently permissive of her self-destructiveness, but equally, the indelicate application of a knowing stance can be experienced as intrusive and so be counter-productive.

The suggestion to work more actively and knowingly in the acute stages does not mean that one should not at times also be using what would be considered to be more traditional analytic technique. Technique should always be attuned to the patient's rhythms and symptomatic presentation, but even in moments of psycho-education, deeper work is also taking place to some extent. The unconscious is never inert and there are no impervious partitions within the mind. As the treatment progresses this knowing stance becomes unnecessary and one can work as one usually would do, moving from a knowing stance to one of openness to discovery.

But let us go back a bit and consider why a knowing stance might be necessary. I argue this to be the case when on a conscious and preconscious level there are a set of particular ideas and fantasies, linked to a specific and complex defensive structure, that keep anorexia in place. It is important that these are kept in mind and worked with. This network of thoughts and fantasies that need to be accessed in the room amount to a defensive denial of the realities that one must accept as part of some significant degree of Oedipal resolution. These are the realities of life and death, the differences between the sexes and the internalisation of the creative parental couple. These facts of life must be tolerated so that one is able to move into mature genitality and adulthood (Chasseguet-Smirgel, 1988).

A structured madness

With anorexics who have not managed sufficient Oedipal resolution, there is often a fantasy that involves the idea of freezing time, a delusion of the possibility of living in a state of eternal waiting-to-be, until she feels ready to continue with the process of maturation. This fantasy finds expression in the childlike pubertal appearance of anorexics. It is as if, in her mind, the anorexic has crawled into a time capsule and she will decide when and if she will come out. In the meantime, in fantasy, she can just stop all of the tortuous demands placed upon her to grow up and become an adult woman. Almost without exception, anorexic patients express their wish not to grow up. Linked to this fantasy of freezing time is a delusion of a-mortality, the idea that she can deny the basic bodily need for adequate nutrition but not suffer the mortal consequences. The feeling is conveyed that she is somewhere between life and death and is still deciding which it will be.

An example of how a knowing stance could be used in response to the patient's insistence, in a manner that feels impervious to a more reflective approach, is that despite severe food restriction or binge-purging, she is in perfect health. The clinician might use psycho-education to try to challenge this, sharing information such as the fact that anorexia can cause death, either through the consequences of dramatic weight loss and the effects of starvation, or through long-term, chronic body damage that can lead eventually to organ failure. One could say that although she feels well (this is, of course, a relative term in this context) she cannot know the state of her organs. One can include information such as the fact that brain atrophy and heart damage, should they happen, will be permanent, that these conditions begin at a certain stage of the illness, the course and timing of which cannot be precisely predicted. One can mention famous cases of anorexics who have died after overt recovery as a result of the damage accrued in the body over time. One can share any other such psycho-educative information that would be helpful; however, this should always be done carefully and appropriately and should never become a bombardment.

Of course, beneath the anorexic symptomatology is an individual whose psychological functioning has become severely compromised. Anorexia is often a way to distract others from a deep sense of personal insufficiency; anorexic patients may feel that they do not know how to be a human being, how to live in the world, while others appear to manage this with seeming ease. The eating disorder is experienced as a sort of compromise. Anorexia is a perpetual brinkmanship with death, operating to fend off the terror of real madness and the constant fear of being seen (Steiner, 2011), which in fantasy is tantamount to the mortifying exposure of appalling personal inadequacy. Writers note specific trends such as omnipotent fantasies (at any and all levels of consciousness), *charged*, obsessional thoughts and pressing control needs, as well as pleasure at the physical sensations of starvation that are an attempt at countering these feelings of terrible helplessness and inadequacy (Bruch, 1973, 1978; Lawrence, 2002).

Pathological organisations and psychic retreats

I have found John Steiner's (1987, 1993) concept of pathological organisations and psychic retreats to be cogent conceptual tools allowing an envisioning of the structure and operation of the defensive organisations present in the anorexic complex. Using Steiner's concepts, anorexia can be considered as a manifestation of a particular structuring of defences, one of the purposes of which is to facilitate psychological relief from terrible internal turmoil. The psychic retreat element is enabled through feelings of omnipotence brought about by various aspects of the symptom complex. Steiner envisages pathological organisations as emergency measures that arise as a desperate defense against annihilatory anxiety.

In anorexia this grouping of defense mechanisms solidifies into a well-organised psychic economy, often with a sadomasochistic cast. Once in place, this constellation is far more than the sum of its parts and is often described by patients as having a life of its own (Tierney & Fox, 2010). Empirical research underlines the necessity of early intervention in anorexia (preferably within the first six months); it has been observed that during this time individuals are far more amenable to therapeutic interventions. For this paper's argument, this is the period during which a self-sustaining defensive structure is amalgamating, after which it becomes entrenched. Once anorexia is habitual, its amelioration demands years of dedicated work, and at best only half of anorexics make a good and lasting recovery (Zipfel, Lowe, Reas, Deter, & Hertzog, 2000).

I give the following example as another illustration of how one might work with the knowing stance I am proposing. Maddie, 15, discussed a conversation in which she was questioned by her grandmother about her refusal to eat enough. Her manifestly triumphant reply was that she didn't ask to be born so she has by definition not agreed to take care of herself. In this situation it felt important to convey my awareness of the internally and externally directed sadomasochism, the thrilling nature of this and also the reality that she was on a path leading to a mortal end. As previously mentioned, this is not something that is really, consciously *known* by the anorexic. The therapist needs to make the patient aware of the sadomasochistic element by speaking to the part of the patient who doesn't want to die. An alliance must constantly be forged with this part of her. After conveying understanding of the sadomasochistic elements, and that this affects her awareness of her physical vulnerability, one can say something like: "You and I must work together to fight for your life." This sort of intervention conveys the message that the therapist knows what the patient is doing (which the patient both knows, and simultaneously doesn't quite know), and that others who have struggled with anorexia have done this before her. As a balancing element to this message, the therapist should offer to help the patient to discover what she really wants, who she really is, and can be. With an anorexic patient this is not an unambivalently tempting proposition. This is due to pronounced anxieties about her internal world, what she is *really* made of.

There is a need to directly dislodge the delusion that protects against these anxieties, what I call the "admirability factor," that is, the idea that what she is doing is special/superhuman.[4] This thrilling sadomasochistic idea underpins the psychic retreat aspect, which makes it essential that it is confronted. A patient, Jocelyn, expressed: "Anorexia makes me special. People admire how strong I am, how much willpower I have."

Delicious death grip

Freud (1920) famously said that there can be no symptom without there being pleasure in it. In the drive for massive bodily control the anorexic patient is literally *eating into* a body that is being related to as a representation. Many compare anorexia to drug addiction, even regarding it as an addiction. Despite certain similarities, it seems important not to miss the important distinctions. In anorexia the pleasure, or *high*, is psychogenic, located within and part of the patient's psychic economy unlike drugs, which are independently psychoactive. These basic distinctions have important significance but are beyond the scope of this paper. In any event, the wasting-away anorexic patient is caught up in an addictive, sadomasochistic thrall. As a pay-off for her draconian bodily control the anorexic is able to feel superior to others and without needs. There is a disparagement of being human in the sense of being bodily. The fantasy of freezing time is present in all the anorexics I have worked with or whose treatment I have supervised.

Steiner's (1993) notion of a psychic retreat is very apt for this aspect of the illness. He suggests that through adherence to a sadomasochistic defensive structure, the individual feels entitled in fantasy to withdraw to a safe place in the mind, an island of calm where all anxieties can be suspended. Awareness is drawn away from the individual's premorbid conflicts, frustrations and object relational difficulties. Anorexia funnels energy away from these areas of distress, drawing it rather to a single quest: a drive for thinness. The seeming advantage of this quest is that it is entirely self-determined and circumscribed, literally demarcated by her body. The anxieties, which have led to the crisis, feel overwhelming and unpredictable; they are relational and so cannot be managed within the self. In a sort of psychic *debt consolidation*, all energies can be focused on a single self-determinable goal; however, its relentless pursuit demands inhumane efforts to satisfy an insatiable internal taskmaster. This reconfiguring of anxieties allows an avoidance of the anxieties associated with being human, a creature of the flesh, and therefore mortal. An anorexic patient seen by Birksted Breen (1989) expresses the draconian tone and the sense of one part of the self, pitted against another: "She [the patient] said she can only eat if she has got a reason to eat. If she tells herself that there is a reason for keeping a certain weight, then she is justified to eat, but then she thinks it is just a trick so that she can eat, and then she can't eat" (p32).

In anorexia there is a sadomasochistic torturing of self and others who must watch the patient waste away. Yet ironically, if this sadomasochistic element is not strongly present there is a very poor prognosis (Glasser, 1998). One can't work with the patient in this way because they are frankly suicidal. An example of this was seen with Emily, an inpatient in a unit with high success rates, especially with primary refeeding interventions. Newly married and in her twenties, Emily came alone to the unit, which was a two hours' drive from her home. Till the end of her life she denied she was anorexic and would at no time entertain the idea that she had a symptom, never mind that there was meaning to her illness. Her only narrative in her therapy was that she had some sort of digestive complaint and lack of appetite, although all biological causes had been ruled out. During her stay she had very infrequent telephone contact with her mother and none with her husband or anyone else. Ultimately, it seemed that Emily's anorexia was far more frankly suicidal than sadomasochistic in its underlying impetus and sadly she did die in hospital despite the heroic attempts of the staff.

Conclusion

In this paper I have suggested that clinicians treating anorexic patients in the acutely symptomatic phase of the illness must set up an extended frame in their case management, before therapeutic work can take place. I have further suggested that in the life-threatening stages of the disorder, the clinician should use a knowing stance to complement her reflective receptiveness. This knowing stance is used to manage dangerous fantasies and ideas, manifestations of the defensive organisation that drives the self-destructive behavior. After this phase of the illness has passed, the suggested intermittent use of a knowing stance makes way for the predominance of typical analytic technique.

Notes

1 My gratitude goes to Professor Susan van Zyl for her valuable counsel.
2 I am referring to patients suffering from either sub-type of anorexia, that is, purging or non-purging types.
3 In this chapter I use the feminine pronoun because anorexia is still far more prevalent in women than men (Hoek & van Hoeken, 2003).
4 Unfortunately, the current socio-cultural impellent that promotes thinness, almost as the loftiest life aspiration there is, means that anorexia is less socially denounced than it has been at other times in history. Several writers have contributed very meaningfully to our understanding of the nature and influence of contemporary social phenomena on women generally, and on the prevalence of eating disorders (Chernin, 1983; Lawrence, 2008; Malson, 1998; Orbach, 1978).

References

Andersen, A. E. (2008). Ethical conflicts in the care of anorexia nervosa patients. *Eating Disorders Review, 19*, 1–4.

Bick, E. (1968). Experience of the skin in early object relations. *International Journal of Psychoanalysis, 49*, 484–486.

Bion, W. R. D. (1967). Notes on memory and desire. *The Psychoanalytic Forum, 2*(3), 272–80.

Birksted-Breen, D. (1989). Working with an Anorexic patient. *The International Journal of Psychoanalysis, 70*, 29–40.

Boris, H. N. (1984). The problem of anorexia nervosa, *International Journal of Psychoanalysis 65*, 435–442.

Brody, S. (2002). *The development of anorexia nervosa*. Madison, CT: International Universities Press, Inc.

Bruch, H. (1973). *Eating disorders, obesity, anorexia nervosa and the person within*. New York: Basic Books.

Bruch, H. (1978). *The golden cage: The enigma of anorexia nervosa*. Cambridge: Harvard University Press.

Chasseguet-Smirgel, J. (1988). From the archaic matrix of the oedipus complex to the fully developed oedipus complex: Theoretical perspective in relation to clinical experience and technique. *Psychoanalytic Quarterly, 57*, 505–527.

Chernin, K. (1983). *Womansize: The tyranny of slenderness*. London: The Women's Press.

Farber, S. K. (2000). *When the body is the target: Self harm, pain and traumatic attachments*. New York & Lanham, MD: Jason Aronson, Rowman & Littlefield.

Freud, S. (1920). XVII: The meaning of the symptoms. In *Part three: General theory of the Neuroses: A general introduction to psychoanalysis*.

Glasser, M. (1998). On violence: A preliminary communication. *International Journal of Psychoanalysis, 79*, 887–902.

Hoek, H. W., & van Hoeken, D. (2003). Review of the prevalence and incidence of eating disorders. *International Journal of Eating Disorders, 34*, 383–396.

Kadish, Y. A. (2011). Autistoid psychic retreat in anorexia. *British Journal of Psychotherapy, 27*, 19–36.

Kadish, Y. A. (2012a). Pathological organizations and psychic retreats in eating disorders. *The Psychoanalytic Review, 99*, 227–252.

Kadish, Y. A. (2012b). The role of culture in eating disorder. *British Journal of Psychotherapy, 28*, 435–453.

Kadish, Y. A. (2013). Two types of psychic encapsulation in anorexia. *Psychoanalytic Psychotherapy, 27*, 60–76.

Kadish, Y. A. (2015). Pathological organisations and psychic encapsulation in eating disorders: A contemporary consideration. *Psychoanalytic Psychotherapy in South Africa, 23*, 1–36.

Kavaler-Adler, S. (1992). Anais Nin and the developmental use of the creative process. *Psychoanalytic Review, 79*, 73–88.

Lane, R. C. (2002). Anorexia, masochism, self-mutilation, and autoerotism: The spider mother. *The Psychoanalytic Review, 89*, 101–123.

Lane, R. C., & Chazan, S. E. (1989). Symbols of terror: The witch/vampire, the spider, and the shark. *Psychoanalytic Psychology, 6*, 325–341.

Lawrence, M. (2001). Loving them to death: The anorexic and her objects. *International Journal of Psychoanalysis, 82*, 43–55.

Lawrence, M. (2002). Body, mother, mind, anorexia, femininity and the intrusive object. *International Journal of Psychoanalysis*, *83*, 837–850.
Lawrence, M. (2008). *The Anorexic mind.* The Tavistock Clinic Series. London: Karnac.
Likierman, M. (1997). On rejection: Adolescent girls and anorexia. *Journal of Child Psychotherapy*, *23*, 61–80.
Magagna, J., & Goldsmith, T. P. (2009). Complications in the development of a female sexual identity. *Journal of Child Psychotherapy*, *35*, 62–80.
Malson, H. (1998). *The thin woman: Feminism, post-structuralism and the social psychology of anorexia nervosa*. New York: Routledge.
Micali, N., Hagberg, K. W., Petersen, I., & Treasure, J. L. (2013).The incidence of eating disorders in the UK in 2000–2009: Findings from the general practice research database. *BMJ Open*, *3*, e002646, doi:10.1136/bmjopen-2013–002646
Orbach, S. (1978). *Fat is a feminist issue*. London, Arrow Books.
Plaut, E. A., & Hutchinson, F. L. (1986). The role of puberty in female psychosexual development. *International Review of Psychoanalysis, 13*, 417–432.
Risen, S. E. (1982). The psychoanalytic treatment of an adolescent with anorexia nervosa. *The Psychoanalytic Study of the Child, 37*, 433–459.
Ritvo, S. (1984). The image and uses of the body in psychic conflict: With special reference to eating disorders in adolescence. *Psychoanalytic Studies of the Child, 39*, 449–469.
Rolland, J. (2006). A young woman's distress. *International Journal of Psychoanalysis*, *87*(6),1433–1442.
Shipton, G. (2004). *Working with eating disorders: A psychoanalytic approach*. Basingstoke: Palgrave Macmillan.
Sours, J. A. (1974). The anorexia nervosa syndrome. *International Journal of Psychoanalysis*, *55*, 567–576.
Spignesi, A. (1983). *Starving women: A psychology of anorexia nervosa*. Dallas, Texas: Spring Publications.
Steiner, J. (1987). The interplay between pathological organizations and the paranoid – schizoid and depressive positions. *International Journal of Psychoanalysis*, *68*, 69–80.
Steiner, J. (1993). *Psychic retreats: Pathological organisations of the personality in psychotic, neurotic and borderline patients*. London: Routledge (*The new library of psychoanalysis*).
Steiner, J. (2011). *Seeing and being seen: Emerging from a psychic retreat*. London: Routledge (*The new library of psychoanalysis*).
Swift, W. J., & Stern, S. (1982). The psychodynamic diversity of anorexia nervosa. *International Journal of Eating Disorders*, *2*,17–33.
Taipale, V., Tuomi, O., & Aukee, M. (1971). Anorexia nervosa: An illness of two generations? Acta paedopsychiatrica. *International Journal of Child & Adolescent Psychiatry*, *38*, 21–25.
Tierney, S., & Fox, J. R. E. (2010). Living with the anorexic voice: A thematic analysis. *Psychology and Psychotherapy: Theory, Research and Practice*, *83*, 243–254.
Williams, G. (1997a). *Internal landscapes and foreign bodies*. London: Duckworth.
Williams, G. (1997b). Reflections on some dynamics of eating disorders: 'No entry' defences and foreign bodies. *International Journal of Psychoanalysis*, *78*, 927–941.
Williams, G., Williams, P., Desmarais, J., Ravenscroft, K. (Eds.) (2004). *Exploring eating disorders in adolescents: The generosity of acceptance, Volume II*. London: Karnac.
Winnicott, D. W. (1960a). The theory of the infant – parent relationship. *International Journal of Psychoanalysis*, *41*, 585–595.
Zerbe, K. J. (2008). *Integrated treatment of eating disorders: Beyond the body betrayed*. New York: W.W. Norton & Company.
Zipfel, S., Lowe, B., Reas, D. L., Deter, H., & Hertzog, W. (2000). Long-term prognosis in anorexia nervosa: Lessons from a 21-year follow-up study. *The Lancet*, *355*, 721–722.

7

HEATHEN TALK

Psychoanalytic considerations of eating disorders and the dissociated self

Judith Brisman

Early in my career, I heard professionals speak of anorexia as a disorder that was "happening" to the patient. Promoted by researchers at the Maudsley Hospital in London (Le Grange, 2005), families and patients were enlisted to fight the "ED" that was overtaking their child. As one of the pioneers in the field of eating disorders and immersed in analytic training at the William Alanson White Institute in Manhattan, I listened with curiosity – and derision.

What happened, I wondered, to consideration of historical dynamics, questions regarding expression of internal experience and capacity to self-soothe? How could externalizing the symptomatic behavior allow for an understanding of self? I found this treatment direction maddening. It disenfranchised analytic thought from the treatment arena and completely erased exploration of one's internal and unconscious world.

But, having faced years of work in the trenches with anorexic and other eating-disordered patients and their families, I too now say things like: "The eating disorder is fierce – we have to go into war mode". Or "ED is tricky – it's going to make you feel like you are a failure if you eat". I disembody the eating disorder; I treat it like an abusive lover; I tell family and patient alike that it is an insidious disease.

And yet, I consider my work to be fully analytic. What has happened – and why?

Where we began

When the epidemic of eating disorders first crashed into our culture in the 1980s, for many, traditional psychoanalytic thinking significantly informed clinical intervention. Starving, bingeing or vomiting were understood as expressions of internal conflict having to do with fear and suppression of sexuality, desire and anger (Wilson, Hogan, & Mintz, 1983). Clinical work was interpretation based, with the belief that exploration and understanding of psychological dynamics would allow for symptom reduction and change. There was no direct intervention with eating behaviors because any attempt to abate the eating disorder was seen as an unwitting repetition of an authoritative and controlling exchange with the patient. If the symptoms were to be prematurely thwarted, surely other problematic ways of expressing inner turmoil would emerge. The work of treatment thus was to focus on internal unconscious conflicts, not the eating itself.

Indeed, in those early years I actually had a patient who had previously been in a three-year analysis in which the protruding hip bones in her severely emaciated anorexic frame were interpreted to be a wish for a penis.

While this example was extreme even in those days, traditional psychoanalytic thinking in modified forms has continued to inform work with the eating-disordered patient. Kernberg (1995), for example, has considered that eating disorders are manifestations of conflicts having to do with separation-individuation; bingeing sprees allow the patient at once to deny dependency on others while expressing rage at fantasied or real abandonment (p. 42). Chessick (2000) considers that the rituals and soothing activities of disordered eating are a protective means of negotiating feelings. Here, separation fears and desire for connection can be managed by turning to food where one can oscillate between appeasing the longing (i.e., bingeing) or wanting nothing at all. Kaddish (2012) describes eating disorders to be a psychic means of adaptation in which the isolation of the eating disorder is an anchor of sorts that is called upon in the face of overwhelming stress or anxiety. The patient pulls out of the land of the living and into the safety of bingeing, vomiting or starving.

In this trajectory of thinking, eating-disordered symptomatology is merely a concretization of a much larger problem, that of negotiating what it means to be human. The therapeutic work thus is to explore and understand internal conflict, emotional regulation and relational interactions. The work is not to intervene with the symptom itself – that is left in the hands of other treatment providers, if dealt directly with at all.

However, immediate questions and contradictions arise.

When words don't work

Interpretive work, the base of traditional analytic thinking, is grounded in the belief that understanding allows for change. But this is tricky business with a population of patients for whom words do not encapsulate or communicate internal experience. For these patients, as Kuriloff (2004) has noted, words fail.

Early parent/child connections allow for words to take on meaning. As Bromberg (Chefetz & Bromberg, 2004) describes, "if a parent is emotionally accessible to the child's communication, his or her meaning is not as much 'understood' as it is affectively 'recognized.' Through the parent's reciprocal affective aliveness to the child's vocal and gestural efforts to communicate, the child's emerging sense of self develops" (p. 418) and words symbolically attach to experience. When this does not happen, when parents unintentionally react to their child as if his or her state of mind at that moment has no meaning, "the child's ability to hold and express certain of its own self-states as a communicable 'I' can be destroyed. Words die as an effective means of expressing aspects of self and 'not-me'; dissociated self-states evolve as containers of unacknowledged experiences and feelings" (p. 418).

When words lose meaning, use of language in the analytic arena indeed becomes suspect. For these patients, words are not means of communicating experience or emotion; words are action, commodities used to control, demand or barter love and connection. Being the counterpoint to another's desire is the endgame of a relational engagement. Words finesse the deal. As a 16-year-old patient of mine says, "I know how to talk to people, to seem like I am really interested. I know how to get people to like me. By the end of the day though, I'm exhausted. I just want my time alone".

Seemingly involved and self-aware, these patients can be maddeningly ensconced in a world of psychic withdrawal, more alone, disconnected and unreachable than may appear at first glance.

What does analysis mean when the most simple of queries is heard as a demand, when a question such as "Are you hungry?" is a provocation (to eat – or not eat) and actually not heard as a question at all?

Questions abound

Bruch (1973, 1985) laid the groundwork for expansion of analytic thinking with the eating-disordered patient. She questioned the use of interpretation, wondering how exploration of conflict could be of use when someone has no sense of one's internal life. Knowing the self was hard enough; experiencing and understanding conflict was completely out of reach. While not using the concept of dissociation directly, Bruch nonetheless understood that, for these patients, just getting to know one's experience separate from that of others, to recognize the array of cut-off parts of self, was the first order of business.

"I'm cold", a patient reports her mother demanding, in a concretization of a myriad of interpersonal moments. "Put on a jacket".

For the eating-disordered patient, being attuned to others' wishes and demands (be it one's mother, a scale or the culture at large) supplants one's own experience of knowing one's self.

No question this laser-sharp awareness gets re-enacted in the therapy room. The therapist's even unspoken belief that talk of food and weight avoids discussion of more pertinent issues may well be intuited by the patient and will be experienced as a demand to "act differently" – which the patient will do. Ironically, this sets the stage for the authoritative/submissive intermix that traditional analysts hoped to avoid. Without direct intervention with the eating, the therapist unwittingly assumes an authoritative stance that quietly communicates that the therapist knows better than the patient what it is that she needs.

Here's the bind though. If we merely listen to the patient and focus on what seemingly hurts – that is, one's body, one's eating, one's weight – aren't we in other ways dangerously missing a broader scope of who this patient is and why she is in trouble? As Zerbe (2016) urges, "sharing one's personal story and having an interested witness (i.e., the therapist) to contain and help metabolize the elements is the only cure I have ever found to alleviate personal anguish" (p. 15).

Action and inquiry: an integrated approach

Consider Bromberg's (1998) discussion of a supervisee's patient, who, months into treatment, felt she was being missed. Therapist and patient had indeed been discussing the eating disorder but, as the patient noted, just talking about the eating disorder didn't help. "You ought to know . . .", the patient said, railing at her therapist "that when I'm talking . . . as long as I'm still fat, it's only my good self that's talking and that I'm doing something self-destructive that you are not even caring about . . . only in my silence do I feel real. If I do talk, it's not my fat self talking. So you have to find her by noticing the fat and not pretending that you don't" (p. 247).

How do we notice the fat self? How do we even talk to her? Perhaps that is where heathen talk comes into play.

In previous papers, I have argued for an approach that attempts to integrate both the language of patient and that of therapist while at the same time searching for the part of the patient who is yet to enter the room (Brisman, 1992, 1995).[1]

This integration of behavioral and interpretive work is hardly new. Hoffman (1992), for example, writes "Every interaction . . . is experienced by the analyst as a psychoanalytic interaction. There are no exceptions. Whether the analyst is reacting emotionally, talking about the weather or talking about the patient's childhood, the stamp of the analytic situation should never be lost on the participants" (p. 302). In this regard, Wachtel (1993) adds: "[Active interventions] are often a means of deepening the process of exploration and promoting greater access to warded-off parts of the self" (p. 600). "[T]hey are not just imports of foreign goods; they are relational events and the exploration of the meaning to the patient is a crucial part of their effective utilization" (p. 597). In this regard, any interaction in the analytic field can allow for "grist for the analytic mill of exploration". Frank (1993) too has encouraged integration of action-oriented techniques within a psychoanalytic frame. "These techniques" he notes, "can become an active part of an in-depth analytic experience, providing valuable material for a complex analytic exploration that results in new ways not only of relating but also of experiencing self and others" (p. 537).

Indeed, analysts in truth are always engaged in action-oriented techniques – they often just don't label them as such. What psychoanalyst, in his or her own way, has not said some version of "Why don't you just cut it out for now?" Isn't this really just a version of "Why don't you stop bingeing tonight and figure out what else is going on"? As Adler (1993) notes: "[F]ew analysts can claim to have conducted an analysis so technically 'pure' as to be devoid of attempts directly to influence the patient's relations to the interpersonal world" (p. 581).

That said, the question I am inevitably asked by supervisees is: "All this sounds right. But just HOW am I supposed to do this with my eating-disordered patient? Wouldn't a vicious fight between my patient and her mother trump talk about food?"

The "how" of this work initially involves a keenly behaviorally oriented focus on direct management of food and weight, a focus that may indeed initially err in the direction of exploring bodily obsessions at the cost of understanding any bigger picture. For indeed the patient's full frame of experience when entering treatment is completely interwoven with food. A fight with one's mother actually will feel less important than the weight gained from the binge following the fight. Patients tell me they can't stop thinking about food and weight. Everything else is peripheral – and that indeed is the point of an eating disorder: the relentless thinking, the torment, the defensive overlay of thinking about food instead of one's mother (or anyone else in one's social arena). Thus, early work requires getting to know the full extent of the eating disorder's reach, listening for the inevitable other issues, but appreciating the primacy of disordered eating and thinking in the patient's world.

In that spirit, an exquisite focus is needed on the specific moments the patient is involved with symptomatic behaviors (bingeing, purging, bodily obsession or the like) and/or thinking.

The therapist actively joins the patient in an assessment of what is and isn't eaten, when food and body are turned to and what can be done instead. Ways of listening to one's self, putting feelings into words instead of actions, and attempting to express and regulate one's internal experience, without food, starving or bodily obsession, are the goals. This initial work is detailed, painstaking and often tedious – for that is the world within which these patients live. But this is only a start. More is needed for the disowned self, the "fat self" (or anorexic or purging self) to emerge.

A 17-year-old talked endlessly about throwing up. It meant nothing to me somehow. As we engaged in a detailed exploration of the bingeing, however, the patient became anxious in the session. Details of the binge unfolded, anxiety mounted and the patient began to engage in what he called a "sort of addictive" behavior – he began to pick his toenails to a bloody core. With his feet strewn on my pillow-laden couch, toes ravaged – only then did I have a momentary entrance into an aspect of this young man that had otherwise been whitewashed, banished from both of our experiences. I was at once horrified and repulsed.

By intricately exploring with the patient the moments of food horror or body despair, I am using the most gritty details of the eating to allow a different part of the patient to emerge. With this patient, when disgust filled the room, clearly, momentarily, the work of the therapy had expanded. I was no longer treating a symptom. I was getting to know the reality of this complicated young man's life and experience. Why repulsion would be part of my experience of him, of course, would open the door to later exploration. For now, what was of importance was that more of him had dared to enter the room.

As Levenson (1983) writes: "Perhaps the key to therapy is for the therapist to experience the patient in some real way, even if with contempt, disdain, or total boredom" (p. 46). With the eating-disordered patient, the therapist's genuine repulsion may be the first sign that therapy is working.

A patient talks about how eating an ice cream cone became a prelude to a binge. The work in this case would not have been to question in general what was on the patient's mind that night. The work, in the most exquisitely exacting way, would be to consider the very moment that things went awry. The patient went for ice cream with a friend. She was okay, feeling good, she reports. She started to order the ice cream and still felt fine. But one friend got chocolate, another vanilla – and she couldn't make up her mind in terms of what she wanted. In a moment's flash, she ordered a double scoop with both flavors. That moment – the moment she said, "I'll have a double scoop" – would be the moment to fully expand and explore. That would be the moment that a different part of the patient would have emerged and would need to be known. Just who was it, who wanted ALL? And how do we get to better know that hungry, insistent part of her, this patient? Only then can we ask, why this night? Why that moment? In a brief second's time, there is much to explore.

Witch (which?) hunt

More traditionally, the search for the dissociated aspects of self takes place within the therapy room, with the therapist using one's own experience in the room to notice and locate disowned aspects of the patient's self.

Take, for example, Chafetz (2015), Bromberg (1994, 1996, 1998) and Howell and Itzkowitz (2016), who (among many) have written extensively about the engagement of dissociated aspects of self in the analytic arena. Traditionally, this is a long-haul process. Exploring and recognizing dissociated aspects of the patient takes place over many sessions (Chafetz, 2015). Slowly the therapist needs to invite the parts of the patient that are laden with disturbing affect into the room. Only when the therapist (often against his will) feels the enacted voices of his patient's dissociated self-states as alive in himself, is there hope of those parts being found (Chefetz & Bromberg, 2004). Prompted by countertransference reactions that are lodged in the body, the therapist may first notice that something has gone unspoken in the psychotherapeutic work because of physical sensations, gestures, postures, or aches and pains that occur during the patient's treatment hours or when the therapist reflects on a particular patient (Zerbe, 2016). In this spirit, the therapist's self-exploration and experience is key to the unfolding of the analytic journey. The goal is that of rebuilding links between unacknowledged aspects of the self and building links between these aspects of self and other people, including, of course, the analyst (Bromberg, 1996).

But what if, with the eating-disordered patient, this process just takes too long?

Culturally, we are living in crucible times. Eating disorders are disrupting and disabling girls (and boys now too) at younger and younger ages (Levine & Smolak, 2006). In this culture gone awry, not only is there a critical surge in the number of those falling to disordered eating, but, of importance, research has shown that the most significant factor affecting recovery is early intervention (Fairburn, 2005; Lask & Bryant-Waugh, 1999). In this case, early intervention means direct behavioral change. For the eating-disordered patient (many of whom are teens), there just is no time to allow dissociated aspects of self to slowly emerge in the treatment arena. In a bit of a blasphemy regarding our training, we, almost literally, need to run out fast – and find them.

The other concern with this population, and perhaps in general imbedded in contemporary theory regarding dissociation, is that, unwittingly, an implicit hierarchy in the therapeutic arena underlies the implications for change and may well disempower our patients. Particularly with the eating-disordered patient for whom severe trauma is not laden in one's history, it is possible that shut-off parts of self are unexpressed not because they are not known – but because they are not allowed.

Analytic work has often implied that it is the analyst who uses one's self and body in the treatment arena to nudge and coax more frightened aspects of the patient's self into the room. This trajectory is changing with the work of Fonagy & Target (1997) and others (Skarderud, 2007; Bateman & Fonagy, 2010). Here, a collaborative patient-therapist relationship is established in which two partners have an equal responsibility in understanding the mental process. The patient is empowered to work almost literally side by side with the analyst, in an investigative role that allows the patient as much responsibility as the therapist in understanding.

With the patient who is bingeing or starving daily, the patient must be heartened to question what – and who – is involved in the moments of food and bodily torment. As much work happens outside the therapeutic arena as does within. Here, even contemporary notions of analytic thinking are fast paced, and a post-feminist expansion of analytic thought, in which therapist and patient act as mutual explorers, is urged.

In this spirit, it is not a jagged jump for the patient and therapist to give the eating disorder form and substance, allowing the patient a safety to more boldly look. Here, one might consider the eating disorder to be a "drug pusher" who seduces the patient into eating. Is the "ED" an abusive boyfriend? A friend gone mad? Even the use of the name "ED" (Schaefer, 2003) allows the eating disorder to be anthropomorphized and concretized. How does ED urge the patient to binge, to starve? What is the exact moment that ED appears? What is said? Who exactly is in the room? The patient is emboldened to face the eating disorder, to look, to see who ED is and to find out how this intrusive other can be understood, taken care of and known.

For one bulimic teen, ED wasn't a male abusive lover but a wild child girl of 10 who wanted what she wanted. She was furious that no one listened to her, no one understood how tough things were for her. She would bellow into the room, tantruming through binges and violent episodes of purging. When the wild child was present, the patient's "real" life was completely smashed. Evenings were lost, schoolwork was left unfinished, wanton sprees could last for days, with hidden candy gulped at every turn. "I try to keep her in a prison box off to the side most of the time", the patient said as we started to get to know this wanton kid.

"If you were a mom, is that how you would treat her?" I ask. The patient is a thoughtful teen, known for being a caring babysitter. "This kid you are taking care of is tough. What are you going to do with her? How can we listen to what she wants without letting her go on a rampage?"

This patient and I, in a detailed exploration, look to the very moment the ED child breaks free. Why that moment? Why now? This work is not a global assessment of what the bingeing or purging means (of course, it is a means of expression, a way of soothing one's self, a thwarted means of self-care). Instead, a refined Sullivanian-type detailed inquiry is used: moment-to-moment, who is patient when the ED lurches forward? Of importance, note that the language of the patient and the language of the therapist soon begin to intertwine. ED is a disruptive other; ED is part of one's self. Does the thought of food start in school, hours before the actual binge and vomiting? Does she reach for a second helping at dinner when Dad picks up his cell phone annoyingly yet again? What is the exact moment any part of the symptomatic behavior is turned to?

"Now" I will ask the patient to attend to when outside the sessions and about to turn to food or restriction or bodily obsession. "Who are you now?"

If the eating disorder is concretized by the "not-me" ED, the patient is allowed the safety to look around corners, to follow this "other self" into the kitchen; the bathroom; yes, even the bedroom; to observe. Shame and blame are reduced; curiosity is enhanced. Conceptually this is interesting. Many patients are able to observe once allowed to look. They know well who they are at these moments. Relationally, however, they have never been entitled to look, and, as a result, self-observation and understanding have been thwarted by relational constraints and consequent immediate behavioral enactments.

Ongoing, the patient is asked to consider what alternative behaviors can replace eating, purging or restricting. If the patient weren't thinking about food or weight, what else would she be thinking about? What else is needed? As the patient begins to consider concrete alternatives to symptomatic behavior, "contracts" are developed between patient and therapist. Transitional objects of sorts, contracts are agreements made between therapist and patient regarding the substitution of "alternative behaviors" for disordered-eating behaviors or thinking. Here, the ED other and the ED self collapse.

This kind of direct work not only attempts to address unacknowledged aspects of self, but it also focuses on the question of developmental capacity for self-care. For many of our patients, direct work is often needed to develop means of self-soothing, emotional regulation and modulation of food intake (Goodsitt, 1983). Behavioral focus and contracts with the patients allow the therapist to function as a self-object of sorts, encouraging the development and integration of skills previously unlearned. Interpersonally, I am giving the patient permission to think about her own needs. Is she cold? Does she need to put on a jacket?

A patient agrees, very specifically, not to binge and throw up on a Sunday night between weekly sessions. She is going to text a friend from her treatment group if she wants to eat or purge. She will write in her journal, email me (I'll let her know I've read the email – but the goal is for her to remember the part of her that wants to recover). A labyrinth of possibilities emerges in terms of other potentially soothing or distracting behaviors. The patient's goal is to agree to turn to these behaviors before sneaking downstairs and bingeing, to get more information about who she is when she wants to turn to food and to question where others are at these moments. The patient enthusiastically agrees – and then arrives for the next session reporting that the night was a "disaster".

What happened?

The questioning of "what happened" is what allows for further integration of the language of the patient and that of the emerging relationally oriented language of the analyst. What was this patient thinking, feeling when she made the agreement? Was she pleasing me the way she pleases others? Was the dissociated part of herself – the wild, rageful, bingeing part of herself – sitting quietly off to the side with no voice when she and I were talking? The contract is a means of exploring the patient's relation not just to food but to people – in this case, to the therapist, with whom she has made a verbal, negotiated agreement. It is also a direct means of giving voice to the dissociated non-self, the part of her who has yet to enter treatment. What the patient doesn't do with the contract is as important as what she does put into play.

Of course, for some, the contract is immediately rejected. The work, regardless, remains the same. Why won't a contract work for this person? Questions regarding the intermingling of control and support come to the foreground. Regardless of what the patient actually does – or doesn't do – with the contract, this proposed connection between patient and therapist allows for fertile ground to consider what happens when two people, with potentially different needs and goals, are having an exchange.

When a patient outright refuses contract work, I'll often ask specifically what is one step the patient feels he or she can take. When the answer (sometimes) is: "I don't know. That's why I'm here", we are full force lurched into the complicated attachment interplay between the two of us. The insistence on not taking hold of one's life, even for one step, the terror of separation, the anger at not being cared for, the role of disordered eating and thinking, come center stage. Why is bingeing or starving preferable to any other means of listening to one's self or turning to others? No question, for many, this is where the work of the treatment begins.

Theology is a fortress

The goal of treatment thus is not merely symptomatic change (though one certainly hopes for that). The goal is the eventual exploration of what happens between patient and analyst as this concrete directed work is done. Who is talking to whom? And how can the potential repulsion, fear, outrage allow for an introduction of a part of the patient into the room?

Herein lies the potential for analytic conceptualization – not primarily with interpretation of internal conflict or inner life, but with the focus of interpretation on what actually happens between two people – and, of course, with the question of which two people are actually in the room.

"What is going on around here?" Levenson (1983) asks in an iconic representation of the interpersonal analytic exchange. What happens when two people are in the room, when they make an agreement together? Who is present? Who is being embraced, discarded, kicked out of the room?

Work with an 18-year-old with a history of both unintended parental neglect – and bulimia – involved weeks of jagged work, contracts made, contracts broken. The patient initially white-knuckled treatment, acing the therapy the way she had aced all her coursework in school, her gymnastics. After years of bingeing and purging (yes, she was 18 and already had been bingeing and vomiting for five years), through the work with contracts, behavioral structuring and our both listening hard, she maintained five months of non-bulimic behavior, with tentative attempts to listen to herself and better meet her needs at moments of difficulty. But a sudden boyfriend crisis resulted in a back-peddling to the symptoms once more. As part of our work, we turned once again to the contract. The patient was to take one day between sessions to engage in the self-care behaviors we had established, to listen to the unacknowledged parts of herself that previously had never been heard.

But this time, the next session started atypically with a failed contract.

"That didn't work at all", she tells me with disdain. "There's no way the contract will help". She laughs derisively, surprisingly (who *is* this person in my room?) when I suggest we think about what else could work, how can we listen harder to what is needed.

"I've done everything I could. I feel like nothing will help me at all".

This, of course, made me think of the helplessness that was likely at the core of her disordered eating. When this patient was 12, her brother had been destructively involved with drugs. Her parents had been frantic and she had been unwittingly but profoundly overlooked. She knew these moments well and we had discussed them at length. Yes, the "good" self talking.

"No one ever can reach you at these moments, can they?" I wondered.

"What if the feeling of helplessness never goes away?" she asks. She and I both know it won't ever really go away for good. It is part of her, that previously disowned experience, the part she has escaped by bingeing, throwing up, thinking about her body. I know the question is not "will it go away", but instead, "what will she do about it? Now what?"

The patient is furious, frightened, hopeless. Quiet.

Silence.

Without words, I know we are finally talking. She is sitting side by side with the part of her that wants to give up, wants to hide out, wants to rage and binge.

"Nothing's going to help", she finally says. And I know. And she knows I know.

Words, food, silence and disdain intermingle. What will follow will be moments when we tangle with the "good" self, edging forward with self-care moments, the "fat" self screaming at me, frantically, quietly, heroically. There will be many moments of neither the patient – nor I – being reached.

"Tell me more", I say.

With a kaleidoscope of moments and people in the room, with the inevitability of our interactions and focus changing from moment to moment, the work of the therapy has now truly begun.

Note

1 Note that with any eating-disordered patient, restoration of medical stability, no matter the treatment approach, is urgently the first order of business. This paper focuses on the patient who is medically stable enough to make use of outpatient care. Note too that the treatment of anorexia always involves weekly weigh-ins, the goal of weight gain and active nutritional guidance. See Siegel, Brisman, and Weinshel (2008).

References

Adler, E. (1993). Commentary on Frank's "Action, insight, and working through" from the perspective of Freudian analysis. *Psychoanalytic Dialogues*, *3*(4), 579–588.

Bateman, A., & Fonagy, P. (2010). Mentalization based treatment for borderline personality disorder. *World Psychiatry*, *9*, 11–15.

Brisman, J. (1992). Bulimia in the late adolescent: An analytic perspective to a behavioral problem. In J. O'Brien, D. Pilowsky, & O. Lewis (Eds.), *Psychotherapies with children: Adapting the dynamic process*. Washington, D.C.: American Psychiatric Press.

Brisman, J. (1995). Psychodynamic psychotherapy and action-oriented technique: An integrated approach. In I. Yalom & J. Werne (Eds.), *Treating eating disorders* (pp. 31–70). San Francisco: Jossey-Bass Publishers.

Bromberg, P. (1994). "Speak! that I may see you": Some reflections on dissociation, reality, and psychoanalytic listening. *Psychoanalytic Dialogues*, *4*, 517–547.

Bromberg, P. (1996). Hysteria, dissociation, and cure: Emmy von N revisited. *Psychoanalytic Dialogues*, *6*(1), 55–72.

Bromberg, P. M. (1998). "Speak! that I may see you": Some reflections on dissociation, reality, and psychoanalytic listening. In P. M. Bromberg (Ed.), *Standing in the spaces: Essays on clinical process, trauma, and dissociation* (pp. 241–266). Hillsdale, NJ: The Analytic Press.

Bruch, H. (1973). *Eating disorders, obesity, anorexia nervosa and the person within*. New York: Basic Books.

Bruch, H. (1985). Four decades of eating disorders. In D. Garner & P. Garfinkel (Eds.), *Handbook of psychotherapy for anorexia and bulimia* (pp. 7–18). New York: Guilford.

Chefetz, R. (2015). *Intensive psychotherapy for persistent dissociative processes: The fear of feeling real*. New York: Norton.

Chefetz, R., & Bromberg, P. (2004). Talking with "Me" and "Not-Me"- a dialogue. Psycho 40(3), 409–464.

Chessick, R. (2000). *Psychoanalytic clinical practice*. London: Free Association Books.

Fairburn, C. G. (2005). Evidence-based treatment of anorexia nervosa. *International Journal of Eating Disorders*, *37*, 26–30.

Fonagy, P., & Target, M. (1997). Attachment and reflective function: Their role in self-organization. *Development and Psychopathology*, *9*, 679–700.
Frank, K. (1993). Action, insight, and working through: Outlines of an integrative approach. *Psychoanalytic Dialogue*, *3*, 553–577.
Goodsitt, A. (1983). Self-regulatory disturbances in eating disorders. *International Journal of Eating Disorders*, *2*, 51–60.
Hoffman, I. (1992). Some practical implications of a social-constructivist view of the psychoanalytic situation. *Psychoanalytic Dialogues*, *2*(3), 287–304.
Howell, E., & Iskowitz, S. (2016). *The dissociative mind in psychoanalysis: Understanding and working with Trauma*. London: Routledge.
Kaddish, Y. (2012). Pathological organizations and psychic retreats in eating disorders. *Psychoanalytic Review*, *99*(2), 227–252.
Kernberg, O. (1995). Technical approach to eating disorders in patients with borderline personality organization. *Annual of Psychoanalysis*, *23*, 33–48.
Kuriloff, E. (2004). When words fail: Psychosomatic illness and the talking cure. *Psychoanalytic Quarterly*, *73*(4), 1023–1040.
Lask, B., & Bryant-Waugh, R. (1999). Prepubertal eating disorders. In N. Piran, M. Levine, & C. Steiner-Adair (Eds.), *Preventing eating disorders* (pp. 476–483). Philadelphia: Taylor & Francis.
Le Grange, D. (2005). The Maudsley family-based treatment for adolescent anorexia nervosa. *World Psychiatry*, *4*(3), 142–146.
Levenson, E. (1983). *The ambiguity of change*. New York: Basic Books.
Levine, M., & Smolak, L. (2006). *The prevention of eating problems and eating disorders: Theory, research, and practice*. Mahweth, NJ: Lawrence Erlbaum Associates.
Schaefer, J. (2003). *Life without ED: How one woman declared independence from her eating disorder and how you can too*. London: Routledge.
Siegel, M., Brisman, J., & Weinshel, M. (2008). *Surviving an eating disorder: Strategies for family and friends* (3rd ed.). New York: Harper Collins.
Skarderud, F. (2007). Eating one's words: Part III. Mentalisation-based psychotherapy for anorexia nervosa- an outline for a treatment and training manual. *European Eating Disorders Review*, *15*, 323–339.
Wachtel, P. (1993). Active intervention, psychic structure, and the analysis of transference: Commentary on Frank's " Action, insight, and working through". *Psychoanalytic Dialogues*, *4*(3), 589–604.
Wilson, C. P., Hogan, C., & Mintz, I. (1983). *Fear of being fat: The treatment of anorexia and bulimia*. New York: Jason Aronson, Inc.
Zerbe, K. (2016). Psychodynamic issues in the treatment of binge eating: Working with shame, secrets, no-entry, and false body defenses, *Clinical Social Work Journal*, *44*(1), 8–17.

8

TO KNOW ANOTHER INSIDE AND OUT

Linking psychic and somatic experience in eating disorders

Danielle Novack

Patients with eating disorders often fixate on the body, perseverating concretely on pounds, inches and "feeling fat." The body is the locus of pain or numbness, excess and deficiency. These somatically preoccupied patients are especially challenging for the psychoanalytic therapist who believes that it is complex inner experience that must be explored and understood for change to occur. How is one to access a patient's inner life in the face of such externalization?

Eating disorders are, among other things, disorders of affect regulation. The ability to formulate, verbalize and regulate emotional experience develops in the context of attuned and responsive caregiving relationships that allow for the intersubjective processing of affect (Aron, 1998). Many patients with eating disorders have had early attachment experiences that were unattuned, inconsistent and/or traumatic, and thus were forced to self-regulate prematurely, often in concrete, stereotypic ways. With patients who use food to attempt to cope with unprocessed trauma and emotions that reside in the body, the therapeutic task includes connecting to their bodily experience, which is facilitated by the analyst's use of her own body as a medium for nonverbal communication. Within the psychoanalytic relationship, somatic experience can be gradually and mutually metabolized into mental representations that can be shared and modulated (Wallin, 2007). In this chapter, I explore the role of the body in psychoanalytic psychotherapy, illustrated through my work with Julia, a college student with a history of anorexia.

Self-regulation and mind-body differentiation in development

In earliest life, the infant comes to know and respond to the world through concurrent processes of dyadic and self-regulation (Beebe & Lachmann, 1998; Gianino & Tronick, 1988; Sander, 1977, 1983; Tronick, 1989). Nonverbal exchanges between caregiver and infant shape experiences and expectations of relatedness. Attuned and coordinated interactions provide the infant with the sense that she has been and will continue to be recognized and responded to in contingent, consistent and synchronized ways (Beebe, Lachmann, & Jaffe, 1997).

Inevitably, in the context of a "good enough" (Winnicott, 1953) mothering environment, the infant comes to experience titrated moments of maternal unavailability or misattunement. According to Tronick's Mutual Regulation Model (Cohn & Tronick, 1989; Gianino & Tronick, 1988; Tronick, 1989, 2003), these relational "misses," rather than indicating an inadequate caregiving environment, are "the interactive and affective 'stuff' from which co-creative reparations generate new ways of being together" (Tronick, 2003, p. 477). The infant must, by necessity, learn to fill in the maternal gaps by entering into "potential space," the safe, protected realm existing between self and other in which she can begin to construct an internal reality (Winnicott, 1951). For Tronick (2003), the process of adjusting to or repairing moments of mismatch results in a "dyadic sense of consciousness" that allows the individual out in the world to experience a sense of connection to others, a feeling that one is "larger than oneself" (p 476). According to Beebe and Lachmann (1994), it is through the disruption and repair process as well as the experience of consistent, optimally coordinated interactions over time that the child comes to experience different aspects of being in relation to others.

If mental health has been associated with the ongoing development of resilient and adaptive coping through early positive attachment experiences, psychopathology later in life has been associated with disturbances in attachment, characterized by deficits in coping with novelty and stress (Schore, 2001). For those who go on to develop eating disorders, there have often been pathological failures in early maternal responsivity, as well as maternal impingements. Bruch (1973), one of the first psychoanalysts to theorize about and treat eating disorders, noted that often, these patients have what she calls an interoceptive problem – difficulty distinguishing between inside and outside *and* between self and other – as the result of having their mothers' needs imposed upon them throughout development. As a result, the potential, or transitional space, never achieved as a space between two people, becomes an embodied, or "in-myself" space (Boris, 1984).

McDougall (2001) observed that mothers of those who go on to develop addictions (including eating disorders) often wish to maintain dependency in their children, stemming from their own dependency needs. In turn, the child develops an addictive need for the mother. The child cannot establish inner caregiving representations, and so cannot provide herself with self-care or self-soothing. Later, a solution is sought in the external world, through substances such as food or drugs. These objects may temporarily relieve psychic and physical distress by fulfilling a maternal function that was not provided, and thus was not internalized.

In early life, mind and body are closely linked, perhaps even indistinguishable. Winnicott (1949) emphasized the genesis of the human as a psyche-soma, and questioned the assumption that the mind is contained in the head or brain. Rather, he conceived of an early mind-body entity, which gradually, through a process of "mutual interrelation" with the caregiver, gives rise to the capacity for self-care. In his theory of the skin-ego, Anzieu (1985) explored how the first experiences of being touched by the mother allow for the formation of a psychic space to hold mental representations. The physical touch of the mother was seen as instrumental to the child's developing capacity for psychic containment. Krystal (1988) suggested that affects are initially experienced as bodily sensations that gradually become differentiated and articulated as psychic states that can be expressed verbally. Empathy and appropriate verbal and nonverbal responsiveness on the part of the caregiver facilitate the eventual experience of subjective feeling states that can be conveyed through words.

When this process goes awry, it can result in a disturbance in the mind-body connection and the individual's capacity for self-care. According to Winnicott (1949), maternal failure can lead to the psyche's prematurely withdrawing into the mind and away from its original intimate relationship with the soma. In such cases, the child must rely on thinking in order to care for herself in the absence of maternal caretaking. This kind of premature mind-body split can result in what Bach (2016) calls the "disembodied self" – patients who received little touching or affective engagement from their caregivers tend to be interpersonally avoidant and experience bodily detachment and depersonalization. Wallin (2007) has suggested that therapy with such "dismissing" patients who "live in their heads" and feel disconnected from somatic sensations must include working towards "resomatization," or the reclaiming of a sentient body that feels and experiences. This occurs through a therapeutic relationship that helps the patient to attend to and take interest in her body.

On the other end of the continuum lie those who did not achieve sufficient, adaptive mind-body separation, as a result of overstimulating caregiving environments that were intrusive and overwhelming, even abusive. These patients experience their bodies as belonging to another, and so are overly dependent on others for soothing and regulatory functions (Bach, 2016). This is consistent with Bruch's (1973) observation that patients with eating disorders have trouble distinguishing between inside and outside and self and other, as a result of intrusive maternal experiences. In cases in which mind-body differentiation is not appropriately achieved, Wallin (2007) recommends a focus on "desomatization," which includes identifying and containing bodily sensations and affects, and then articulating and understanding them through words. "Desomatization" is a concept originally developed by Krystal (1988) for use with traumatized patients.

I view both de- and resomatization as important in working with eating disorders, and neither process can be seen as distinct from the other. While many anorectic and bulimic patients describe themselves as feeling disconnected from their bodies, or even like heads without bodies, they are also trapped in an inability to differentiate affect from bodily state, as evidenced through difficulty articulating feelings verbally (see Krystal, 1988 on alexithymia), and the use of food and the body as the primary or only means of self-expression.

The body in treatment

By linking in-session somatic experience to words and images that can be reflected on in the therapeutic relationship, we can foster the "self-reflexivity" (Aron, 1998) that is essential for psychic change. Bucci (1985) suggests that an important task of adult psychoanalysis is to translate between verbal and nonverbal modes of expression. For this to happen, the therapist must tune in to the patient's "subsymbolic processes" (Bucci, 2011), which occur across motoric and sensory modalities. Good enough mothers respond to their infants' cues through their own proprioceptive sensory experience, or what Bucci (2011) calls "the wisdom of the body" (p. 48). Good mothers, most of the time, smile in response to their infants' smiles, reflect their infants' distress in their own faces, and provide physical and verbal soothing in response to what they sense their infants need, and not solely in response to their own anxiety or desire. This attuned emotional expression both reflects and creates what Stern (1983) calls "state sharing," in which the mother and infant feel the same, and "state complementing," in which one responds affectively to the other's signals. The same phenomena occur in therapy. Bromberg (2011), discussing the concept of moment-to-moment affective state-sharing (Schore, 2003), notes that it is through this process that a good psychoanalytic "match" is created.

For therapists, it is a bit like tuning in to two different but related frequencies, using two different but related receivers. We are always using our minds, but we also must learn to use our bodies as finely tuned psychotherapeutic instruments (Stone, 2006) that can help us connect to and co-process our patients' "unformulated experience" (Stern, 1983). To use our bodies to receive patients' nonverbal signals, we must observe our own bodily experience as closely as we observe that of the other. While we can rely on sight and hearing to pick up on some of our patients' nonverbal cues (vocal acoustics, facial and postural expressions, motoric activation and inhibition), we have at our disposal additional modes of sensing; changes in our own breathing and heart rates, our own digestive tracts and our own musculoskeletal systems can tell us something about what is occurring in the analytic relationship that may not meet the eye. We feel fatigued, sexually aroused, cold, sweaty, restless. We have coughing fits, difficulty breathing (Stone, 2006), aches and pains and abdominal rumblings (Da Silva, 1990). We notice that our arms are crossed, or that we are eagerly leaning forward. The therapist's in-session somatically based experience is essential for receiving and understanding patients' nonverbal communications.

Reich (as cited in Sletvold, 2011) was one of the first analysts to recognize the importance of the body, noting that what is expressed nonverbally via movement and voice can at critical points become more important than the verbalized content. Sletvold notes that according to Reich, "The patient's expressive movements involuntarily bring about an imitation in our own organism. By imitating these movements, we 'sense' and understand the expression in ourselves and, consequently, in the patient" (p. 458). This phenomenon has been demonstrated by researchers Ekman, Levenson, and Friesen (1983), who found that an adult onlooker, observing a particular facial expression in another adult, matches that expression and exhibits a similar state of physiological arousal.

Nebbiosi and Federici-Nebbiosi (2008) take imitation a step further, using it purposefully in their clinical work by miming their patients in their absence. They see efforts toward understanding what is communicated through body rhythms as bridging the gap between the body and the construction of an emotionally meaningful relationship. Specifically, through their technique of actively miming patients, they seek to explore what they view as the ongoing dialectic between implicit and explicit processes (Federici-Nebbiosi & Nebbiosi, 2001), which they relate to the concept of the third in psychoanalysis (Benjamin, 1988). They write:

> Furthermore, if imitation is a process, there is an ongoing interaction between miming a patient and going back to being in a relationship with him or her after miming him or her. The way we "see" changes, we pay different and greater attention to all the implicit aspects. Rather than concentrate solely on listening to the verbal contents, an effort is currently being made to keep a focus on the processes of interaction between bodies, which language is unable to describe.
>
> *(p. 434)*

Miming not only gives the analyst a body-knowledge of the patient's experience, but it also contributes to the co-construction of the unique patient-therapist relationship as the therapist, the patient and the space they create together is altered by the experience of miming itself.

Ogden (1994) has written of his own in-session body-centered reveries as clues to the patient's unconscious experience. Using his in-the-moment somatic or psychic experiences as a starting point, Ogden views his own reveries as having the potential to reveal important aspects of the intersubjective experience existing in the space created by the analyst and patient. His sensory and bodily experiences during sessions with patients become elaborated through fantasy, which ultimately can be used to help understand something that is occurring within the dyad. This is made possible by his exquisitely attuned inner listening, occurring in the context of listening to and being with his patient. Rather than viewing such inner listening as narcissistic self-involvement or a barrier to analytic attunement, Ogden sees it as a way of allowing an intersubjective experience to be created. Thus, he is both finding and creating what he refers to as the "analytic third," akin to the potential space that exists between mother and infant, in which they are at once one entity and two beings. Ogden conceives of the third as a subjectivity that is continually co-created through the implicit and explicit interactions of analyst and analysand, and that is at the same time, creating analyst and analysand. He writes:

> Each time my conscious attention shifted from the experience of 'my own' reveries to what the patient was saying and how he was saying it to me and

> being with me, I was not 'returning' to the same place I had left seconds or minutes earlier. In each instance, I was changed by the experience of the reverie, sometimes only in an imperceptibly small way.
>
> *(p. 9)*

This is quite similar to what Nebbiosi and Federici-Nebbiosi described, that going "back" to a patient after miming him or her amounts to a changed analyst going back to a changed patient.

Ogden emphasizes that he uses his own experience "in and of the third" (p. 17) internally, and as a kind of lens through which to understand the experience of the patient. He does not invite the patient to reflect on her perceptions of the analyst's subjectivity. This is an important point at which Ogden's third diverges from that of Jessica Benjamin. For Benjamin (1990), the achievement of intersubjectivity depends on the infant's gradually coming to see the mother as a subjective other, and no longer just an object to satisfy her own needs. In the therapy situation, this translates to the patient's acquisition of the capacity to see the therapist as a subject, and to reflect on her subjectivity. A view of the third as a space for mutual recognition between two subjects is, for Benjamin, "crucial for a relational psychoanalysis" (p. 35). Thus, where Ogden's communication of his reverie-informed experience of the patient occurs only at an implicit level, another analyst might choose to do so more explicitly, inviting the patient to reflect upon the analyst's reveries or somatic experiences and communications.

The process of coming to see the other as a subjective self in her own right requires something analagous to Tronick's process of disruption and repair in the early mother-infant dyad. The analyst's role is not to provide perfectly attuned caregiving to compensate for the failures of the patient's early experiences. Benjamin (2010), referencing Tronick, notes that through therapeutic enactments/ruptures and their ensuing repair, the shared project of surviving and negotiating "therapeutic 'mistakes' (misattunements, failures in regulation) [is] what actually allow[s] development and change to occur" (p. 115). To relate this to the treatment of eating disorders, I refer to Bromberg (2001), who notes that through the process of rupture (interpersonal enactment) and repair in the analytic dyad, there arises "an opportunity to co-construct a transitional reality in which the patient's impaired faith in the reliability of human relatedness can be restored, and eating can become linked to appetite rather than to self-protection" (p. 891).

Julia: a body turned inside out

Julia's anorexia first surfaced in high school. By the time she began seeing me as a college student, she had already had some therapy and had made notable improvements. Her eating was less restrictive and she was able to maintain a normal weight, although she occasionally binged on healthy foods such as rice cakes or fruit. In high school, she had struggled to maintain boundaries with her anxious, depressed mother, as well as friends who took advantage of her. She had managed others' demands by becoming smaller, taking up less and less space emotionally and physically. Recently, she had become an avid practitioner of Pilates. She felt safer and stronger, less permeable in her hard, well-muscled body.

A primary focus of the first two years of treatment was Julia's relationships with others. She wanted a more active social life, but sometimes isolated herself in her room rather than go out with friends, despite many invitations. She worried that others would think she was boring if they spent much time with her. The same applied to romantic relationships. She believed that once men really got to know her, they would see that she was "not the smartest, funniest or the most interesting," and would lose interest.

As time went on, Julia was able to share that it wasn't simply that she thought others found her boring. She believed there was "something disgusting" about her that people discovered after a while, and that would result in rejection if she let them get too close. It had partly to do with her eating disorder, a shameful, gross part of her that she believed others could sense, even though she looked normal. But the "something disgusting" felt bigger and older than the eating disorder alone. It was her disgustingness that had caused the eating disorder in the first place. It had been there for as long as she could remember.

This "something disgusting," diffuse and ineffable, was not apparent in the transference-countertransference. Julia was smart, attractive and well-liked. She was doing well in school and had a bright future ahead of her. Why was she so unhappy with herself? What was this rotten, festering part of her that I knew about, but didn't actually know? I struggled to understand her conviction that she was disgusting, unlovable and undeserving of meaningful relationships. In fact, it was this very factor, my disconnect from her sense of disconnection from others, that contributed to a growing sense of mutual alienation in the therapy.

There was a fragility about Julia, notwithstanding her strong muscles. Small things, like the coldness of winter days or indecision about whether to go out with friends on a given night, could plunge her into a state of anxious despair. I was concerned that therapy was making things worse. Despite my efforts to contain and empathize, she often left appearing more upset than when she arrived. When I asked about this, she became more upset still. No, she had thought therapy was helping. But now that I'd raised this, what if I was right? Again, she left in a state of agitated distress, leaving me helpless and flustered. It felt as though the harder I tried to connect to her internal state, the more tenuous our connection became.

In "The Rotten Core" (1980), Ruth Lax described the puzzling presentation of women who complained of great suffering despite having lives and relationships that appeared adaptive, even gratifying. They all had in common a belief that their suffering arose from "something rotten within," resulting in a pervasive sense of doom. Similar to Balint's "basic fault" (1968), the "rotten core" stems from a rupture in the early mother-child relationship, often resulting from maternal depression. For Lax, during the rapprochement phase of development, these children did not receive the necessary combination of loving acceptance and ambivalence required for autonomous growth. Instead, the self-representation became subsumed by a "bad" introject, which fused with "bad" aspects of self to form the rotten core.

Tronick (1989), in studying dyadic behavior patterns with infants and depressed mothers, repeatedly observed that the mother fails to appropriately track and respond to the infant's affective cues. As a result, the infant becomes more and more preoccupied with self-regulation and the management of her own distress states. It was as though my attempts to track and respond to Julia's affective states resulted in more distress, not less, indicating that she may have lacked early experiences that allowed for the safe internalization of maternal soothing and regulatory functions. She withdrew into herself or turned to food to reduce aversive stimulation and to give herself the comfort she could not take in from others.

Julia's mother had struggled with periodic depression and overeating, using food to try to quell her emotions. From a young age, Julia recalled her mother explicitly telling her to eat when she felt sad. She had also instructed babysitters and preschool teachers to feed Julia if she cried. Negative feelings were signs of "low blood sugar" or hunger, and were treated as such. Not surprisingly, Julia had difficulty differentiating between bodily and mental states. Later, in adolescence, she coped with burdensome relationships by restricting her food, as though she felt physically stuffed, filled up by interpersonal impingements. Then, through exercise, she built up a tough muscular armor to help protect herself from further violation. But none of this lessened the inexorable rottenness at her core, and my efforts to reach it felt futile.

Two years into treatment, sudden, severe abdominal pain led to Julia's having the first of two emergency surgeries. Weeks later, she shuffled into my office, hunched and pale. "It was basically a C-section," she said dully, "but they took out half my colon." The incision had become infected, and she had to clean and pack the open wound daily. This was both physically painful and psychically distressing. The "something disgusting" was now on the outside of Julia's body, and required continual tending. Perhaps most upsetting was the fact that afterwards, the surgeon had told her that it had been particularly difficult to cut through her unusually thick abdominal wall. All that hard work in Pilates was gone with the slice of the surgeon's knife. She wondered whether it would ever be possible to rebuild her body, now that it had been unalterably breached.

As we spoke, I became acutely aware of a sensation of tightness in my own abdominal scar, the result of two cesarean sections. This awareness of my body brought me back to how I had felt following my first C-section, ten years earlier. My pregnancy had been normal and healthy, and I had diligently attended childbirth classes where we watched videos of indigenous women squatting in the woods, delivering easily and with little pain. I planned to deliver as naturally and with as little intervention as possible. Instead, after a failed induction and twelve hours of labor, I ended up on the operating table. My recovery was difficult, and I experienced an unusual amount of pain. Listening to Julia, I felt myself return to that time. I remembered how painful it had been to rise out of bed to attend to the crying baby that I could barely lift. I remembered how shocked I'd been that this had happened to me, when I'd been so certain it would not. I felt like a failure. I'd relived the labor over and over in my mind, wondering if I could have pushed harder, been stronger.

Relating to Julia's physical pain provided access to something of her psychic pain that had previously eluded me. In that session, I felt connected to her, as though through a shared umbilicus, and I recognized that this might be a point of entry through which to reach her. I understood her fear of being jostled as she walked down the street, and I knew that little things, such as sneezing and sitting down, could be excruciating. I knew how it was to be vulnerable and in pain, and to have to carry on nonetheless. We spoke together about what it was like to have the "something disgusting," once hidden, now on the outside of her body. Being turned inside out was bewildering, revolting, a nightmare come true. She sat on my couch crying, and we both knew it hurt to cry.

Julia was terrified that her colon might reopen, leaking toxic, "disgusting" fluid into her body. Eating felt dangerous, and old restrictive patterns resurfaced. Unable to exercise, Julia feared gaining weight despite having lost quite a bit after the surgery. I asked whether she would like to go back to meeting twice a week. We had previously met twice a week, until a demanding semester had necessitated reducing to weekly sessions. But she became upset when I proposed increasing the frequency. No, that was not what she wanted at all. "Talking about this doesn't help; it just makes me feel worse," she complained.

"I wonder whether talking, and my saying I think we should do more of it, feels like I'm poking holes in you, like that surgeon," I reflected.

"Yes," she snapped, "that's exactly what it feels like." I was getting it, even though she was pushing me away at the same time.

Soon after that, Julia emailed that she was back in the hospital, following a second surgery. She said she was in a "bad place" and asked for a phone session. Instead, I offered to visit her in the hospital, and she agreed. The floor she was on also served maternity patients, and the nurse at the desk asked cheerily whether the patient I was visiting had had a baby. Julia looked pale and gaunt beneath her hospital gown. We walked down the hall to a place where we could speak privately, her IV stand trailing along. Wires and tubes protruded from her body. In striking contrast, cheerful new mothers pushed clear plastic bassinets down the hall behind us. "People keep asking if I had a baby," Julia said. We sat together, and in a flat, monotone voice, she told me about the pain and vomiting that had preceded this latest procedure, the removal of an obstruction that had formed as a consequence of her first surgery. The efforts she had been making to resume her life had been violently disrupted. She felt helpless, afraid she would never again live a normal life. "If this happens again, I'll kill myself," she confided.

When she was able to return to my office, Julia complained that her mother didn't want to hear that she was sad, frustrated or scared. She told her to smile more and to think of happier things to focus on. Things could have been much worse, and she was lucky to be alive. Her father kept making suggestions, telling her to try various things to distract herself from the pain and bad feelings. "I just want someone to listen to me, not fix things," she said. Yet my attempts to be that listener seemed only to anger her. She was getting hungry late at night and eating sweet potatoes and bananas. Baby food, I thought. "I shouldn't be eating so late at night, I am out of control. I need tools; I want you to tell me what to do!"

I felt helpless and stuck. If I told her what to do, then I was being like her father. If I "just" listened and offered support, I wasn't doing enough. I recalled the months after my own surgery. My newborn daughter had cried for four months straight. Nothing I did seemed to soothe her. She would calm down enough to nurse, but then would scream afterwards. At night, I would nurse her for an hour, then walk around with her for another hour, trying to get her to settle. Stepping on a creaky floorboard was enough to wake her up and start the whole process over again.

Working with Julia at this juncture felt like trying to soothe a colicky baby. Nothing I did or didn't do seemed to help. However, I found that my ability to relate to her physical state, and the internal reverie that ensued, gave me a kind of perspective on things that allowed me to patiently ride out the storm. Previously, my difficulty understanding her distress had led to the affective misattunement that results from trying too hard to make sense of things. Now, I had a body-knowledge that mirrored something of her experience, inside and out. We found a new language that reflected both bodily and mental states: we spoke of "poking holes," "healing," and "scars" as they related to her psyche-soma.

Our new, shared language helped Julia find ways to link bodily experience and affective states. She wearied of people's comments that she looked frail or ill, and wished she could "create a bubble" around herself that no one could penetrate. She noticed that feeling tired or vulnerable or closed off might be a physical state or a mental one, or perhaps both. She observed that she now felt less worried about people thinking there was something wrong with her. "It's out there, they all know," she said. "I can say, 'I feel ugly,' or 'I'm afraid to eat this,' and it doesn't sound like an eating disorder, because there's a physical reason for it." There was, paradoxically, less shame around how she felt about her body.

My experience with Julia also helped me help her see the link between her food behaviors and her connections to others. My suggestion that her nighttime eating might be related to loneliness was received enthusiastically. "Now that I think about it," she added, "I don't binge when I'm dating someone." She recalled that when she had trouble sleeping as a child, she and her mother would snack together. She began to see that food was offered when there was an emotional need. And food was linked to mother – late-night snacking was a pleasure that they shared. She acknowledged that her ritual of nighttime snacking had been going on for years, but that she felt more able to think and talk about it now.

I also asked her many more questions about her bodily experience than I had before. How does your body feel right now? Where do you feel bloated/achy/ugly? I inquired how her second scar was healing, and she explained that there was only one scar. The first one had been reopened and resutured during the second surgery, and it was actually healing much better the second time around. It was fully closed and she did not have to clean and pack it. My second, planned, C-section had also been much less stressful than the first, and my doctor had removed my first scar and left a new one that had also hurt less and healed better. Struck by this parallel in our experiences, I spontaneously and uncharacteristically told her about it. As I did so, I wondered what had gotten into me, and I chastised myself internally for committing such a blunder, breaking the frame in this way.

After a moment, Julia said that she'd had three successive thoughts in reaction to my revelation. The first was, "*Two* C-sections? That's awful!" The second was, "Oh, you understand what this is like; you understand me." And finally, the third was, "I haven't had a C-section, and you haven't had my surgery. So you might understand something about it, but no one can fully understand someone else's experience, because everyone's experience is different."

"I think you got that just right," I answered. Her words reflected what Ogden (1994) says of the dialectic inherent in viewing mother and infant at once as one entity and two separate beings, and how this relates to the analytic third: "The intersubjectivity of the analyst-analysand coexists in dynamic tension with the analyst and the analysand as separate individuals with their own thoughts, feelings, sensations, corporal reality, psychological identity and so on" (p. 4). With her three thoughts, Julia had said: This is you, this is us and this is me.

Upon later reflection, I realized that my uncharacteristic self-disclosure had been a response to feeling unseen in the therapy. I believe my decision to visit her in the hospital had also been related to a desire to have her see me as helpful and caring. My enacting a wish to be seen in a particular way may also have reflected an aspect of Julia's experience. For much of the treatment, I had struggled to understand how she felt, but never got it quite right. She, too, may have felt unseen and unrecognized by me and by others in her life, in a way that she could not articulate; perhaps this feeling was held in her bodily experience but not as a mental construct that could be expressed through words. In addition, the shame and self-berating that followed my impulsive disclosure mirrored the shame and self-hate she experienced so much of the time. I had done something messy, shown her my own version of inner disgustingness, and I could not do anything to cover it back up.

Further, I worried that Julia was not ready, in a developmental sense, to view me as a subjective other, to make the transition from object relating to object usage (Winnicott, 1969). She rarely referred to me or our relationship. When I did occasionally say or ask something about the relationship, or attempted to explore her dissatisfaction with the therapy, she changed the subject or became more distressed. My interjecting my own experience and history in such an unaccustomed way could have resulted in withdrawal or dissociation. Thus, her sharing of her three thoughts following my disclosure reflected a greater capacity for intersubjectivity than I had realized.

In the next session, she spoke of a noisy roommate who left her belongings all over their apartment. Thinking anxiously of my self-disclosure and having trouble finding words, I said awkwardly, "People keep putting their . . . their stuff in your space. Did it feel like I did that too, telling you about my surgeries?" She said that it did not, but that "putting their stuff in my space" was exactly her experience with many people. Whether it felt that way with me too, something new was happening, because we were talking about it together, and I was showing her through my words and my affect that I cared about how my revelation had felt for her. And we were talking about the interaction in terms ("stuff," "space") that captured its physical as well as its psychical essence. Together, we were growing a vocabulary for the places where affect and soma intersected, where interpersonal struggles were felt in the mind and the body, and where we could reflect together on how we impacted each other.

Julia came to speak about her "three thoughts" following my self-disclosure (you – us – me, overlapping but distinct) as a "three-part guide to relationships." Her ability to take in and make use of what had happened between us amazed me. She spoke of a friend who had canceled plans with her at the last minute. "I've always experienced things like that as abandonment," she reflected. "But maybe that's not what it is for the other person. It could be something else, like maybe she isn't good at time management." We continued to refer to her "three-part guide" as it applied to other relationships, and revisited how it had emerged from ours. We had both learned something about holding the tension between inside and outside, how to use your inside to know the other, all the while knowing that you can never truly be inside someone else's experience.

Discussion

While attending to somatic communication is an important aspect of any treatment, it is particularly salient in the treatment of eating disorders, disorders of self-regulation that center on the body. In this chapter, I have attempted to show how attunement to somatic communication allowed for important changes in the psychoanalytic process with Julia. A physical sensation of tightness in an old scar simultaneously signaled and created a new resonance between us, a body-to-body mirroring that allowed me, powerfully, to connect to something that Julia was feeling in her own body. This led to an internal reverie in which I found myself a new mother once again, coping with the dual stressors of recovering from abdominal surgery and caring for a baby who wouldn't stop crying. My reverie lined up uncannily with the experience of going to visit Julia in the hospital and finding myself in a maternity ward, surrounded by new mothers and faced with Julia's disjunctive experience of having others think she was one too. Against the background of all that hopeful newness, her loss and anguish were thrown into high relief.

I continued to draw upon my body-generated reverie to help me ride out the storm of Julia's implacable distress for weeks after the surgeries. Bromberg (2011) refers to this kind of process as " 'living through the mess' – a mess that can be affectively felt as such by the analyst and through which he hangs in relationally" (p. 80). Gradually, as I worked to contain both Julia's affective storm and my own worry over her anger toward me, I came to recognize the part I had played in the enactment, doing certain things that were unusual for me, out of a need to be seen. It was the same need to be seen that arose from four months of desperately trying to calm a baby who wouldn't calm down. It was the same need to be seen that Julia herself had experienced throughout her life, with her parents, her friends and eventually her therapist. Finally, I think I did see her, or saw a part of her I hadn't seen before, and this allowed her to see a new part of me too. I felt the "something disgusting," that which could not be put into words, in my own flesh, and I revealed it to her through my messy self-disclosure. Together, we found a mind-body language in which to communicate, part of a developing "relational unconscious – a shared therapeutic space in which old truths can be reorganized into new patterns of self/other meaning" (Bromberg, 2011 p. 97).

Julia's case tangibly illustrates the relationship between the psyche and the soma in psychoanalytic psychotherapy. Her inchoate inner pain and disgustingness came to manifest as a festering wound on the outside of her body, more accessible but no less deep. In treatments that do not take such dramatic turns, the use of our own body experiences to connect to and understand those of our patients is still important, even crucial, as more subtle body states are good places for dissociated aspects of self to hide. By living through our "mess," a process of relational and bodily rupture and repair, we found connection that had been wanting earlier in the treatment. At the same time, as Julia so wisely reminded me, we could understand each other only if we recognized the limits to that understanding. The child, in the context of a good enough caregiving relationship, experiences moments of mismatch that help her come to see the mother as a subjective other. In the potential space between self and other, she gradually and safely learns to self-regulate. For Julia and me, it was in going from outside to inside, from skin to psyche, that we found a way of being both inside and outside each other.

References

Anzieu, D. (1985). *The skin ego*. New Haven, CT: Yale University Press.

Aron, L. (1998). The clinical body and the reflexive mind. In L. Aron & F. S. Anderson (Eds.), *Relational perspectives on the body* (pp. 9–37). Hillsdale, NJ: Analytic Press.

Bach, S. (2016, April). *The disembodied self: Dysregulation and feelings of unreality*. Paper presented at the Norbert Freedman Memorial Lecture at the Institute for Psychoanalytic Training and Research, New York.

Balint, M. (1968). *The basic fault: Therapeutic aspects of regression*. London, England: Tavistock.

Beebe, B., & Lachmann, F. (1994). Representation and internalization in infancy: Three principles of salience. *Psychoanalytic Psychology*, *11*, 127–165.

Beebe, B., & Lachmann, F. M. (1998). Co-constructing inner and relational processes: Self- and mutual regulation in infant research and adult treatment. *Psychoanalytic Psychology*, *15*, 480–516.

Beebe, B., Lachmann, F. M., & Jaffe, J. (1997). Mother-infant interaction structures and presymbolic self- and object representations. *Psychoanalytic Dialogues*, *7*, 133–182.

Benjamin, J. (1988). *The bonds of love*. New York: Pantheon.
Benjamin, J. (1990). An outline of intersubjectivity: The development of recognition. *Psychoanalytic Psychology, 7S*, 33–46.
Benjamin, J. (2010). Where's the gap and what's the difference? The relational view of intersubjectivity, multiple selves, and enactments. *Contemporary Psychoanalysis, 46*, 112–119.
Boris, H. N. (1984). The problem of anorexia nervosa. *International Journal of Psycho-Analysis, 65*, 315–322.
Bromberg, P. M. (2001). Treating patients with symptoms – and symptoms with patience: Reflections on shame, dissociation, and eating disorders. *Psychoanalytic Dialogues, 11*, 891–912.
Bromberg, P. M. (2011). *The shadow of the tsunami and the growth of the relational mind*. New York: Routledge.
Bruch, H. (1973). *Eating disorders: Obesity, anorexia nervosa, and the person within*. New York: Basic Books.
Bucci, W. (1985). Dual coding: A cognitive model for psychoanalytic research. *Journal of the American Psychoanalytic Association, 33*, 571–608.
Bucci, W. (2011). The interplay of subsymbolic and symbolic processes in psychoanalytic treatment: It takes two to tango – but who knows the steps, who's the leader? The choreography of psychoanalytic interchange. *Psychoanalytic Dialogues, 21*, 45–54.
Cohn, J., & Tronick, E. Z. (1989). Specificity of infants' response to mothers' affective behavior. *Journal of the American Academy of Child and Adolescent Psychiatry, 28*, 242–248.
Da Silva, G. (1990). Borborygmi as markers of psychic work during the analytic session: A contribution to Freud's 'Experience of satisfaction' and to Bion's idea about the digestive model for the thinking apparatus. *International Journal of Psycho-Analysis, 71*, 641–659.
Ekman, P., Levenson, R., & Friesen, W. (1983). Autonomic nervous system activity distinguishes among emotions. *Science, 221*, 1208–1210.
Federici-Nebbiosi, S., & Nebbiosi, G. (2001). The experience of another body on our body in psychoanalysis: Commentary on Paper by Jon Sletvold. *Psychoanalytic Dialogues, 22*, 430–436.
Gianino, A., & Tronick, E. (1988). The mutual regulation model: The infant's self and interactive regulation and coping and defensive capacities. In T. Field, P. McCabe, & N. Schneiderman (Eds.), *Stress and coping* (pp. 47–68). Hillsdale, NJ: Erlbaum.
Krystal, H. (1988). *Integration and self-healing*. Hillsdale, NJ: The Analytic Press.
Lax, R. F. (1980). The rotten core: A defect in the formation of the self during the rapprochement subphase. In R. F. Lax, S. Bach, & J. A. Burland (Eds.), *Rapprochement: The critical subphase of separation-individuation* (pp. 439–456). New York: Jason Aronson, Inc.
McDougall, J. (2001). The psychic economy of addiction. In J. Petrucelli & C. Stuart (Eds.), *Hungers and compulsions: The psychodynamic treatment of eating disorders and addictions* (pp. 5–26). New York: Jason Aronson, Inc.
Nebbiosi, G., & Federici-Nebbiosi, S. (2008). "We" got rhythm: Miming and the polyphony of identity in psychoanalysis. In F. S. Anderson (Ed.), *Bodies in treatment: The unspoken dimension*. New York: Analytic Press.
Ogden, T. H. (1994). The analytic third: Working with intersubjective clinical facts. *International Journal of Psychoanalysis, 75*, 3–19.
Sander, L. (1977). The regulation of exchange in the infant-caretaker system and some aspects of the context-content relationship. In M. Lewis & L. Rosenblum (Eds.),

Interaction, conversation, and the development of language (pp. 133–156). New York: Wiley-Blackwell.
Sander, L. (1983). Polarity paradox and the organizing process in development. In J. D. Call, E. Galenson, & R. Tyson (Eds.), *Frontiers of infant psychiatry* (pp. 315–327). New York: Basic Books.
Schore, A. N. (2001). Effects of a secure attachment relationship on right brain development, affect regulation, and infant mental health. *Infant Mental Health Journal, 22*, 7–66.
Schore, A. N. (2003). *Affect dysregulation and disorders of the self.* New York: Norton.
Sletvold, J. (2011). "The reading of emotional expression": Wilhelm Reich and the history of embodied analysis. *Psychoanalytic Dialogues*, *21*, 453–467.
Stern, D. B. (1983). Unformulated experience: From familiar chaos to creative disorder. *Contemporary Psychoanalysis*, *19*, 71–99.
Stone, M. (2006). The analyst's body as tuning fork: Embodied resonance in countertransference. *Journal of Analytical Psychology*, *51*, 109–124.
Tronick, E. (1989). Emotions and emotional communication in infants. *American Psychologist*, *44*, 122–119.
Tronick, E. Z. (2003). "Of course all relationships are unique": How co-creative processes generate unique mother-infant and patient-therapist relationships and change other relationships. *Psychoanalytic Inquiry*, *23*, 473–491.
Wallin, D. J. (2007). *Attachment in psychotherapy*. New York: Guilford Press.
Winnicott, D. W. (1949). *Through paediatrics to psycho-analysis* (pp. 243–254). New York: Basic Books, 1975.
Winnicott, D. W. (1951). *Playing and reality* (pp. 1–25). New York: Basic Books, 1971.
Winnicott, D. W. (1953). Transitional objects and transitional phenomena: A study of the first not-me possession. *International Journal of Psycho-Analysis*, *34*, 89–97.
Winnicott, D. W. (1969). The use of an object. *International Journal of Psychoanalysis*, *50*, 711–716.

9

ON TARGETING EMOTION REGULATION DEFICITS IN EATING DISORDERS THROUGH DEFENSE ANALYSIS[1]

Timothy Rice

Introduction and proposal

Introduction

Adolescent anorexia nervosa is among the deadliest of psychiatric disorders (Arcelus, Mitchell, Wales, & Nielsen, 2011). Despite its morbidity and mortality, a restricted range of therapeutic options exists for individuals with this disorder. Existing approaches leave room for improvement (Lock, 2011). The predominantly behavioral, family-based options often yield modest clinical gains (Campbell & Peebles, 2014) and may not deliver optimal change beyond core behavioral constructs. Given the high level of need in this patient population, why are so few treatment options available?

One reason may derive from the negative reactions that adolescents with anorexia nervosa commonly invoke in their treating clinicians. These responses may drive clinicians away from working in individual psychotherapy with this population. Clinicians across professional disciplines often experience very negative emotions in working with individuals with anorexia nervosa and other eating disorders (Thompson-Brenner, Satir, Franko, & Herzog, 2012). Feelings of frustration, hopelessness, incompetence, and worry are common. In fact, "emotional exhaustion" is the most common reason for burnout in the treatment of individuals with eating disorders (Warren, Schafer, Crowley, & Olivardia, 2013). Trainees and early-career professionals may be particularly susceptible to this fate (Satir, 2013). This burnout-susceptible younger generation may also be the one most open to engaging in research that could create evidence-based psychodynamic approaches, which creates a problem for the survival of psychodynamic treatment approaches in the field of eating disorders.

Instead, the academic field of eating disorders remains mostly behavioral- and family-based. These approaches deemphasize the patient-provider relationship as the medium of change, which allows both therapist and patient to distance themselves from emotions that are difficult to tolerate. Working through the family provides further distance, as does the rational algorithmic relatedness emphasized in traditional behavioralism. Whereas these parameters may enable clinicians to protect themselves from burnout, they fail to understand the patient-provider relationship as a valuable point of entry to effecting change.

Attachment-based psychodynamic psychotherapies

Despite the challenges psychodynamic psychotherapy faces in working with individuals with eating disorders, valuable contributions have been made. Tasca and Balfour (2014) authored an elegant portrayal of a psychodynamic model based on attachment theory. Their use of attachment theory provides a validated, promising framework for their model (Bucci, Roberts, Danquah, & Berry, 2015). Their model also gracefully incorporates intrapsychic concepts of affect and defense (p. 266). Insecure attachments are seen as promoting disordered affect regulation strategies and as predisposing patients to reverting to defensive eating-disordered behaviors.

In her thoughtful discussion of Tasca and Balfour's model, Thompson-Brenner (2014) notes that though attachment insecurity may promote disordered affect regulation strategies, the relationship of both to eating disorders is in all probability multidirectional. That is, affect regulation deficits may be of equal importance in the maintenance of eating disorders. In fact, they may even be more important. Thompson-Brenner writes, "If one factor such as emotion regulation proves to be the strongest predictor of eating-disordered symptoms and a stronger influence on attachment insecurity/reflective functioning than vice versa, then an approach that specifically and directly promotes the skills of emotion regulation may be a more direct route to improvement across domains" (p. 279). Though future research examining this proposition of a "more direct route" would be of interest, we know now that both disordered attachment and emotion regulation deficits may warrant address in individual work with patients with eating disorders. Contemporary psychodynamic approaches may benefit from the flexibility to address both.

A proposal: targeting the emotion regulation deficits of eating disorders through operationalized defense analysis

This paper proposes that, as a complement and balance to two-person, attachment-oriented developments in psychodynamic psychotherapy, a defense-focused approach to patients with anorexia nervosa shows promise. A defense-focused approach offers an opportunity to address the emotion regulation deficits observed in individuals with eating disorders.

This approach involves an empathic procedure in which the provider assumes an experience-near relatedness to the patient that recognizes and respects the patient's self-protective measures. This is in contrast to older analytic models of bypassing the defenses, such as going for "deep" interpretations and playing the game of trying to guess what's on the patient's mind or failing to recognize and respect the patient's means of self-protection as their best mode of survival. This approach highlights empathy and discourages defensiveness and direct confrontation with the patient. This assists the clinician in acknowledging his or her own negative feelings as often products of a patient's defenses and thus promotes the clinician's empathy for the patient.

This approach is theorized to address emotion regulation deficits. This proposition originated with the observation of the similarities between the psychodynamic defense mechanism construct and the implicit emotion regulation system (Rice & Hoffman, 2014). This observation enables a theoretical means for a psychodynamic approach to be based within a neurobiological developmental framework. Testing of this hypothesis through assessing for change in validated rating scales of emotion regulation capacities through a defense-focused approach is under way. Future assessment of changes in the underlying defined neural correlates of implicit emotion regulation through this approach is possible.

In the defense-focused model, clinical dysfunction in individuals with eating disorders is understood to arise from too rigid a reliance upon a restricted set of maladaptive defense mechanisms. For example, an adolescent with bulimia nervosa may purge to provide relief from painful feelings. In many cases, the adolescent employs defense mechanisms, such as criticizing, provoking, or attacking the clinician, to avoid processing painful material. Addressing these defense mechanisms provides a point of entry into the patient's maladaptive self-regulatory style. Persistent and gentle noticing with the patient of the patient's maladaptive defenses will lessen the rigidity and tenacity by which the individual is forced to aggressively defend. Alternate self-regulatory styles will develop when the self-defeating styles are divested of their power. Through maintaining a stable presence and resisting enactment, the clinician demonstrates that the feared painful affect from which the eating-disordered individual defends will not overwhelm the clinician, nor the patient. The painful, defended feeling can begin to be accepted, and when these feeling states are less fiercely defended against, the patient will begin to explore and to integrate alternate modes of self-regulation. These interventions occur upon a background of developmental help (Freud, 1974).

In the parallel language of affective neuroscience, blockades in the normative developmental thrust of the implicit emotion regulation system become undone. Adopting this language for contemporary psychodynamic psychiatry yields benefits. A brain-based, dimensional framework of health and illness is in greater synchrony with contemporary directions in research and funding (Insel, 2014; Insel et al., 2010). This offers a psychodynamic approach an exceptional advantage in contemporary models of care delivery, as well as the ability to integrate services with modern medicine. The neuropsychiatric foundation of the emotion regulation system may become the target of biological agents and targeted procedures such as transcranial magnetic stimulation; it would be of benefit to the field of psychodynamic psychiatry to position a targeted psychotherapy as among those procedures.

The implicit emotion regulation system and defenses against painful affect

Emotion regulation is defined as the capacity to shape which emotions one has, when one has them, and how one experiences or expresses them (Gross, 2014). There is a rich history of research and development of this construct dating back now over three decades (Gross, 2013). The more recent definition of the implicit branch of the emotion regulation system (Gyurak, Gross, & Etkin, 2011) is important for psychodynamic psychiatry. This sub-system has defined neural correlates that are distinct from explicit emotion regulation processes: more ventromedial regions of the prefrontal cortex regulate lower limbic reactivity and hyperarousal (Etkin, Büchel, & Gross, 2015). What we observe clinically are the system's automatic constituent processes that function to regulate emotion "without the need for conscious supervision or explicit intentions" (Koole & Rothermund, 2011).

These processes are similar to the analytic concept of defense mechanisms (Freud, 1936). The observation of this similarity (Rice & Hoffman, 2014) has previously been absent in the modern defense literature (Hentschel, Smith, Draguns, & Ehlers, 2004) but is apparent when formulating defenses as protective measures against painful affective states. This unique conceptualization originates within the clinical developments in child analysis of Berta Bornstein (1945, 1949) and the subsequent line of work of child analysts to the present (Becker, 1974; Hoffman, 2007). Hoffman's leadership in driving the development of an operationalized form of this procedure (Hoffman, 1989, 2000, 2007, 2014) yielded an approach capable of manualization (Hoffman & Rice with Prout, 2016). Overlaying defense analysis with the implicit emotion regulation system offers one opportunity to integrate psychoanalytic theory with affective neuroscience, a potentially meaningful pursuit (e.g., Kernberg, 2006).

Integration with an attachment-based approach

Just as Tasca and Balfour's model (Tasca & Balfour, 2014) incorporates the role of emotion regulation deficits, this defense-focused approach also incorporates a two-person, attachment-based model of the mind. Developmental delays in the emotion regulation system derive from a combination of constitutional and environmental influences in the form of the caregiver-child interaction (Calkins & Hill, 2009). Environmental influences in the shape of dyadic interactions have been an interest in the psychoanalytical literature since the time of Anna Freud. Her concept of developmental lines underscored dyadic exchanges between mother and child around positive and negative affect (pleasure and pain) as formative for regulatory control and development (Freud, 1963). Recognition of the importance of "the emotional rapport of the mother's nurturant care" and emotional mutual cueing (Mahler, 1968) remained salient up to and including recent psychoanalytically informed thinking (Fonagy, Gergely, Jurist, & Target, 2004).

The defense-focused approach assumes this developmental perspective and aims to advance normative development of self-regulatory capacities. In the analytically informed literature, Phebe Cramer (1991, 2006) showed a normative developmental progression of defense mechanism style and flexibility from infancy to adulthood. Parallel findings of developmental progression exist in the neuroscience literature on emotion regulation (Stegge & Terwogt, 2007). Each individual likely has a unique mix of constitutional and environmental contributions to developmental delays in self-regulatory capabilities. These are the targets of a defense-focused approach that serve to complement and to flexibly integrate into the work of attachment-based therapies as one productive psychodynamically informed intervention among many.

Considerations that support the applicability of a defense-focused approach to individuals with eating disorders

Negative clinician feelings

The defense-focused approach originated in working with young children with disruptive behavior disorders (Hoffman & Rice with Prout, 2016). Importing this approach to adolescents and other individuals with eating disorders has face validity. Despite the superficially different picture of the adolescent with anorexia, often female and with internalizing symptoms, and the disruptive child, usually a male child with externalizing symptoms, these two groups share important similarities. Caring for both populations is defined by mostly behavior- and family-based approaches. For example, just as parent management training (PMT) is the mainstay treatment of oppositional defiant disorder (ODD) and other externalizing disorders of childhood (Steiner & Remsing, 2007), there exists the aforementioned dominance of behaviorism and family-based therapy (FBT; Lock & Le Grange, 2013) in the eating disorder field.

It has been noted that these qualities of the healthcare delivery system may be a product of negative clinician reactions to working with these individuals. In work with disruptive, taunting, and oppositional children, failures to understand aggression and disruptive behavior as children's means of protecting themselves against painful affects – "the best defense is a good offense" – leads to negative feelings in the clinician (Hoffman & Rice with Prout, 2016). Whereas in some individuals with eating disorders attacks are direct, in others these attacks may be covert or directed towards the self. The distribution of aggression may exist in a spectrum that includes patients with bulimia nervosa, anorexia nervosa, binge-eating disorder, and other unspecified eating disorders.

Regardless of the mode of aggression, the defense-focused perspective suggests that the destructive relatedness and behaviors of some individuals with eating disorders may best be understood as the individual's means of self-preservation. This empathic stance allows clinicians to understand the meaning and function of their negative feelings. This may reduce clinician defensiveness, experience of distress, and ultimately, burnout. When these negative affects are so prevalent in the eating disorder field and may drive avoidance, this may generate new possibilities for further development in psychodynamic approaches to the treatment of eating disorders

Historical and contemporary precedents in the psychiatric literature

There is a historical precedent to understanding eating disorders as disorders of impaired emotion regulation. In the earliest modern descriptions of anorexia nervosa, the defensive aspect of the refusal to eat was emphasized. Anorexia nervosa was first described in a modern scientific manner by Lasègue and Gull (Vandereycken & van Deth, 1989). Lasègue, writing from France, described the anorexic as "a young girl . . . [who] suffers from some emotion which she avows or conceals" (Lasegue, 1873). In contrast to his contemporary Englishman Sir William Gull (1874), whose remedies were medicinal and included cinchona, bichloride of mercury, and citrate of quinine, Lasègue formulated the lack of appetite as a wish to avoid pain. Whereas Gull focused on the medical, Lasègue went into great detail into the disorder's psychological aspects and its associated family dynamics. Elements of this unfortunate split in understanding of the disorder exist to this day.

These two early modernist perspectives did not integrate anorexia nervosa into hysteria and other contemporary illness constructs. This set an additional precedent for modern psychiatry (Lawrence, 2008). Even today anorexia nervosa and other eating disorders are in a section of their own in major classification systems (American Psychiatric Association, 2013). This separation from other disorders of anxiety and affect may have impeded the role of delayed emotion regulation in the disorder: the focus falls on the eating behavior rather than on the commonalities of this disorder with other psychiatric conditions of disturbed affect regulation.

The emerging interest in the Research Domain Criteria (RDoC) project of the National Institute of Mental Health (Insel, 2014; Insel et al., 2010) may mend this split. This perspective provides categorical psychiatric disorders a fresh opportunity to become increasingly understood within a transdiagnostic, brain-based perspective. There is emerging evidence that anorexia nervosa is tightly integrated with deficits in emotion regulation (Racine & Wildes, 2013, 2015a, 2015b), which builds on contemporary formulations concerning the importance of disordered affect regulation in the maintenance of eating disorders (Taylor, Bagby, & Parker, 1997; Wildes, Ringham, & Marcus, 2010). A recent review of anorexia nervosa and bulimia nervosa (Lavender et al., 2015) demonstrates that emotion regulation deficits are important in both disorders, and that it may in fact be differences in emotion regulation that distinguish these two eating disorders from each other.

Historical and contemporary precedents from the psychodynamic literature

Freud himself, in the case history of the Ratman (Freud, 1918), initiated the concept of defensive avoidance in the analytic literature when he briefly mentioned anorexia nervosa as a normative neurosis in girls at puberty in which a fear of sex leads to anorexia nervosa (p. 106). This "regression" hypothesis neglects the importance of affect. The sexual and aggressive drive focus on early psychoanalytic models are a barrier to integration with the affective neurosciences and more contemporary models of academic psychiatry (Kernberg, 2006).

Theory developed through Freud's understanding of anorexia nervosa as a "normal" neurosis of childhood (Lawrence, 2008). This influenced Anna Freud's evaluation of the disorder in her efforts to understand normative childhood development. Anna Freud helped move the early emphasis strictly on sexual development into an evaluation of ego functions and adaptation. Her emphasis on defense (Freud, 1936), and the later incorporation of this perspective by Berta Bornstein (1945, 1949), forms the foundation for a defense-focused approach.

Bornstein's approach understood defenses as protective measures against painful feelings in children. This approach demonstrated that addressing the child's defenses against painful emotions instead of directly confronting the child's unwelcome thoughts and fantasies, will promote a connection with the child in a much more sensitive and, thus, effective way. With this approach, it is the child's defensive maneuvers against painful feelings, rather than the painful feelings themselves, that are the focus of exploration. These maneuvers are respected and are only eventually communicated to the child in a careful, respectful, and developmentally appropriate way, with the goal of approaching a situation where the child feels less threatened by painful feeling states. The child then feels in greater control of him or herself, leading to greater mastery of affects and more adaptive interactions with the environment.

In the psychodynamic eating disorders literature, it was the foundational work of Bruch (1963a, 1963b, 1973), and later Goodsitt (1983) and Grotstein (1999) which described deficits in affect acceptance/awareness and regulation in individuals with eating disorders. Much of the contemporary psychodynamic thought in eating disorders was influenced through the developments of Katherine Zerbe (Zerbe, 1993a, 1993b, 2008, 2015) and are of great value.

In a defense-focused approach, the lessons of these works are valued while a focus on defense analysis is also maintained. Developmental interventions and a broad range of contemporary psychodynamic techniques are included within a framework of "developmental help" (Freud, 1974). Within this background, the operationalized focus on defenses remains in the forefront. This operationalized approach, grounded in the work of Bornstein, is paralleled by the "affect phobia" model (Mccullough, 1997) in the short-term psychodynamic psychotherapeutic literature. There, defense is also understood as one means of avoiding a feared or painful affect or anxiety. Modern, empirically supported models of defense mechanisms also inform the work (Vaillant, Bond, & Vaillant, 1986), as do these models' further developments (Bond, 1986; Bond & Perry, 2004; Perry & Cooper, 1989). Phebe Cramer's empirical studies (1991, 2006) concerning the development of defenses in children and other systematic work regarding defenses in children (Laor, Wolmer, & Cicchetti, 2001; Wolmer, Laor, & Cicchetti, 2001) have also been informative.

Contemporary examples

Hoffman (2014) notes that many writers employ defense analysis. This is indeed the case in the eating disorders literature. For example, Goodsitt (1983) posits that starvation, binging, vomiting, and hyperkinetic activity may be understood as a means to drown out states of overstimulation or fragmentation. Bers and colleagues (2013), informed by Blatt (2008), understand restriction as a defense against anaclitic longings. The appearance of this conflict in the transference is understood as the mechanism of change. Washington (2004) identifies resistances in the anorexic individual against threatening stimuli, depressive anxieties, and conflicts as the central organizing principle of working with these individuals. Ritvo also supports a defensive orientation through identifying anger and rage as the feared affect (Ritvo, 1976). Perspectives that emphasize defense extend beyond ego psychology and its derivatives. Steiner (1990), for example, writes from a post-Kleinian perspective about defenses against unbearable guilt and anxiety. Boris (1984a; Boris, 1984b) also works from a Kleinian perspective in identifying hunger and weight-related obsessions as a manic defense against excessive pain and longing (Lawrence, 2001).

Identification of defense analysis as a consistent theme among multiple perspectives yields further indication that an evidence-based approach organized around this psychodynamically informed paradigm is of value. When psychoanalysis risks some loss through fragmentation via pluralism, the commonality of defenses among all these approaches may be of value.

Case illustration: a defense-focused approach in an adolescent with anorexia nervosa

Introductory considerations

A focused illustration of work with an adolescent with anorexia nervosa follows. This case history is provided to show the approach as a model of working with individuals with eating disorders.

In working with individuals with eating disorders, myriad defenses are at play. These include acting out, rationalization, denial, withholding, and lying (Wilson, 1988). Projective identification is also common and is the means by which the eating-disordered individual defends against perceived therapeutic intrusions into autonomy and independence.

Malan (1979) describes how the structure of the patient's conflict permits the individual to choose either the experience of anxiety, the experience of the avoided painful affect, or the employment of defense. In the individual with anorexia nervosa, we might understand the food restriction to be a defense against a myriad of hidden and unacceptable feelings to the individual. We might also understand it to be the means by which the anorexic attacks when threatened of his or her autonomy. Through defenses analysis, the aggression of the individual with anorexia nervosa can be met without unduly inflicting painful narcissistic injury. Rather than bypass defense and directly confront the unmetabolized and unwelcome thoughts and fantasies, the therapist comments on defense, thereby connecting with the adolescent in a more sensitive and effective way.

The defense-focused approach is systematically applied in an operationalized manner. A focus is always maintained upon the defenses. Through a sustained focus on defenses and affect regulation, this approach organizes the patient and keeps the focus in the here and now. This can be especially helpful for individuals with eating disorders who may tend to dissociate, intellectualize, or use other avoidance behaviors to detach from the treatment. This approach also enables clinicians to address the patient's full complement of concerns rather than restricting intervention to disordered eating alone. Anorexia nervosa is highly comorbid with anxiety and depressive disorders. A focus upon affect regulation deficits enables these commonly comorbid conditions to be addressed as well.

Individuals are complex, and despite the fact that this procedure is operationalized and capable of manualization for individuals, including adolescents with eating disorders, it is flexible enough to target the full range of each individual's needs in a way that protocols focused upon disordered eating alone cannot. This is in alignment with the emerging models of psychiatric care that are transdiagnostic, dimensionally focused and rooted in brain-based biology. It is hoped that the following material illustrates this flexibility.

Case material

An anxious teenager of seventeen with diagnoses of anorexia nervosa and obsessive compulsive disorder was referred for individual therapy when she was deemed inappropriate for ongoing academic specialty care because, among many reasons, she was "too angry."

Following an onset of clinically significant symptoms of anorexia nervosa around age thirteen and their worsening around age fifteen, this adolescent was enrolled in a specialized family-based program at sixteen. She fought with the program and proved to be a "difficult" patient. No-shows were common and weight loss accelerated. The patient was ultimately hospitalized when palpitations onset secondary to severe malnourishment and self-starvation.

Her inpatient program facilitated weight restoration. At the end of a nearly three-month-long inpatient stay and once weight had been restored, she was prescribed the antidepressant medication fluoxetine to target her anxiety. She was felt to be inappropriate for ongoing care in her established program owing to the intensity with which she attacked her cognitive behavioral therapist in angry rages. Her family declined a recommendation for residential treatment.

In response a new support team was created. This team included weekly visits with an adolescent nutritionist, every-two-week visits with a pediatrician, and ultimately, twice weekly visits with a psychiatrist. An intervention that addressed the meanings of the adolescent's anger was felt to be crucial to her recovery and, thus, the approach described in this paper was chosen.

In her first session, the teen immediately assumed an angry and attacking posture. Her offensive began on the topic of her medication adherence. She taunted the clinician that "You can't make me take it; I will stop it . . . I will weigh nothing, and I will die." This was the pattern that had been reported by her previous treatment team. The clinician moved quickly to help the teen see the patterned quality of her behavior. The intent was to later move to the meaning behind her repetitions of this stance; for now it was to remain experience-near. The clinician said that it was easier to provoke and attack the provider (defense) than to simply look at the issue of the medication (feared affect). With discussion she was helped to see that many (unknown) feelings surrounded the issue of the medication, and that it was easier to avoid these by attacking the clinician. In trying to put words to these feelings, issues of her autonomy came up. She was helped to see how far she was willing to go to avoid these painful concerns about her autonomy, even to the limit of death. Though the clinician could not force the patient to take the medication, he could help her to understand the factors that made up her wish to reject it, helping her to make a better-informed decision on her own. Of course, her obstinacy over her medication mirrored her refusals to eat.

To facilitate the patient's understanding of her tendency to fight as a means of avoiding more painful feelings, the provider discussed with the patient the merits of inviting her mother into a session to review the new collaboratively developed plan for the patient's medication adherence. The clinician explicitly invited the patient to reflect upon her own behavior and anger once the mother entered the room, anticipating that the loud escalations between the mother and child that were described by the cognitive behavioral therapists would immediately manifest. As anticipated, the patient entered a rage. She said that no one, and especially not her mother, could make her take her medication. The adolescent in the session to this point and in prior telephone conversations around scheduling had been quite organized, responsible with keeping times and following up on paperwork, and quite adept in her ability to alienate an entire specialty eating disorder division; now, she stuck out her tongue at her mother, parroted her mother's language in a mocking tone, and regressed into a babyish whine. The mother's introduction into the session, though an untraditional intervention for a teenager in psychodynamic psychotherapy, underscores the flexibility of this approach. It tested the clinician's emerging hypothesis that the patient's angry behaviors served to protect her from severe regressions to dependency that, for reasons to be explored, wrought shame, discomfort, and other severe negative affects. This clinician's experience of the repetitive, attacking pattern employed by the patient provided further reassurance that, moving forward, he could take comfort and refrain from becoming defensive, even when he felt he had made mistakes and was criticized and attacked for them.

Following that first session the patient chose to continue with her medication. In fact, over the course of approximately two months, she took ownership of it. She accepted its titration from a moderate level (30mg) to its maximum daily dose (80mg). She recognized that the medication helped to reduce her anxieties, intrusive thoughts, and experiences that she described as panic attacks. Repeated commenting upon her tendency to fight to avoid emotional distress relieved some of the intensity of her upset in these sessions. She gradually began to be able to acknowledge her anger and to describe the things that made her so angry in her life.

As treatment continued, the patient's mother continued to be engaged through separate parent meetings and telephone conversations. The patient attended all sessions and developed a closer engagement with the clinician. Very quickly she ceased fighting with the clinician and spent much of the time in sessions expressing her frustration about feeling isolated from her family and friends, who didn't "get" her and her eating. In contrast the provider "seemed to always know just what to say." Often, the clinician just reflected back and listened. This switch from fighting to idealization was not addressed until it became problematic to the treatment. Increasingly, the patient would end her associations by abruptly stopping and saying, "Oh, I'm not ready to share that." At those times she would in humor change the topic in a stereotyped way (e.g., "So, how about the weather!"). This demonstrated her insight into her reliance on defenses against uncomfortable affects; she became capable of poking fun at herself and of accepting her imperfections.

At the same time, she described profound isolation after sessions. She would say that she hated attending her sessions, yet she felt she never had enough time with the provider. Ultimately, the patient arrived for one of her standing sessions at the correct time of day but exactly 24 hours early. The provider had 15 minutes before another patient on that day. There were several options. The clinician considered speaking to the patient in the waiting room, having the patient into the office for a brief check-in, or not speaking to her at all. Her presentation was understood as meaningful; her act may have been related to a wish to be seen or be close that, if directly experienced, could trigger intense shame and put the patient at risk for not showing for her appointment the following day. As such, the clinician opted to invite her into the office for brief support and interventions intended to increase the chances that she would still present for her session on the following day. The risk of the loss of the tight adherence to the treatment structure was felt to outweigh the benefit of being able to show to the patient that she need not be embarrassed.

The reaction of the front desk staff at the clinic where she was treated had already clued her in to the incorrect timing. As anticipated, she arrived in a near panic, unable to understand how she could have made such a mistake. "I don't understand; this is so unlike me. I always get everything right; how could I make this mistake," she said. The provider did not interpret but, instead, simply said that he would look forward to seeing the patient for a full session at their scheduled time. He asked her to recognize the part of her that will wish to stay home and to do exactly the opposite by attending. This directive and supportive stance was felt to better help the patient than a defense interpretation of her new tendency to beat herself up instead of attacking the clinician. This interpretation would be left for the following session.

The following day the patient did arrive on time. She was in an excruciatingly anxious state. She verbalized how badly she had desperately wanted not to show up, but that she knew that the provider would be disappointed in her had she not. Favoring the defense interpretation over the transference interpretation, the provider remarked that it was easier to attribute her disappointment to the clinician than to herself. The patient was asked whether she understood any meaning in her mistake. She associated that she had returned that night and eaten a cookie from her mother's kitchen. When asked, she clarified that she understood this as loosening of her caloric restrictions. She reported that it evoked for her fears of reversion to the uncontrolled binging and vomiting which she had engaged in leading up to her hospitalization. She reported that she then felt miserable about her choice, commenting that she felt she was losing control of herself. When asked if the clinician played a role in this, she could only say that she feared the clinician thought that she appeared fat.

The clinician felt that a connection was now clear between her dependency wishes, their unacceptability, her resultant anxieties, and her defensive retreat into concerns about appearance and weight. Yet the clinician did not want to make this "experience distant" interpretation. Instead, he asked if the patient felt that her association to the story of the cookie had any relevance to what she was feeling in the room.

The patient went on to say that she no longer could stand feeling so alone in her life and that she had romantic interests for the clinician. She was fearful that her love would destroy her treatment. The patient was reminded that in therapy there was safety to talk about these feelings without acting on them. She went on to describe feeling that she was "black inside," that if she allowed the clinician to truly see how disturbed she was, he would be horrified and terminate the treatment, and then she would be left alone. The clinician reminded the patient that though her frequent fighting had led her to often feel abandoned, only her inability to maintain a safe weight or other safety concerns would provoke an interruption to the care. After leaving the hospital while awaiting establishment of her new outpatient treatment team, the patient had been eating only 200 calories a day: black coffee in the morning, a hard-boiled egg and coffee at lunch, and tidbits of toast at dinner. She was reminded that she had not only maintained her weight since beginning the current treatment but that she was, in fact, slowly and consistently gaining weight and emotional strength.

The clinician anticipated that his scheduled vacation in about a month from that time would require processing in advance with the patient. The themes presented by the patient, including her unlovability and her need to protect the clinician, were further developed while her ambivalence about the clinician was repeatedly pointed out. She idealized the clinician yet reported that she hated coming to sessions, for example, and though she reported hating to maintain and gain weight, she continued to do so.

Soon the patient became able to express anger at the clinician in a way that did not serve a defensive purpose. Her tentative criticisms of his messy office, his personal shortcomings, and his inability to satisfy all her needs were accepted and validated. She was helped to do this by moving her out of displacement; initially, she spoke through the displacement of a giraffe stuffed animal, who felt all these frustrations in the treatment room. She allowed herself to regress more fully in the treatment, accepting the whiny, babyish part of her self that could play with toys in the room, demand more care and comfort, yet respect the endings of session with less feelings of deprivation and shame upon returning.

That the clinician could be all-knowing yet capable of destruction by her aggression was another discrepancy pointed out but not further explored along the lines of her omnipotent fantasies, rages, and their relation to her anxieties. At the end of one session that marked four sessions before the clinician's vacation, the potential conflict that the vacation might present was discussed at length. At this point, the clinician made an error by moving beyond what the patient was experiencing at that time, that is, beyond the experience-near stance of the approach described in this paper. This may have occurred because of the clinician's guilt over his vacation. These feelings were magnified because of the strength of the patient's desire for total care and satisfaction and her rage at the clinician for failing to satisfy these desires. Processing these reactions internally helped the clinician to proceed with the treatment when the patient was ready.

After this mistake, the patient failed to show for the first of the four remaining sessions. She resurfaced for the second of the four. At that session she again appeared acutely anxious. She did not bring up her failure to show despite it standing in stark contrast to her near-complete session adherence. Instead, she began with the revelation that she had discontinued her medication four days prior, just after the time of the last session. She stated with confidence that she would no longer be taking it. The clinician felt trapped between the pull to tend to the medical problems that her abrupt discontinuation at her low weight might present and the pull to guide her in an exploration of the reasons for her oppositional nonadherence. The patient's safety was assessed as of primary importance, though it was felt that space for processing could be made in the course of the symptom-focused discussion. It was pointed out that all this medical talk prevented the provider and the patient from continuing their psychotherapeutic work. The patient admitted that this was so.

The clinician returned to the content of the first session with the patient by reminding her that she would retain control of whether to take the medication or not so long as she was safe and with her mother's consent. It was offered that perhaps she had returned to the stance of fighting. She agreed. The patient knew that the medication had significantly helped her anxiety, but that at 80mg had caused heartburn that was related to food restriction. She would make no firm commitment. The clinician opted to make a directive intervention that 60mg rather than 80mg of fluoxetine would be called in to the pharmacy for her to take should she make this choice, and that they would revisit her decision at the next session. The clinician offered that it would perhaps be of greater importance to their work together to understand the reasons for nonadherence and put aside the struggle over the medication. She agreed.

Though once again moving beyond the patient's immediately registered experience, the clinician brought up the impending weeklong break for his vacation. The risk of moving the patient beyond her immediate experience outweighed the benefit of immediately processing this threat to her adherence to the treatment. This was made more pronounced by the issue of her medication adherence. Her act of not showing also communicated that she was likely in fact very aware of the vacation and registering this already. When asked if she had remembered the vacation, the patient said yes, but quickly interceded that it would be wonderful to have the time off. Her tendency to state this after expressing feelings that the clinician was wonderful was pointed out, and she was asked if this defense was maybe easier for her to employ than experience uncomfortable feelings about the clinician. She admitted that it was so. Notably, the quality or type of feelings were not pointed out, be they anger, dependency, worry, sexual, or many other possibilities that the clinician could not know. The focus was on the defense.

The patient spent much of the session expressing disbelief that the clinician would care about her while he was gone. In response the clinician attempted to develop her emerging sense of object constancy. He reminded her that though he would be gone, that the patient would be in his thoughts. Though there would be no treatment or contact in that period, their work and its fruits would not cease to exist. The patient was encouraged to recognize her changes over the break in her everyday interactions as a means of maintaining that constancy of connection with the work. The patient left anxious, still never resolving whether she would resume her medications. With the patient's permission, the clinician called her mother to update her on the patient's break from medication adherence and to provide coverage considerations for emergencies over the clinician's vacation.

The following session, the second to last before the break, the patient failed to show. The patient's mother left a voicemail received just before the session absence. She reported that the patient had returned home after the last session, saying that she was now determined to have all four of her wisdom teeth removed at once. Though this had been discussed previously, the decision was spontaneous and impulsive. The mother admitted in the voicemail not reflecting on the many possible meanings of this behavior and accommodated her wish. The patient chose an appointment for extraction that directly conflicted with the second-to-last session before the break. The mother also reported in the voicemail that she would likely be in such pain and suffering that she would not make the final session before the vacation. At the same time, the mother reported that the patient had also indeed resumed her medication and had been taking the 60mg consistently since the last session.

The clinician returned the mother's call and clarified the details and timeline of these events. The masochistic quality of this enactment was not interpreted. Instead, the clinician left a voicemail with the patient on her cell phone in which he emphasized that it was a loss to the treatment to have had the patient not show for the session that day, that he was aware of the wisdom tooth extraction and her medication adherence, and that despite these challenges he still hoped to see her at the final visit before the scheduled week interruption in their work together.

The clinician did not address the passive into active element of the patient's behavior: that she had abandoned the clinician to save herself from feeling abandoned because of the upcoming vacation. Nor did he address her rage and decision to inflict pain upon herself, condoned by the controlled and ostensibly productive act of tooth removal. What was felt to be most important was to help the patient return to treatment and to convey a consistent, reflective, and caring attitude. On the morning of the final session before the vacation, the mother called and left a voicemail with the clinician to confirm that the patient had received his voicemail and would not attend the session.

The clinician, unexpectedly, arrived at the clinic that afternoon to find the patient in the waiting room. A full session was had in which the patient, uncomfortable and appearing modestly unwell in her pain, spontaneously said that, though she hated coming for her sessions and had had full intention that morning not to attend that afternoon, she also recognized the value of her treatment and made the committed choice to attend. Rather than get into the details of the events on the eve of the clinician's vacation, the patient was supported for her strength in facing her uncomfortable feelings and in stopping a painful enactment so that she could continue her progress in the treatment.

Discussion

This short vignette suggests that the approach described in this paper may be effective for individuals with eating disorders. Through a focus on defenses, the patient moved from a rigid reliance on fighting to a wider and more flexibly employed range of defenses, including humor. These changes coincide with a greater capacity to accept and to explore previously unacceptable affects.

The defensive maneuvers employed by a patient in psychotherapy are often present from the start. They are directly and often clearly apparent. Because they are often behavioral or associated with behavioral or mental status changes, such as a change in affect, facial expression, or shift in the thought process, they can be objectively noted and shared with the patient. Respect for the patient's self-protective defenses offers a means of nonconfrontational engagement. This may be especially productive in working with individuals, and particularly adolescents, with eating disorders. This case vignette illustrates this clinically.

The matter of the patient's decision to extract her wisdom teeth is a good focus for discussion. It shows the stance of remaining experience-near and avoiding "deep" interpretations that the defense-focused model provides. It also reveals the flexibility of this model to defer the focus on defense analysis when needed. In the place of defense analysis the therapist employed interventions from a range of the eating disorders literature and from a "developmental help" model. Whereas the defense interpretation focus is understood as the primary operationalized intervention in promoting the development of emotion regulation capabilities, global development through a broad range of interventions remains of key importance to progress.

There is literature dating to Freud (Freud, 1900) concerning the meanings of teeth (Lorand & Feldman, 1955) and their loss (Lorand, 1948; Schneck, 1979). Early writings pertained to dream content, psychosexual conflict, and castration anxieties. These symbolic translations of content are "experience-distant"; that is, they are not likely close to the patient's mind. This may be particularly the case in individuals with eating disorders; as psychodynamic psychiatry broadens to care for individuals beyond the restricted neurotic realm, its techniques must accommodate a broader range of patients and their needs. Earlier formulations of symbolism are also unhelpful in their language rooted in drive theory rather than the more contemporary affect theory that enables cross-talk with other disciplines in the natural brain sciences (Kernberg, 2006).

From the perspective of this model, it is unwise to try to "guess" what is on the patient's mind. There may be several overdetermined conflicts in the concreteness of teeth and, in particular, their loss or removal. Even when the clinician's guess is correct, the intervention does little for the patient. Such a maneuver does not respect the patient's self-protections and may leave them vulnerable to painful feelings. Patients with eating disorders may be particularly vulnerable to negative affects (Engel et al., 2013) and from the perspective of this therapeutic model should only gradually be helped towards their exploration through defense analysis.

In the case of this teen, the behavior can be understood within the restricted sphere of her fixation upon issues of weight. Her wisdom teeth's extraction may have served on the one hand as a means of enabling an unimpeachable potential for weight loss. Her pain and mechanical discomfort would impair her ability to eat, and any accusations from family or providers at weight loss would take on an uncomfortably sadistic aspect given the medical realities of the procedure. Simultaneously, the pain inflicted by the extraction served to continue a self-restrictive punishment upon the patient. By extension, it deprived her of the wished-for and feared presence of the therapist. It deprived the clinician of the security of knowing her well-being in advance of his vacation. It enabled an expression of her sadism and rage in physicality outside of sessions rather than through speech within. The extraction of the teeth served as a means not only of avoiding attendance at the sessions but also enabled a re-engagement with the mother, who through collusion enabled the patient to act out the conflict in real life. Among many other readings, the act retained many complicated dynamics in the symbolic language of oral regressive conflicts that was well known to the patient, given her eating-disordered symptoms.

The experience-near elements of the act were of greater value to address in the treatment than an introduction of any of these considerations to the patient. Instead of discussing masochistic or sadistic elements, the defensive functions of passive-into-active and identification with the aggressor of her behavior were instead communicated. This kept the focus on the here and now with the clinician, which permitted further exploration of the underlying affects within the safety and consistency of the therapeutic frame. However, this exploration was deferred until following the clinician's vacation. In alignment with Bruch's "fact-finding" interventions (Bruch, 1963c, p. 47), such an exploration is deferred when the patient is vulnerable. Vulnerability may be from risk of starvation or, in this case, disrupting the treatment. This teen's treatment had the privilege of proceeding after weight reconstitution and alongside a pediatrician and nutritionist who helped to carry and support the teen from the dangers of starvation and collapse. Abandonment of the treatment remained a real risk that required the attention of the psychiatric clinician. This was more pronounced at the time of the teen's wisdom tooth extraction given the timing of the break introduced by the vacation and the regression to enactment by the wrenching out of her teeth.

In the words of Bruch, "authoritative, simple statements as to basic facts of life, knowledge of which these patients have failed to acquire under the confusing conditions of their early development" are made before interpretation (Bruch, 1963c, p. 56). Though the defense analysis model described in this paper does not agree with Bruch's emphasis on consistently placing interpretations after these reorienting interventions – it is the interpretation of defenses against painful affect that engages the teen and allows the clinician to work with the negative affects that can threaten treatment – this model understands and incorporates these engrained lessons from the eating disorders literature. Thus in this situation, the teen's strength, courage, and resilience evidenced in her ability to present to the session was reflected back to her. She was supported and cared for. The time frame of the upcoming vacation was concretely sketched out, and she was helped to anticipate stressors. She was respected in a way that, owing to her deficits in development, she had not yet internalized a capability to do for herself. The intent was to help her continue to internalize self-care and self-respect that might in the future promote her ability to better tolerate the painful affects that led to her controlled masochism.

Similarly with the parent, while retaining an understanding and supportive relatedness, the therapist reminded the mother that she retained the authority to determine whether to schedule the visit. She was helped to bring from preconsciousness to consciousness her decision that to allow the tooth extraction would impair the patient's ability to attend sessions. Helping the mother to understand the consequences and implications of her decision helped her to retain a sense of agency and to move toward a stance where behaviors had meanings. Over time, such interventions help to prevent impulsive acting and to develop a stronger internal state where options can be considered. This mentalizing stance towards herself and towards her daughter was intended to break a family cycle of impulsive decision-making. These interventions took a flexible approach to individual work that respected the importance of working with the parent (Novick & Novick, 2013).

We know that psychodynamic psychotherapy can produce neurobiological changes in emotion regulation circuits (Buchheim et al., 2012). By remaining calm and remaining with the patient despite enactments that are occurring while reminding her of her strength in presenting for the final session preceding the vacation, a dyadic regulation was undertaken as a means of promoting the patient's own internalized internal implicit emotion regulation. Washington (2004) describes "resistance to 'take in' physically and emotionally." This can present "adamant refusal of treatment, fierce rejection of the practitioner and formidable systems of defense" (p. 418). The patient, in her presentation, appeared to be showing at least at this moment that she had developed some improved capacity to face and tolerate uncomfortable feelings rather than experience anxiety or maladaptively defend in a self-defeating manner. Though much work was to come, the patient's progress in a short period was notable.

Conclusion

Academics are often dismissive of psychodynamic approaches in contemporary models of care. This may be because of a lack of an empirical base for psychodynamic approaches, particularly in the eating disorders literature. This is not to say that there is no evidence for dynamic approaches in eating disorders. Focal psychodynamic psychotherapy has recently been shown to have important benefits relative to treatment as usual and cognitive behavioral therapy in the *Lancet* (Zipfel et al., 2014). It was the focal, operationalized nature of this intervention that allowed its inclusion in a major clinical trial. Despite accomplishments, the authors write of psychodynamic approaches that there remains a need to "refine our treatments further (p. 136)."

An operationalized, defense-focused approach to individuals with eating disorders has been suggested in this paper to provide an opportune means of providing a modular intervention that may be particularly adept at addressing some of the barriers to working psychodynamically with individuals with eating disorders. It may be incorporated into existing approaches to individuals with eating disorders, or it may be manualized for further study and development. Several elements make it adept for use in a trial for hypothesis testing. Such a manualization has occurred in similar work with children with externalizing behaviors (Hoffman & Rice with Prout, 2016) where clinical trials are under way. The additional ability to structure this approach within a Research Domain Criteria (RDoC)-compatible neuropsychiatric functional system that has broad relevance for eating disorders is an additional benefit. Its ability to incorporate the existing eating disorders literature and exciting developments in recent attachment-based developments are hoped to encourage clinicians to integrate defense analysis in creating an optimal model for psychodynamic work with individuals with eating disorders. It offers a means to address the emotion regulation deficits of individuals with eating disorders (Lavender et al., 2015) that may be just as important and worthy of intervention as these individuals' disordered attachment styles (Thompson-Brenner, 2014).

Satir (2011), who incorporates attachment theory and a relational perspective (Greenberg & Mitchell, 1983) to provide focus on alliance (Safran & Kraus, 2014), is exemplary for her use of a short-term orientation bookended by pre- and post-standard clinical measures. Satir's approach, termed *alliance-focused therapy* (AFT; Satir, 2011), has evidence through the use of an experimental single-case phase change design. Her accomplishment shows that single-case experiments are valuable contributions at this time to the psychodynamic psychotherapy literature. Her notice of the need for additional studies is a motivation for this paper. By offering some preliminary evidence regarding the utility of defense analysis in working with individuals with eating disorders, this paper is one step towards the objective of building an evidence base for a comprehensive psychodynamic model of eating disorders. In that it is primarily an intrapsychic, biological model with bridges both to two-person attachment models and to psychopharmacology and other brain-based medical interventions, it may provide a nice complement to the existing literature to be incorporated and used productively.

Without such therapeutic approaches and the creation of an evidence base, psychodynamically informed treatments will continue to find little mention in major academic reviews of the eating disorders treatment literature (Hay, 2013; Watson & Bulik, 2013). It is currently the case that the lack of emphasis on such empirical approaches has not only failed to represent psychodynamic psychiatry among the contemporary approaches to anorexia nervosa but also facilitated mischaracterizations and biases against the rich tradition of psychodynamic work. The Maudsley approach considers itself "a radical break from the traditional treatment of the illness" because it does not embrace "the culture of blaming the family for the patient's illness," which they suggest "remains commonplace even to this day (p. xv)." This appears to be a misunderstanding and mischaracterization of contemporary psychodynamic treatments. This misunderstanding fails to incorporate the development of psychodynamic approaches since their earliest times. It may be that the large omission of psychodynamics from evidence-based journals promotes this perspective among academics and contemporary mental health providers and recipients. These misconceptions should be clarified through work in psychodynamic research that is acceptable for entry into the academic literature. These are goals that will take time and perseverance. Fortunately, focuses on negative clinician reactions and alliance may help young clinicians and paradigm developers prevent the "burnout" to which they are susceptible (Satir, 2013;

Warren et al., 2013) and go on to develop the offerings of psychodynamic psychiatry for individuals with eating disorders. This work and recent developments hope to show that psychodynamic treatments are very diverse and have much to constructively offer. Even when the patient is "angry," care is possible.

Note

1 I am grateful to Dr. Leon Hoffman, MD, for his mentorship that produced this work. I am additionally appreciative to Drs. Dana Satir, PhD; Tracy Prout, PhD; and Rachel Ritvo, MD, for their constructive comments on an earlier draft of this work.

References

American Psychiatric Association. (2013). *Diagnostic and statistical manual of mental disorders* (5th Ed.). Washington, DC: American Psychiatric Press.

Arcelus, J., Mitchell, A. J., Wales, J., & Nielsen, S. (2011). Mortality rates in patients with anorexia nervosa and other eating disorders. A meta-analysis of 36 studies. *Archives of General Psychiatry*, *68*(7), 724–731. doi:10.1001/archgenpsychiatry.2011.74

Becker, T. E. (1974). On latency. *The Psychoanalytic Study of the Child*, *29*, 3–11. Retrieved from www.ncbi.nlm.nih.gov/pubmed/4475440

Bers, S. A., Besser, A., Harpaz-Rotem, I., & Blatt, S. J. (2013). An empirical exploration of the dynamics of anorexia nervosa: Representations of self, mother, and father. *Psychoanalytic Psychology*, *30*(2), 188–209. doi:10.1037/a0032512

Blatt, S. (2008). *Polarities of experience: Relatedness and self-definition in personality development, psychopathology, and the therapeutic process*. Washington, DC: American Psychological Association.

Bond, M. P. (1986). Defense style questionnaire. In G. E. Vaillant (Ed.), *Empirical studies of ego mechanisms of defense*. Washington, DC: American Psychiatric Press.

Bond, M., & Perry, J. C. (2004). Long-term changes in defense styles with psychodynamic psychotherapy for depressive, anxiety, and personality disorders. *American Journal of Psychiatry*, *161*(9), 1665–1671. doi:10.1176/appi.ajp.161.9.1665

Boris, H. N. (1984a). On the treatment of anorexia nervosa. *The International Journal of Psycho-Analysis*, *65* (Pt 4), 435–442.

Boris, H. N. (1984b). The problem of anorexia nervosa. *The International Journal of Psycho-Analysis*, *65*(Pt 3), 315–322. doi:10.1056/NEJM192808231990808

Bornstein, B. (1945). Clinical notes on child analysis. *Psychoanalytic Study of the Child*, *1*, 151–166. Retrieved from www.ncbi.nlm.nih.gov/pubmed/21004307

Bornstein, B. (1949). The analysis of a phobic child-some problems of thoery and technique in child analysis. *Psychoanalytic Study of the Child*, *3*, 181–226.

Bruch, H. (1963a). Disturbed communication in eating disorders. *The American Journal of Orthopsychiatry*, *33*, 99–104.

Bruch, H. (1963b). Psychotherapeutic problems in eating disorders. *Psychoanalytic Review*, *50D*, 43–57.

Bruch, H. (1963c). Psychotherapeutic problems in eating disorders. *Psychoanalytic Review*, *50*, 573–587. Retrieved from www.ncbi.nlm.nih.gov/pubmed/14073180

Bruch, H. (1973). *Eating disorders: Obesity, anorexia nervosa and the person within*. New York: Basic Books.

Bucci, S., Roberts, N. H., Danquah, A. N., & Berry, K. (2015). Using attachment theory to inform the design and delivery of mental health services: A systematic review of the literature. *Psychology and Psychotherapy: Theory, Research and Practice*, *88*(1), 1–20. doi:10.1111/papt.12029

Buchheim, A., Viviani, R., Kessler, H., Kächele, H., Cierpka, M., Roth, G., . . . Taubner, S. (2012). Changes in prefrontal-limbic function in major depression after 15 months of long-term psychotherapy. *PloS One*, *7*(3), e33745. doi:10.1371/journal.pone.0033745

Calkins, S. D., & Hill, A. (2009). Caregiver influences on emerging emotional regulation: Biological and environmental transactions in early development. In J. J. Gross (Ed.), *Handbook of emotion regulation* (pp. 229–248). New York: Guilford Press.

Campbell, K., & Peebles, R. (2014). Eating disorders in children and adolescents: state of the art review. *Pediatrics*, *134*(3), 582–592. doi:10.1542/peds.2014-0194

Cramer, P. (1991). *The development of defense mechanisms: Theory, research and assessment*. New York: Springer-Verlag.

Cramer, P. (2006). *Protecting the self: Defense mechanisms in action*. New York: Guilford Press.

Engel, S. G., Wonderlich, S. A., Crosby, R. D., Mitchell, J. E., Crow, S., Peterson, C. B., . . . Gordon, K. H. (2013). The role of affect in the maintenance of anorexia nervosa: Evidence from a naturalistic assessment of momentary behaviors and emotion. *Journal of Abnormal Psychology*, *122*(3), 709–719. doi:10.1037/a0034010

Etkin, A., Büchel, C., & Gross, J. J. (2015). The neural bases of emotion regulation. *Nature Reviews Neuroscience*, *16*(11), 693–700. doi:10.1038/nrn4044

Fonagy, P., Gergely, G., Jurist, E., & Target, M. (2004). *Affect regulation, mentalization, and the development of self*. New York: Other Press.

Freud, A. (1936). *The ego and the mechanisms of defense*. New York: International Universities Press.

Freud, A. (1963). The concept of developmental lines. *The Psychoanalytic Study of the Child*, *18*, 245–265. Retrieved from www.ncbi.nlm.nih.gov/pubmed/14147280

Freud, A. (1974). A psychoanalytic view of developmental psychopathology. In *The writings of Anna Freud, VIII* (pp. 119–136). New York: International Universities Press.

Freud, S. (1900). The interpretation of dreams. In *The standard edition of the complete psychological works of sigmund freud, Volume IV (1900): The interpretation of dreams (First Part)*.

Freud, S. (1918). From the history of an infantile neurosis. In *The standard edition of the complete psychological works of Sigmund Freud, volume XVII (1917–1919): An infantile neurosis and other works* (pp. 1–287). London, England: The Hogarth Press and the Institute of Psychoanalysis.

Goodsitt, A. (1983). Self-regulatory disturbances in eating disorders. *International Journal of Eating Disorders*, *2*(3), 51–60. doi:10.1002/1098-108X(198321)2:3<51::AID-EAT2260020305>3.0.CO;2-N

Greenberg, J., & Mitchell, S. (1983). *Object relations in psychoanalytic theory*. Cambridge, MA: Harvard University Press.

Gross, J. J. (2013). Emotion regulation: taking stock and moving forward. *Emotion (Washington, D.C.)*, *13*(3), 359–365. doi:10.1037/a0032135

Gross, J. J. (2014). *Handbook of emotion reguation* (2nd ed.), ed. J. Gross. New York: Guilford Press.

Grotstein, J. S. (1999). Foreword. In J. T. Graeme, R. M. Bagby, & J. D. A. Parker (Eds.), *Disorders of affect regulation: Alexithymia in medical psychiatric illness* (pp. xi–xiix). Cambridge: Cambridge University Press.

Gull, W. W. (1874). Anorexia nervosa (apepsia hysterica, anorexia hysterica). *Transactions of the Clinical Society of London*, *7*, 22–28.

Gyurak, A., Gross, J. J., & Etkin, A. (2011). Explicit and implicit emotion regulation: A dual-process framework. *Cognition & Emotion*, *25*(3), 400–412. doi:10.1080/02699931.2010.544160

Hay, P. (2013). A systematic review of evidence for psychological treatments in eating disorders: 2005–2012. *The International Journal of Eating Disorders*, *46*(5), 462–469. doi:10.1002/eat.22103

Hentschel, U., Smith, G., Draguns, J. G., & Ehlers, W. (2004). *Defense mechanisms: Theoretical, research, and clinical perspectives*. Amsterdam: Elsevier.

Hoffman, L. (1989). The psychoanalytic process and the development of insight in child analysis: A case study. *The Psychoanalytic Quarterly*, *58*(January), 63–80. Retrieved from www.ncbi.nlm.nih.gov/pubmed/2704773

Hoffman, L. (2000). Letter: The exclusion of child psychoanalysis. *Journal of the American Psychoanalytic Association*, *48*(4), 1617–1618. Retrieved from www.ncbi.nlm.nih.gov/pubmed/11212203

Hoffman, L. (2007). Do children get better when we interpret their defenses against painful feelings? *The Psychoanalytic Study of the Child*, *62*, 291–313. Retrieved from www.ncbi.nlm.nih.gov/pubmed/18524096

Hoffman, L. (2014). Berta Bornstein's "Frankie": The contemporary relevance of a classic to the treatment of children with disruptive symptoms. *The Psychoanalytic Study of the Child*, *68*, 152–176. Retrieved from www.ncbi.nlm.nih.gov/pubmed/26173332

Hoffman, L., Rice, T., & Prout, T. (2016). *Manual for regulation-focused psychotherapy for children with externalizing behaviors (RFP-C): A psychodynamic approach*. New York: Routledge.

Insel, T., Cuthbert, B., Garvey, M., Heinssen, R., Pine, D. S., Quinn, K., . . . Wang, P. (2010). Research Domain Criteria (RDoC): Toward a new classification framework for research on mental disorders. *The American Journal of Psychiatry*, *167*, 748–751. doi:10.1176/appi.ajp.2010.09091379

Insel, T. R. (2014). The NIMH Research Domain Criteria (RDoC) project: Precision medicine for psychiatry. *The American Journal of Psychiatry*, *171*(4), 395–397. doi:10.1176/appi.ajp.2014.14020138

Kernberg, O. F. (2006). Psychoanalytic affect theory in the light of contemporary neurobiological findings. *International Congress Series*, *1286*, 106–117. doi:10.1016/j.ics.2005.10.011

Koole, S. L., & Rothermund, K. (2011). "I feel better but I don't know why": The psychology of implicit emotion regulation. *Cognition & Emotion*, *25*(3), 389–399. doi:10.1080/02699931.2010.550505

Laor, N., Wolmer, L., & Cicchetti, D. V. (2001). The comprehensive assessment of defense style: measuring defense mechanisms in children and adolescents. *The Journal of Nervous and Mental Disease*, *189*(6), 360–368. doi:10.1097/00005053-200106000-00003

Lasegue, E. (1873). De l'anorexie histérique. *Archives Générales de Médicine*, *1*, 385–403.

Lavender, J. M., Wonderlich, S. A., Engel, S. G., Gordon, K. H., Kaye, W. H., & Mitchell, J. E. (2015). Dimensions of emotion dysregulation in anorexia nervosa and bulimia nervosa: A conceptual review of the empirical literature. *Clinical Psychology Review*, *40*, 111–122. doi:10.1016/j.cpr.2015.05.010

Lawrence, M. (2001). Loving them to death: The anorexic and her objects. *The International Journal of Psycho-Analysis*, *82*(Pt 1), 43–55. Retrieved from www.ncbi.nlm.nih.gov/pubmed/11234113

Lawrence, M. (2008). *The Anorexic mind*. London, England: Karnac.
Lock, J. (2011). Evaluation of family treatment models for eating disorders. *Current Opinion in Psychiatry*, *24*(4), 274–279. doi:10.1097/YCO.0b013e328346f71e
Lock, J., & Le Grange, D. (2013). *Treatment manual for anorexia nervosa*. New York: Guilford Press.
Lorand, S. (1948). On the meaning of losing teeth in dreams. *The Psychoanalytic Quarterly*, *17*(4), 529. Retrieved from www.ncbi.nlm.nih.gov/pubmed/18121418
Lorand, S., & Feldman, S. (1955). The symbolism of teeth in dreams. *The International Journal of Psycho-Analysis*, *36*(3), 145–161. Retrieved from www.ncbi.nlm.nih.gov/pubmed/14366798
Mahler, M. (1968). *On human symbiosis and the vicissitudes of individuation*. New York: International Universities Press, Inc.
Malan, D. (1979). *Individual psychotherapy and the science of psychodynamics*. London: Butterworth.
Mccullough, L. (1997). *Changing character: Short-term anxiety-regulating psychotherapy for restructuring defenses, affects, and attachment*. New York: Basic Books.
Novick, K. K., & Novick, J. (2013). Concurrent work with parents of adolescent patients. *The Psychoanalytic Study of the Child*, *67*, 103–136. Retrieved from www.ncbi.nlm.nih.gov/pubmed/26072560
Perry, J. C., & Cooper, S. H. (1989). An empirical study of defense mechanisms. I. Clinical interview and life vignette ratings. *Archives of General Psychiatry*, *46*(5), 444–452. Retrieved from www.ncbi.nlm.nih.gov/pubmed/2712663
Racine, S. E., & Wildes, J. E. (2013). Emotion dysregulation and symptoms of anorexia nervosa: The unique roles of lack of emotional awareness and impulse control difficulties when upset. *The International Journal of Eating Disorders*, *46*(7), 713–720. doi:10.1002/eat.22145
Racine, S. E., & Wildes, J. E. (2015a). Dynamic longitudinal relations between emotion regulation difficulties and anorexia nervosa symptoms over the year following intensive treatment. *Journal of Consulting and Clinical Psychology*, *83*(4), 785–795. doi:10.1037/ccp0000011
Racine, S. E., & Wildes, J. E. (2015b). Emotion dysregulation and anorexia nervosa: An exploration of the role of childhood abuse. *The International Journal of Eating Disorders*, *48*(1), 55–58. doi:10.1002/eat.22364
Rice, T. R., & Hoffman, L. (2014). Defense mechanisms and implicit emotion regulation: a comparison of a psychodynamic construct with one from contemporary neuroscience. *Journal of the American Psychoanalytic Association*, *62*(4), 693–708. doi:10.1177/0003065114546746
Ritvo, S. (1976). Adolescent to woman. *Journal of the American Psychoanalytic Association*, *24*(5 Suppl), 127–137. Retrieved from www.ncbi.nlm.nih.gov/pubmed/803140
Safran, J. D., & Kraus, J. (2014). Alliance ruptures, impasses, and enactments: A relational perspective. *Psychotherapy*, *51*(3), 381–387. doi:10.1037/a0036815
Satir, D. A. (2013). The role and meaning of eating disorder therapist experience level. *Psychotherapy (Chicago, Ill.)*, *50*(4), 570–572. doi:10.1037/a0030572
Satir, D. A., Goodman, D. M., Shingleton, R. M., Porcerelli, J. H., Gorman, B. S., Pratt, E. M., Barlow, D. H., & Thompson-Brenner, H. (2011). Alliance-focused therapy for anorexia nervosa: integrative relational and behavioral change treatments in a single-case experimental design. *Psychotherapy (Chicago, Ill.)*, *48*(4), 401–420. doi:10.1037/a0026216
Schneck, J. M. (1979). Dreams of loss of teeth symbolizing aging and disintegration. *The Journal of the American Academy of Psychoanalysis*, *7*(3), 447–451. Retrieved from www.ncbi.nlm.nih.gov/pubmed/457514

Stegge, H., & Terwogt, M. (2007). Awareness and regulation of emotion in typical and atypical development. In J. J. Gross (Ed.), *Handbook of emotion regulation* (pp. 269–286). New York: Guilford Press.

Steiner, H., & Remsing, L. (2007). Practice parameter for the assessment and treatment of children and adolescents with oppositional defiant disorder. *Journal of the American Academy of Child and Adolescent Psychiatry*, *46*(1), 894–921. doi:10.1097/01.chi.0000246060.62706.af

Steiner, J. (1990). Pathological organizations as obstacles to mourning: The role of unbearable guilt. *The International Journal of Psycho-Analysis*, *71*(Pt 1), 87–94.

Tasca, G. A., & Balfour, L. (2014). Eating disorders and attachment: a contemporary psychodynamic perspective. *Psychodynamic Psychiatry*, *42*(2), 257–276. doi:10.1521/pdps.2014.42.2.257

Taylor, G., Bagby, R., & Parker, J. (1997). Eating disorders. In *Disorders of affect regulation: Alexithymia in medical psychiatric illness* (pp. 190–215). Cambridge: Cambridge University Press.

Thompson-Brenner, H. (2014). Discussion of "Eating disorders and attachment: A contemporary psychodynamic perspective" does the attachment model of eating disorders indicate the need for psychodynamic treatment? *Psychodynamic Psychiatry*, *42*(2), 277–284. doi:10.1521/pdps.2014.42.2.277

Thompson-Brenner, H., Satir, D. A., Franko, D. L., & Herzog, D. B. (2012). Clinician reactions to patients with eating disorders: A review of the literature. *Psychiatric Services (Washington, DC)*, *63*(1), 73–78. doi:10.1176/appi.ps.201100050

Vaillant, G. E., Bond, M., & Vaillant, C. O. (1986). An empirically validated hierarchy of defense mechanisms. *Archives of General Psychiatry*, *43*(8), 786–794. Retrieved from www.ncbi.nlm.nih.gov/pubmed/3729674

Vandereycken, W., & van Deth, R. (1989). Who was the first to describe anorexia nervosa: Gull or Lasègue? *Psychological Medicine*, *19*(4), 837–845. doi:10.1017/S0033291700005559

Warren, C. S., Schafer, K. J., Crowley, M. E. J., & Olivardia, R. (2013). Demographic and work-related correlates of job burnout in professional eating disorder treatment providers. *Psychotherapy (Chicago, Ill)*, *50*(4), 553–564. doi:10.1037/a0028783

Washington, M. (2004). On the issue of resistance in anorexia. *Psychoanalytic Psychotherapy*, *18*(4), 418–431. Retrieved from http://doi.org/10.1080/14749730412331318658

Watson, H. J., & Bulik, C. M. (2013). Update on the treatment of anorexia nervosa: review of clinical trials, practice guidelines and emerging interventions. *Psychological Medicine*, *43*(12), 2477–2500. doi:10.1017/S0033291712002620

Wildes, J. E., Ringham, R. M., & Marcus, M. D. (2010). Emotion avoidance in patients with anorexia nervosa: Initial test of a functional model. *International Journal of Eating Disorders*, *43*(5), 398–404. doi:10.1002/eat.20730

Wilson, C. P. (1988). The psychoanalytic treatment of anorexia nervosa and bulimia. In B. B. Chaitin, & R. Goldstein (Eds.), *The eating disorders*. New York: PMA Publishing Corp.

Wolmer, L., Laor, N., & Cicchetti, D. V. (2001). Validation of the Comprehensive Assessment of Defense Style (CADS): Mothers' and children's responses to the stresses of missile attacks. *The Journal of Nervous and Mental Disease*, *189*(6), 369–376. Retrieved from www.ncbi.nlm.nih.gov/pubmed/11434637

Zerbe, K. (1993a). *The body betrayed: Women, eating disorders, and treatment*. Washington, DC: American Psychiatric Publishing.

Zerbe, K. (1993b). Whose body is it anyway? Understanding and treating psychosomatic aspects of eating disorders. *Bulletin of the Menninger Clinic*, *57*(2), 161–177. Retrieved from www.ncbi.nlm.nih.gov/pubmed/8508154

Zerbe, K. (2008). *Integrated treatment of eating disorders: beyond the body betrayed.* New York: W. W. Norton & Company.

Zerbe, K. (2015). Psychodynamic theory of eating disorders. *The Wiley Handbook of Eating Disorders*, 253–268. doi:10.1002/9781118574089.ch20

Zipfel, S., Wild, B., Grob, G., Friederich, H. C., Teufel, M., Schellberg, D., . . . Herzog, W. (2014). Focal psychodynamic therapy, cognitive behaviour therapy, and optimised treatment as usual in outpatients with anorexia nervosa (ANTOP study): Randomised controlled trial. *The Lancet*, *383*, 127–137. doi:10.1016/S0140-6736(13)61746-8

10

EATING DISORDERS, IMPAIRED MENTALIZATION, AND ATTACHMENT

Implications for child and adolescent family treatment

Starr Kelton-Locke

Introduction

Although many models exist for the treatment of eating disorders, therapeutic outcomes remain variable and less than optimal (Keel & Brown, 2010; Steinhausen, 2002). The large number of patients who prematurely leave treatment, frequently relapse, maintain residual depressive and anxiety symptoms, and show poor social functioning even after multiple treatments demonstrate that improvements in therapeutic effectiveness are still needed. Evidence suggests that interventions based on coherent theories and identified risk factors offer the best potential for improved treatment outcomes (Pennesi & Wade, 2016). Some of the consistently identified risk factors for the genesis and maintenance of eating pathology include negative self-evaluation, general psychopathology, negative mood states, internalization of the thin ideal, ineffectiveness/lack of agency, pathological body dissatisfaction, and poor social support (Stice, 2002; Striegel-Moore & Bulik, 2007). Identified risk factors predictive of treatment outcomes include patients' motivation to recover, severity of eating disorder pathology, psychiatric co-morbidity, age of onset, illness duration, interpersonal functioning, and familial problems (Vall & Wade, 2015). Pennesi and Wade (2016) argue that distal risk variables for eating disorders, specifically those related to developmental antecedents, are lacking in many theories used to inform treatment. Rather than develop new models, however, they recommend the revision of existing treatments to include new therapeutic elements that consider the developmental characteristics that place patients at risk. They also advise integrating into treatment the expanding neurobiological evidence related to eating disorder pathology.

This chapter aims to address these recommendations by reviewing the multidimensional model of mentalization-based treatment (Allen & Fonagy, 2006; Allen, Fonagy, & Bateman, 2008) and its application to understanding and treating eating disorders (Skarderud, 2007a, 2007b, 2007c; Skarerud & Fonagy, 2012). *Mentalization*, or *mentalizing*, is a term that refers to the human capacity to understand one's own and others' behavior in relation to states of mind. Mentalization-based treatment (MBT) is grounded in theory and research from the fields of developmental psychology, neurobiology, attachment theory, and psychodynamic and systems theory. Specifically, mentalization treatment focuses on the developmental antecedents of psychopathology, the child/caregiver attachment system, and how affect regulation, self-agency, and self-identity develop and go awry. These foundational hallmarks of MBT meet Pennesi and Wade's recommendations for improving treatment outcomes for eating disorders: theoretical coherence, integration of developmental and neurobiological factors involved in the onset and maintenance of emotional disturbances, and interventions designed to address these factors.

MBT was originally formulated in the United Kingdom by Peter Fonagy and his collaborators for the treatment of borderline personality disorder and has since been expanded to treat depression, anxiety, drug addiction, adolescents, infant/parent problems, family dysfunction, and eating disorders (Bateman & Fonagy, 2012). MBT's application to the treatment of eating disorders (MBT-ED) proposes that these disorders are manifestations of an underlying self-disorder, with deficits in mentalizing capacities, emotional regulation, interoceptive awareness, self-cohesion, self-agency, and self-esteem regulation (Skarderud & Fonagy, 2012). These deficits are considered by some researchers as domains of attachment functioning that are possible risk factors for the pathogenesis of eating disorders and predictors of therapeutic processes and outcome (Tasca & Balfour, 2014). Specifically, a review of current research on attachment and eating disorders showed that compared with controls, eating-disordered individuals had higher levels of attachment insecurity and disorganized mental states, as well as lower reflective functioning in anorexic patients (reflective function is the quantified index of attachment-related mentalization). Prospective studies support these conclusions with evidence that insecure attachment and reduced mentalizing capacities are associated with the onset of eating pathology (Jewell et al., 2015; Rothschild-Yakar et al., 2010; Rothschild-Yakar & Stein, 2013). Further support for the relationship between mentalizing capacities, self-deficits, sociocognitive functioning, and eating disorders comes from neuroscience research into the neural regions involved in these processes. Cortical activity relating to self-knowledge and perspective-taking in both recently ill and long-term recovered women with anorexia nervosa showed differences in functional magnetic resonance imaging (fMRI) activation compared with healthy controls (McAdams & Krawczyk, 2014; McAdams et al., 2016), as well as decreased activation of network regions during both general social cognition (McAdams & Krawczyk, 2011) and social interaction tasks (McAdams, Lohrenz, & Montague, 2015). Given these findings, it appears that self-deficits, difficulties in understanding one's own and others' states of mind, and attachment functioning may be some of the more important developmental factors that should inform new therapeutic elements.

The therapeutic interventions of MBT-ED focus not only on behavioral symptom remission but also on the therapeutic relationship, impaired mentalizing capacities, the concretization of inner reality, difficulties in relationships, and deficits in self-regulation, agency, and emotional regulation. The primary aim of MBT – to strengthen the ability to understand mental states in self and others – appears especially warranted for eating disorders treatment given that improvements in interpersonal relationships, including the capacity to understand others' perspectives, are shown to be associated with long-term recovery in patients (McAdams et al., 2016; McAdams et al., 2015; Nilsson & Hagglof, 2006). Moreover, given its emphasis on developing mentalizing interactions that increase emotional regulation skills, attachment security, trust, and interpersonal problem-solving, an MBT family treatment model for adolescents and children with eating pathology has significant implications for treatment process and outcome, including reducing iatrogenic effects in treatment, lowering drop-out rates, and choosing an appropriate treatment method. For example, parents' inability to understand and tolerate their child's emotional reactions may contraindicate the choice of a family-based therapy (FBT) that focuses mainly on refeeding because of the increased emotional demands placed on the family during this challenging process. Additionally, the attachment style of the child and parental dyad may contraindicate certain types of family treatment interventions. Specifically, an FBT intervention that aims to "raise parental anxiety and concern so that they can take appropriate action" to help their child eat (Lock et al., 2001, p. 47) could lead to iatrogenic treatment effects in a family with an anxious-ambivalent child and an anxious-preoccupied parent that have pre-existing maladaptive interactional patterns in the relationship. To address these potential attachment-related vulnerabilities, a thorough pre-treatment assessment of these factors may warrant a modified family model that treats the parents separately from the child/teen, or if conjointly, immediately focuses on strengthening mentalizing capacities in the family during emotionally charged attachment relationship exchanges.

To address the need for using mentalization-focused interventions in all populations of eating-disordered patients, the theoretical rationale and key interventions of the MBT eating disorder model used in a multicenter research and treatment project is discussed, and an adapted mentalization-based family treatment model for adolescents and children with eating pathology is outlined. The adapted model, MBFT-ED, is proposed to address the developmental and neurobiological risk and maintaining factors of attachment insecurity, affect dysregulation, negative self-states, ineffectiveness/lack of agency, and mentalizing vulnerabilities in the identified patient, as well as the interactional patterns, mentalizing vulnerabilities, and regulation of emotional distress in the family system. Additionally, the adapted model is intended to address important risk factors predictive of treatment outcomes, such as motivation to recover, interpersonal functioning, family problems, and early intervention to decrease the length of illness. The proposed model could be implemented as a stand-alone treatment, or used adjunctively in existing eating disorders treatment models to address impairments in mentalizing.

Mentalization: definition, processes, development, neurobiology

The concept of mentalization, or mentalizing, refers to the fundamental human capacity to recognize and interact with each other as beings with minds. Broadly speaking, it is a form of social cognition, but specifically defines the ability to understand behavior in relation to intentional mental states, such as personal desires, needs, feelings, beliefs, and motivations (Bateman & Fonagy, 2012). The originators of the concept underscore that mentalization is not a "static and unitary" faculty of the mind, but rather is a dynamic process influenced by stress, emotional arousal, and attachment relationships (Fonagy, Bateman, & Luyten, 2012). Furthermore, this aspect of mind is considered a developmental achievement that is established within the intersubjective matrix of early caregiver/infant interactions and depends on the child's successful development of "a symbolic representational system for mental states" (Fonagy, Gergely, & Target, 2007, p. 289).

Most mentalizing activity occurs on the procedural (implicit) level of consciousness and is a rapid, reflexive response to interpersonal exchanges. An example of implicit mentalizing is when we preconsciously decode the motivations of another by reading his or her facial expressions and body language. Conscious, deliberate and reflective mentalizing (explicit) is an effortful mental process that helps us understand and explain our thoughts, feelings, and intentions, as well as consciously consider the possible mental states of others. Fonagy and Bateman (2011) have expanded the concept to include four dimensions, or polarities of mentalization: cognitive/affective, automatic/controlled, self-oriented/other-oriented, and internally focused/externally focused. Each dimension represents a range of possible levels of functioning, with psychopathology manifesting in dominance at either end of the poles, or inability to shift states when warranted by social/interpersonal demands. For example, rigid dominance in two of the poles, automatic and affect-driven mentalizing, are core features of borderline personality disorder and a prime factor in these patients' interpersonal difficulties (Bateman & Fonagy, 2010).

Mentalization, at its core, is a theory of mind paradigm that is rooted in Bowlby's attachment theory and its more recent incorporation of neurobiological ideas related to the hard-wired brain processes that promote the organization and expression of social cognition (Gergely & Unoka, 2008). During the past two decades, much progress has been made in understanding the interaction between brain development and the attachment relationship (Sroufe, 1996; Schore, 2001; Cozolino, 2014). In short, the intersubjective matrix of attachment not only serves a safety and security function as Bowlby hypothesized but, as neuroscience now shows, is also critical to social brain development (Fonagy, 2008). Fonagy and his collaborators have extensively reviewed the application of attachment and developmental psychology to the origins of mentalizing (Fonagy et al., 2002; Sharp & Fonagy, 2008; Sharp, Fonagy, & Goodyer, 2008; Fonagy et al., 2007; Fonagy &

Target, 2007). In this substantial body of work, they argue that there is an evolutionary selective advantage in the neural development of mentalizing. The capacity to anticipate and interpret mental and emotional states and behavior not only serves social cooperation but also provides a competitive edge. This argument is borne out in evolutionary biology's evidence that competition for resources and survival among humans requires skill in understanding, outsmarting, and even deceptive behaviors accomplished by the "quick and expert *reading of intention in others*" (Wilson, 2012, p. 56, italics added). Conversely, social learning about cooperation, reciprocity, altruism, and trust can be safely assimilated within the noncompetitive, attachment relationship (Fonagy, 2008).

The attachment system and its associated neural circuits, neuropeptides, and brain regions have been well defined by fMRI studies and neuroscience studies in animals and humans (Bartels & Zeki, 2004; Porges, 2003). Specifically, the neural circuits of reward and motivation, including the mesocorticolimbic dopaminergic reward circuit (Young & Wang, 2004), and the interaction of oxytocin, arginine vasopressin (AVP), and dopamine are thought to facilitate maternal pair-bond and adult pair-mating formation (Bartels & Zeki, 2004). The same neural circuits, brain regions, and primary neuropeptides involved in pair-bonding (attachment) overlap with the areas of the brain that support the development of social cognition, learning, and the capacity to "read" others' intentions and emotions (mentalizing). Foundations of attachment and social learning, however, are not just products of neurons, hormones, and genetically programmed brain functions. Rather, there is an interactive process whereby these neurobiological components are shaped by and in turn shape the human species (Cacioppo, Bertson, & Decety, 2010). The full expression of the social cognitive regions of the brain is an emergent property of the infant/caregiver relationship. Likewise, Fonagy and colleagues propose that the faculty of mentalization is not a constitutional given, but rather a developmental achievement acquired within the intersubjective matrix of the attachment relationship (Bateman & Fonagy, 2004; Fonagy et al., 2002). In this relationship, affect regulation, attentional control, and origins of the self, including coherent self-structure and self-agency, are acquired. Moreover, impairments in social cognition, especially in mentalizing capacities, are primary factors in the development of various psychiatric disorders, including borderline personality disorder (Bateman & Fonagy, 2004), antisocial personality disorder (Bateman & Fonagy, 2008), and eating disorders (Skarderud, 2007b, 2007c).

Consequences of impaired attachment, mentalization, and eating pathology

Early disruptions in attachment experience, whether resulting from constitutional or environmental influences, can create long-term vulnerabilities in a child that may never abate (Mikulincer & Shaver, 2007, 2012; Glaser, 2000). An inability to express and regulate emotions, difficulties in interpersonal relationships, disruptions in self-agency, cognitive and social cognition deficits, and poorly established mentalizing capacities are some of the main bio-psycho-social consequences of attachment disruptions. As stated, prospective studies suggest that insecure attachment and its associated psychological sequelae may be a risk factor for the development of eating pathology (Jewell et al., 2015; Rothschild-Yakar et al., 2010). The consistent finding that eating-disordered patients suffer in the areas of self-directedness, self-awareness, and self-understanding, and that they evidence inflexible, externally oriented thought processes (Bishop, 2006) may be related to these attachment vulnerabilities. Eating-disordered patients are also vulnerable to relationship difficulties and self-referential ruminations about their shape and size. Some of these ruminative tendencies are due to the biological consequences of starvation. For many patients, however, these proclivities predate the onset of the disorder. This narrowed point of view of self and other often results in rigid and stereotyped behaviors and thoughts that leave little room for the creative expression of emotional and relational drives and needs. Thus, there is a "disconnect from self and others" and an over-reliance on "emotional escapism" (Bishop, 2006, p. 35) that creates suffering for the patient and results in poor treatment outcome.

The vulnerabilities mentioned previously and other underlying psychological processes of eating-disordered patients support the need for making these factors a primary treatment goal in addition to, and just as importantly as, nutritional and health restoration. Researchers in the field of mentalization-focused treatment developed MBT's interventions to treat these types of psychological vulnerabilities and address self-disorders, dysfunction in emotional regulation, and deficits in social cognition (Skarderud & Fonagy, 2012). Specifically, MBT-ED interventions address problems with self-agency, self-esteem, interoceptive awareness, self/other relationships, cognitive rigidity, and affect regulation in attachment relationships. Interventions are also designed to target reduced *embodied mentalizing*. Embodied mentalizing refers to the broader use of the mentalization concept to include impairments in patients' kinesthetic and sensory experiences of their bodies (Skarderud & Fonagy, 2012). For example, most patients report an inability to tolerate any bodily sensations of fullness after eating a meal. Rather than experiencing fullness as a normal facet of the digestive process, patients report feeling pain, disgust, and guilt about eating, as well as conviction that their bodies are suddenly "bulging," "swelling," and "huge." These types of phenomenological experiences not only hamper recovery of normalized eating patterns but also reflect impairments in the ability to experience one's body as predictable, integrated, and understandable.

Mentalization theory assumes that the absence of fully functioning mentalization, whether because of temperament or attachment vulnerabilities, is most evident in the re-emergence of pre-mentalistic modes of thinking and representing subjectivity. Three forms of pre-mentalistic, or non-mentalistic, reality can be experienced and described in eating disorders. The first, psychic equivalence, is when an individual assumes that his mental states are direct representations of reality (Fonagy & Target, 2006; Fonagy et al., 2002). This concept comes from developmental psychology studies that show mind-world isomorphism in young children's perceptions of mental states. Psychic equivalence (PE) accounts for a core feature of eating disorders: the bodily concretization of inner reality. Mental states, deprived of symbolic representation as thoughts or feelings, are communicated instead in the material realm of the body (Skarderud, 2007a). Specifically, somatic sensations and external bodily characteristics (hunger, desire, shape, size) are expressed literally and lack experiential meaning. Eating-disordered patients' descriptions of their bodies as "disgusting" and "fat" and their desire to be "skinny" despite all costs are hallmarks of PE. As Fonagy and his colleagues explain, "physical attributes such as weight come to reflect states such as internal well-being, control, sense of self-worth, and so on, far beyond the normal tendency for this to happen in adolescence" (2002, p. 405). Concretized expressions of self-states are also common. For example, if the patient feels bad about something, this emotion is often experienced as, "*I* am bad."

The second pre-mentalistic mode of thinking observed in eating disorders is called *pretend mode*, which is the opposite of psychic equivalence. When functioning in pretend mode (PM), thoughts and emotions are devoid of meaning and detached from felt experience. Ideas do not serve to link inner and outer reality, and feelings do not correspond with thoughts (Fonagy & Target, 2006; Fonagy et al., 2002). In early development, PM is evident in young children's imaginative or pretend play. This normative activity serves as a source of creativity and joy at this stage of life. For example, a child in PM might use a bath towel as her superhero cape for flying across the sky. For another child, a bowl full of water, sticks, leaves, and dirt can be stirred to make a magic potion. This world of creativity and pretend is maintained by a mental process of separating these fantasies from the reality of the physical world (Gopnik, 1993). In adulthood, the inability to unite inner and outer reality is not adaptive as in childhood and can have dire consequences for navigating the larger social world. Two forms of PM are relevant to eating disorder treatment: hypermentalization and pseudo-mentalization. Hypermentalization, frequently seen in patients with bulimia nervosa, is when the patient is so outer-directed that she is prone to obsessively interpreting others' minds, but not in an accurate way. Hypermentalized fantasies about another's mind is an effort to meet and satisfy that person's perceived desires and needs (Buhl, 2002; Skarderud, 2007c), and based on inaccurate interpretations of self/other mental states because of attachment anxieties. Similarly, pseudo-mentalizing is when the patient appears to be expressing or talking about feelings and thoughts, but the narrative lacks emotional connection. Instead, words and expressions are empty of meaning and serve to defend against feelings of worthlessness, insignificance, or desolation (Skarderud & Fonagy, 2012).

The most developmentally primitive mode of non-mentalistic thinking is what Fonagy calls the teleological stance (TS). In healthy development, TS refers to the child's representational expectations about self-agency and agency of the other. Because of the child's immaturity, the understanding of agency and intention of self and other is restricted to the physical world, as opposed to mental outcomes.

In adulthood, TS manifests in an inability to "accept anything other than a physical action as a true expression of someone's intentions" (Bateman & Fonagy, 2012, p. 45). Communication of internal mental states and understanding of others' minds occurs mostly through behaviors. Ideas and feelings, and their symbolic representation through language, are not available for the person as a means of understanding and expression. Few clinical conditions illustrate the concept of teleological stance better than eating disorders. The clinical expression of TS is seen in eating-disordered patients' modification and subjugation of the body as an effort to achieve feelings of self-worth and acceptance from others (Skarderud & Fonagy, 2012).

Overview: MBT-ED treatment model

MBT-ED treatment structure, goals, and interventions are all guided by the underlying assumption that problems in affect regulation and self-experience interfere with the development of mentalization. The interventions and process of this model are designed to repair these developmental deficits in mentalizing, strengthen the therapeutic alliance, and prevent dropout from treatment (Skarderud & Fonagy, 2012). Symptom reduction and changes in eating-disordered behaviors are a primary goal, as are emotional regulation, improvement in body image, interpersonal skills, and reduction in self-injurious behaviors. One of the model's strengths is the way it approaches problems of embodied mentalizing: how patients' mental states shift from the concrete to the symbolic realm. A close tracking of small changes in physical and psychological states in the patient, followed by an exploration of the causal chain of interpersonal interactions that led to these shifts, is but one recommendation for improvement of these problems (Skarderud & Fonagy, 2012).

The structure of the ongoing MBT-ED treatment and data collection in the United Kingdom and Norway consists of weekly individual and group therapy, time-limited psychoeducational groups, and ongoing medical management. One important feature of MBT-ED is the systematic use of a case formulation for guiding the treatment process. The case formulation is co-created between the individual therapist and patient, utilizing input from the treatment team gathered during the assessment phase. Defined goals and approaches in treatment, management of risk, specific target behaviors, central interpersonal and self-concerns, and anticipation of the trajectory of the treatment process are all outlined in a written document with the patient's input. Having the patient participate in this process is meant to increase the patient's responsibility and sense of agency regarding treatment compliance (Skarderud & Fonagy, 2012). The case formulation is continually referred to and reformulated throughout the treatment to increase the patient's motivation and investment in recovery.

Weekly group therapy is called the Implicit Mentalizing Group. This group targets issues such as non-participation in treatment, patients' compliance with others' ideas, and body comparisons. It also serves as a primary format for helping eating-disordered patients learn to mentalize unformulated self and other experiences. Other activities include experiential exercises for body and interoceptive awareness and therapeutic meals (Skarderud & Fonagy, 2012). The psychoeducational group is called the Explicit Mentalizing Group. Typically, eight educational sessions take place, with some conducted during the assessment phase. Because the overall aim of MBT-ED is to strengthen mentalizing capabilities, this objective is clearly and explicitly explained in this context from the onset of therapy. Other goals include addressing interpersonal problems and intolerance of others' perspectives and ideas.

MBT-ED therapy process and interventions

MBT-ED utilizes the fundamental components that define adherence and competence in MBT skills (Bateman, Bales, & Hutsebaut, unpublished manual, n.d.), with a few exceptions based on the specific needs of eating-disordered patients (Skarderud, 2007c). Research has shown that adherence to these precepts is critical to transforming mentalizing capacities in patients (Moller, Karlgren, Sandell, Falkenstrom, & Philips, 2016). The defining therapeutic processes of MBT-ED include the therapist stance of "not-knowing," adjusting interventions to match patients' mentalizing capacities, and a steadfast focus on stimulating mentalizing throughout the treatment. Curiosity and a "not-knowing" attitude in the therapeutic exchange encourage reflective functioning or mentalizing. Additionally, a non-interpretive approach is recommended. Profound and sophisticated interpretations are avoided because they can create confusion and in general are ineffective and counterproductive to mentalizing in vulnerable patients. The primary focus should be on the present emotional state of the patient. The MBT manual offers the following questions for therapists as a method to reflect on the intersubjective process: "What is happening now? What makes the client say this now? Why do I feel as I do now? What has happened recently in the therapy that may justify the current state?" (Bateman & Fonagy, 2007).

Treatment process: emotional arousal

Neuropsychological evidence has shown that overly heightened emotional states are not conducive to effective therapeutic intervention (Carryer & Greenberg, 2010; Lane et al., 2015). One potential factor related to this ineffectiveness is that emotional arousal and stress severely inhibit mentalization. Controlled mentalization, identification and understanding of emotional reactions, and emotional-regulation are significant problems for eating-disordered patients. In general, bulimia nervosa patients show problems in emotional hyperarousal and flooding. The opposite, a dominance of detached and flattened affect, is typically seen in patients with anorexia nervosa. One of MBT-ED's core therapeutic values is gauging all therapeutic interventions on the level of functioning and emotional arousal of the patient. If the patient is highly emotional, mentalizing is severely compromised, and perceptions are skewed in a direction that further escalates reactivity. The MBT-ED recommendation is for the therapist to interrupt and explore the therapeutic exchanges that evoked the emotional reaction. This intervention helps both patient and therapist return to a mentalizing state. Conversely, for those trapped in the corporal realms of experience, the careful exploration and identification of emotional signals are necessary to invoke emotional arousal. Actively pursuing clarifications and challenging patients about concrete explanations for emotional processes can potentially increase suppressed affect and clarify emotional experience (Skarderud & Fonagy, 2012).

Interventions: non-mentalizing activity

In general, all interventions in MBT-ED are designed to be simple, concise, and focused on the therapy process as opposed to the patient's commentary. Therapeutic interventions should also target the current subjective experiences of the patient, particularly in relation to present events or interpersonal interactions. Misunderstandings and enactments that occur within the therapeutic relationship are also key opportunities for reflecting on different perspectives and states of mind. Moreover, ruptures in the therapeutic alliance are considered a failure of mentalizing on the part of both patient and therapist. Bateman and Fonagy (2007) recommend that the therapist first review his/her role in the problem as a way of modeling self-reflection, as well as discuss with the patient the events that led to the breach. Unlike the cognitive behavioral therapy (CBT) technique of correcting cognitive distortions, no assumptions are made in MBT about the greater validity of the therapist's point of view. Instead, the goal of the therapeutic process and interventions is to help patients reflect upon implicit representations, mentalize emotional states, and achieve representational coherence.

The central purpose of MBT's interventions is to interrupt the pre-mentalistic or non-mentalizing flow of content and activity occurring during sessions. Patients are stopped and asked to go back and consider their stated perspective, think about the stance they are taking, and be curious about possible alternatives. Again, this technique differs from the CBT intervention of delineating and correcting cognitive distortions. Instead, the aim of the MBT intervention is to create a meta-cognitive process of reflecting on thought processes, shift from rigid and polarized views of self and other, and realize that multiple perspectives are possible. The term, "Stop, Rewind, and Explore" designates the group of interventions for this process (Bateman & Fonagy, 2007).

MBT-ED does align with the psychodynamic tradition that eating-disordered behaviors such as starving, purging, binge eating, and excessive exercise convey symbolic meaning for the patient, but are primarily viewed as maladaptive attempts to defend against painful self and emotional states. The life-threatening nature of behaviors seen in eating disorders, however, especially starvation and purging, calls for a modification of the original MBT model's recommendation that the patient's mind, not behaviors, be the focus of treatment. Skarderud and Fonagy (2012) address this difference in therapeutic need by explicitly stating that MBT-ED interventions must also actively target symptom reduction. In the present MBT-ED model, however, there are no techniques specified for shaping these behaviors other than a brief description of "negotiating the non-negotiables" of eating requirements for anorexic patients (p. 380). The term *negotiating the non-negotiables* refers to a process whereby the therapist takes a firm, but flexible stance when discussing expectations about eating and weight restoration. It is unclear how this negotiation process would be enough to modify the entrenched compulsive behaviors of restriction and purging to restore health, especially in an out-patient treatment where there is minimal or no ongoing supervision. Further empirical investigation of the clinical application of this model will likely determine whether additional behavioral-shaping techniques are necessary for remission of severe eating disorder behaviors.

Mentalizing the body

Preoccupations about weight, shape, and size and the concretization of self and somatic experience demonstrate an impoverished ability to symbolize psychic experience. Skarderud and Fonagy (2012) introduced the concept of *embodied mentalizing* to describe the corporal aspects of the mentalizing process and help define problems in this domain. Specifically, they suggest that interoceptive confusion and body image distortions are forms of impaired embodied mentalizing and expressions of pre-mentalistic thinking. For example, psychic equivalence demonstrates how patients' painful self and affect states are expressed through extreme body hatred and the mistaken belief that being "skinny" will bring them self-acceptance, "confidence," and agency. The teleological stance explains the obsessive drive for thinness as a method to obtain self-acceptance and the approval of others. In short, subjugation of the body is a confused attempt to gain mastery and control over feelings of ineffectiveness and lack of self-worth.

Mentalizing the body, from an MBT-ED standpoint, means helping the patient translate concrete experiences into language that symbolizes these processes as "*metaphors for the mind*," not physical objects (Skarderud, 2007a, 2007b). The therapist engages the patient in an exploration of how he/she experiences things but also connects the concrete and literal explanations to primary affective experience and its symbolic meaning. MBT's recommendations to accomplish this goal include focusing on triggers for bodily sensations, identifying shifts in mental states that lead to physical discomfort or body image distortions, and tracking the chain of interpersonal events that induce feelings and ideation about the body (Skarderud & Fonagy, 2012). In short, the phenomenological world of the patient is explored, understood, and connected to subjective experience.

Implications for treatment of eating disorders in children, adolescents, and the family context

Skarderud (2007a) first adapted MBT theory to eating disorders treatment for a qualitative study on the relationship between reflective function and concretized metaphors in patients with anorexia nervosa in Norway. The small cohort of female patients (n=10) ranged from 16 to 35 years of age. Results of the study suggest impaired reflective function (RF) as a core psychopathological trait in anorexia nervosa. (RF signifies quantified index of attachment-related mentalization.) Skarderud used the initial findings to outline a treatment and training manual for the application of MBT for eating pathology (2007c). Subsequently, Robinson and his colleagues (2015) in the United Kingdom conducted the first randomized controlled trial of the MBT-ED model for eating-disordered patients with co-existing symptoms of borderline personality disorder. This research, known as the NOURISHED study, investigated the efficacy and cost effectiveness of MBT-ED for patients 18 years and older. Preliminary results suggest that the approach could be successfully adapted to treat eating disorder symptoms and justified further research investment. In this study, impaired mentalizing resulting from unmanageable emotional states and problems in relationships was found to be a primary precipitant to the onset and escalation of eating disorder symptoms. Thus, MBT, which targets deficits in interpersonal relations and emotional regulation, appears to be well suited for treatment of mentalizing vulnerabilities in this patient population.

The preliminary outcome of the MBT-ED research, although conducted on adult patients (18 years and older), and the existing MBT adolescent, child, and family therapy models offer an opportunity for an adapted version of MBT-ED for the treatment of these patient categories. Mentalization-based treatment for adolescents (MBT-A) primarily focuses on strengthening mentalization in the context of emotionally charged attachment relationships (Bleiberg, Rossouw, Sharp, & Fonagy, 2012). A fundamental feature of the MBT-A model is the provision of "social scaffolding" (Masten & Obradovic, 2006) to support and increase the teenager's mentalizing capacities in this stage of life. *Social scaffolding* refers to an environment that provides clear and consistent boundaries that support maturation. A second guiding principle of MBT-A is to help the parents and family establish mentalized interactions with the adolescent that increase trust, security, attachment, and better communication.

MBFT, the family treatment model, specifically focuses on helping the family members increase their understanding of one another, effectively handle their emotional reactions in relation to one another, and increase effective problem solving. Another principal aim is to assist the family members in increasing empathy for one another (Asen & Fonagy, 2012). Likewise, mentalization-based treatment for children (MBT-C), which includes the parents in the treatment process, aims to facilitate mentalizing capacities, emotional and self-regulation, and self-agency in the child (Zevalkink, Verheugt-Pleiter, & Fonagy, 2012). These two adapted versions of MBT, both in theory and technique, take into consideration the developmental antecedents of certain forms of psychopathology, as well as how the attachment relationship presents advantages and disadvantages for mentalizing activity. The attachment relationship offers an evolutionary context for learning about minds (Fonagy, 2008). Parents' capacity for reflection (Ruffman, Perner, & Parkin, 1999), ability to discuss emotions (Gottman, Fainsilber Katz, & Hooven, 1996), and parenting style (Vinden, 2001) positively correlate with a child's ability to understand mental states. At the same time, there is neuroimaging evidence that some attachment phenomena can temporarily suppress mentalizing capacity. In two studies, activation of brain regions that mediate maternal and adult pair-bonding suppressed brain activity in areas that mediate cognitive control and understanding of others' intentions and emotions during times of negative emotions (Bartels & Zeki, 2000, 2004). This research explains why people in close relationships are frequently unaware or mistaken about the mental states of one another and often the most critical and judgmental about one another.

These findings have critical implications for the treatment of eating pathology in children and adolescents, particularly in the context of family treatment. There is no question that one of the most stressful situations parents can face is the illness of a child. Threat to their child's well-being, uncertainty about the cause of the problem, and helplessness can understandably cause parents to become emotionally distraught and unable to effectively problem solve. Moreover, given that eating disorders are one of the most difficult psychiatric problems to treat (Kaplan & Garfinkel, 1999), it stands to reason that all parties involved in treatment, including the therapist, will struggle with emotional reactivity, interpersonal strife, and impaired mentalizing. In addition to the typical developmental limitations of mentalizing in children and adolescents, the onset of eating psychopathology interrupts any rudimentary forms of mentalizing that the child/teen has developed up to that point in time and contributes to treatment resistance. These factors point to the need for treatment models to include interventions that assist the identified child/adolescent patient (IP) and family members with mentalizing impairments that existed before the onset of the disorder or are due to the stressful experience of the illness.

Proposed model: mentalization-based family therapy – eating disorders (MBFT-ED)

The Academy for Eating Disorders (AED) has taken a position on the important role of the family in eating disorders treatment, except in cases in which family involvement may be clinically contraindicated (LeGrange, Lock, Loeb, & Nicholls, 2010). Examples of contraindication include severe parental psychopathology, lack of parental competencies, parental non-compliance, or history of adverse or traumatic events in the family or child. MBT's empirically supported effectiveness in the treatment of severe psychopathology, as well as its successful work with families and children with trauma at the Anna Freud Centre, offers the field a model that bridges this gap in treatments that work with troubled families. Moreover, MBT's focus on rehabilitation of coercive, non-mentalizing cycles in family interactions meets the need for interventions that aid families that lack the competencies for handling the challenges of the child/adolescent's disorder. An evaluation of attachment-related mentalizing impairments during the assessment phase could inform the choice of optimal treatment modality and interventions based on the identified patient's developmental and attachment needs, as well as the family's vulnerabilities in meeting these needs during times of extreme stress.

The following outline for such a model is based primarily on the treatment protocols used at the Anna Freud National Centre for Children and Families and the Menninger Clinic's MBT adolescent treatment program. The overarching goals and objectives of the proposed MBFT-ED model are to aid the family to commit to treatment, develop and maintain mentalizing processes within the family context, and assist the affected child or adolescent back to physical health and developmental continuity. Other goals and objectives include symptom remission and behavioral change, improved emotional regulation for all family members, and improved body image, self-esteem, and self-agency for the identified patient (IP). Interpersonal vulnerabilities in the IP are another target of treatment, as is self-injury, if present.

Phase I: assessment

The initial assessment phase of MBFT-ED includes a clinical and medical evaluation of the IP to diagnose and determine the severity of the eating pathology and evaluate the impact of the problem on the family. An introduction to the MBFT-ED principles and methods is provided to the family and includes discussion of treatment goals, treatment commitments, and an initial treatment plan. During this evaluation period, an assessment of the mentalizing capacities of all family members can be determined. Fonagy and his associates developed a new self-report measure, the Reflective Functioning Questionnaire (RFQ), which holds promise for this purpose. The measure was validated in three studies and shown to correlate with measures of empathy and perspective-taking (Fonagy et al., 2016). In addition to assessing mentalizing, the interviews should also gather information on the family members' attachment histories and an evaluation of their capacities for empathy, emotional regulation, methods of handling stress, and parenting style. The trajectory and symptoms of the eating disorder and its impact on the family should also be determined. A thorough assessment of these factors and the level of mentalization are necessary to guide the treatment plan and address the risk factors that interfere with treatment outcomes. A full "mentalizing profile" (Luyten et al., 2012) will continue to evolve throughout treatment, and goals and interventions can be adjusted accordingly. Formal training in MBT theory and technique provides clinicians with the knowledge necessary for assessing levels and forms of mentalizing activity. In general, however, mentalizing capacities can be determined by the patients' ability or inability to flexibly reflect on their own and others' minds in an open and curious manner.

All information gathered during the assessment process will define the goals and objectives for the mutually composed case formulation. This written document serves as a guide to how treatment will progress, how interventions will help the family address the eating disorder behaviors, management of conflicts over limit-setting and other interactions, and problem-solving strategies for nutritional rehabilitation. Central relationship concerns, including the impact of the eating disorder on social isolation in the family and IP, are anticipated in the written document, as are potential problems in the therapeutic relationship. These situations are likely to create lapses in mentalizing because of the inordinate amount of emotional distress the family will undergo when implementing the strategies needed to help the child or adolescent. Thus, the formulation also contains educational information and an outline of other resources that support the treatment, including working with the team of professionals that eating disorder syndromes often require (medical management, nutritional advice, and psychiatrist). The case formulation also includes a crisis management plan.

A primary aim of the assessment phase is to educate the family on what mentalizing is and how it assists them in their efforts in recovery. These psychoeducational details are included in the final case formulation and reviewed with the family before Phase II of treatment begins. A truncated version of the plan related to health care needs is given to other team members (physician, psychiatrist) for consensus on goals. Initially, some eating-disordered patients will be reluctant to fully contribute to the creation of the formulation, especially on topics related to weight restoration or monitoring for purging behaviors. Regardless of the IP's response, having him or her participate, even reluctantly, helps increase the IP's commitment to treatment and provides an in vivo experience for the family of taking a firm stance on how health-related behaviors will be handled.

Case example

Dr. A, a pediatrician, referred "S," age 14, for therapy because of a significant weight loss that occurred over her summer break from school. During the medical evaluation, S explained to the pediatrician that she had decided to become vegetarian because of her love of animals and that the weight loss resulted from her lack of understanding of how to incorporate enough vegetarian protein into her diet. At first, the pediatrician recommended a consultation with a nutritionist to educate S about adequate sources for a healthy diet. After a month of these efforts, S was found to have lost even more weight and ceased menstruating.

At that time the pediatrician recommended they consult with a therapist to determine possible emotional causes for the weight loss and conflicts in the family over S's eating patterns.

During the first assessment session, S's father repeatedly stated he believed S had lost weight only because she went "slightly overboard" in her efforts to save animals and have a healthy lifestyle. He felt he alone understood his daughter's belief system because he too was an "activist." Although S's mother did not directly challenge his assertions, she kept requesting that the therapist provide "tools" to get their daughter to eat more. S's brother, R, age 16, barely responded to questions, but eventually stated that he did not want to be at the appointment. The therapist continued to focus on gathering the history and symptoms of the presenting problem and the impact it had on S's functioning and the family. The goal was to have all members of the family reflect on what had happened to bring them to this point in time. As mom began to describe S's progression into odd and rigid behaviors around food, social isolation, and emotional outbursts, dad interrupted to counter with explanations for her changes in behavior. During these parental interactions, both teens remained mostly disengaged but became visibly anxious as the conversation ensued. Because of the parental disagreement on what was happening to cause S's weight loss and the teenagers' increasing anxiety about their disagreement, the therapist decided not to "increase the anxiety" of the parents to activate them into action against the eating disorder, a common family-based therapy (FBT) intervention for denial of the problem. Instead, the therapist invited the family to collaborate on a way to restore S's health, regardless of the etiology of the weight loss. By moving the focus of the discussion to "thinking together" about possible helpful actions, the anxiety and discord in the family gradually subsided. By the end of the session there was growing consensus that the family needed "a bit more help" in this process because of lack of progress to date in restoring S's health.

In subsequent sessions, the measures of assessment the family had been given to complete were reviewed, and further evaluation was made of the family's emotional regulation skills, stress tolerance, parenting styles, and S's eating behaviors and symptoms. Over the course of these sessions a consistent pattern developed of mom becoming very anxious in session about S's "meltdowns" at the table, her inability to get S to eat, and her argument with dad that S had an eating disorder. Dad would challenge these assertions and say that mom was "making a mountain out of a molehill" and causing S's outbursts by her insistence that she eat. He continued to maintain that the weight loss was due to

S's tendency to put a "110% effort" into everything she did. Moreover, he felt that "everyone was overreacting" and that the therapist had a "vested interest in making it a problem." In an individual assessment session with S, she admitted to body shape and size concerns, interpersonal and academic pressures, and distress over how her family interacted. She refused, however, to openly discuss these concerns with the family. Brother, R, eventually stated that he thought something was wrong with the way his sister was eating, but his main concern was that mom and dad were arguing over what to do about it.

After reviewing the information from the assessment, the therapist's initial goals included engaging the family in treatment, further explaining how MBT's model would approach the issues they outlined, and inviting the family to formulate a conjointly agreed-upon treatment plan (case formulation). Problems to be immediately addressed that would interfere with helping the IP recover included parental disagreement about diagnosis, the emotional conflicts and distress related to this difference, the level of anxiety in the family about how to help S, and mentalizing capacities of all family members when in distress and conflict. Risk factors that needed immediate focus included S's health and emotional consequences of the starvation and medical assistance to aid in recovery. Other treatment objectives included dad's lack of trust in the therapist's motivation for helping S and his difficulty in seeing S as possibly having different thoughts, needs, and motivations than his. Brother R's disengagement in the treatment was tentatively understood as his attempt to deal with the family tension and his confusion over what was happening with his sister. Initial goals to assist him included engaging his strengths as an older brother, while at the same time supporting him through this family crisis.

In the formal assessment measures, mom revealed that she grew up with a depressed mother. Dad's father was an alcoholic, which he said taught him to "stand on (his) own two feet." From the attachment measures, mom was assessed as having a preoccupied/anxious attachment style. As a result, she had difficulty providing calm and effective soothing in her responses to S's fears and bodily discomfort, and ultimately would increase S's anxiety. The father was assessed as having dismissing/avoidant style, thus making it also difficult for him to provide sensitive responses to S, especially when it related to seeing her as a person with her own mind. His responses also pointed to his difficulty in understanding mom's distress and need for assistance in dealing with their daughter, which he viewed as "weakness" and exaggeration. Additionally, both teenagers showed indications on the measures of anxious attachment. This information was used to tailor treatment objectives and interventions for the family.

Phase II: treatment framework and session structure

There should be a collaborative effort between the therapist and family in setting the agenda for each session. Choosing what subjects to discuss provides an opportunity for the family to regain a sense of agency and effectiveness in knowing how to help the IP. Each family member starts with suggestions on topics to discuss in the session, as well as input on residual issues from prior sessions that require further attention. Examples of potential subjects in the early stages of therapy include battles over the IP not eating enough, over-exercising, water-loading before medical appointments, and throwing away food. Although these problems may require behavioral intervention, the underlying aim of MBFT-ED is to help the family mentalize during the interactions and situations that induce intense emotional distress. These family discussions, if guided in a safe and productive manner, also offer the IP an opportunity to mentalize the unformulated emotional experiences manifest in these destructive behaviors.

In general, sessions should address communication difficulties, difficulties in handling emotional arousal in the IP and parents when conflicts arise, and ways to understand and reflect on the differences in perspectives and ideas in the family. Exploration, curiosity, and a "not-knowing" stance on the part of the therapist are necessary to model effective mentalizing, especially in the face of the refusal by the IP to eat what is needed, decrease compensatory behaviors, and allow the family to help her/him. The therapist does not take an authoritarian and expert stance in these situations by telling the parents what to do to re-feed their child/teen, which no doubt families in distress will request. Rather, the therapist continually probes and responds in such a way that helps the family think through their process, explain what is happening in these moments of distress, and develop effective solutions to their problems. Examples of questions the therapist might ask the family members to facilitate this process include, "What just happened to cause you to say that to X?" "When you got back into the car, after the last weigh-in, things seemed to fall apart. What do you think you were feeling before leaving the doctor's office? "You said you feel helpless in figuring out how to get her to eat. Let's stop and see if anyone else can help you think through this problem and come up with ideas that might help." The aim is to have the therapeutic action take place between the family members. "What if" questions (Asen & Fonagy, 2012) are also useful for helping parents and the IP reflect on interactions that repeatedly cause fights and arguments. For example, "What if she continues to refuse to eat her dinner? Let's stop and think through what might be helpful in working with this situation?" Again, the therapist does not tell the family what to do, but instead helps the family mentalize in a systematic way.

As recommended in the MBFT model, the MBFT-ED treatment sessions are guided by certain hypotheses about the mentalizing difficulties the family has when interacting with one another. Asen and Fonagy (2012) recommend the following questions to assist the therapist in formulating the hypotheses: "Which mentalizing problem is the most relevant for the family to work on at this time?"

"Which mentalizing problem (PE, PM, TS) might be involved in causing, maintaining, or exacerbating the problematic interaction?"(p. 116). The working hypotheses are discussed with the family, mutually agreed upon, and illustrated with examples from the family's narratives. The strengths of the family members are also outlined in this process. These interactive cycles of conflict and non-mentalizing are explained as maintaining factors, and are not implied as the direct cause of the problem. This explanation helps diminish shame, which in turn increases the capacity to reflect on internal states of mind.

Case example

At the end of the assessment period, the therapist gave the family members a written draft of the formulation to read, discuss, and refine. In the document was a summary of background information provided by the family, a history of S's change in behavior around eating, and current problematic interactions reported by the family. Brief developmental history experiences and attachment history were linked to existing coping skills, mentalizing capacities, interactional patterns in the family, and S's symptoms. A description, using the family's own language, was provided on how the family handled stress and emotional arousal in difficult interactions. Mentalizing vulnerabilities were described in this context. Strengths and positive interactional strategies in the family were also listed. The draft formulation was then used to discuss whether a commitment to treatment was feasible. Dad's doubt about the necessity of therapy was a central topic of discussion at this point. The discussions around this theme were also used by the therapist to intervene on mentalizing vulnerabilities in family interactions and regulating emotional intensity. Once the revisions were completed, the therapist asked S to decide what to call the family's formulation to model curiosity of S's independent mind. S chose the title, "Working Plan for the Family." The therapist highlighted the flexible and open tone of her chosen title.

The "Working Plan" was to be used by the family to help them think through how to address the physical reality of S's weight loss and their previous inability to get her to eat. To that end, the consulting physician's warning about a higher level of care or hospitalization was listed for consideration, as was the family's anxiety and conflict about the best approach to prevent this. For S, objectives included normalization of eating, restoration of weight, and return of menses. Specific mentalizing vulnerabilities highlighted in the formulation included difficulties in understanding one another's perspectives about what was going on for S, a lack of trust in the therapist's motivations to help, and how emotional strife and stress led to helplessness, frustration, and blaming. With the therapist's prompting, the teenagers listed specific recommendations for their parents about how to respond more effectively to the teens' emotional distress. The therapist's intention in this suggestion was to find a way for the family to reflect on assumptions being made about one another's needs, desires, and motivations.

A pivotal point in the initial phase of treatment appeared to result from the therapist asking a "what if" question. In response to a declaration by dad that he thought S had enough information to "know" she needed to eat more, the therapist asked, "What if S continues to refuse to eat and lose weight? What do you think you will do then?" Dad appeared stumped by the question, while mom spiraled into predictions of disaster. Although this increased the anxiety in the family and clearly upset mom, the moment was used to interrupt pre-mentalistic modes of thinking and have the family reflect on problem solving and agreeing on what to do should this happen. After this session, the family agreed that it behooved them to find a way to work in unison to help S. Dad continued to stress, however, that the therapist and doctor had "no right" to determine what type of care was provided to S in the future should she continue not to eat. This form of pre-mentalistic thinking, psychic equivalence, and its underlying emotional states were a central focus in the remaining treatment.

Therapeutic process

Two of the defining features of MBT are the "not-knowing" stance of the therapist and a dedicated focus on fostering mentalizing throughout the treatment process. Treating eating disorders, however, also requires a committed focus on "keeping the symptoms in mind" and restoration of health because of the high risk of short- and long-term medical complications (Skarderud & Fonagy, 2012). One of the safeguards "for keeping the symptoms in mind" includes consistent medical monitoring by a physician trained in these disorders. There should be a close collaboration with this team member on the health status of the patient, weight restoration targets, and consensus on treatment goals. For the therapy process, "keeping the symptoms in mind" entails having a clear idea of when mentalizing assists with symptom management and when other modalities may be necessary to change dangerous behaviors. The developers of MBT-A (Bleiberg et al., 2012) have recommended incorporation of adjunctive forms of therapy that also address the multiple neuropsychiatric problems seen in adolescent patients. In the case of eating disorders, behavioral shaping techniques may also be necessary to reduce compulsive behaviors such as purging and over-exercising. Exposure therapy techniques could also be beneficial in treating food refusal and other eating-related anxieties. The mentalizing framework of promoting and enhancing mentalizing in children/adolescents and their families, however, is the core goal of the MBT models, even when adjunctively using behavioral and cognitive techniques. The primary objective in the choice of all interventions in MBT is to increase a reflective process of mentalizing.

MBT-ED techniques for enhancing mentalizing

Once the hypotheses on mentalizing difficulties are generated and discussed with the family, the therapist needs to take an active stance in intervening in these processes. Unlike some eating disorders family treatment models, MBFT-ED assumes that these underlying psychological problems need to be addressed from the onset of therapy, in addition to symptom management, if the family is going to be successful at moderating their emotional distress, and the distress of the IP, invoked during efforts to help the child. As mentioned earlier, the deactivation of the attachment system under states of emotional arousal not only suppresses mentalizing activity but also decreases the capacity to see attachment figures as benign. In such cases, this makes it difficult to trust one another's motivations and intentions. This could explain why many parents view their child's eating disorder behavior as "manipulative," "attention-seeking," and intentional. Additionally, many children and adolescents have described their parents' efforts to help them as "controlling," "making the problem worse," and intended to "punish" them. Some models explain these responses by the IP as "the eating disorder talking" in order to wrest control away from the parents. From an MBFT-ED standpoint, however, helping the parents view these types of reactions as efforts to regulate fear or confusion within the parent/child (attachment) relationship can evoke empathy for the child, while still holding firm on required behaviors for recovery.

To address lapses in empathy and emotional reactivity in the treatment process, Asen and Fonagy (2012) have described several techniques for restoration of mentalizing. Two methods are outlined, followed by illustrations in the case example. The first intervention is called the "five-step loop." The imagery of a "loop" is used to capture the repetitive process inherent in social learning and also in the therapeutic process. The intervention starts with the therapist making an observation about an interaction that has just occurred in the session. Next, the therapist checks to see if the family agrees with the observation, or refutes it. If rejected, more discussion is elicited to determine the family's perspective on what they think happened. If the family accepts the observation, the next step is to "*mentalize the moment*" (p. 120). The therapist's questions and interest in the viewpoints of all family members facilitates this process. By understanding each person's perspective, the family has an opportunity to reflect on the thoughts, feelings, and motivations of each member. Essentially, this is a form of meta-communication about mental states that helps reduce emotional reactivity and generate better understanding. It is important that the family conducts this process with one another, instead of only engaging with the therapist. The last step of the "loop" is for the therapist to invite the family to review their experience of the interaction. This serves as an opportunity to reflect on how engaging in such a process outside of the sessions could help them in future interpersonal exchanges.

Case example

S, brother, and parents were discussing in session the previous week's efforts to help S eat her meals with the family, as opposed to eating alone in her room as she had done during the time she lost weight. S's brother, R, stated that his mom and dad were not "tough" enough on S to keep her at the table. R also said that he "knew" S was giving food to the dog and throwing it out her window when mom served her in her bedroom instead of having her come to the table as was agreed in the last session. When R said this, mom immediately became upset and told the therapist that she was "all alone" in trying to get the family meal going because dad "never" helped her with "anything." S sat silently looking out the window, as the three other members exchanged words and glances regarding this topic. The therapist understood this recurring pattern as not only mom and dad disagreeing about how to help S, but as inducing emotional states that led to pre-mentalistic modes of thinking. In short, mom reported feelings of being abandoned, while dad accused her of exaggerating to get him to capitulate. R's reaction to the distress resulted in him serving as the "family therapist" and pointing out the inconsistencies and conflicts. S withdrew altogether from any interactions (a pattern of behavior described by mom in the history taking about early attachment experiences). The therapist stopped the interaction by stating, "I notice that whenever the three of you start to talk about this subject that S seems to leave the room. In this case, she goes away by staring out the window. Does anyone else notice this?

R immediately interjects that he agreed; mom notes how S also withdraws from everyone at home by going into her room to "watch Netflix." Dad disagrees by saying, "I think it's normal for teenagers to want to get away from their parents." Because of this disagreement and the increase in the tension in the room, the therapist asks how each member understands this difference in perspective. R volunteers first and says that dad "always sides with S" whenever she has a disagreement with mom. Dad denies this and elaborates that S does not need help speaking for herself. The therapist uses this opening to ask S if she has an opinion on these differences. Despite S's answer of, "I don't know," the therapist continues the recursive steps of the "loop" by asking if she could try imagining what mom might be thinking and feeling when she sees her staring out the window during the session. S hesitates at first, then answers, "I guess she's wondering what I'm looking at." Mom says with a quiver in her voice, "Yes, I'm always wondering what you are thinking about because I'm really interested in what's important to you; it's just so hard to tell." S finally looks at her mother but does not reply. The therapist points out that better understanding S's thoughts and feelings, as well as helping her express them, seems important to her getting better. She asks if they agreed and if they thought it was important to continue to find ways in session to work on this together.

In a subsequent session, during a disagreement mom and dad were having over what would be an adequate breakfast for S's health, S reminded dad that he had previously said she "did not need help speaking" for herself. She then told her mother that she wanted oatmeal for some of her breakfasts next week. Mom thanked her for the suggestion and added that the oatmeal would also need nuts and raisins to meet her nutritional needs. S said that would be "okay for a while." The therapist observed that something had just happened to help S directly tell her parents what would help her, as opposed to them guessing and disagreeing over what might be in her mind. The therapist then asked, "Is that the way you see it?" Mom quickly turned to S and said that she appreciated knowing that S was willing to add the raisins and nuts without "creating a stink." Dad stated that he had told mom that S "could handle" other breakfast choices and that mom just needed to stop worrying and constantly nagging S to eat more. The therapist responded with, "It seems that mom feels that S's input on food choices lowers her worry that they will get into an argument, whereas dad feels mom needs to quit asking S for input. Do you recognize this as something that happens at home when you are trying to decide on how to help S eat? Everyone agreed that this was a frequent discussion/disagreement at home. The therapist then asked if they would explore what changed or was different today when S spoke up about what she wanted for breakfast. Mom responded first by telling S that knowing her thoughts helped her know "how to help more effectively." R added that S speaking her mind kept mom and dad from "getting into it." The "getting into it" theme was used repeatedly in future sessions to help the family interrupt an argument, step back, and reflect on one another's perspectives, rather than make assumptions.

Another useful intervention for MBFT-ED families is called "Stop and Stand" (Bateman & Fonagy, 2007). The primary purpose of the intervention is to reinstate mentalizing when it fails, in either the patient(s) or the therapist. The therapist interrupts the family's escalating argument with a challenging question or observation. They are then asked to examine the problematic emotional interaction. The goal is to create a focal moment in which a less emotionally charged exploration of the problem can occur and mentalization can be restored. Essentially, the observation "stops" the severe non-mentalizing and confronts or takes a "stand" on the position the person is taking. This intervention can be helpful in family sessions when one member is making extreme assumptions about another person, including the therapist. The investigation of the underlying emotional state that was motivating the non-mentalizing activity follows the intervention.

Case example

During this session, mom started talking about what happened at the last doctor's appointment and how S had not gained weight that week, despite her best efforts at helping her eat. At this point, dad started glancing at his cell phone. Eventually, mom began to sigh and express how alone she felt in the effort to get S well. R's attention oriented towards mom and he seemed to become concerned about her distress, while S shifted her gaze to the window. The therapist, at this point, stopped the flow of content by saying, "S is clearly expressing something by looking out the window again, while the rest of us are talking about the doctor's visit. Can anyone help her with this, because I wonder if she's trying to tell us something about how she feels about the doctor's appointment or something else? Does anyone want to try and help her see if she can tell us what she's thinking?" (This is meant not only to "stop" the process, but also to try and engage S.) Dad immediately steps in for S and says, "She's a very private person. Like me, she doesn't wear her feelings on her sleeve. *You* keep forgetting that (referring to the therapist)." The therapist responded, "Help me understand how you came to that conclusion – that I keep forgetting how private S is?" (Challenge was used to intervene on dad's continued problem with understanding others' minds, including the motivations of the therapist.) Dad says, "Well, you keep asking her what she's *feeling* (tone of disgust)." The therapist responds, "I can see how that question could imply that I keep forgetting and might bother her. Would you be interested in my intention when I continue to ask S questions?" Dad says, "Maybe she would too." Therapist, "Oh, yes, that's right. (Turning to address S, as well as dad). S, would it be okay if I explained my actions? (S nods in agreement.) I continue to ask you questions because I do not want to make assumptions about what you might be feeling and thinking, and yet I'm genuinely interested in knowing what you think." S does not immediately respond but does look at the therapist and smiles. The therapist turns to dad and says, "I'm also interested in what you feel. In this case, could you let me know what your concerns are about how I interact with S?"

Assigned activities and tasks

Requesting that the family work on mentalizing between sessions is necessary for progress. To this end, is it important to collaboratively establish goals, tasks, and activities the family can use to target problematic interactions and communications. "Homework" assignments are helpful for this process and can address specific problems and areas of concern for the family. One well-received activity for families from the MBT family model is called the "mind-brain scan." The family members are each given a large sheet of paper that contains artwork of a cross-section of the human brain. The image of the brain has several large and small empty spaces on it, symbolizing ventricles of the brain, where family members are asked to write descriptions of thoughts and feelings about the assigned task. For example, a disengaged teenager might be asked to, "Imagine this is your mom's brain or mind. Write in all the thoughts and feelings you think she might be having at this moment. In the larger ventricles, or spaces, you can put in obvious feelings and thoughts. In the smaller spaces or ventricles, put the less obvious, or maybe secret, thoughts and feelings she could have." Other members of the family are told to do the same about that person, or another member. A discussion follows on how accurately each family member can "mind-read" the internal lives of one another. This intervention has different variations, including having the family "mind-read" about a specific problematic interaction or speculate about thoughts and feeling that might come up in the future (Asen & Fonagy, 2012).

Case example

The family was making progress in helping S eat her full meals, almost reach the doctor's weight goal range, and have fewer "meltdowns" during meals. During a session, the parents were describing this progress. Dad stated that he thought therapy was no longer needed since S was doing so well. This statement seemed to upset mom, as she began to shift around in her seat. As this was going on, the therapist noticed that

S was looking out the window again. The therapist noted this interaction by saying, "I am noticing that as we are talking about the progress you have made, that you are looking out the window again. I know you are a private person, but I am guessing you might be trying to communicate something to us by looking out the window. I may be completely wrong, so let me know." S was not that forthcoming with information, so the therapist said, "Since we're getting close to the end of the session today, I've got a suggestion I would like the family to try." The brain-scan exercise was explained to the family, along with its purpose. The brain "images" were given to the family to complete at home, with the request not to confer with one another before or after filling in the "ventricles" with imagined thoughts and feelings about certain members of the family that each one selected to "mind-read."

The family brought the "brain scans" to the following session and after taping them up for examination, the therapist asked a member to read aloud the "contents" of another family member's mind. An exploration of how "accurately" each person could "mind-read" another family member followed. During this process, mom and R both agreed that S was the "best mind-reader of Dad's brain." The therapist asked dad, "Do you agree, that S understands the most about what you are thinking and feeling?" For the first time since therapy began, Dad's response softened as he said, "Yes, but I didn't realize I was coming across so strongly." The therapist asked dad if he could tell S more about what he meant by "coming across so strongly." He said, "S, I didn't realize you felt that I was always telling you what you think."

Final phases of treatment and termination issues

The final phase of MBFT-ED contains the goals of increasing independence and responsibility and consolidating gains made during treatment. Working on ending the therapeutic endeavor is also a primary focus. The exact timing of this phase will depend on the achievement of the goals set out from the beginning of treatment for symptom remission, restoration of health and weight, and the ability of the IP to meet his or her nutritional needs without parental supervision. It can be helpful to reduce the sessions in a graduated process, such as going from once-a-week therapy to every other week, to monthly meetings, to periodic check-ins. Additionally, because of the severity of some forms of eating disorders, additional individual work may be necessary to address continued body image problems, social difficulties, or other problems for the IP. Referrals for individual treatment should be framed as an indication of the child/teen's ability to work independently and not as a lack of success in the family's efforts.

Case example

At the beginning of the session the family was given an opportunity to decide what to cover in the session. Dad brought up that S had been given medical clearance by the physician and that he thought this was the perfect time to end therapy because the original goal for treatment had been reached. As the family engaged in a discussion of this topic, the recurring pattern emerged of mom becoming anxious, dad becoming insistent on his point of view, R trying to restore calm in the family, and S "leaving the room." At this point, these patterns had been described, agreed upon as problematic, and understood in a more reflective way. The therapist intervened by interrupting the process and saying that it felt as if "a stuck place" was coming up. She asked the family to look at what was going on and if anyone could think of ways they learned from the "Working Plan for the Family" that they could use to help them out of the "stuck place." These terms had been devised by the family for use in communicating better about conflicts. S was the first one to come up with the idea about someone in the family taking a turn at mind-reading her thoughts about reaching her weight goal and ending therapy. Mom volunteered to go first and began by asking S for immediate feedback if she was making "assumptions." Mom stated that she thought S was probably "ready" for therapy to end some time ago, but also probably worried about her parents handling things on their own. Mom then asked, "Am I reading you right, or missing something?" S acknowledged the accuracy of this. R immediately chimed in that he has "wanted to end therapy from the start!" Everyone laughed, but S reminded him that it was *her* mind that was being read, not his. (The therapist laughed the loudest at this comment.) Dad took his turn by saying that he realized he had spoken for everyone and that he wanted to start again by having a discussion about the decision. The family discussed all options, including having S attend individual therapy, but ultimately decided that further family work was needed. Dad's input that he wanted to still reduce the number of sessions "bit by bit" was also accepted by all.

Conclusion and recommendations

Mentalization-based family treatment for eating disorders (MBFT-ED) offers a multidimensional approach for the treatment of eating disorders in children and adolescents. It not only addresses the AED's recommendation for the involvement of the family in treatment but also its theoretical grounding in theory and research from the fields of developmental psychology, neurobiology, and attachment theory meet the recommendations for addressing the developmental complexities in eating-disordered patients, treating related co-morbidities in this population, and improving treatment outcomes. Moreover, given that MBT's foundational framework is premised on the caregiver/child attachment system, as well as how affect regulation, self-agency, and self-identity develop within this matrix, it offers a unique perspective on how these developmental tasks go awry and contribute to the etiology and maintenance of eating pathology. MBFT-ED interventions are specifically designed to address these self-deficits, as well as support the family in restoring the child or teen back to physical health.

The adaptation of the MBT-ED for treating adolescents and children in the family context was proposed as a stand-alone model or adjunctive treatment focus to use in other existing treatment models. Given the multi-factorial causation of eating disorders, it is likely that impaired mentalizing and attachment insecurities have an interactional relationship in the etiology of eating disorders for many patients (Jewell et al., 2015). Moreover, the mentalizing construct holds promise for informing advancements in effective interventions that address the developmental and neurobiological risk factors of eating pathology. Specifically, recent neuroscience research into the neural regions involved in socio-cognitive functioning in eating-disordered patients shows that improvements in interpersonal relationships, including the capacity to understand others' perspectives, are associated with long-term recovery (McAdams et al., 2016). To that end, this paper offers an initial proposal of an adapted version of MBT for the needs of families involved in the treatment of their children and adolescents with eating pathology that merits further development and eventual empirical investigation into its efficacy and cost-effectiveness.

References

Allen, J. G., & Fonagy, P. (Eds.) (2006). *Handbook of mentalization-based treatment*. Chichester, England: Wiley & Sons.

Allen, J. G., Fonagy, P., & Bateman, A. W. (2008). *Mentalizing in clinical practice*. Arlington, VA: American Psychiatric Publishing.

Asen, E., & Fonagy, P. (2012). Mentalization-based family therapy. In A. Bateman & P. Fonagy (Eds.), *Handbook of mentalizing in mental health practice* (pp. 107–128). Washington, DC: American Psychiatric Publishing.

Bartels, A., & Zeki, S. (2000). The neural basis of romantic love. *NeuroReport*, *11*(17), 3829–3834.

Bartels, A., & Zeki, S. (2004). The neural correlates of maternal and romantic love. *Neuroimage*, *21*, 1155–1166.

Bateman, A. W., Bales, D., & Hutsebaut, J. A. (n.d.). Quality manual for MBT, Unpublished.

Bateman, A. W., & Fonagy, P. (2004). Mentalization-based treatment of borderline personality disorder. *Journal of Personality Disorder*, *18*, 36–51.

Bateman, A. W., & Fonagy, P. (2007). *Mentalization-based treatment for borderline personality disorder: A practical guide*. Oxford: Oxford University Press.

Bateman, A. W., & Fonagy, P. (2008). Comorbid antisocial and borderline personality disorders: Mentalization-based treatment. *Journal of Clinical Psychology*, *64*(2), 181–194.

Bateman, A. W., & Fonagy, P. (2010). Mentalization-based treatment for borderline personality disorder. *World Psychiatry*, *9*(1), 11–15.
Bateman, A. W., & Fonagy, P. (Eds.) (2012). *Handbook of mentalizing in mental health practice*. Washington, DC: American Psychiatric Publishing.
Bishop, E. R. (2006). *The path to coherence: Resolving the mind-body problem in eating disorders*, Unpublished Manuscript.
Bleiberg, E., Rossouw, T., Sharp, C., & Fonagy, P. (2012). Adolescent breakdown and emerging borderline personality disorder. In A. Bateman & P. Fonagy (Eds.), *Handbook of mentalizing in mental health practice* (pp. 463–509). Washington, DC: American Psychiatric Publishing.
Buhl, C. (2002). Eating disorders as manifestations of developmental disorders: Language and capacity for abstract thinking in psychotherapy for eating disorders. *European Eating Disorders Review*, *10*, 138–145.
Cacioppo, J. T., Berntson, G. G., & Decety, J. (2010). Social neuroscience and its relationship to social psychology. *Social Cognition*, *28*, 675–685.
Carryer, J. R., & Greenberg, L. S. (2010). Optimal levels of emotional arousal in experiential therapy of depression. *Journal of Consulting and Clinical Psychology*, *78*(2), 190–199.
Cozolino, L. (2014). *The neuroscience of human relationships: Attachment and the developing social brain*. (2nd ed.). New York: Norton.
Fonagy, P. (2008). The mentalization-focused approach to social development. In F. N. Busch (Ed.), *Mentalization: Theoretical considerations, research findings, and clinical implications*. (pp. 3–56). New York: The Analytic Press.
Fonagy, P., & Bateman, A. (2011). The widening scope of mentalizing: A discussion. *Psychology and Psychotherapy: Theory, Research, and Practice*, *84*, 98–110.
Fonagy, P., Bateman, A. W., & Luyten, P. (2012). Introduction and overview. In A. Bateman & P. Fonagy (Eds.), *Handbook of mentalizing in mental health practice* (pp. 3–42). Washington, DC: American Psychiatric Publishing.
Fonagy, P., Gergely, G., Jurist, E., & Target, M. (2002). *Affect regulation, mentalization, and the development of the self*. New York: Other Press.
Fonagy, P., Luyten, P., Moulton-Perkins, A., Lee, Y., Warren, F., Howard, S., Ghinai, R., Fearon, P., & Lowyck, B. (2016). Development and validation of a self-report measure of mentalizing: The reflective functioning questionnaire. *PLoSOne*, *11*(7). (Published online).
Fonagy, P., & Target, M. (2006). The mentalisation-based approach to self pathology, *Journal of Personality Disorders*, *20*, 544–576.
Fonagy, P., & Target, M. (2007). The rooting of the mind in the body: New links between attachment theory and psychoanalytic thought. *Journal of the American Psychoanalytic Association*, *55*, 411–456.
Gergely, G., & Unoka, Z. (2008). Attachment and mentalization in humans: The development of the affective self. In E. J. Jurist, A. Slade, & S. Bergner (Eds.), *Mind to mind: Infant research, neuroscience, and psychoanalysis* (pp. 50–87). New York: Other Press.
Glaser, D. (2000). Child abuse and neglect and the brain – A review. *Journal of Child Psychiatry and Allied Disciplines*, *41*(1), 97–116.
Gopnik, A. (1993). How we know our minds: The illusion of first-person knowledge of intentionality, *Behavior and Brain Science*, *16*(1), 1–14.
Gottman, J. M., Fainsilber Katz, L., & Hooven, C. (1996). Parental meta-emotion philosophy and the emotional life of families: Theoretical models and preliminary data. *Journal of Family Psychology*, *10*(3), 243–268.

Jewell, T., Collyer, H., Gardner, T., Tchanturia, K., Simic, M., Fonagy, P., & Eisler, I. (2015). Attachment and mentalization and their association with child and adolescent eating pathology: A systematic review. *International Journal of Eating Disorders, 49*(4), 354–373.
Kaplan, A. S., & Garfinkel, P. E. (1999). Difficulties in treating patients with eating disorders: A review of patient and clinician variables. *Canadian Journal of Psychiatry, 44*, 665–670.
Keel, P. K., & Brown, T. A. (2010). Update on course and outcome in eating disorders. *International Journal of Eating Disorders, 43*, 195–204.
Lane, R. D., Ryan, L., Nadel, L., & Greenberg, L. (2015). Memory reconsolidation, emotional arousal, and the process of change in psychotherapy: New insights from brain science. *Behavioral and Brain Sciences, 38*, 1–80.
LeGrange, D., Lock, J., Loeb, K., & Nicholls, D. (2010). Academy for eating disorders position paper: The role of the family in eating disorders. *International Journal of Eating Disorders, 43*(1), 1–5.
Lock, J., LeGrange, D., Agras, W. S., & Dare, C. (2001). *Treatment manual for anorexia nervosa*. New York: Guilford Press.
Luyten, P., Fonagy, P., Lowyck, B., & Vermote, R. (2012). Assessment of mentalization. In A. Bateman & P. Fonagy (Eds.), *Handbook of mentalizing in mental health practice* (pp. 43–66). Washington, DC: American Psychiatric Publishing.
Masten, A. S., & Obradovic, J. (2006). Resilience in children. *Annals of the New York Academy of Sciences, 1094*, 13–17.
McAdams, C., & Krawczyk, D. (2011). Impaired neural processing of social attribution in anorexia nervosa. *Psychiatry Research: Neuroimaging, 194*, 54–63.
McAdams, C., & Krawczyk, D. (2014). Who am I? How do I look? Neural differences in self-identity in anorexia nervosa. *Social Cognitive and Affective Neuroscience, 9*, 12–21.
McAdams, C., Lohrenz, T., & Montague, P. R. (2015). Neural responses to kindness and malevolence differ in illness and recovery in women with anorexia nervosa. *Human Brain Mapping, 36*, 5207–5219.
McAdams, C., Jeon-Slaughter, H., Evans, S., Lohrenz, T., Montague, P. R. & Krawczyk, D. (in press). Neural differences in self-perception during illness and after weight-recovery in anorexia nervosa. *Social Cognitive and Affective Neuroscience*.
Mikulincer, M., & Shaver, P. R. (2007). *Attachment in adulthood: Structure, dynamics and change*. New York: Guilford Press.
Mikulincer, M., & Shaver, P. R. (2012). An attachment perspective on psychopathology. *World Psychiatry, 11*(1), 11–15.
Moller, C., Karlgren, L., Sandell, A., Falkenstrom, F., & Philips, B. (2016). Mentalization-based therapy adherence and competence stimulates in-session mentalization in psychotherapy for borderline personality disorder with co-morbid substance dependence. *Psychotherapy Research, 19*, 1–17.
Nilsson, K., & Hagglof, B. (2006). Patient perspectives of recovery in adolescent onset anorexia nervosa. *Eating Disorders, 14*(4), 305–311.
Pennesi, J. L., & Wade, T. D. (2016). A systematic review of the existing models of disordered eating: Do they inform the developments of effective interventions? *Clinical Psychology Review, 43*, 175–192.
Porges, S. W. (2003). Social engagement and attachment: A phylogenetic perspective. *Annals of New York Academy of Sciences, 1008*, 31–47.
Robinson, P., Hellier, J., Murphy, C., Barrett, B., Rutterford, C., Lemonsky, F., Schmidt, U., . . . Fonagy, P. (2015, April). *A randomized controlled trial of mentalization-based therapy (ED) against specialist supportive clinical management (ED) in patients with*

both eating disorders and symptoms of borderline personality disorder: The nourished study. Poster session presented at the International Eating Disorder Conference, Boston.
Rothschild-Yakar, L., Levy-Shiff, R., Fridman-Balaban, R., Gur, E., & Stein, D. (2010). Mentalization and relationships with parents as predictors of eating disordered behavior. *Journal of Nervous and Mental Disease, 198*(7), 501–507.
Rothschild-Yakar, L., & Stein, W. A. (2013). Mentalizing in self versus parent representations and working models of parents as risk and protective factors from distress and eating disorders. *Journal of Nervous and Mental Diseases, 201*(6), 510–518.
Ruffman, T., Perner, J., & Parkin, L. (1999). How parenting style affects false belief understanding. *Social Development, 8*(3), 395–411.
Schore, A. N. (2001). The effects of early relational trauma on right brain development, affect regulation, and infant mental health. *Infant Mental Health Journal, 22*(1–2), 201–269.
Sharp, C., & Fonagy, P. (2008). The parent's capacity to treat the child as a psychological agent: Constructs, measures and implications for developmental psychopathology. *Social Development, 17*(3), 737–754.
Sharp, C., Fonagy, P., & Goodyer, I. M. (Eds.) (2008). *Social cognition and developmental psychopathology*. Oxford: Oxford University Press.
Skarderud, F., & Fonagy, P. (2012). Eating disorders. In A. Bateman & P. Fonagy (Eds.), *Handbook of mentalizing in mental health practice* (pp. 347–384). Washington, DC: American Psychiatric Publishing.
Skarderud, F. (2007a). Eating one's words, Part I: Concretised metaphors and reflective function in anorexia nervosa – an interview study. *European Eating Disorders Review, 15*, 163–174.
Skarderud, F. (2007b). Eating one's words, Part II: The embodied mind and reflective function in anorexia nervosa – theory. *European Eating Disorders Review, 15*, 243–252.
Skarderud, F. (2007c). Shame and pride in anorexia nervosa: A qualitative descriptive study. *European Eating Disorders Review, 15*, 81–97.
Sroufe, L. A. (1996). *Emotional development: The organization of emotional life in the early years*. New York: Cambridge University Press.
Steinhausen, H. C. (2002). The outcome of anorexia nervosa in the 20th century. *American Journal of Psychiatry, 159*(8), 1284–1293.
Stice, E. (2002). Risk and maintenance factors for eating pathology: A meta-analytic review. *Psychological Bulletin, 128*(2), 825–848.
Striegel-Moore, R. H., & Bulik, C. M. (2007). Risk factors for eating disorders. *American Psychologist, 62*(3), 181–198.
Tasca, G. A., & Balfour, L. (2014). Attachment and eating disorders: A review of current research. *International Journal of Eating Disorders, 47*(7), 710–717.
Vall, E., & Wade, T. D. (2015). Predictors of treatment outcome in individuals with eating disorders: A systematic review and meta-analysis. *International Journal of Eating Disorders, 48*(7), 946–971.
Vinden, P. G. (2001). Parenting attitudes and children's understanding of mind: A comparison of Korean American and Angelo-American families. *Cognitive Development, 16*(3), 793–809.
Wilson, E. O. (2012). *The social conquest of earth*. New York: Liveright Publishing.
Young, L. J., & Wang, Z. (2004). The neurobiology of pair bonding. *Nature Neuroscience, 7*, 1048–1054.
Zevalkink, J., Verheugt-Pleiter, A., & Fonagy, P. (2012). Mentalization -informed child psychoanalytic psychotherapy. In A. Bateman & P. Fonagy (Eds.), *Handbook of mentalizing in mental health practice* (pp. 129–158). Washington, DC: American Psychiatric Publishing.

PART III

Contemporary issues related to eating disorders

11

THE LOW SPARK OF HIGH-HEELED 'GIRLS'

Hyperdeadness and hyperawareness with eating-disordered patients

Jean Petrucelli

Our culture follows an unspoken, yet quietly accepted, code of behavior and set of rules when it comes to women in the limelight in that they are required to be thin. Not eating a normal diet is seen as 'normal,' and not even dangerous. Eating disorders, or disordered eating, is regrettably culturally normalized, especially in celebrity and popular culture. Few acknowledge that it's not healthy, and potentially fatal (Hughes, 2015). Americans are obsessed with obesity, yet people that are actually overweight are largely absent from our cultural landscape. Most of the people who are overweight – in the media or pop culture – hate their bodies, with few exceptions. Shows such as "The Biggest Loser" parade contestants around like circus animals – celebrities – who are vocal about being overweight and flog themselves in nationally televised weight-loss commercials. We have come to expect the spectacle of the miserable overweight person and to expect that emaciated bodies are culturally sanctioned or 'normal'. However, both result in negative body image, low self-esteem, and increased body dissatisfaction. On either end of the spectrum of body size, a person's shame is held in secret eating and the eating of their secrets. It is, or has become, a radical idea to love your body without losing weight. It is an even more radical idea to appreciate untapped imperfection.

Bodily esteem and body size have become one and the same. Eating disorders fall in line with what society 'expects' of people in the spotlight – a love of 'thinness' while simultaneously conveying that they are immune to, or even repulsed by, the *means* of achieving it. Throughout visual culture, objectification – which we might think of as relational impingement, if not as relational trauma – reminds women that they are being scrutinized and sexualized. It supports women feeling both cut off from their bodies as they regard them as mere aesthetic wrappers of the self, and at the same time deeply preoccupied with their bodies, as they perceive them as central signifiers of identity (Baker-Pitts, 2014; Petrucelli, 2015).

The focus on one's own body as an object inhibits self-awareness and leads to stultifying self-consciousness.

Eating disorders are a silent form of destruction: a destruction of vitality and the hope for a meaningful existence. They create the illusion of time stopping. Past, present, and future collapse: the insidious negative self-talk is too loud, and/or the aftermath of trauma too pervasive and/or the affects too overwhelming. The body itself becomes the theater of war (McDougall, 1989) wherein the feelings, memories, longings, and stories that have led to the symptoms feel so dangerous that they are dissociated from the behaviors themselves. The largeness of a life that we see on stage with celebrity limelight can be paradoxically personally myopic.

Consider the tragic death of British music performer Amy Winehouse. She died in 2011 from what was officially stated as alcohol poisoning; however, various other factors were involved. Her body was also weakened and medically compromised from her known-but-not-discussed eating disorder and the complications relating to bulimia. This was a 'secret' known by many and reported in the media on several accounts from interviews with family members (Day, 2013). On the night of her death, she drank two bottles of vodka, while watching YouTube videos of herself. As well-documented as her struggles with alcohol and drug addiction were, the under-reported fact of her severe, untreated, decade-long bulimarexia, was rarely mentioned (Hughes, 2015).

We can learn much from Amy's painful life, and among these things are the ways in which her dependence on alcohol, drugs, and disordered eating – in other words, her compulsive reliance on 'substances' – were attempts at regulating a profoundly compromised experience of self. Anxious, isolated, alone – yet sparkling, kind, and immensely talented – her vitality was quashed as her fame increased. And one can easily speculate as to how the 'fame' provided her with a kind of pseudo-company – the illusion of companionship and love – that only highlighted on the other hand, her dreadful aloneness and lack of any real or sustaining support or connection. It is a substance-induced high, rather than a sturdy vitality; a binge-on whip cream, rather than a satisfying meal; the illusion of contact, rather than authentic relatedness (Schoen, 2016, personal communication). Amy's struggles and death show us how the low spark of this high-heeled girl only flickers and is then extinguished.

A person struggling with an eating disorder keeps their rituals and disordered behaviors secret – it is a double life of sorts – and the behaviors themselves could be thought of as a maladaptive attempt at a solution. The symptoms are used to maintain a state of mind, full of fantasies of the possibilities of a 'moment 'or a 'life,' without what '*feels*' unbearable (Petrucelli, 2004, 2010, 2015). The person, in the eating disorder (ED) 'body-state,' truly believes that there is no other way. However, there is clearly a kind of knowledge borne of the absence of experience. An anorexic patient refuses food in order to keep her desire 'alive' – rather than saying she does not eat anything – because maybe by the act of refusing food – which results in the absence of the experience of eating – she keeps some space for her desire to live (Fink, 2004). If she says she eats 'nothing,' then nothing is the object that holds her desire . . . and in some ways, keeps her 'feeling' something.

We could ask a person struggling with an ED to truly *imagine* what it is like to have a healthy, stable body that can be trusted. Or can someone struggling with an ED know what it feels like to be alive with feelings of longing and desire? The ED becomes a patient's hyperaware 'solution' to not facing the consequences of living life in her body if she *does not* and *cannot* know – what that experience is. The resulting hyperdeadness, an anesthetization of sorts, that follows from starving, bingeing, or purging forces her to focus on nothing but her symptoms even if she would '*prefer*' not to. It allows her to ultimately believe that in being symptomatic she is 'getting away with something' (Phillips, 2010). But it is only the illusion of getting away with it – and in reality, she has just protracted the torture and deferred the moment of punitive truth of accepting imperfection because, in the illusion of pseudo desire, appetites and their bodies can *seem* bearable.

> I can have all the food I want and never face the idea of the thing not chosen.
> I can be thin and control my body and no one can hurt me.
>
> *(many voices)*

Regardless of the symptom, patients with eating disorders feel they are at the mercy of their feelings and enslaved by their felt inability to contain desire as a regulatable affect, rather than as an overwhelming state in which one wishes and hopes to have everything all the time – a state of mind commonly known as 'greed.' Greed – particularly with regard to human contact – is overwhelming to the eating-disordered patient, who attempts to control her 'appetite.' In this way, she tries to eliminate the potential for traumatic rupture in human relatedness by replacing relationships with food, a solution that is largely self-contained and thus not subject to betrayal by the other (Bromberg, 1998). The problem with greed, or the desire to have it all, is that it inevitably runs into the necessity – the pressure and need to choose. The realization of the need for choice creates either a refusal – no more appetite and frustration – or if the eating-disordered patient manages to make the choice, she always has to contend with the feeling of loss of the thing not chosen. The issue of greed and the unbearable loss of the thing not chosen – unbearable, as Bromberg (personal communication, 2016) would say, because the external indifference and non-recognition that it is indeed a loss – leads to their own dissociative 'indifference' to loss by making sure that loss becomes impossible because desire is foreclosed.

To make a meaningful choice, one must feel meaningfully related to others. To feel meaningfully related to others, one must give up omnipotent fantasies of being able to have it all (or alternately deprive oneself of all), and deal with the losses that reality – and by this I mean real dependency needs and the pleasures and pains of real relationships – entails.

But what is so tricky clinically is that a person with an ED can be of 'many minds' that are not supposed to interfere with one another, and when these patients try to protect themselves in this way, self-development and a sense of coherence is derailed. Rather, they feel stuck, trapped in a narrow, isolated world of loneliness and despair. In contrast, when a person's self and body-states are linked – and when these links do not threaten core, internalized attachment relationships – they have access to all parts of the self and can smoothly transition between them without succumbing to the narrow tunnel of a particular self or body-state filled with shame or self-loathing. This capacity also allows for real contact with others – for the ability to take in what they have to offer and survive how they may fail or disappoint. In treatment, the body speaks in part through the patient's narrative, but it is the felt experience one has within one's own body and between bodies, that is ultimately the vehicle for discourse. The patient's hyperawareness of the outside as a potential threat or impingement and the deadness and lack of vitality on the inside are excruciating, and these states are passed back and forth between patients' varied internal states and between patient and therapist.

Amy Winehouse's story reminds me of my patient, Bella. Bella's desires, like Amy's, were never met and transformed in the mutually regulating context of good enough caretaking. When my patient Bella's mom was pregnant with her, she (Bella's mom) was told she was having twins. During the pregnancy, one of the babies died. The way the family story was told was that 'due to the way the babies were positioned, Bella *ate* all the food' or 'Bella was so hungry that she ate her twin in utero.' Her father chided her, 'You ate your twin with your ravenous appetite!' Bella believes her lost twin was a boy and feels a mixture of guilt and glee.

As a child, Bella preferred to do pirouettes rather than math problems. The middle child of two other sisters, Bella carved her identity out of negative attention-seeking behaviors. From forest-fire setting at age 10, to car crashing under the influence at 17, she had two hospitalizations in her early 20s. She has oscillated between alcohol and opiate addiction, bingeing, purging, restriction, and exercise addiction. Bella's appetite for trouble was as voracious as her craving for food. Physically, she is strikingly beautiful, feisty, antsy, and jumpy. She pulls for images like a 'white rabbit,' with long blonde hair and a petite body. And in fact, when recounting her drug history, she resorts to quoting the Jefferson Airplane lyrics that one pill makes you larger, another small, and the ones mother gives you do nothing at all. In one jangling chorus, it was also her way of forewarning me: I was to be in for a wild ride and nothing I could or would 'give her' would work. Bella lacks empathy and self-reflexivity. She is extremely competitive and also condescending with her sisters. Her thinking is black and white, and her actions are impulse driven. Her first dream in treatment involved 'her sister vomiting in the bathroom in their Hamptons beach house and not cleaning up her vomit.' Bella's association? 'What an amateur she is!'

Bella does whatever she can to anesthetize her unfettered energy and anxiety. The intergenerational transmission of body dissatisfaction and her inability to live in her body is profound. Her mother has had seven cosmetic surgeries; with her mother's suggestion, by the age of 24, Bella had four surgeries, including breast reduction and then implants. She has lost sensation in her breasts, and her breasts have become objects of someone *else's* pleasure. This is one of the many ways Bella sees and treats herself as an object. In her career, as a performer – and perform she does for all around her – she caters to the whims of the narcissistic others who surround and rule her. When not on stage she isolates, avoids social interactions and commitments, and does not make sustainable friendships. She would rather preserve the integrity of an initial encounter by denying herself further ones.

When Bella entered treatment with me, she had two failed residential treatments, had been through several therapists, and was now bingeing and purging four to six times a day, with a 'driving under the influence' charge. I saw her twice weekly and in my group. We made a contract to use her birthday, which was six months away, as a timeline to decide that, if her symptoms hadn't changed, she would consider rehab for a third time. We focused on stopping the alcohol first, utilizing AA, and group therapy. Alcohol was added calories, a secondary gain in her mind, and she was able to stop drinking and has remained sober for the past five years. This was partly because alcohol was not her primary addiction – food was. At this time, she also stopped all her ED symptoms for three months. This was short lived. Her body was slowly starting to digest on its own as her metabolism was sorting itself out. She gained a few pounds as is to be expected but she could not tolerate her 'new' body, so she started to binge and purge once a day. We made another contract. This time it was that she could binge and purge up to one to two times a week – no more. We explored why she had stopped her ED symptoms for three months, and she revealed that her desire to be the 'good girl' in the therapy group was motivating to her but not sustainable because her sense of agency and integrity had not yet developed.

Bella had an extremely needy and intrusively unaware mother whose own mother died when Bella's mother was 12. Nurturing and self-care conflicts abound, and so when I do a contract with Bella it's tricky and often does not work. I try to help her establish a sense of her own agency and integrity, which could slowly extend into other areas of her life as well – having her own voice, doing performances that were healthy with manageable schedules, setting boundaries, identifying her anger, regulating her self-care, and saying no when necessary. But try as I might, it often failed. We considered again if she should do residential treatment. Instead, she immediately got pregnant and had an abortion. How do we understand that? One thought is that she was letting me know that her body was still enacting self-harm while trying desperately in a maladaptive way to change her situation. If she got pregnant, she could quit performing and someone new – this guy, not her parents or her manager – would take care of her, but she did not really want to be with him. She just did not know how to get out of her current rut. For her, words did not work; behaviors up the ante as actions have always spoken louder. Fast forward another year, Bella remained sober, and went from purging three to six times a day to sometimes once a week. She finished her performing tour but was holding on desperately to her 'old solution': the possibility of purging when overwhelmed and not able to deal. It was her body-state that believed she could purge if she *needed* to, even though she truly intellectually and even emotionally now knew it didn't work. She wanted more in life, but there was this '*just in case I need it*' idea that still floated in her head and body.

Contracting put a pressure on her and she was terrified of failing so she typically fails in advance, so we stopped officially contracting. But it didn't mean we stopped talking about it, because we didn't. And then one day, I repeated something to her I had said months before. She asked, "Am I ever going to stop purging?" And I answered playfully, something like, 'Well . . . you can't be my only patient that NEVER stops purging!' (We can bookmark my narcissism here which was clearly in the mix, even though I was playing with her.) But in this moment, she said, 'OMG! I have been your BEST WORST patient.' The realization hit us both, that the enactment was that she found a way to be "the best" at something with me – without failing in advance. As long as she stayed symptomatic she maintained her BEST WORST status – that I had unconsciously validated by giving her a platform to feel 'special with me' through her maintaining her symptomatology and her title of BEST WORST – clearly not my intent. I felt terrible but also strangely excited, as did she. It was *her* realization . . . with agency. Being headstrong served her now. She stopped purging and she just celebrated a four-year anniversary of being ED free.

Real recovery from an ED takes a long time. Our patients struggle to tolerate ambiguity and uncertainty – as do we, both members of the dyad, confronted with their limits and vulnerability. As clinicians, we are taught to remain 'rock' steady (Hoppenwasser, 2008). But steadiness means doing this work in a way that we remain keyed into our own experiences of being in and out of sync, of recognizing our shortcomings, becoming aware of our moments of dissociation, shifts in our self and body-states, and the collision of our dissociative lapses with our patients. There is no leaving the self out. And, there is no seeing yourself either. The whole thing is a messy complexity, but the beauty is in seeing the mess from the vantage point of human imperfection. This not only helps in not perpetuating more shame-based feelings in our patients by owning our pieces and having the courage to stay real, but it also provides what can be the first experience of feeling real, in other words, of vitality for these patients.

In moments of intense vulnerability, new relational experiences can be taken in and superficial relating can become sustaining connection. Sometimes this occurs in playfully poignant ways. As a clinician, I have often thought being Italian and Jewish gives me an advantage because it affords me two 'luxuries': *tsuris* and *agita*, or the ability to worry and to have guilt and not question the existence of either as I move between the two. During a heated exchange with a patient in 'recovery' whom I was extremely worried about, she turned to me and said daringly in an irate huff:

> Do you know what my name means in Hungarian?!! . . . STORM!!!!!! . . . and I could destroy you and blow you away!

> To which I replied, "Okay . . . but do you know what *my* name means in Italian? . . . LITTLE ROCK!!!!! . . . and I'm not moving . . . so there!
>
> *(Petrucelli, 2016)*

And we laughed. Over time, over cultures, between 'our names,' between us, a bedrock of mutative impact was able to be built because holding steadfast to helping people is the business we are in. Together, we inspire, we enliven, we infuse, we care, we struggle, we metabolize, we digest, we frustrate, we cry together, we succeed, and we fail. Yet we endure. And it was also quite clear with this patient, as it is with many, that the experience of our names was also a felt experience of our bodies. It was an embodied experience, not a fleeting performance, or manic escape – the kind of experience that singer Amy Winehouse never had a chance to develop in an impoverished, abusive, relational world.

It is my hope that this chapter touches on the complex dialectical relationship between patients' bodily experiences and the loss of their vitality, so that maybe we can assure as the song lyrics go that 'the spirit is something that no one destroys – and that the sound that you're hearing is only the sound of the low spark of high-heeled . . . 'girls.'

References

Bromberg, P. (1998). *Standing in the spaces: Essays on clinical process, trauma, and dissociation*. Hillsdale, NJ: Analytic Press, p. 206.

Bromberg, P. (2016). personal communication.

Day, E. (2013). Growing up with my sister Amy Winehouse. *The Guardian*, June 22, 2013.

Fink, B. (2004). *Lacan to the letter*. Minneapolis: University of Minnesota. Press, p. 60.

Hoppenwasser, K. (2008) Being in rhythm: Dissociative attunement in therapeutic process. *Journal of Trauma & Dissociation*, *9*(3), 349–367.

Hughes, K. (2015). We need to talk about Amy Winehouse's eating disorder and its role in her death. *The Guardian*, September 6, 2015.

McDougall, J. (1989). *Theaters of the body*. New York & London: W.W. Norton & Company.

Petrucelli, J. (2004). Treating eating disorders. In R. H. Coombs (Ed.), *Handbook of addictive disorders: A practical guide to diagnosis and treatment* (pp. 312–352). Hoboken, NJ: John Wiley & Sons, Inc.

Petrucelli, J. (2010). Things that go bump in the night: Secrets after dark. In J. Petrucelli (Ed.), *Knowing, not-knowing & sort-of-knowing: Psychoanalysis and the experience of uncertainty* (pp. 135–150). London: Karnac.

Petrucelli, J. (2015). Mermaids, mistresses & medusa: 'Getting inside out and outside in' the relational montage of eating disorders. In J. Petrucelli (Ed.), *Body-states: Interpersonal/relational perspectives on the treatment of eating disorders*. London: Routledge.

Petrucelli, J. (2016). Body-states, body-image, and dissociation: When not-me is "Not-body'. *Clinical Social Work Journal*, *44*(1), 18–26.

Phillips, A. (2010). *On balance*. New York: Farrar, Straus, & Giroux.

Pitts, C. (2014). Look at me – what am I supposed to be? In J. Petrucelli (Ed.), *Body-states: Interpersonal/relational perspectives on the treatment of eating disorders*. London: Routledge.

Schoen, S. (2016). personal communication.

12

PSYCHODYNAMIC IMPORTANCE OF "CYBER" AND "IN THE FLESH" FRIENDS IN PSYCHOTHERAPY WITH COLLEGE-AGED ADOLESCENTS WITH EATING DISORDERS

F. Diane Barth

In this chapter we consider the relationship among social media, friendship, and the development of eating disorders in adolescents. We look at the idea that social media has both potential risks and benefits in terms of helping adolescents establish friendships and to navigate the attachment-individuation phase of development. We further consider how these issues can be brought into clinical work and what clinicians can do to counteract the negative and reinforce the positive aspects of these influences.

Clinical material from therapy with two college students with eating disorders illustrates the discussion. Questions about the role and use of social media in therapy also are addressed.

The word "friend" has become so utterly void of meaning in a world governed by social media. How can anyone truly claim to have 1,100 friends? In my book, that would involve making time to meet at least three of them every day of the year (Morritt, 2014).

Nineteen-year-old Kate started talking as she walked through my office door. "I hate my body," she said, "hate it, hate it, hate it." She sat down and added, "And don't try to tell me that I look fine. That's what my mother does. I hate that too. I don't look fine."

Although Kate looked more than fine – she was a petite young woman with huge brown eyes and thick, straight dark hair, a terrific figure, and glowing skin – I knew better than to offer reassurance, which would do nothing to soothe her and would, at least on the surface, simply reinforce her belief that no one, not even her therapist, could understand her. On the other hand, I also knew that she would experience a nonresponse as my silent agreement with whatever criticism she was currently directing toward her physical appearance. There had been some evidence that she had occasionally, albeit silently, accepted some of the statements I had made contradicting her self-criticalness, as long as the comments were both genuine on my part and also took into account her negative feelings in some way. Like most 19-year-olds I have worked with, she was not interested in nor comfortable exploring any aspect of the transference. However, I had found some ways to verbalize, often as lightly as possible, some of what I understood about her conflicts and concerns within the context of our relationship, which she sometimes seemed to find helpful.

I said, "I know that you are feeling angry at yourself, and I'm not trying to take that away. But I think it's important for you to at least know that from the outside, I can't see any reason at all for you to hate your body the way you do." She nodded. "But why don't you tell me what you are so unhappy about. What has this body of yours done to you to deserve all of this fury?"

"Ugh," she said. "I just got a Snapchat with me and some of my friends. I am sooo short. And my nose is so fat. And my hair looked awful." She hesitated, and then she added, "And I hate how my arms look. I knew it was a mistake to wear that tank top."

This explained the long-sleeved sweater Kate was wearing despite the warmth of the day. She was, as she often did, hiding her arms, which she viewed as "fat and floppy." Kate had struggled with an eating disorder since her freshman year of high school, when she had gone on such a rigid diet and lost so much weight that she had to be hospitalized. Within a short time she had begun eating again and had maintained a healthy weight. But in her senior year she developed bulimia, bingeing and forcing herself to throw up daily. Her freshman year of college had been so difficult that her bingeing and purging had increased dramatically. In my experience, this is not unusual. With the mixture of separation from family, academic pressure, and complex social relations that is relatively common during this transitional phase of adolescent life, the transition to college often fosters eating disorders in freshman and sophomore students (Barth, 2015a; Defeciani, 2016; Petrucelli, 2016; Zerbe, 2008, 2016). Kate came to see me for help not only with the eating symptoms but also with the depression and anxiety that had invaded her life.

In our early sessions I learned that Kate had many friends who she "saw" both in person and on social media. Her relationships with these friends were important but not always either positive or supportive. Despite the pain of comparing herself to her peers, Kate spent hours a day looking at images of her friends engaged in a variety of activities both with and without her, an activity that stirred up a variety of complicated emotions. Girls she knew either in person or in cyber space shared information about boyfriends, girlfriends, social activities, and school. They also discussed their weight, need to diet, successful exercise regimens, and weight loss. Images of lost or gained weight, fat thighs, skinny arms, flat bellies, and flabby upper backs were part of her daily electronic diet. As she read texts and looked at their pictures, Kate felt envious, anxious, competitive, and inadequate all at the same time, although often she could not sort out the different emotions. I suspected that she coped with these feelings by bingeing and purging, but when I suggested this idea to Kate, she said, "Maybe. But that doesn't help me stop."

I agreed. Numerous authors have discussed the importance of integrating psychodynamic understanding with behavioral techniques when working with clients with eating disorders (e.g., Barth, 2014; Connors, 2006; Frank, 1999; Schutz & Paxton, 2007; Wachtel, 1997; Zerbe, 2008). I explained to Kate that understanding this function of her eating symptoms would not make them go away but could give us an opportunity to think about other tools for self-soothing. When I asked her to tell me some of the ways she made herself feel better, she had no idea at first and then said, "Drinking. Shopping. Talking and texting with my friends." I said that we would try to find some other techniques that she could add to her toolbox, so that she had more alternatives available when she did feel the need to soothe herself. She asked what kinds of techniques. I said that for some people, warm showers, bubble baths, using good-smelling body lotion, listening to music, watching dumb television shows, and giving themselves manicures and pedicures helped. Puzzles, dumb books, knitting, and doing artwork were other techniques that I told her sometimes helped. She liked some of these ideas, and we agreed that she would focus on one or two to use the next time she felt like bingeing.

I told her that these techniques would not always work as a perfect substitute, and that one of our jobs would be to talk about what did and did not work for her, and how she could make them more useful. I encouraged her to try not to beat herself up when she was not successful at avoiding a binge. I explained that both time and more talking in therapy would help her get better at some of the alternative techniques. Then I said that for many people, talking to friends could be soothing, but I said that sometimes friends could actually make things a little worse. She nodded vigorously. I asked if we could talk about how this worked for her. She said she did not know. I said maybe we could start by trying to get a sense of how talking and texting with her friends soothed her.

"I don't know. It's just what I do. If I'm feeling bad, I like to see what they're doing, or . . . I don't know, just talk with them." Although my initial instinct was to suggest that Kate substitute some of the activities we had just discussed for this behavior as well, it was important for me to recognize that despite the often-negative impact that these interactions had on Kate, and the ways that they frequently led to binge/purge behavior, there was also some positive value to these "friend" contacts. For instance, they were an intricate part of her relational world and part of the developmental process of becoming individuated while also beginning to find ways to develop adult forms of attachment (see Lyons-Ruth [1991] for a discussion of "attachment-individuation" as a developmental model). I reminded myself that the fact that social media and related "friendships" were woven into her life did not mean that she was "addicted" to them. These connections are part of contemporary adolescent culture (see Mishna, Bogo, Root, Sawyer, & Khoury-Kassabri, 2012). Research shows that 45 percent of American teens use social media[1] every day, and that some are on entertainment media up to nine hours a day (Rideout, 2015). Fortunately, Kate did not fit into this latter category. But could I, a member of an older generation not steeped in her culture, ever fully understand not only the meaning of social media in her life but also the positive influences that it had on her? Could I help her begin to explore possible links between her eating disorder, her unhappiness, and her cyber-social life? And were there ways that I could help her engage differently with friends in both the electronic and "in the flesh" worlds?

In this chapter I consider the relationship among social media, friendship, and the development of eating disorders in adolescents. I look at the idea that social media has both potential risks and benefits in terms of helping adolescents establish friendships and navigate the attachment-individuation phase of development. I further consider how these issues can be brought into clinical work and what clinicians can do to counteract the negative and reinforce the positive aspects of these influences.

Vulnerability to the influence of friends has long been recognized as having an impact on these disorders (Bunnell, 2016; Petrucelli, 2016; Sands, 1991, 2016; Zerbe, 2008, 2016). The impact of "friendfluence" can be magnified by social media and the cyber world (Sales, 2016; Wooldridge, 2014). One area in which social media has both potential risks and benefits is that of establishing friendships and navigating the attachment-individuation phase of development (Bunnell, 2016; Lanzieri & Hildebrandt, 2016; National Public Radio, 2016; Sales, 2016). Friendships conducted through social media and electronic tools can have significant effects not only on how these young people feel about their bodies, their selves, and their general sense of the world in which they live but also on their specific eating behaviors (Bunnell, 2016; Defeciani, 2016; Lanzieri & Hildebrandt, 2016; Sales, 2016).

When working with young college students with eating disorders, it is important not only to understand and counteract the negative but also to reinforce the positive aspects of the influence of friends, both in the cyber world and the "real" world. Adolescents often casually but regularly mention friends in the course of a session. Following Sullivan (1953), I encourage therapists to listen carefully to even the most insignificant details of these comments and to gently probe for more information. How do these friendships impact a client's life? What do they do together?

Kate, for example, spent hours of every one of her days with her friends. They ate together, did homework together, and even slept in one another's dormitory rooms. This kind of easy camaraderie is often so much a part of the college experience that it is taken for granted by clients and never even brought into therapy as a topic. Other college students may spend surprising amounts of time with groups of sorority sisters or fraternity brothers, teammates in college athletics, or peers in special interest groups, such as occur in the theater, environmental science, or language departments of many colleges and universities. Interestingly, once a client begins to bring the small details of these friendships into therapy, evidence begins to emerge that there is overlap between in-person and cyber-connections. Keep Me Posted, a web series from writer-producer Hillary Berkowitz Nussbaum, takes a tongue-in-cheek approach to contemporary women's friendships as three women, two of whom are roommates, communicate almost exclusively through texts, social media, and other electronic forms of communication.

How and when a clinician brings the cyber world into therapy will depend on many factors, including his or her own comfort with this world and each client's specific needs and dynamics. An integrative approach is a useful tool in this process, helping a clinician both understand these dynamics and respond directly to some of the needs for support and affirmation that are filled by technologically based and "in the flesh" friendships. In this chapter I am not able to address all of the different ways in which this can be done. Instead, I look at some sample clinical interactions that may be enhanced by taking into account the influence of social media platforms on a client's internal and relational dynamics. I hope the applicability of this small sampling to a broader range of situations will be fairly obvious.

The world of cyber technology poses particular problems for adolescents with eating disorders. Significant data show that eating disorders commonly develop in adolescence, who may be especially susceptible to the impact of messages conveyed by social media (Defeciani, 2016; Lanzieri & Hildebrandt, 2016; Sales, 2016). No longer limited to a small segment of the population, these behaviors now occur in a wide range of ethnic and socio-economic groups. They also are appearing in increasing numbers of adolescent males (Bunnell, 2016; Defeciani, 2016; Lanzieri & Hildebrandt, 2016; Swanson et al., 2011). Contemporary theorists differ on the impact of technology on these symptoms, as conflicting data report harmful, helpful, or simply neutral impact on both contemporary adolescent development and the development of eating-related symptomatology (e.g., Boyd, 2014; Hicks, 2010; Koutamanis, Vossen, Peter, & Valkenburg, 2013; Kross et al., 2013; Sales, 2016). What is clear is that no matter what one thinks about these new forms of communication, they are here to stay. What is also clear is that contemporary therapists need to take these factors into account when working with this population, since many of the developmental dynamics and conflicts that can lead to eating disorders in adolescents are often played out through social media platforms. Yet even while clinicians, parents, and educators recognize (and often complain) about the important, almost critical role that these platforms play in the lives of contemporary young people, we all too frequently neglect them as either a topic for exploration or a tool within a therapeutic setting.

Convergence of factors in adolescent development: separation, attachment, identity formation, friends, social media, and eating disorders

Friends are an important part of child and adolescent emotional and psychological development. From Sullivan's (1953) recognition of the significance of same-sex friends, or "chums," and Erikson's (1980/1959) discussion of friendships and identity to Kohut's (1971) thinking about twinship and contemporary discussions of attachment, theorists and clinicians have continued to find evidence that peer relationships contribute to a sense of identity separate from family, a capacity for both intimacy and empathy, an ability to manage conflict, and a sense of belonging (Rubin et al., 2004; Sroufe et al., 1999).

For Kate, as for many adolescents, socializing was both important and filled with conflict. A good student, she was far more emotionally focused on friends than on schoolwork. The binge eating and drinking were a way of managing many feelings, including her social anxiety, need for social approval, and severely critical self-image, often projected outward onto peers, who she imagined were as unforgiving of her as she was of herself. Interpreting these as triggers of her problematic behaviors is only part of the work, as most young people, like Kate, have difficulty translating cognitive knowledge into behavioral change. Offering behavioral substitutes such as those I suggested to Kate, or those described by Albers (2009, 2015) can be extremely helpful, especially when integrated with understanding about why such behaviors are so difficult to change.

It is also helpful to recognize that conflicts and anxieties about friends are common and age-appropriate for adolescents. Yet, adolescents today struggle with a kind of peer pressure that has been magnified by both traditional and social media. Friendships among twenty-first century children and adolescents are perhaps more complex and complicated than at any time in recent memory. Not only do books, movies, and television offer wildly divergent images of teens in the world but also, because real relationships between adolescents today develop not only in person but also through social media, impressionable youngsters are also subject to wildly unrealistic and often unmanageable demands from people they may not know at all. When it comes to eating disorders, both peer pressure and social focus on weight and size have long been recognized as having an impact on the development of eating disorders in children and adolescents.

Friends affect not only how these young people feel about their bodies, their selves, and their general sense of the world in which they live but also their specific eating behaviors. A number of authors (e.g., Boyd, 2014; Ornstein, 2016; Sales, 2016) detail some of the ways that young women use social media to measure self-worth and regulate self-esteem. Much of this activity goes on outside the purview of adults, the dynamics often played out on websites and apps unknown to parents and teachers. In fact, almost as soon as adults discover the programs popular with teens, another comes along that is even better hidden from the sight of adult overview. From the moment of my writing this chapter to the time that the book is published, for example, new and old programs such as Snapchat, Instagram, Twitter, Tumblr, Reddit, Pinterest, Vine, Kik, Pheed, Wanelo, 4Chan, Ask.fm, Whatsapp, GroupMe, iMessage, Periscope, Tinder, and Yik Yak sites may be long gone, traded in for new formats that are, whenever possible, unknown to adults.

There is a point to this hidden life of adolescents. It is part of the developmental progression of separation from parents and using peers to help discover one's individual identity. Yet there are, of course, hidden dangers in the unsupervised and unstructured exploration of this aspect of self. One of the crucial questions for clinicians, educators, and parents today is how to help young men and women navigate the critical developmental issue of separation and individuation (or, using the phrase suggested by Lyons-Ruth [1991], which I believe more aptly captures the dynamics of this developmental process, "attachment and individuation") so that they can be healthy, both physically and psychologically, have a good body image and sense of self, and a healthy capacity to connect to others. This is a tall order at any time, but perhaps particularly difficult in today's world, where, according to some research, the amount of time a girl spends on Facebook, "where contributing factors such as the influence of media and pressure from peers are merged," might be linked to her risk of developing an eating disorder (Sales, 2016, p. 91). Borzekowski, Schenk, Wilson, & Peebles (2010) suggest that social media may have more of an impact on body image than traditional media because the messages and images may be more specifically targeted (see also Lanzieri & Hildebrandt, 2016). Messages that are believed to come from "friends," for instance, are perceived as particularly meaningful. Thus the world of social media and cyber friends and the developmental issues that contribute to eating disorders come together to make the world of contemporary adolescents fertile ground for the development of eating symptoms.

Not surprisingly, Borzekowski et al. (2010) found that those with less exposure to rational, clear messages from supportive adults are more at risk. This is an important point for clinicians to keep in mind. Where parents' voices may not be experienced as either rational or supportive, a therapist's voice might be. But to provide support, many clinicians must overcome their negative transference to social media. To address this issue, let us look a little more closely at some of the factors that may link both social media and friendships with eating disorders.

Social media, eating disorders, and friendship

When it comes to eating disorders, both peer pressure and social focus on weight and size have long been recognized as having an impact on the development of eating disorders in children and adolescents (Sales, 2016; Stice, 2016). Friends affect not only how these young people feel about their bodies, their selves, and their general sense of the world in which they live but also their specific eating behaviors (Jacobi & Fittig, 2010; Jacobi, Hayward, De Zwaan, Kraemer, & Agras, 2004). For many adults, this dependence on others for self-esteem appears to be an emotional failure. Blaming social media for the difficulty can interfere with a clinician's ability to empathize with a client's struggles and to recognize some of his strengths within this context. Adolescents who struggle with eating and related disorders have traditionally used eating behaviors both to manage and to avoid conflict-laden social situations. Many, like Kate, restrict food intake before a party in order to feel good about their bodies, but then end up bingeing at the party because alcohol removes inhibitions and makes them less able to control their food intake. Others binge and then feel too uncomfortable and/or too fat or ugly to go to the activity. Today, however, avoiding an activity does not necessarily protect an adolescent from painful feelings about themselves, since pictures of friends and acquaintances having what looks like a wonderful time are instantly broadcast on their smartphones, tablets, watches and computers, stimulating FOMO, or a fear of missing out. Thus, painful, confused, and distressing feelings in relation to peers are stimulated all the time, not only in person but also through social media.

Further complicating the picture is the fact that some "friends" are never met in person or seen "in the flesh," yet there is no question that they have an impact on the psyches and the developmental progress of these youngsters. Cyber "friends" reinforce cultural demands to conform to particular body images and dress codes. "Squadgoals" (the expectation of working toward goals, such as weight loss and fitness, in tandem with friends) and "twinning" (the demand to be like a particular leader or friend) demand conformity to one style, often chosen by a specific leader. Hicks (2010) lays the blame for increased childhood obesity on the long hours that many adolescents spend sitting at computers instead of getting physical exercise. Problems of cyber bullying and Internet overuse and addiction are serious, and the risks of making mistakes online are real. Some authors have suggested that the media is having a specific impact on how adolescents manage the developmental struggles that have traditionally led to eating disorders (e.g., Borzekowski et al., 2010; Sales, 2016). Ranging from collegecandy.com, which discusses everything from star gossip to "butt contouring" to dating, clothing, and dieting tips, and the pro-ana and pro-mia sites which provide support and guidance about how to maintain, respectively, symptoms of anorexia and bulimia, these platforms offer a sense of community and connection that can, unfortunately, reinforce problematic symptoms and psychological difficulties (Jett, LaPorte, & Wanchisn, 2010; Wooldridge, 2014).

To intervene effectively, a clinician needs to walk a fine line between reality-testing some of the problems caused by cyber technology while avoiding criticizing the platforms through which these young people are developing. Therapists can get help finding a working balance from the evidence that the impact of social media is not all negative. Some authors (e.g., Boyd, 2014; Steinberg, 2013) suggest that social media is simply the environment in which adolescents are working through age-appropriate developmental tasks of identity development, individuation, and peer relationships. Others have found a significant degree of healthy and developmentally progressive interaction is derived from electronic communication (Lenhart, 2015; Jett et al., 2010). The Pew Research Center (Lenhart, 2015), for instance, suggests that a majority of teens feel more connected not only to friends but also to their friends' feelings through social media. According to this research, 68 percent of teen social media users report having received support during "tough or challenging times" through social media platforms (Lenhart, 2015). Adolescent boys, a growing part of the eating disorder population (Bunnell, 2016; Defeciani, 2016; Lanzieri & Hildebrandt, 2016) report finding greater support and connectedness to friends through social media, perhaps because of the sense of joint activity, and perhaps because boys are more comfortable sharing feelings online than in person (Lenhart, 2015). A recent program on National Public Radio (2016) reports:

> Increasingly, there are challenges [on social media platforms] designed to spread self-esteem, kind of like a modern-day chain letter.
>
> On Facebook, for example, users are called on to post three confident selfies and to tag 10 people the users feel should share their beauty with the world. "And then, there will be like 10 people [commenting] 'Awww, oh my God, you're so beautiful,'" says 18-year-old Billy Cruz, Caitlyn's [one of the show's teen reporters'] boyfriend. "It's really cool, because it's like, here, I'm being confident, and then you guys all be confident now. And they're like, 'OK, we're all confident now let's pass it on to other people!'"
>
> *(material in brackets added; NPR March 2016)*

Thus, not only is there evidence of positive uses of social media, but also it seems more accurate to suggest that these platforms, while having an impact on eating disorders, do not create them. Yet Kate is not, in my experience, unusual. Even college students, who we think might have developed some important skills for living with and managing cyber relationships, are vulnerable to many of the issues that she brought into her therapy. I have found, however, that social media can become both an important factor and a teaching tool in therapy with this population. In particular, it can be extremely useful for focusing on, exploring, and even altering the significant vagaries of friendships both in the flesh and in cyberspace, and the impact of these connections on eating behaviors.

Clinical approach to social media

Adolescence is famously a time of identity confusion. Intimate peer relationships are supposed to aid in the developmental processes of separation and building self-esteem. But although some college students develop a group of friends who provide support and camaraderie during this stage of life, an internal, often hidden sense of incompetence and fraudulence can make it difficult for others to build meaningful bonds with peers. Even when they appear to be highly social, closer examination shows that many of their connections are somewhat superficial. Because they keep aspects of themselves out of these interpersonal interactions, friendships in the "real" world can feel ingenuine or incomplete. Social media can make these adolescents feel less alone in that they offer an opportunity to engage with part-objects who affirm the parts of self that have been split off or kept out of "in person" friendships. Yet these part-object connections can simultaneously contribute to anxieties and self-doubts by leaving other aspects of the self out of the connection. Adolescents often do not believe that their peers struggle with the painful worries that they struggle with (Barth, 2015b; May, 2000; Qualter, Quinton, Wagner, & Brown, 2009), and nothing a clinician says will convince them otherwise. Yet, this is one of the places where a therapist can use social media to clinical advantage. It is first important to establish a climate in which we have made it clear that we both use and appreciate the value of the cyber world. This can be done in many different ways, but most easily through a willingness to communicate with clients in their own chosen medium, at least to some extent. A discussion about the privacy issues involved in different communications can be highly profitable, as when a therapist shares that she will text or use WhatsApp with a client, but that she will not use Snapchat or Instagram (or other rapidly appearing and disappearing platforms that have more than one recipient at a time), because they are visible to others, and she wishes to protect her client by keeping communication between them as private as possible. If a clinician truly believes that the only really safe form of communication is by phone, then she will need to clarify with an adolescent that this is not a criticism of the client, who may be much more comfortable with non-voice contact.

Once a clinician has established that he is not criticizing everything about social media, he can do some reality testing with young clients. For instance, as May (2000) points out, adolescents tend to believe the public persona put out by their friends. They generally do not recognize underlying conflicts or contradictions and therefore assume that no one else feels as conflicted, confused, unattractive, socially inadequate, or lonely as they do. Feelings of self-doubt and isolation are often magnified by posts on social media that show friends and acquaintances having fun, looking good, and appearing special. I encourage clients to question these images, both by asking what they put up, and by sharing things like the quote from Morritt at the beginning of this paper, which is usually good for both a laugh and as a reminder that social media friendships are not always "real."

Adolescents often tend to believe that social media provides far more privacy than it does. Their tendency to share information about themselves with social media "friends" often seems like an anomaly to adults (except for those who are equally unboundaried in their electronic communications). As one *New York Times* writer puts it, "the urge to share a private moment with potentially millions of strangers is now endemic to being a teenager" (Hess, 2016). Opening up our concerns about these boundaries in therapy with college students can irritate them and make us feel inadequate, fussy, and old. It can remind them and us that we do not always speak the same language (Lepisto, 2012), but it can also initiate useful discussions not only of the topics I have mention herein but also of the very essence of friendship as well. The cyber world, which is part of our clients' lives, affects them in a wide variety of both positive and negative ways. The question is not whether to address these issues in therapy, but when and how to do so. For instance, do we accept young clients' requests (or expectation) that we communicate with them by texting? Do we "friend" them on Instagram or Facebook?

I have informally surveyed colleagues on this question for years. My information is totally nonscientific, but what I have gathered from conversations with a wide range of professionals is a general ambivalence about the world of technology. Protecting our own boundaries as well as those of our clients would appear to dictate that we not engage in such communication, but how much of that need is countertransferential anxiety? We wonder how they would feel if they knew we were "following" them on Facebook or Instagram, but we also worry about their seeing aspects of our private lives posted in the cyber world. What is out there about our private lives anyway? And do we have any control over it? Lepisto (2012) writes that many therapists today have to deal with being immigrants in a world in which our young clients are native-born speakers. In a moving example of integrating boundaries while simultaneously meeting a young client in her own technological world, she describes how she gracefully utilized social media, text, email, and phone communications not only with a troubled adolescent but also in family work with the girl's parents. Few of us are able to do such integration smoothly, but even our awkward efforts to do so can be a powerful tool for engaging adolescents with eating disorders as they struggle with questions about boundaries, self, and other in the process of conquering their symptoms.

Let us turn briefly to another client, a young man who was entering his sophomore year of college. Jeffrey had been on his high school rowing team and had hopes of rowing in college, but learned that he was not quite big or heavy enough to get a seat on his school's heavyweight crew. He decided to try out for the lightweight team, which meant dieting to lose a significant amount of weight. He won a seat on the lightweight crew, but then had to maintain the lower body weight at which he had been accepted. The challenge was thrilling for Jeffrey. He lost more weight and felt a sense of control over his body that he had never felt previously. As he continued to take off pounds, however, his coaches became concerned. He was losing muscle mass and becoming a less competent team member, but they were also worried about his psychological state. Jeffrey was incensed when they told him he would have to begin to regain some of the lost weight in order to remain on the team, but when they spoke to him about his loss of strength he agreed they might have a point. Yet, he could not bring himself to eat enough to begin the process. One of his coaches worked with him to set up a reasonable daily food regimen, but Jeffrey could not follow it. He was still losing weight when he came to see me.

"I've read some of your stuff online," he said almost immediately after sitting down in my office. "You have some interesting things to say."

I told him I was glad he had been looking at my "stuff" and asked him if he could tell me what he had found interesting. After he told me a little about what he had read, he said, "It looks like you're pretty comfortable with the Internet world and that kind of thing." I nodded and asked him if that made a difference. "Yeah. I mean, so many adults avoid it. They think it's bad."

This kind of comment is an entrée to a client's initial transference to a therapist. Both positive and negative transference can crystallize around many different facets of a clinician's personality, particularly with adolescents and young adults, but they can often be difficult to explore with this population. A discussion of issues directly related to electronic communication can bring this material into awareness without making clients uncomfortable. It is important for clinicians to be comfortable with our presence in the social media world, whether we are active users or silent observers. I use some social media platforms myself, albeit not to the extent of any adolescent I know. I appreciate the fact that I can communicate with family and friends all over the world. However, I carefully guard what I post in order to protect my own boundaries and those of family members, which is something I share with clients and open up for discussion with them. I also believe that the fact that young clients and family members are able to remain engaged in ongoing communication with high school and college friends who they no longer see on a daily basis enhances and enriches their relational world. Clients quickly learn of and respond to both positive and painful events in their friends' lives because of social media, and as a result learn important social skills, including how to support friends at times of loss, how to encourage them when they are feeling inadequate, and how to protect their own space and boundaries.

With clients, and perhaps particularly with those with eating disorders, a non-judgmental but honest discussion of social media can open up important areas that are often otherwise unavailable for discussion. Issues such as boundaries, limit-setting, self-esteem, and self-value, as well as empathy and respect for others, can all be addressed within this context. Even a discussion of HIPPA rules and regulations can open up the question of boundary violations and confidentiality and how secure electronic communications might be. I have had numerous discussions with adolescents who complained about my "old-fashioned" worries about their privacy, which led to an opportunity to explore issues of boundaries, privacy, self-protection, and impulse control. I have also talked about my own desire to protect my privacy while also engaging in social media. The question of how to balance a wish to connect with an ability to set limits and to respect the limits set by others is a crucial topic in their world. I believe that exploring these issues with young clients, bringing in an adult perspective without being critical of their behavior (not an easy task), can affect not only social media interactions but also behaviors in the real world. Learning that it is not only acceptable but also healthy to set and accept limits can impact eating and drinking disorders among young people who often feel that there are, or should be, no limits on them or on any aspect of their lives. It is also a crucial interpersonal tool for both men and women living in a world in which 15 percent of college women report being raped during their freshman year, frequently at a time when they are incapacitated from alcohol and/or drugs (Barth, 2015a; Carey, Durney, Shepardson, & Carey, 2015).

I would suggest that to explore these issues with our young clients, many clinicians must pay close attention to our own feelings, both positive and negative, about the world of social media. Countertransferential responses can range from overt criticism and negativity to unthinking acceptance. Neither extreme makes room for the complex issues that adolescents are working out with both their eating behaviors and their social relationships, in person and in cyber space. Let us return one final time to Kate.

Like many college students, Kate was not able to maintain a consistent appointment schedule, and she did not always act as though she found anything I said to be meaningful. I sometimes had doubts as to whether therapy was helping her. However, although we frequently had to change our meeting time, she kept and arrived on time for almost all of her appointments. She revealed over time that her binges had diminished except when she was under stress. And she was even able to talk about what kinds of situations made her feel more stressed than others. She had a terrific sense of humor, although she kept it under wraps much of the time, hidden by an attitude that was simultaneously deeply serious and worrisomely cynical. We had established that the eating disorder was a way that she soothed herself when she felt depressed. It was also a way that she managed her fears of being rejected. She talked about sometimes staying home from a social event because she had binged the night before and was feeling fat. She said that she hated going out with her friends because she felt unattractive and uninteresting around them. At times when she did go out partying, she would binge drink, consuming several alcoholic beverages in a very short time because, as she put it, "I'm much more social when I've been drinking." This is not an uncommon phenomenon.

Binge drinking has reached epic proportions on college campuses in recent years and often performs many of the same functions as eating disorders (Bruce, Curren, & Williams, 2011; Stewart, Svolensky, & Eifert, 2002). Thus, like many other college students with eating disorders, Kate would often also binge drink, both as an attempt to control her anxiety in social situations and also as a way of managing her food intake. Yet as often happens, the drinking backfired, in that at some point she would lose her inhibitions about eating. "And then I just stuff myself," she said. "So it's better if I stay home. But that doesn't always work, since I start scrolling through my phone, and I see what everyone else is doing, and I feel left out and miserable. And then I eat."

I said, "You're damned if you go and damned if you don't go." The solution seemed simple to me. I said, "Would it be possible not to look at your phone?" She looked at me like I had grown an extra head. "What?" I asked. "What does that look mean?"

"Sometimes," she said, "you sound just like my parents."I laughed. "I guess that makes sense," I said. "But really, can you explain to me why you need to look at your phone when you know it's going to make you feel miserable?"

She said, "I need to know what I missed. I need to know what everybody will be talking about tomorrow."

In this interchange, my belief that the phone should not be considered part of the human body initially interfered with my ability to empathize with Kate's dilemma. Acknowledging that my reaction had to do with generational differences was easy with Kate, who, as I said earlier, had a great sense of humor. But what was most important was that Kate began working out with me, in the therapy, some of the conflicts between her parents' "adult" view of her friendships and her own, more immediate need for social contact, no matter how painful or conflicted. As we explored my "old-fashioned" nature, for instance, when I asked her to put aside her phone so that she could focus on what we were discussing in a session, we also began to put into words some of her needs, worries, and the ego strengths that would gradually get her through this time of her life. One day she came into a session and said, "I realized the other day after our session that I can get through 45 minutes without seeing what everyone else is doing. And I hate to admit this to you, because you'll get very big-headed about it, but I actually even see that it can be a good thing to be able to pay attention to other things." She grinned. "I made my friend Ginny put her phone down yesterday when we were having dinner together. And I put mine down. We had a great time!!! We giggled and talked and didn't look at what anybody else was doing for a full hour." The icing on this cake was that although it was her habit to binge during and throw up after a dinner with friends, Kate did neither on this occasion. I asked if she had any idea what had made this possible. She replied, "I'm not going to say it was because we weren't looking at what everyone else was doing. But maybe it was because I was so comfortable with Ginny. Not criticized, not comparing myself. It was just really nice."

Conclusion

It is well established that friends are an important part of child and adolescent emotional and psychological development. Peer relationships contribute to a sense of identity separate from family, a capacity for both intimacy and empathy, an ability to manage conflict, and a sense of belonging. However, twenty-first century friendships are different from those of any previous era, in that some friends are never actually seen "in the flesh." Yet, both "real" and "cyber" friends continue to have an impact on the development and maintenance of eating disorders. Friends affect not only how these young people feel about their bodies, their selves, and their general sense of the world in which they live but also their specific eating behaviors.

There is much material within the therapeutic relationship that can be gleaned for clinical work on friendship, trust, boundaries, and self-esteem in both the "real" and the "cyber" worlds of college students, but this population is famously resistant to exploration of transference and countertransference material. In this chapter we have looked at how a clinician can bring these issues into clinical work with this population. The importance of examining and accepting our own conflicted feelings about social media platforms is considered. Clinical material from therapy with two college students with eating disorders illustrates the discussion. Questions about the role and use of social media in therapy are addressed.

Note

1 Although I realize the words have different meanings, in this chapter I will use "social media," "cyber technology," and "electronic technology or communication" as overarching terms for the ever-changing sites for social networking such as Facebook, LinkedIn, and Google Plus, as well as for information – and media – sharing sites such as Twitter, Instagram, and Tumblr and for other forms of communication such as texts, Skype, Facetime, and even cell phone use.

References

Albers, S. (2009). *50 ways to soothe yourself without food.* Oakland, CA: New Harbinger Publications.

Albers, S. (2015). *50 more ways to soothe yourself without food.* Oakland, CA: New Harbinger Publications.

Barth, F. D. (2014). *Integrative clinical social work practice: A contemporary perspective.* New York: Springer.

Barth, F. D. (2015a). Alexithymia, affect regulation and binge drinking in college students. *Journal of College Student Psychotherapy, 29*, 132–146. doi:10.1080/87568225.2015.1008369

Barth, F. D. (2015b). Social media and adolescent development: Hazards, pitfalls and opportunities for growth. *Clinical Social Work Journal, 43*, 201–208. doi:10.1007/s10615-014-0501-6

Borzekowski, D. L. G., Schenk, S., Wilson, J. L., & Peebles, R. (2010). e-Ana and e-Mia: A content analysis of pro-ED websites. *The American Journal of Public Health, 100*, 1526–1534. doi:10.2105/AJPH.2009.172700

Boyd, D. (2014). *It's complicated: The social lives of networked teens.* New Haven, CT: Yale University Press.

Bruce, G., Curren, C., & Williams, L. (2011). Alexithymia and alcohol consumption: The mediating effects of drinking motives. *Addictive Behaviors, 37*(3), 350–352. doi:10.1016/j.addbeh.2011.11.024

Bunnell, D. (2016). Gender socialization, countertransference and the treatment of men with eating disorders. *Clinical Social Work Journal, 44*, 99–104. doi:10.1007/s10615–10015–10564-z

Carey, K. B., Durney, S. E., Shepardson, R. L., & Carey, M. P. (2015). Precollege predictors of incapacitated rape among female students in their first year of college. *Journal of Studies on Alcohol and Drugs, 76*(6), 829–837. doi:10.15288/jsad.2015.76.829

Connors, M. (2006). *Symptom-focused dynamic psychotherapy.* Hillsdale, NJ: Analytic Press.

Defeciani, L. (2016). Eating disorders and body image concerns among male athletes. *Clinical Social Work Journal, 44*, 114–123. doi:10.1007/s10615-015-0567-9

Erikson, E. (1980/1959). *Identity and the life cycle.* New York and London, England: W.W. Norton.

Frank, K. A. (1999). *Psychoanalytic participation: Action, interaction, and integration.* London, England: Routledge.

Hess, A. (2016, April 8). The awkward charm of the promposal. *The New York Times Magazine.* Retrieved from www.nytimes.com/2016/04/08/magazine/the-awkward-charm-of-the-promposal.html?smid=nytcore-ipad-share &smprod=nytcore-ipad&_r=1

Hicks, M. R. (2010). *The digital pandemic: Reestablishing face-to face contact in the electronic age.* Far Hills, NJ: New Horizon Press.

Jacobi, C., & Fittig, E. (2010). Psychosocial risk factors for eating disorders. In W. S. Agras (Ed.), *Oxford handbook of eating disorders* (pp. 123–136). New York: Oxford University Press.

Jacobi, C., Hayward, C., De Zwaan, M., Kraemer, H., & Agras, W. S. (2004). Coming to terms with risk factors for eating disorders: Application of risk terminology and suggestions for a general taxonomy. *Psychological Bulletin, 130*, 19–65. doi:10.1037/0033–2909.130.1.19

Jett, S., LaPorte, D. J., & Wanchisn, J. (2010). Impact of exposure to pro-eating disorder websites on eating behaviour in college women. *European Eating Disorders Review, 18*, 410–416. doi:10.1002/erv.1009

Kohut, H. (1971). *Analysis of the self: Systematic approach to treatment of narcissistic personality disorders*. New York: International Universities Press.

Koutamanis, M., Vossen, H. G. M., Peter, J., & Valkenburg, P. M. (2013). Practice makes perfect: The longitudinal effect of adolescents' instant messaging on their ability to initiate offline friendships. *Computers in Human Behavior, 29*, 2265–2272. doi:10.1016/j.chb.2013.04.033

Kross, E., Verduyn, P., Demiralp, E., Park, J., Lee, D. S., Lin, N., . . . Sueur, C. (2013). Facebook use predicts declines in subjective well-being in young adults. *PLoS One, 8*, e69841. doi:10.1371/journal.pone.0069841

Lanzieri, N., & Hildebrandt, T. (2016). Using objectification theory to examine the effects of media on gay male body image. *Clinical Social Work Journal, 44*, 105–113. doi:10.1007/s10615-015-0562-1

Lenhart, A. (2015). *Teens, technology and friendships: Video games, social media and mobile phones play an integral role in how teens meet and interact with friends*. Washington, DC: Pew Research Center. Retrieved from www. pewinternet.org/2015/08/06/teens-technology-and-friendships/

Lepisto, B. L. (2012). My space, your space, whose space? The use/abuse of technology in the treatment of an adolescent. *Journal of Infant, Child and Adolescent Psychotherapy, 11*, 113–120. doi:10.1080/15289168.2012.673405

Lyons-Ruth, K. (1991). Rapprochement or approchement: Mahler's theory reconsidered from the vantage point of recent research on early attachment relationships. *Psychoanalytic Psychology, 8*, 1–23.

May, R. (2000). Basic requirements and survival strategies for a college psychotherapy service. *Journal of College Student Psychotherapy, 15*, 3–13.

Mishna, F., Bogo, M., Root, J., Sawyer, J. L., & Khoury-Kassabri, M. (2012). "It just crept in": The digital age and implications for social work practice. *Clinical Social Work Journal, 40*, 277–286. doi:10.1007/s10615-012-0383-4

Morritt, A. (2014). *Impromptu scribe*. Paxanax Press.

National Public Radio. (2016). *Teen girls flip the negative script on social media*. Retrieved from www.npr.org/sections/alltechconsidered/2016/03/24/470686073/teengirls-flip-the-negative-script-on-social-media

Ornstein, P. (2016). *Girls & sex: Navigating the complicated new landscape*. New York: HarperCollins.

Petrucelli, J. (2016). Body-states, body image and dissociation: When not-me is "Not body." *Clinical Social Work Journal, 44*, 18–26. doi:10.1007/s10615-015-0539-0

Qualter, P., Quinton, S. J., Wagner, H., & Brown, S. (2009). Loneliness, interpersonal distrust, and alexithymia in university students. *Journal of Applied Social Psychology, 39*, 1461–1479. doi:10.1111/j.1559–1816.2009.00491.x

Rideout, V. (2015). *The common sense census: Media use by tweens and teens*. Retrieved from www.commonsensemedia.org/sites/default/files/uploads/research/census_executivesummary.pdf

Rubin, K. H., Dwyer, K. M., Booth-LaForce, C., Kim, A. H., Burgess, K. B., & Rose-Krasnor, L. (2004). Attachment, friendship, and psychosocial functioning in early adolescence. *The Journal of Early Adolescence, 24*, 326–356. doi:10.1177/0272431604268530

Sales, N. J. (2016). *American girls: Social media and the secret lives of teenagers*. New York: Knopf.

Sands, S. (1991). Bulimia, dissociation and empathy: A self-psychological view. In C. L. Johnson (Ed.), *Psychodynamic treatment of anorexia nervosa and bulimia* (pp. 34–50). New York: Guilford.

Sands, S. (2016). Eating disorder treatment as a process of mind – body integration: Special challenges for women. *Clinical Social Work Journal*, *44*, 27–37. doi:10.1007/s10615-015-0540-7

Schutz, H. K., & Paxton, S. J. (2007). Friendship quality, body dissatisfaction, dieting and disordered eating in adolescent girls. *British Journal of Clinical Psychology*, *46*, 67–83. doi:10.1348/014466506X115993

Sroufe, L. A., Carlson, E. A., Levy, A. K., & Egeland, B. (1999). Implications of attachment theory for developmental psychopathology. *Development and Psychopathology*, *11*, 1–13. doi:10.1017/S0954579499001923

Steinberg, L. (2013). *Adolescence*. New York: McGraw Hill.

Stewart, S. H., Svolensky, M. J., & Eifert, G. H. (2002). The relations of anxiety sensitivity, experiential avoidance, and alexithymic coping to young adults' motivations for drinking. *Behavior Modification*, *26*, 274–296.

Stice, E. (2016). Interactive and mediational etiologic models of eating disorder onset: Evidence from prospective studies. *Annual Review of Clinical Psychology*, *12*, 359–381. doi:10.1146/annurev-clinpsy-021815–093317

Sullivan, H. (1953). *The interpersonal theory of psychiatry*. New York: W.W. Norton & Co.

Swanson, S. A., Crow, S. J., Le Grange, D., Swendsen, J., & Merikangas, K. R. (2011). Prevalence and correlates of eating disorders in adolescents: Results from the National Comorbidity Survey Replication Adolescent Supplement. *Archives of General Psychiatry*, *68*, 714–723. doi:10.1001/archgenpsychiatry.2011.22

Wachtel, P. (1997). *Psychoanalysis, behavior therapy and the relational world*. Washington, DC: American Psychological Association.

Wooldridge, T. (2014). The enigma of Ana: A psychoanalytic exploration of pro-anorexia Internet forums. *Journal of Infant, Child, and Adolescent Psychotherapy*, *13*(3), 202–216. doi:10.1080/15289168.2014.937978

Zerbe, K. (2008). *Integrated treatment of eating disorders: Beyond the body betrayed*. New York: W.W. Norton & Company.

Zerbe, K. (2016). Psychodynamic issues in the treatment of binge eating: Working with shame, secrets, no-entry, and false body defenses. *Clinical Social Work Journal*, *44*, 8–17. doi:10.1007/s10615-015-0559-9

13

THE ENIGMA OF ANA

A psychoanalytic exploration of pro-anorexia Internet forums

Tom Wooldridge

Legal Disclaimer
The names and identifying details have been changed to protect the privacy of individuals. At the time of writing, all of the online data was freely available for anyone to access.

Introduction

In the form of chat rooms, newsgroups, and websites, pro-anorexia has emerged in recent years as a cultural movement that takes an at least partially positive attitude toward anorexia nervosa and other eating disorders. Most pro-anorexia (commonly referred to as "pro-ana") forums offer guidelines for beginning and maintaining anorexia, tips for rapid weight loss, dieting competitions, ways to avoid detection by family and friends, and motivational images ("thinspiration") to inspire further weight loss (Strife & Rickard, 2011). More than 500 forums exist at a given time, though estimates are unreliable because forums are frequently shut down by their hosts and reopened at new locations (Atkins, 2005; Bardone-Cone & Cass, 2007). This number vastly exceeds that of recovery-oriented forums (Chesley, Alberts, Klein, & Kreipe, 2003).[1]

It's hard to describe the startling, visceral experience of visiting a pro-ana website for the first time. You're immediately confronted with diatribes against medical and mental health treatments, accompanied by photos of emaciated adolescents that convey a strange combination of starvation and sexuality. In a universe of part objects, participants share their particular obsessions: the space between the thighs, protruding ribcages, hipbones like boomerangs. Upon further investigation, you'll find disquieting discussion about how to improve and maintain eating disorders. How do you throw up without choking on your own vomit?

How to "water load" so your doctor won't know you've lost weight? How to curb the insistence of the body's appetite?

Like anorexia nervosa itself, pro-ana sites confront visitors with what has been described as "the spectacle of not eating" – words and images conveying profound degrees of emaciation and embodied images of suffering (Warin, 2004). But to the surprise of the media and the medical community, which has almost uniformly condemned pro-ana sites, there's more to the story. As you continue to read, you'll find that participants are making real attempts at connection. "You're a good person," they say to each other, "and we want to support you whether you get worse, stay the same, or eventually recover." And there's a palpable sense of appreciation in the community. Participants speak of their loneliness and how, on these sites, they've found true peers for the first time.

The pro-ana community does not reflect a single, coherent philosophy. On the contrary, each site has its own unique perspective of what it means to have an eating disorder – for example, whether eating disorders are a lifestyle or a medical condition (Strife & Rickard, 2011), a positive or negative experience (or both), an experience to be cultivated or to be avoided. In some ways, the pro-ana community is defined in opposition to its adversaries. When an outside user posts an attack on a pro-ana forum or a site is shut down by its host, the resistance of its users and their shared goals and beliefs are strengthened (Giles, 2006).

Pro-ana sites have raised intense controversy. Effectively a movement of resistance against conventional conceptualizations and treatments of eating disorders (Giles, 2006), they have raised concern among both health professionals and parents, who express alarm that these forums harm vulnerable individuals (Paquette, 2002). In many cases, visitors encounter images of emaciated women (and men), often semi-naked, juxtaposing eroticism and sterility, beauty and suffering, femininity and its repudiation.

What is the impact of pro-ana forums on participants? The deleterious effects of pro-ana participation, including decreased self-esteem, self-efficacy, and perceived attractiveness, as well as increased negative affect and perception of being overweight, have been documented (Bardone-Cone & Cass, 2007). Recent research, however, has taken a more nuanced point-of-view, suggesting that participation has benefits, including social support, a way to cope with a stigmatized illness, and a means of self-expression (Yeshua-Katz & Martins, 2012). Another study suggested that participants who sought emotional support on pro-ana forums experienced benefit, whereas those who use the sites for sustaining an eating disorder without seeking emotional support were harmed (Csipke & Horne, 2007).

I believe that we have much to learn from pro-ana forums. After all, the fact that they appear to have benefits for some participants is a bracing discovery. If we understand why these sites are appealing to individuals with eating disorders as well as the mechanisms through which they provide benefit, we will understand both more about the psychodynamics of eating disorders as well as the complex relationship between cyberspace and mental health.

No doubt cyberspace has introduced a dramatic change into our cultural understanding of reality (Hartman, 2011). However, the nature of that understanding is still a matter of ongoing debate. Does cyberspace offer a potential space, an avenue for personal development and growth, or a venue for psychic retreat (Lingiardi, 2008)? In other words, cyberspace has been envisioned as a "funhouse mirror, trapping the wary and vulnerable in pseudo-reality," while at the same time offering others an opportunity for creative fantasy and imagination (Malater, 2007).

In this paper, I argue that pro-ana forums are a double-edged sword. On the one hand, they may provide participants with a potential space (Winnicott, 1971) that fosters further psychological development. On the other, they may provide the opportunity for psychic retreat (Steiner, 1993), in which cyberspace becomes an escape from relatedness, a kind of dissociation.

Clinical case

I present excerpts from a psychoanalytic psychotherapy with Sara, a woman in her late teens with a severe case of anorexia who was an avid user of pro-ana websites. Although our work together was extensive and involved the exploration of numerous dynamic themes, in the following section I focus primarily on the development of Sara's relationship with pro-ana forums and the impact of that relationship on our clinical work together.

In our initial hours together, Sara began to describe her earliest memory, vague and uncertain but elaborated by her parents' joy in retelling it at family gatherings.

> When I was young – maybe two or three – I'd call out in the night because I was upset. But I didn't scream for my mother or father. I'd wake up at 2am and yell, 'cookie! cookie!' I've never been able to understand that, why I didn't want my mother or my father. The only source of comfort I could imagine was a cookie.

In demanding a cookie, was Sara asking for her mother? Or was she simply asking for a cookie? Over time, analytic inquiry increasingly suggested the latter. For Sara, the dialectic between fantasy and reality had collapsed in the direction of reality, foreclosing her capacity to make use of potential space (Ogden, 1985). Early on, comfort and soothing became equated with concrete objects – in most cases, with food – and the symbolic aspect of food, insofar as Sara's yearning for cookies representing a yearning for maternal comfort, was entirely obliterated.

Further exploration revealed that an immensely controlling and hypochondriacal mother had foreclosed Sara's capacity for transitional object use in early life. With regard to a child's first transitional object, Winnicott (1953) wrote, "The parents get to know its value and carry it round when travelling. The mother lets it get dirty and even smelly, knowing that by washing it she introduces a break in continuity in the infant's experience, a break that may destroy the meaning and value of the object to the infant." As Sara learned from her mother, she'd tried to appropriate an old doll that had belonged to her grandmother, "carrying it around everywhere" and "always kissing and hugging it." Within a few weeks, Sara's mother had taken that "smelly, dirty thing away and thrown it in the trash bin," and in fact continued to replace Sara's toys entirely every few weeks so they would be "clean and hygienic."

Over time, Sara and I discovered that this story was a prototypical example of her mother's own lack of capacity to make use of potential space. Sara's mother, it seems, didn't have the ability to consider that the doll, though dirty, represented an object of immense importance to Sara. Put differently, mother lacked the capacity for reverie, for making meaning of Sara's communications by gradually sifting through her own experience (Bion, 1962). Over time, Sara's mother's failure to serve as a "protective shield" against the premature introduction of reality gave rise to cumulative trauma (Kahn, 1963). Repeatedly, the dialectical process of fantasy and reality, potential space, collapsed toward the reality pole (Ogden, 1985).

As a child, Sara was unable to tolerate fantasies of longing for maternal comfort and increasingly turned to concrete (reality-based) objects both to defend against these fantasies and because it was the closest approximation available. Later in our work, Sara said:

> Growing up I would think of food endlessly – at home in my bed when I was going to sleep, on the way to kindergarten. I remember it so vividly. I would think about how it could be arranged, the cookies and muffins and candy, what order to eat things in and what tastes would go together, and all of this would calm me.

Food became a symbolic equation (Segal, 1957) for comfort. Without the capacity to generate potential space, Sara was unable to think about or intuit the meaning of her cravings and, therefore, to access the fantasies they kept out of her awareness. In thinking about food – how it would be ordered, ingested, and taste, as well as the comfort, albeit temporary, it would bring – Sara bolstered the illusion of omnipotence.

This dynamic immediately made its way into the therapeutic relationship and persisted for approximately the first year. When I suggested possible meanings to Sara's associations, she often became angry and withdrawn. These interactions culminated on several occasions with Sara curling up tightly in her chair, yelling while tears ran down her face that I was "cold and cruel." In our first iterations of this interaction, I found myself feeling defensive and embarrassed, searching myself for any sign of irritation with Sara. In time, I came to recognize a strong dissonance between Sara's description of me and my own experience of extending myself in an effort to understand her experience. In short, I recognized my desire to offer her nourishment and her need to reject it.

The experience of being heavily projected into the countertransference often reflects the patient's experience of having received profoundly intrusive projections in early development (Grinberg, 1962). As we discovered more about Sara's early life, we quickly learned that this had indeed been the case. Sara remembered one incident that represents the intensity of her mother's projective identifications. Around age eight, Sara had been eating a pear in her family's kitchen. When her mother walked in and saw "the juice running down [Sara's] chin," she became extremely distraught and insisted that her daughter explain her overt exhibition of sexuality. Sara found herself filled with immense shame that persisted to the current day whenever she ate fruit or other "juicy" foods. As we see later, it also had a significant impact on her relationship to her own sexuality as a young adult and contributed to her interest in "thinspiration" images.

Traumatic levels of intrusion through projective identification such as Sara experienced inevitably lead to a closing down of potential space. As Winnicott (1953) noted, in less healthy states early transitional object usage may develop into "fetishism, lying and stealing, the origin and loss of affectionate feeling, drug addiction, the talisman of obsession rituals, etc." Soon after this incident, Sara convinced her parents and pediatrician that she was deaf for almost six months. As she said, "I can remember clearly that I could hear what people were saying to me. But for some reason I didn't want them to know that." I suspect this was Sara's best effort, given her limited capacity for play, to symbolize her experience, though in a strikingly concrete way.

Repeated experiences of intrusion led Sara to develop a no-entry system of defenses (Williams, 1997), making it difficult for Sara to take in nourishment through either food or relational connection. After the incident with the pear, Sara became increasingly preoccupied with restricting her food intake and, by the beginning of the following year, her interpersonal relationships had ceased to provide her with a felt sense of connection. Furthermore, this incident became a prominent topic of discussion, especially in relation to Sara's developing sexuality:

Sara: At 15 I first tried to have sex with my then-boyfriend. And it didn't work.

Therapist: What about it didn't work?

Sara: I couldn't get wet, to be honest. It's embarrassing for me to say that to you. We tried several times but it just wasn't going to happen.

Therapist: We've talked a lot about your relationship with your then-boyfriend and a lot about what was going on between you, but we haven't talked much about your sexual relationship with him.

Sara: Sex is disgusting to me. The whole thing is just really gross.

Therapist: I wonder if it feels intrusive, in the same way it felt intrusive when your mother would walk into your room without knocking and see you without clothes on, for example.

Sara: Or like when I was eating the pear, when my mother got so upset that time.

Therapist: For your mother, the juice from the pear showed that you were being too open with your sexuality. And with your ex-boyfriend, it felt gross and disgusting to show, in an outward way, signs of sexual interest.

In this dialogue, Sara is beginning to understand the impact of her mother's projective identifications on her developing sexuality. Growing up, Sara internalized her mother's representation of her sexuality; all overt displays of sexual excitement were to be restricted. (Notably, Sara also restricted her all-too-rare consumption of food to times when she was alone. Eating, she felt, was a deeply sensual act and brought embarrassment when done in the company of others.) And consistent with her no-entry system of defenses, Sara is understandably anxious about penetration, which to her is a concrete representation of intrusion.

With this compromised capacity for relational connection, Sara was drawn to the ethereal world of pro-ana around age twelve. When she first came for treatment, Sara visited these forums several times daily, spending hours each night posting and responding to the comments of her online friends. Pro-anorexia forums first came to life in our work together when I learned that Sara was strongly drawn to so-called "thinspiration" on pro-ana forums and that these images had great meaning for her. The following dialogue occurred almost a year into treatment:

Sara: It's not sexual at all, really, but the images are of really pretty women, so beautiful. It's not that I feel attracted to them like that, though, or to anybody really. . .

Therapist: They don't bring up sexual feelings for you.

Sara: They're just so . . . empty, you know.

Therapist: Empty . . . of what?

Sara: When I look at them, I think what they must feel like, so peaceful and empty, so clean, and I think that I could feel that way too, maybe, if I keep on not eating like this.

Therapist: You imagine that you'd feel peaceful, finally, if you could empty out what's inside of you like they seem to have done.

In these images, Sara was hoping for a transformational experience and developing an ongoing relationship to objects that signified her yearning for transformation (Bollas, 1979). More than an idealized split between thinness and fatness, lightness and heaviness, these images suggest Sara's search for a particular kind of object relation, which she associated with the capacity to remain impervious to insidious maternal projective identifications, as well as a nascent knowledge of an urgent, internal demand for ego repair. I suspect, too, that these images allowed Sara to maintain some connection to her sexuality. Indeed, thinspiration is the epitome of sexuality without excess; though often semi-naked subjects also appear, in Sara's words, "empty" and "clean," epitomizing the self-control and self-sufficiency Sara idealized.

Several months later, Sara began to discuss her experiences participating in pro-ana forum discussions. Over time, we learned that these forums served several purposes for her. At times, Sara's participation on pro-ana forums served as what Steiner (1993) has called a psychic retreat, a place to withdraw from overwhelming emotional pain. Indeed, Sara was subject to the same ruminations and fixations as in real life and often used these venues for perseverative thinking separate from relationship. For example, over periods of weeks she would recount posting virtually identical material, often focused on the specifics of calories ingested, calories expended throughout the day, and current body weight. It seemed to me that was done not in hope of relational response but as a primitive way of containing her anxieties.

I want to comment on Sara's use of these sites in relationship to me. Throughout our work together, this was an ongoing thread of exploration. At times, I felt that Sara worried I couldn't handle the more disturbed parts of her psyche and so reserved them for her online interactions. At other times, Sara seemed to be saying, "You are too threatening, but pro-ana forums are controllable." By remaining invested in pro-ana forums, Sara minimized, and at times nullified, the emotional importance of our relationship and thus protected herself from a repetition of her earlier experiences of feeling controlled and invaded. Many times, Sara attempted to emerge from her claustrophobic retreat but found the anxiety overwhelming:

Sara: I feel like my world is so small sometimes. There is nothing for me to look forward to, no future in any of this.
(*long silence. . .*)

Therapist: It's so small, so restricted, in the world you're living in, yet coming out and being seen is terrifying. You've found a way to shield yourself from that terror, but at a great cost.

Sara: If I gave it up, there'd be no going forward, either.

Over time, however, Sara also found herself able to develop a kind of mutuality (though at a sufficient distance) in her online relationships, which she was not been able to do in the real world. As we explored this, we discovered that pro-ana forums provided Sara with a good enough environment for play; the computer and its connection to cyberspace was sufficiently removed from the exigencies of reality without becoming pure fantasy, a space on the "border between self and not-self" (Turkle, 1997, p. 30). As Gabbard (2001) has written:

> The person sending an e-mail message is alone, but not alone. The apparent privacy allows for freer expression, but the awareness of the other receiving the e-mail allows for passionate attachment and highly emotional expressiveness.
>
> (*p. 734*)

Pro-ana forums became, at times, a form of potential space for Sara precisely because they were a move toward relatedness away from purely omnipotent fantasy while retaining an element of omnipotence. As Lingiardi (2008) has written, "Spoken dialogue, more than written exchange, seems to confer 'reality' on a phenomenon" (p. 120). Sara began to find a way to play with her thoughts and feelings in a space between reality and fantasy, in which her fears of traumatic intrusion could be kept at a distance. With this emergence of the capacity to generate potential space, Sara began to engage in increasingly imaginative dialogue with her peers:

Sara: A lot of the time when I'm on there, when I'm having a bad day or when I'm not doing well in recovery, I talk about how many calories I had today or how much my weight has changed.

Therapist: You get stuck going around and around, like we've talked about happening in here when you're talking to me.

Sara: Yeah, it's exactly like that. But you know sometimes I talk about what it's like to get better, and what it might be like to really be healthy – you know, normal weight and happy, if that's possible – and people really listen, you know, they get it, how scary that idea is.

Therapist: You're able to think about getting better, maybe to even prepare yourself for the idea a little. And you're able to let people in, just a little.

Sara: Yeah, I mean, I'm not sure if I can handle it. I know I'd feel fat and ugly and terrible about myself, and my family would still be messed up, but you know, sometimes I talk about the idea on there. . .

For Sara, pro-ana forums served as a space that allowed her to imagine different thoughts, feelings, and ways of being in the world without the commitment real-life action entails or with the same level of vulnerability that face-to-face interaction involved. Over time, Sara's emerging capacity for play made its way into our clinical work. Toward the end of our time together, Sara began to relinquish the forums entirely, in favor of more relational forms of play. I believe the following dialogue captures this transition:

Sara: You know, I haven't been on PT [Sara's primary pro-ana site] in almost a week now.

Therapist: How does that feel?

Sara: I'm not sure. I miss it, but I also know I can always go back. But it's exciting too, because I've connected with Michael [a new male friend], and it feels like we can talk about all the things I talked about on there.

Therapist: And how does it feel to talk to Michael?

Sara: Like I can be myself. Sometimes I'm scared or embarrassed for him to see my family or that he'll think I'm too screwed up for him to be friends with, but so far it hasn't happened. At other times, I find myself thinking about what it'd be like if we started dating, if we became really close, you know?

Therapist: You can envision that when Michael sees everything that's going on with you, everything you've been through, he might be freaked out. And you can also imagine that there's something there he might be attracted to.

Sara: I'm trying to think about whether I can let him in just a little more.

Sara is increasingly able to make use of potential space in face-to-face relationships. This reflects her developing capacity to tolerate the subjectivity of others without consistently retreating to a position of omnipotence, to rely less extensively on psychic retreat, as well as her growing sense that it's possible to develop relationships without a repetition of the traumatic level of intrusion she found in the maternal relationship.

Observations of pro-ana forums

Because of their increasing appearance in clinical work, we conducted a qualitative analysis of pro-ana forums (Wooldridge, Mok, & Chiu, 2014). In the process, I've become extensively familiar with the pro-ana community. I've read thousands of posts and followed the plight of innumerable young men and women over time. I've come to believe that pro-ana forums provide participants with the opportunity to make use of potential space (Winnicott, 1971) for creative play with multiple dimensions of their experience. At the same time, pro-ana forums provide a venue for psychic retreat (Steiner, 1993), an escape from truth and relatedness.

The architecture of pro-ana forums facilitates the generation of both potential space and psychic retreat. Potential space depends on the capacity to maintain a dialectical process between oneness and separateness, fantasy and reality (Ogden, 1985). For this dialectic to be maintained, the participant has to find ways to manage reality as it presents itself. The high level of control afforded to users of Internet-based forums facilitates the management of disturbing aspects of reality, allowing this dialectical process to be maintained and potential space to be accessed. At the same time, when reality becomes too much to bear, this control extends into omnipotence and can be used to facilitate psychic retreat (Steiner, 1993).

As I have spent time on pro-ana forums, I have been repeatedly struck by the experience of alienation so prominent among its participants. Here, young men and women lament their estrangement from friends and family and their extreme loneliness, which is the conscious, affective component of alienation (Burton, 1961). As one participant wrote:

> The nature of the beast being mostly secretive and lonely, it's a comfort to know that others have gone through the same thing. When I first found a similar ED [eating disorder] web site at age sixteen I nearly wept with relief – I had suffered alone in silence for almost five years, and didn't know anyone else who had an ED.

In thinking about this aspect of participants' experiences, I am reminded of Sartre's (1984) elucidation of alienation in his analysis of "the look." When we are engaged in the immediacy of our lives, we experience the world through a first-person perspective in which others are experienced as objects related to our current pursuits. When we become aware of being looked at – in Sartre's words, when our subjectivity is invaded by the subjectivity of another of whose world we are merely a part – we become aware of another, more objective aspect of our nature insofar as it exists as an object in the mind of a separate subjectivity. We become aware that we are alienated from a dimension of our being that resides outside of our immediate experience.

Many participants describe experiencing the other as forcing upon them a disruptively different aspect of reality from their own, subjectively apprehended, experience. In many cases, this experience of having one's subjectivity invaded by the subjectivity of another reverberates with earlier experiences of traumatic intrusion. In the words of one participant:

> Everybody around me thought they knew more about it than I did. I felt like the loneliest person on the planet . . . everyone was telling me what was wrong with me and how I should feel. But its [sic] always been that way for me, even before I had the ED my parents never thought me my own person.

Pro-ana forums present participants with the possibility of retreating from the pain inherent in the experience of alienation. Of course, psychic retreats can serve as both pathological organizations or as temporary, self-regulatory private spaces that foster resilience and reconsolidation (Steiner, 1993). The problem, in other words, is not the retreat itself but how the retreat is used. When we emerge from retreat, are we more equipped to deal with the exigencies of day-to-day living? As one participant wrote:

> When I come on here and talk, I can actually cope, can get through the rest of the day. This place has given me so much strength. Its [sic] given me the support I need to get treatment, to reach out to friends.

In this excerpt, a participant makes use of a pro-ana forum as a temporary retreat that allows him to refuel, emerging again into the world of relationship less battered and more resilient than before. Others, however, use pro-ana forums as extended retreats; in the words of one participant, "Why bother with people? They'll fuck you up and disappoint you. Better to stay on the computer." Thus, pro-ana forums can become a way to avoid relational contact that feels too threatening almost entirely. As Faber (1984) has written:

> [The computer] offers itself to its manipulator as a powerful little world, a powerful little universe, a kind of microcosm, that can be totally mastered, totally controlled, in such a way as to offset, at the unconscious level, early

> narcissistic wounds experienced in the failure to master, to control, the primary caregiver or 'object.'
>
> *(p. 267)*

At their worst, pro-ana forums serve as a purely projective container into which participants evacuate their emotional lives in order to dissociate from them. The containment of the self, in other words, is entrusted to the pro-ana forum and the repetitive behaviors engaged within it. The most common of these repetitive behaviors is declaration of highest weight, current weight, and goal weight. Similarly, participants often repeat their calories eaten or calories burned. These conversations are notable for their lack of involvement with the other; they are posted without expectation of response, and any response that is made is rarely engaged.

Although psychic retreat may be helpful for the ego at times, it becomes problematic when used at great length. As participants become increasingly involved with the ethereal world of pro-ana, they may become increasingly detached from the real world, with the physicality (and frailty) it entails. Consider the following excerpt from one participant:

> I spend all my free time here. . . . I dunno [sic] what I'd do without all you. Don't really have any friends, nothing worth spending time on. This place has saved me.

Beyond the unpredictability of relationship and its risk of loss, pro-ana forums provide a kind of autistic-contiguous experience (Ogden, 1989) in which the sensory experience of the keyboard and monitor, the letters dancing across the screen, provides an environment that is controllable and containing. For some, pro-ana forums may become a fantasized retreat that is preferred over the real world.

Although cyberspace may provide retreat from relational anguish, it also provides the opportunity to make initial steps into a world inhabited by others (Lingiardi, 2008). I have been struck by the intimacy that occurs on these forums as participants make real connections with their peers. The relative safety of cyberspace makes the possibility of relational connection feel within reach for those with fraught histories of emotional intimacy. As one young man wrote:

> Part of why this is the best support site is that people on here are in all stages of [eating] disorders and can come here no matter what they feel about their EDs. I have made real friends here, more than in my RL [real life], where it's so hard.

In this excerpt, we can see a young man who has found "real friends" on pro-ana sites, presumably because of the kinds of experiences that these sites make possible. Indeed, it is because pro-ana sites may protect participants against the experience of a reality that is too much to bear that potential space and, thus, deeper relationships become accessible.

Similarly, the atmosphere of tolerance for experimentation and the relational warmth that accompanies many conversations are remarkable. Consider the following excerpt:

> nice to see you here! i think you'll find that people are accepting of what you're going thru [sic]. a lot of us are in different stages of recovery and a lot of people are still struggling with their sexual orientation gay? bi? straight? it's a question that i'm always asking myself, still no answers.

There is an implicit agreement within the pro-ana community that the differentiation between "real life" and life in cyberspace will not be confronted. This makes play, which depends heavily on the possibility of maintaining illusion, possible (Winnicott, 1953). When this area of illusion is collapsed – through "flames," or comments made by hostile site visitors (O'Dochartaigh, 2002), for example – strong responses are elicited (Giles, 2006). Consider the following example of an outsider's critique:

> I know you probably feel you are doing a deed to those who are afflicted with this illness, but the way in which you go about promoting it is not only wrong, it is contributing to the delinquency of others (most of whom are more than likely minors). Giving "diet tips" and encouragement to eat less than the recommended amount of daily calories could be hindering the health of young girls (and perhaps boys) everywhere. It is people like you who continue to put it in these young women's minds that they aren't good enough, when that is simply not true. You think you are the answer, you think you are doing the right thing; you are not. You are the problem with this world.

In this excerpt, we see an outsider's attack on the pro-ana forum, reflecting a collapse of his own ability to understand what the site represents to its participants. Instances such as these are often reacted to with outright aggression; in many cases, moderators remove them from the forum entirely. When the impingement of reality collapses the illusion necessary for play, participants, both as individuals and as a community, make a concentrated effort at the restoration of illusion. The consensus of the pro-ana community and the omnipotence afforded by modern technology are precisely what makes it possible for this illusion to be maintained with relative consistency.

Questions of identity are inherent in pro-ana forums. Among the questions pertaining to identity that are explored on pro-ana forums, perhaps the most common is, "What does it mean to be anorexic?" Pro-ana websites do not reflect a universally coherent standpoint. On the contrary, each site has its own perspective on what it means, and the term "ana" has become the subject of intense identity negotiation. For example, participants appear to frequently consider whether anorexia is a lifestyle choice or medical condition, a positive experience or a negative one (Giles, 2006).

Individuals with eating disorders find themselves the object of public scrutiny and clinical diagnosis. These individuals must reconcile their own experience of eating disorders as empowering states of distinction with immense symbolic power with the one-sided representation of eating disorders by the media and medical professionals (Warrin, 2004). Deprived of their agency, these individuals are likely to seek alternative forums in which they can reclaim their power from outside agencies. Indeed, pro-ana forums provide such a venue, a potential space in which individuals can engage in what has been called "agency play" (Battaglia, 1997, p. 507), which can be seen in the following excerpt:

> I just wanna [sic] put it out there that I'm tired of being told what I am by my treatment team. They think they know more than me about what I feel. I'm not a diagnosis; I'm a person who carries around ana by myself all day, every day. And maybe ana is not what they think it is, maybe it's both better and worse.

Here, we can see a participant begin to think about various aspects of her identity and, furthermore, resisting having her identify defined primarily by others. In this forum, she can develop a more nuanced perspective about what it means to be "ana" – a perspective that is ultimately more consonant with her experience.

Pro-ana forums also provide a potential space for participants to play with various aspects of identity. As Turkle (1997) argues, the Internet, with its relative anonymity, provides individuals with a laboratory for exploring and experimenting with different versions of self. With this anonymity, participants are free to express themselves and behave in ways that are frowned upon in their day-to-day lives (Bargh, McKenna, & Fitzsimmons, 2002). Indeed, in face-to-face interactions, disclosing or experimenting with one's sense of identity can have serious consequences (Derlega, Metts, Petronio, & Margulis, 1993). In contrast, pro-ana forums provide participants with the possibility of inhabiting a space between fantasy and reality; free to fantasize, they are nonetheless in contact with others, but without the same degree of risk found in the real world.

Perhaps the most striking element of pro-ana forums is visual in nature. In its most common form, "thinspiration," or "thinspo," consists of motivational images of models, actresses and actors, or even site participants, many of whom have been modified to make them appear even more emaciated. As I've browsed innumerable thinspiration images and read the dialogue that accompanies them, I've discovered that these images are used in several ways. As I suggested with Sara, for example, a thinspiration image may serve as a concrete representation of a yearning for a particular kind of psychological state. In many cases, participants develop "favorite" models as sources of thinspiration, and follow and discuss them over time:

> Have you seen the Machinist? I want to look like Bale. he's [sic] got no excess at all, totally ripped. If I could look like that, I think id be happy with my life for good – ahhhh contentment.

Often, participants post images of themselves, providing a visual record of their increasing emaciation over time. In these images, we find a visual representation of the participant's internalized object relationship. Lemma (2010) has written that the body can be open and receptive to the other or it can be shut down, keeping the other out. Drawing on Frank (1991), Lemma (2010) writes of the *monadic body*, which serves as a psychic retreat (Steiner, 1993), an idealized state that can be used to hold the self together and to resist the regressive pull back into a fused relationship with the mother. Consider the following excerpt:

> Im still working on it. No breakfast, coffee only, 3 hours of exercise. Im running seven miles every am. Im going to post some badass thinspo of myself soon! It feels like I barely need food anymore. Its amazing to see!

We might speculate that this participant's "barely needing food" suggests his fight against the allure of dependency. In other cases, thinspiration seems to serve as a kind of communication by impact (Casement, 1991). When I first encountered so-called thinspiration images, I felt intruded upon by the intensity of their suffering and frailty. Because intrusion and invasion are central to the experience of eating disorders (Williams, 1997), these images seem to say, "I feel invaded by your gaze, and I am going to invade you in return."

As I've watched discussions about thinspiration evolve over time, I've noted that some participants eventually lessen and occasionally abandon their preoccupation with these images. Insofar as an internalized object relationship is actualized primarily in the body, it resists finding its way into words. As participants become able to use words to develop a narrative of their experience, they are increasingly able to make tentative steps into the relational world:

> i dunno. i just don't get what I used to get out of thinspo . . . doesnt [sic]do it for me anymore, you know? when I look at those pictures, i feel bad for the people in them. they've suffered like i've suffered, and i wouldn't wish that on anybody.

Surprisingly, much conversation on pro-ana forums is focused on the possibility of recovery. The experience of eating disorders is fraught with ambivalence (Williams & Reid, 2010). In the literature and in clinical practice, patients report feeling uncertain about whether anorexia is a "friend" or an "enemy" and whether it is a problem that needs treatment (Colton & Pistrang, 2004), often spending a great deal of time weighing its advantages and disadvantages (Cockell, Geller, & Linden, 2003). On these forums, participants find a space in which to play with their ideas about the benefits and risks of eating disorders. In the following excerpt, the participant gives voice to a "positive" aspect of the anorexic experience:

> Have any of the people against Ana been fat? It's the worst feeling. When added to physical problems keeping you from adequate exercise, Ana is a godsend. So I feel really grateful to Ana for that, that she's taken that pain away.

In this excerpt, the participant is commenting on the perceived psychological benefits of anorexia. For her, anorexia is experienced as the lesser evil when compared with the feelings of distress she experiences when not actively restricting. In contrast, consider the following post:

> I feel unsure, as well. But I don't want to go on starving. Like, I don't want to have an ED, but I don't want to have to eat, either.

In this excerpt, we see a participant with more overtly expressed ambivalence; although eating is recognized as a fraught experience, starvation is also understood as a deeply unsatisfying experience in significant ways as well.

In some cases, pro-anorexia forums provide the space for sufferers to play with the idea of recovery in all its dimensions, even including weight restoration:

> so what's it like exactly to feel normal weight? I gain a pound and feel fat as all hell so I cant [sic] imagine what itd [sic] be like to be looking like people I see walking around. but then I look at em [sic] and they look happy sometimes, it makes me wonder if its worth it. . . [anorexia].

In this excerpt, the participant is beginning to think about what it might be like to change his relationship to his body and its weight and shape. He is, furthermore, questioning whether the psychological benefits of his disorder justify their cost. In the following excerpt, we encounter a participant who is more motivated toward recovery:

> looking to attempt recovery again, and I'm feeling really fucking passionate about succeeding this time. I'm so done with this chapter of my life, I don't want to restrict and b/p [binge and purge] my brains out all the time. One of the things I've failed to do in the past when attempting recovery is reach out to others doing the same, so I was hoping to find some others on this site who are in whatever stage of recovering just as someone to lean on or even to help encourage. I need all the help I can get!

Indeed, here we see a participant who is strongly motivated to change. He is clearly reaching out for support – an act that may have been made possible through his relationship to pro-ana forums – and has made a connection between receiving emotional support and increasing his chances of recovery.

Conclusion

In this paper, I have suggested that pro-anorexia forums demand the attention of the psychoanalytic community, both because of their increasing prevalence (Custers & Van den Bulck, 2009) and relevance to clinical practice. After reviewing the research on the impact of pro-anorexia forum participation, I have attempted to present a nuanced view of these forums.

I have suggested that, on the one hand, pro-ana forums may provide participants with a potential space (Winncott, 1971) that fosters psychological development. Making use of potential space, participants are able to think creatively about many aspects of their experience, from the experience of alienation that characterizes eating disorders to the possibility of eventual recovery. On the other, they may provide the opportunity for psychic retreat (Steiner, 1993), in which cyberspace becomes an escape from aspects of reality that are too difficult to bear.

As I have written with this paper, I have struggled with the same conflicts inherent in the pro-ana movement. Essentially, pro-ana forums attempt to provide a protected space in which individuals are accepted without judgment. Consider, for example, the following mission statement of one pro-ana forum:

> Imagine you have something within you; something that you think about often; something that consumes such a great part of your life that the general public deems it a disorder because it is something so engrained in you. Imagine having no one to talk to about it. . . . [This] is a place for people who "think a certain way" about their bodies and lives to meet and to talk. About anorexia, about family, about relationships, about anything at all. To talk openly, in the hope that they won't be judged, and in the hope that they will be understood.

In many ways, I, too, have wanted to refrain from judgment. And while I have argued for a nuanced view of pro-ana forums, attempting to understand their potential risks and benefits, I must emphasize that pro-ana forums remain intensely disturbing. In these moments, I remind myself that I have witnessed touching moves toward connection take place within these communities which, in some cases, have resulted in participants taking steps toward recovery.

Note

1 Because of the anonymity the Internet provides, it is virtually impossible to obtain accurate information about the demographics of pro-ana participants. However, the majority of studies that have been conducted suggest that most users are adolescents. For example, one study suggests that 12.6% of female and 5.9% of male students (n = 711) in four secondary schools had visited these forums, often several times daily (Csipke & Horne, 2007).

References

Atkins, L. (2005, November 3). It's better to be thin and dead than fat and living. *The Guardian*. Retrieved November 8, 2012, from www.guardian.co.uk/technology/2002/jul/23/lifeandhealth.medicineandhealth

Bardone-Cone, A. M., & Cass, K. M. (2007). What does viewing a pro-anorexia website do? An experimental examination of website exposure and moderating effects. *The International Journal of Eating Disorders*, *40*(6), 537–548.

Bargh, J. A., McKenna, K. Y. A., & Fitzsimmons, G. M. (2002). Can you see the real me? Activation and expression of the 'True self' on the Internet. *Journal of Social Issues*, *58*(1), 33–48.

Battaglia, D. (1997). Ambiguating agency: The case of Malinowski's ghost. *American Anthropologist, 99*(3), 505–510.

Bion, W. R. (1962). *Learning from experience*. London: Heinemann.

Bollas, C. (1979). The transformational object. *The International Journal of Psychoanalysis*, *60*, 97–107.

Burton, A. (1961). On the nature of loneliness. *American Journal of Psychoanalysis*, *21*, 34–39.

Casement, P. (1991). *Learning from the patient*. New York: Guilford Press.

Chesley, E. B., Alberts, J. D., Klein, J. D., & Kreipe, R. E. (2003). Pro or con? Anorexia nervosa and the Internet. *Journal of Adolescent Health*, *32*(2), 123–124.

Cockell, S. J., Geller, J., & Linden, W. (2003). Decisional balance in anorexia nervosa: Capitalizing on ambivalence. *European Eating Disorders Review*, *11*(2), 75–89.

Colton, A., & Pistrang, N. (2004). Adolescents' experiences of inpatient treatment for anorexia nervosa. *European Eating Disorders Review*, *12*(5), 307–316.

Csipke, E., & Horne, O. (2007). Pro-eating disorder websites: Users' opinions. *European Eating Disorders Review: The Journal of the Eating Disorders Association*, *15*(3), 196–206.

Custers, K., & Van den Bulck, J. (2009). Viewership of pro-anorexia websites in seventh, ninth and eleventh graders. *European Eating Disorders Review: The Journal of the Eating Disorders Association*, *17*(3), 214–219.

Derlega, V. L., Metts, S., Petronio, S., & Margulis, S. T. (1993). *Self-disclosure*. London: Sage.

Faber, M. D (1984). The computer, the technological order, and psychoanalysis: Preliminary remarks. *Psychoanalytic Review*, *71*(2), 263–277.

Frank, A. (1991). For a sociology of the body: An analytical review. In N. Featherstone, M. Hepworth, & B. Turner (Eds.), *The body: Social processes and cultural theory*. London: Sage.

Gabbard, G. O. (2001). Cyberpassion: E-Rotic transference on the Internet. *Psychoanalytic Quarterly*, *70*, 719–737.

Giles, D. (2006). Constructing identities in cyberspace: The case of eating disorders. *The British Journal of Social Psychology*, *45*(3), 463–477.

Grinberg, L. (1962). On a specific aspect of countertransference due to the patient's projective identification. *International Journal of Psychoanalysis*, *43*, 436–440.

Hartman, S. (2011). Reality 2.0: When loss is lost. *Psychoanalytic Dialogues*, *21*(4), 468–482.

Kahn, M. M. R. (1963). The concept of cumulative trauma. *Psychoanalytic Study of the Child*, *18*, 286–306.

Lemma, A. (2010). *Under the skin: A psychoanalytic study of body modification*. New York: Routledge.

Lingiardi, V. (2008). Playing with unreality: Transference and computer. *The International Journal of Psychoanalysis*, *89*, 111–126.

Malater, E. (2007). Introduction: Special Issue on the Internet. *The Psychoanalytic Review*, *94*, 3–6.

O'Dochartaigh, N. (2002). *The Internet research handbook: A practical guide for students and researchers in the social sciences*. London: Sage.

Ogden, T. H. (1985). On potential space. *The International Journal of Psychoanalysis*, *66*, 129–141.

Ogden, T. H. (1989). On the concept of the autistic-contiguous position. *International Journal of Psycho-Analysis*, *70*, 127–140.
Paquette, M. (2002). Bad company: Internet sites with dangerous information. *Perspectives in Psychiatric Care*, *38*(2), 39–40.
Sartre, J. P. (1984). *Being and nothingness. A phenomenological essay on ontology*. New York: Washington Square Press.
Segal, H. (1957). Notes on symbol formation. *International Journal of Psychoanalysis*, *38*, 391–397.
Steiner, J. (1993). *Psychic retreats: Pathological organizations in psychotic, neurotic, and borderline patients*. New York: Routledge.
Strife, R. S., & Rickard, K. (2011). The conceptualization of anorexia: The pro-ana perspective. *Journal of Women and Social Work*, *26*(2), 213–217.
Turkle, S. (1997). *Life on the screen: Identity in the age of the Internet*. New York: Simon & Schuster.
Warin, M. (2004). Primitivising anorexia: The irresistible spectacle of not eating. *The Australian Journal of Anthropology*, *15*(1), 95–104.
Williams, G. (1997). Reflections on some dynamics of eating disorders: 'No entry' defences and foreign bodies. *International Journal of Psychoanalysis*, *78*(5), 927–941.
Williams, S., & Reid, M. (2010). Understanding the experience of ambivalence in anorexia nervosa: The maintainer's perspective. *Psychology & Health*, *25*(5), 551–567.
Winnicott, D. W. (1953). Transitional objects and transitional phenomena: A study of the first not-me possession. *The International Journal of Psychoanalysis*, *34*, 89–97.
Winnicott, D. W. (1971). *Playing and reality*. New York: Basic Books.
Wooldridge, T., Mok, C., & Chiu, S. (2014). A qualitative content analysis of male participation in pro-anorexia forums. *Eating Disorders: Journal of Treatment and Prevention*, *22*(2), 97–110.
Yeshua-Katz, D., & Martins, N. (2012). Communicating stigma: The pro-ana paradox. *Health Communication*, *28*(5), 499–508.

14

TOWARDS SOCIAL JUSTICE

The continuum of eating and body image problems: how social and psychological realities converge into an embodied epidemic

Susan Gutwill[1]

Part one: social causes of eating and body image problems

Today our world is at war with obesity. The preoccupation of the medical community and anxiety in the popular culture have each created a frantic obsession about the dangers of fat, both to individual well-being and to the economic viability of health care institutions, especially the insurance industry. Doctors' offices and hospitals are papered with posters and charts that warn us about the threat of obesity. In the media, fat people, now referred to as "obese," are considered to be contemptible and portrayed as such. Fat women, in particular, are seen as a threat to our society and our very selves. Without strict attention, we too might become like them: slothful, lazy, stupid, selfish, and disgusting, without the backbone of "will power." In a sense, obesity and fat are downright unpatriotic! Female obesity has everyone, including therapists, obsessing about "what to *do*" about fat women given their perceived individual, moral failure. At the same time, women's suffering about feeding themselves and their struggle to live at peace in their bodies remains less recognized in public discourse, if it is acknowledged at all.

In this chapter I explore eating problems[2] and body image pain from several perspectives, all of which, I believe, are required to thoroughly understand and treat those who are suffering. I begin with what women say about their own experiences with food and their bodies, and then discuss social causes of fat hatred and body image shame. The development of the advertising industry and its role in selling diets, style, and beauty, and agribusiness (the journey of food from planting, to processing, to packaging, to selling), are all critical for understanding the proliferation of eating problems today. I explain how women buy into traumatogenic advertising such that it becomes part of their own internal life and guides their behavior. Finally, given what I have documented, I articulate what are, from my experience, several of the best and necessary clinical practices for eating and body image suffering. In this final section, I advance the following elements of practice: 1) working in depth with hunger, satiation, and food choice; 2) pursuing eating and body image experience from its expression to its underlying meaning through the use of detailed inquiry; and 3) working in the inevitable transference and "co-motion" dance regarding eating and body size, shape, and image (Gutwill, 1994).

Experience-near observations of eating and body image suffering in women

For more than 35 years I have run free educational groups about eating and body image concerns for the public and for professionals in the field. I advertise them in local papers, in public libraries, YWCAs, Jewish Community Centers, and sometimes with posters in supermarkets in the towns near my office and in mental health settings for the staff and their development. In this chapter, I relay my observations as an experience-near way to introduce concepts about the prevalence of eating problems, the conscious and unconscious elements of the disordered eating experience, and the continuum of eating problems, from binge eating, to compulsive overeating, to bulimia, anorexia, and orthorexia.

Self-selected attendees represent a range of women: those who are obese, those who are large or somewhat heavy, those who are average-looking (neither very small nor very large), and some who are very small. Some are bulimics, orthorexics, or anorexics, and other women are just worried about their eating. These women represent the full continuum of eating problems, all with significant fear of food and eating and all experiencing body insecurity.

I begin each group with questions such as: "About how many times in an hour, a day, or an evening do you worry about your weight, what you ate, what you didn't eat, or what you promise yourself not to eat again?" "How often in a minute, an hour, a day, do you worry about how you look? Suck in your stomach? Sit up in the chair so your rolls don't show?"

Inevitably the boldest of the group call out, "100 times a day," "90 percent of the time," or "Not a minute passes without those thoughts." The compulsive eaters usually begin in a relatively raucous mood, nervously laughing. The restrictors – anorexics, bulimics, orthorexics, and, here I may surprise you, the seriously large women considered by society as obese – are all quieter, but totally engaged. Not giggling, they look down or stare wide-eyed like an animal caught in headlights, or they have a small, stiff smile. They are the first to show embodied anxiety.

I let a discussion begin and then I ask them to place their minutes, hours, and days of worrying about food and eating into an imaginary pile in the middle of the room. The titters and jokes subside. I ask them to throw in their worries about their "unworthy" bodies. The imagined pile begins to look monumental to most participants, who now become quieter, their faces strained, as if caught by surprise in a dangerous, dark place.

I propose that now, together, we contemplate this pile of pain with *curiosity*, as if we were perhaps anthropologists from Mars who are studying the experiences and feelings of our group. We female Martian investigators (or, if you like, Fairbairn's observing ego) can then see our shared pain with *compassion*, even though it may last only a moment or for the length of the workshop. Now we can work together towards *dignifying* our common pain rather than normalizing it and taking its "authority" for granted.

One might think that my experience with these women is an expected outcome of self-selection, that these women and their worries are not the norm. In fact, though, data show this is exactly what social psychology dictates. These women embody what psychoanalyst and educator Lynne Layton (2006) would call "the normative unconscious," the shame- and anxiety-inducing social values we all *unconsciously* share, precluding the compassion necessary to healing. This is important to note because, even while people are conscious of the hatred of fat – their own and society's – there are also unconscious elements that psychoanalytic practitioners must understand.

In terms of eating and body image, Western consumer culture creates in girls and women a ubiquitous demand for thinness, impossible standards of beauty, and an ever-changing "acceptable" style. These constructs underlie the insecurity and suffering of women – and some men. They are used as a weapon for social control and corporate profit-making at the expense of the minds and bodies of women and girls. People worry about their weight, age, size, and shape without a full understanding of how profitable their worries are to some of our country's biggest industries. After all, it would be too threatening to those in power if women were to become fully conscious of how and why the notion of fat as "disease" has been and continues to be proliferated at their expense.

The question is: how did we get here? How and why does this message persist?

The role of advertising in creating eating and body image problems

Advertising grew apace with immigration in each decade from the 1920s, through and especially after World War II, continuing to leap into many of the most important industries of the 1960s and 1970s. Ever more sophisticated visual and aural strategies were developed to "sell" newly immigrated women their dream: to be a true American and, therefore, to be a "true woman." *Mad Men* is one of the most brilliant shows documenting the ethics, growth, and power of the advertising industry and its sexist internal culture.

One of the most critical strategies in this enterprise was to sexualize and objectify women's bodies to associate "desire" with the product being sold. Historians Stewart and Elizabeth Ewen described this process as "the democratization of the surfaces," meaning that the more a woman bought "the look," acquiring the right clothes, makeup, hair, and size, the more that woman could leave the denigrated category of greenhorn and become a full participant in

America. Only then could she walk where "the streets are paved with gold" (Ewen & Ewen, 1979).

Simultaneously, the more that industry could produce items that working-class families had previously either done without or made themselves – clothes, things for the home, items for the kitchen – the more "The Captains of Industry" became "The Captains of Consciousness," applying emerging tenets of social psychology to understand how to create "consumers" rather than savers. Capital required a dramatic shift of consciousness so that people, led by women, spent their money instead of saving for a rainy day. The advertising industry and its consumption was the way towards an identity that was, ultimately, impossible to achieve.

As artist and critic John Berger argued, women were meant to be the objects of others' desire rather than the subjects of their own desire. As such, they had to discipline themselves to strive daily towards impossible and unreal patriarchal standards, expressly advanced by consumer capitalism for its own gain (Ewen, 1979; Ewen, 1976; Ewen, 1988; Zaretsky, 1986; Gutwill, 1994). This history brings us to its terrible byproducts: the intertwined epidemics of fat hatred, fear of food, and body dysmorphia.

Objective measurements of eating and body image suffering

In this section and its three components, I examine the way that the diet empire, beauty and style corporations, and agribusiness each create and contribute to the intense suffering of eating and body insecurity, manifested across the whole spectrum of eating problems, from obesity, binge eating, compulsive eating, bulimia, bulimarexia, anorexia, and orthorexia.

The diet empire and the diet experience

According to Susie Orbach and Cynthia Bulik, disordered eating behaviors or symptoms consistent with eating problems are reported by 75 percent of participants. That is, three out of four women are afraid of food and insecure or ashamed about their body image. Excluding those in treatment for diagnosed eating disorders, 67 percent of women are trying to lose weight; 53 percent of the dieters are already at a healthy weight and still trying to lose weight; 39 percent of women say concerns about what they eat or weigh interferes with their happiness; 37 percent regularly skip meals to try to lose weight; 27 percent would be "extremely upset" if they gained just five pounds; 26 percent cut out entire food groups; 16 percent have dieted on 1,000 calories a day or fewer; 13 percent smoke to lose weight; 12 percent often eat when they are not hungry; and 49 percent sometimes do (Orbach, 2009, p. 154).

These data help us understand that eating problems and body image shame are the norm for women; hence, it is important to understand *that almost all women* exist on a continuum of eating problems and shared body image shame: very large women, compulsive eaters, binge eaters, anorexics, bulimics, and orthorexics. This is why I and my colleagues use the term *eating problems* rather than *eating disorder*, shifting the focus from an individual medical and mental disorder to a social problem. Eating problems are the overwhelming standard: in psychoanalysis we call this the "unthought known," or "normative unconscious" (Bollas, 1987; Bollas, 1989; Layton, 2006).

A staggering number of women and men reach out to the diet corporation to buy a regimen dictating what to eat and in what quantity. Yet the reality is that diets *create* weight gain in the short and the long run. A 2016 *New York Times* article (Aamodt, 2016) summed up these data. On the TV show *The Biggest Loser*, where obese participants enroll in a strict program of extreme dieting and exercise to achieve massive weight loss, contestants regained 70 percent of their weight loss after six years or less. Moreover, to maintain a stable weight, they would have to eat 500 fewer calories than they would have before their diet to stay at that same weight. Some in the diet industry argued that this was because they lost their weight too quickly or by eating the wrong foods. However, regaining weight happens whether someone dieted "slowly" or "dramatically." Other studies corroborate this: "In 2002, 231 million Europeans attempted a diet, but only 1 percent will achieve permanent weight loss" (Orbach, 2009).

In fact, dieters are more likely to become obese than non-dieters. In young girls, weight anxiety and dieting predict later binge eating and weight gain. When controlling for genetic factors, even a single diet increased the risk of being overweight. Long-term studies show that dieters are more likely than non-dieters to become obese over the next one to 15 years. This is the case for women and men, and across ethnic groups, from childhood to middle age. Ironically, the effect is strongest in those who started in the normal weight range, a group that includes almost *half* of female dieters in the United States. It must also be noted that dieters' weights often "yo-yo," which is particularly detrimental to health, greatly increasing one's risk of heart disease and cardiac arrest.

Why do diets have such antithetical results? One reason is that the brain learns that it must survive on less and "economizes," adapting to what it perceives as starvation conditions. Yet diets provoke more hunger by inducing hormones that increase one's obsession with food. It's a recipe for failure. Psychologically, feelings of shame and stress are increased with every diet failure, as the diet industry has even admitted.

Looking through the lens of actual outcomes in controlled epidemiological studies corroborates what I have seen in my personal and professional life. Most people gain back more than they lose on diets. No wonder, then, that the Diet Empire "is estimated to be worth one hundred billion dollars in the U.S. while the Department of Education budget was just over 127 billion dollars" (Orbach, 2009, p. 154). Meanwhile, if the psychic cost of the diet industry to women could be quantified, it would likely be even greater.

The BMI (Body Mass Index)

Fat terror creates a traumatogenic environment that has intensified with the development and use of the BMI (Body Mass Index) The BMI, a weight-to-height ratio designed as a standardized measure of body fat, was promulgated by the International Obesity Task Force think tank (now World Obesity/Policy & Prevention) (Orbach, 2009, p. 155). Cutoff scores are widely used to "objectively" designate people as underweight (<18.5), in the normal weight range (18.5–24.9), overweight (25–29.9), and obese (>30). In data published for the years 2007 to 2010, the average BMI for American males over the age of 20 was 28.7, and for females over the age of 20, 28.6. According to the BMI, then, most American adults are overweight, nearly obese. As Orbach (2009) points out, the very same organization that advanced the BMI measure also publishes extreme – one might say alarmist – data on the obesity epidemic and accepts funding from pharmaceutical companies seeking to develop drugs that eliminate unwanted fat.

Problems with using the BMI as an indicator of health are numerous. Orbach argues that to accept the BMI as valid in any way, evidence indicates that a 27.5 level, which designates one as overweight, is in fact the most health-protective. Moreover, Orbach notes, studies that claim that 365,000 people in the United States will die from obesity, that one in three children is obese, and that a BMI under 25 is optimal, are incorrect. "In fact, on the National Institutes of Health reanalysis of its own figures, one in 15 children are seriously overweight in the United States and some 26,000 adults will die of obesity-related diseases. Contrast this with the United States figures for smoking-related deaths per annum of 600,000" (Orbach, 2009, p. 100).

Pollution of our internal and external environments

In the 1960s the feminist psychoanalyst and social analyst, Dorothy Dinnerstein (1976), in her book *The Mermaid and the Minotaur*, applied a Kleinian analysis to understand the omnipresent denigration of and violence against women and the earth itself, Mother Earth. She wrote that we all are both biologically and psychologically dependent upon women for life and, because our early and later needs and wishes cannot ever be totally fulfilled, we are all inevitably at least frustrated, if not outright hateful, of women. In retaliation and revenge we want to dominate them – mothers, women, and Mother Earth itself. Joel Kovel, in his book, *The Age of Desire*, also has many thoughtful things to say about this (Kovel, 1981; Gutwill, 1994).

Dinnerstein's analysis holds ever more explanatory power in today's female-hating and controlling public world. In the following section, I describe how the non-stop attack on women's self-worth and bodily integrity are inseparable from the ongoing assaults on our natural environment.

The beauty and style industries

Each person in the United States sees approximately 2,000 to 5,000 images a week of women's bodies that have been digitally manipulated, carefully lit to highlight prized features, smoothed, airbrushed, and stretched. In the March 2008 issue of *US Vogue*, for example, the digital artist and photo retoucher Pascal Dangin changed 145 images: 107 in advertisements, 37 fashion shots, and the cover (Orbach, 2009). Representations of women in popular culture are less realistic than ever, influencing children at younger and younger ages to push their bodies to unattainable ideals.

For this reason, the beauty industry is one of the most successful global businesses, pulling in $160 billion profits in a year. At 7 percent, the beauty industry has an annual growth rate double that of the gross domestic product in countries in the developed world (Orbach, 2009). Through advertising and popular culture, Western standards of beauty are exported around the world, hastening the proliferation of eating problems globally. Larger numbers of women around the globe swell the ranks of those with "eating" and "body dysmorphia," as a result of body ideals they will almost certainly never be able to achieve but are shamed to be without.

So many in our world are "stuffed and starved," to borrow the phrase coined by Raj Patel (2007), whose book of the same name is reviewed herein. In fact, anorexia, bulimia, and compulsive eating are all increasing in prevalence as we focus on the horrors of obesity.

"The hunger of around one billion happens at the same time as another historical first: they are outnumbered by the one and half billion people on this planet who are overweight. . . . Global hunger and obesity are symptoms of the same problem. What's more the route to eradicating world hunger is the way to prevent global epidemics of diabetes and heart disease and to address a host of environmental and social ills" (Patel, 2007).

Agribusiness: malnutrition, starvation and obesity, and overall health

This section concerns the way food is grown, processed, packaged, delivered, and sold. This is the third of three corporate industries that create eating problems. From seed to supermarket, agribusiness not only destroys our natural environment but also contributes to the destruction of our bodies' internal environment and health. Three important books, among many others, document how these corporations function, with special consideration to the way they create eating problems and body image hatred. *Stuffed and Starved* by Raj Patel (2007), *Weighing In: Obesity, Food Justice, and the Limits of Capitalism* by Julie Guthman (2011), and *Seeds of Destruction* by F. William Engdahl (2007) have shown that agribusiness devastates farmers as it destroys the soil. As family farms fail, monstrous industrial farms have grown, interconnected with other monopoly corporations required to bring food from the field to the customer's table. Their business model sacrifices the earth, seeds, and health of populations to the profit motive.

Monsanto, for example, owned by Dow Chemical, develops genetically modified seeds that extend the shelf-life of food, so that after being processed and packaged, it can travel thousands of miles around the world to the stores that sell it. Lawyers are employed by Monsanto and companies like it to challenge and change local and national laws around the world, so as to secure their monopolies against the interests of small farmers in agricultural areas of the Global South. Litigious practices further embed corporate agriculture's dominance of the industry. For example, Monsanto will sue small farmers if their non-genetically–modified seeds travel into Monsanto-owned fields. Meanwhile, Monsanto's genetically modified crops regularly take over locally owned fields surrounding their property (Patel, 2007).

Patel charts an epidemic of suicides among small farmers in India and around the globe related to these practices. These farmers have been declassed; they are forced to sell their own land because they cannot compete with the industrial farming companies while using their centuries-old, sustainable methods. Farm workers and small-farm owners alike, both abroad and in the United States, with its use of migrant labor, become impoverished, quite like indentured servants in past eras. Starving workers, as Patel points out, represent the counterparts of people made obese by poor food quality.

Once fruits, vegetables, and livestock are harvested, they are processed in plants by the same few corporate monopolies that farm the fields. Included in the processing practices of these monopolies is the use of additives such as soy lecithin and palm oil to make meat and other food last until it makes its way to the table. To develop enough soy to meet the demand, entire rainforests have been cut down. Moreover, other additives, according to Guthman (2011), are actually obesogens, chemical additives that may affect metabolism and increase the likelihood of weight gain. For example, Guthman points to the proliferation in food of high-fructose corn syrup EDCs (endocrine-disrupting chemicals).

The food is next sent for packaging, where it will be wrapped in "new and improved" designs, usually plastic, produced from fossil fuels expensively extracted from the earth. Much of this plastic will end up in the oceans, endangering marine life. Chemicals harmful to humans may also be used in packaging; for instance, BPA (bisphenol-A) is a compound found in plastics that mimics estrogen when consumed.

To transport food from farm to processing plant to packaging facility to supermarkets consumes still more fuel, also contributing to the destruction of the natural environment. Even when our food has finally arrived at the point of sale, agribusiness's assault on our bodies and minds continues. Supermarkets have been engineered, based on much social psychological research funded by our consumer dollars, to sell more products to busy consumers. Customers have to travel through the many aisles and shelves loaded with high-sugar, attention-grabbing foods that advertise themselves as treasures, relief, entitlement, and the promise to transform workaday reality, just to get simple items such as eggs.

The very distribution of supermarkets facilitates corporate profits and engenders poor health, especially obesity, in low-income communities. Food deserts, areas where there is no option to buy fresh, healthy foods because supermarkets are lacking or low in quality, are more likely to be found in impoverished neighborhoods. Instead, residents may be forced to rely on cheap processed and packaged foods or fast food. Meanwhile, wealthier communities may have multiple supermarkets to choose from, stocked with organic fruits, vegetables, and meat. Economic inequality is perpetuated when healthy foods are available only to those who can afford them.

The causes of eating and body image problems I have described here – the diet empire, the style and beauty industry, and agribusiness, sold to us through advertising – are connected and reinforcing. It is important to note that food production, processing, and delivery corporations have interlocking directorates with advertising, diet, beauty, and style companies. Huge conglomerates will often own many different parts of the food industry – and its antidotes. For example, in 2000 Unilever, the owner of Noxema, Pond's, and other beauty brands, as well as Ben and Jerry's ice cream, purchased Slimfast. In 2006, the Swiss chocolate manufacturer Nestle acquired the Jenny Craig weight loss brand (Patel, 2007).

To summarize, we are caught by assaults on our minds and bodies from 1) the diet industry and experience, 2) the socio-symbolic realm injected into the culture by the beauty and style industries, and 3) the practices of agribusiness stuffing and starving the world population. These forces create the conditions for the proliferation of eating and body image problems among women. Fear of eating and hatred of fat have become so ensconced in our society that they are the internalized norm for most. The norm is not only simply held by people, but also it is held like a voluminous cheer of "our team" at a huge sporting event. As a large group, we are connected by it.

With so many women suffering with eating and body image problems with deep roots in the culture, we must ask: What are the necessary and best clinical practices to be included when we work with eating and body image problems? We turn to this question in the second half of this chapter.

Part two: clinical considerations

The role of eating, being fed, and held in psychological relational development

Readers of this book will be familiar with Winnicott's (1960) notion of the feeding, holding, and handling situations as the first relational environment in which we must overcome the annihilation anxiety that exists until we learn, over the course of time, that when we are hungry we are not dying and will reliably be fed. For Winnicott, food and the relationship within which it is offered are indivisible.

The "ordinary good enough mother" who can achieve "primary maternal preoccupation" makes her baby safe in the pre-Oedipal period – especially in the earliest months of life. Winnicott then goes on to discuss later stages of development that lead, if all is going well, to the safety of embodiment, or "indwelling." With these and other concepts based on the mother-child relationship, Winnicott spoke of what happens when things go right in development.

However, sometimes things go wrong, and the early caretaker overly frustrates or rejects her baby. In my view, Ronald Fairbairn (1952) best theorized the psychology of what happens when things go wrong, something he considered, to some degree, to be inevitable. Fairbairn focused on how psychic structure develops when the holding environment is insufficient or even abusive. Believing we are all born with "a healthy central ego," our bio-psychological inheritance, Fairbairn imagined that we had to split off a piece of that ego to house frustration or rejection in "ancillary ego structures." By carrying out what Fairbairn termed "the moral defense," we create psychic structure to internalize the fear and depression following serious disappointments at the hands of those early caregivers upon whom we are, like Winnicott's baby, totally dependent. Creating these ancillary ego structures takes up psychic energy and space. We then further split the bad experience into a false-good and false-bad object relationship which, cut off from others, remain in an unending compulsive dance – a tantalizing and exciting experience of relationship alternating with a rejecting and disappointing experience. Through the moral defense we transform painful experience at the hands of a real other into a hope that if we could be better – thinner in this case – we would finally be loved. Yet, there is always the other side of that equation in which we feel that, as we are, *we* are the problem; *we* are worthless, fat and ugly; and therefore we will always be rejected.

It is important to understand that an object relationship is an internalized experience with others embedded in our selves. It is also worth noting that these "parts" of self were a base for what later psychoanalysis and trauma theory came to think of as self-states. Trauma theory teaches us to know these parts and the history from which they evolve; Bromberg (1998) teaches us to stand in the spaces between self-states. Working with eating and body image suffering means working with parts of self – for example, the eater and the berater – to understand and reconnect them.

For Winnicott and Fairbairn, the time of our greatest dependency, the pre-Oedipal period, is when we develop basic psychic structure. Object relational and feminist psychoanalytic and psychological theorists also focus on early dependency relations as central to psychological development. After years of Freudian thinking that deemphasizes the mother of dependency in favor of later Oedipal development centering on sexuality, these theories opened many doors that could be used not only in psychological but in social theories as well.

I believe, with Stephen Mitchell (1988), that the mother-child dyad is also a metaphor for *lifelong* needs people have in relationship to their adult environment. This is particularly relevant when the cultural environment seeps into our sense of self in the traumatogenic way that I outlined in the first half of this chapter. Mitchell criticized psychoanalytic theory for what he called the "developmental tilt," that is, privileging early development at the expense of understanding lifelong struggles all people have. Such issues, he argued, included tensions between merger and autonomy, finding one's own authentic voice versus compliance, and developing a healthy sense of grandiosity while recognizing others and external reality. I argue that in these psychological struggles people are highly affected by the culture at large, and I extend the object relational theories of Winnicott and Fairbairn to develop an understanding of eating problems and in analysis more generally (Gutwill, 1994).

For example, we hear, again and again, some version of the statement, "I could be perfect/better/safer, if I were thinner/younger/more athletic/harder/whiter." This is an example of Fairbairn's notion of the message of the enticing ego, the tantalizing ego. Meanwhile, the notion that "I will never look good enough because I am just a loser/a fat pig/out of control/not sexy/etc." is a perfect example of Fairbairn's rejecting ego. Human minds internalize disappointment and danger into schizoid inner object relationships in order to feel safe. Psychically, we live in an unconscious, unwinnable war with ourselves because it feels safer than realizing how we have been hurt by others. The culture then piggybacks onto early experience, using "the terrain of women" (Orbach, 2009) – their bodies – to offer false solutions to its assaults on our subjectivity.

For Fairbairn, it is the goal of the analytic therapist to enter that schizoid, dissociated, inner object world in order to make a "mutual but asymmetrical" relationship with the pained and isolated parts of self (Aron, 1992). Regarding eating and body image suffering, therapists help patients stay with their obsessive thoughts and feelings to bring them into a therapeutic relationship; in that relationship, we can help translate this internal battle into what it represents in their lives.

As we track the many moments of body hatred and fear of food, we come to understand what was "instantaneously and unconsciously transformed from feeling language into the language of food and fat" (Bloom, Gitter, Gutwill, Kogel, & Zaphiropoulos, 1994). This is related to Winnicott's (1980) notion of the false self that goes into hiding until conditions are safe for it to join up with one's capacity for having a "potential self," an authentic sense of being. Fairbairn would describe it as rebuilding the central ego by integrating the split-off defenses in the ancillary ego/object relationships into the central ego.

The continuum of eating problems

For an omnipresent set of preoccupations, problems, and disorders, there is little professional or popular writing that sees all eating problems as existing on a continuum where compulsive eating, the most common of them all, is included. Historically, many students of eating disorders wrote exclusively about anorexia and bulimia. From the perspective of the Women's Therapy Centre Institute, compulsive overeating, fear of food and eating, and serious body insecurity underlie *all* eating problems. When including compulsive overeating, defined as regularly eating for emotional reasons rather than to match hunger and satiation, the number of women who suffer is enormous: more than 80 percent of all women are living with eating problems and, by some estimates, it may be closer to 90 percent.

It should be noted that, despite the clinical preoccupation with anorexia and bulimia that has been characteristic of psychology, the newest iteration of the *Diagnostic and Statistical Manual*, the DSM-V, includes binge eating disorder. I do think that since the great focus on obesity has emerged, more eating disorder centers are developing programs for all along the continuum.

The power of ideology

Setting aside the impact of the industries discussed previously, we still need to ask why and how women buy the lies about how we are of value only if we are thin, in style, and so on. For this we now turn to the study of the psychosocial and socio-symbolic spheres of life, the study of ideology.

I have asked myself how women buy the lie, how patriarchal social oppression and capitalist greed both work to sell false hopes that assault our embodied psychological, social development and drive how we spend our money. Marx and Engels wrote that in every age, the ideology of the economic and power elites becomes the ideology of the working class (Marx & Engels, 1994). Today, in the language of the Occupy Wall Street movement, we might say that the 99 percent have come to hold the beliefs and values of the 1 percent, whose goal is purely to profit without concern for social responsibility.

Many further formulations have followed. For example, Antonio Gramsci described how we rarely question hegemonic – that is, dominating and ubiquitous – ideas about how and why we are placed in society where we are. According to Gramsci, hegemonic beliefs regulate behavior. Likewise, Althusier, another theorist of ideology, speaks of how members of any hierarchical society feel a "call" that cannot be seen or heard but which nevertheless "hails" them into internalizing the current hegemonic notions about power and one's place. To us, who work with eating and body image insecurity in the era of consumer capitalism, the work of Michel Foucault, a theorist writing about ideology in the 1960s, is central. In his seminal work, *Discipline and Punish,* he questions how we voluntarily punish ourselves, becoming our own jailors so that we fit into the allegorical prisons of social mores. He argued that the ideas of the wealthy class – its politics and its institutions – function as a kind of jail of thought and action. He imagined the structure of this jail: it was a place where all prisoners could be constantly watched by a guard in a high watchtower called "The Panopticon." Under constant surveillance, prisoners would learn to discipline themselves so as not to be punished for misbehavior. In other words, the jailor need not always discipline the prisoners for they learn to police themselves.

In the book *Eating Problems: A Feminist Psychoanalytic Treatment Model*, in addition to extending the perspectives mentioned here and focusing on eating and body fears, I develop an object relational theory about how women "buy the lies." I critically apply Winnicott's and Fairbairn's theories to this end. Lynne Layton, writing at the same time, might call it the study of the "normative unconscious" at the expense of our own embodied and psychological experience.

As discussed previously, according to Fairbairn, we protect ourselves by creating object relationships of which we are unconscious; recall the enticing ego and the rejecting ego. It is significant that the symbols of advertising do the same. They imply, "If you go to Weight Watchers, you can be a lifetime member, you can go on a 'healthy diet' and be who you want to be. Your life, your feelings about yourself, they will improve! You will have your (thin) dream!" They tantalize us on the one hand while they imply, on the other, that we will be fat failures if we don't "get control of ourselves." They say, "Here, you are pictured as lovingly cooking your family's dinner," on one page, and on the other page "Here, you are buying Slim Fast" for yourself. Restrict your needs and desires, but never stop giving to others (Eichenbaum & Orbach, 1983b).

Endless are the ads that tantalize with beauty items you just cannot be without. If you are without them, the implied message goes, you are ugly and shameful. They are the offers we cannot refuse, as the Mafia might say. If you are older, heavier, of color, or have a transgressive sexual or gender orientation, you are in even greater danger – that is, unless your group has created a place for you, wherein to retreat to some extent.

Clinical considerations given social realities – what helps

Hunger, satiation, and food choice

Diets *teach* women to ignore their biological and psychological impulses. These impulses tell us when to eat, how much to eat, and what foods our bodies want and need. We have a natural biologically and neurologically determined internal environment, just as we have an external physical environment. Diets, fat phobia, and the drive for profit despoil both these environments, which I consider to be a matter of social injustice.

Physiological hunger tells us when to eat and produces enzymes to properly digest the food we need. Satiation, which is not the same as being stuffed, tells us when to stop eating until the next time hunger returns. Hunger manifests on a continuum, from feeling hungry to stomach rumbling, growling, or stomach contractions, which can come and go and then come back again with greater intensity. Patients need to explore and identify their own hunger continuums. Satiation too, like hunger, exists on a continuum, from eating just enough to stop hunger to different stages of a feeling of comfortable fullness. Stopping at satiation frequently produces anxiety and can be infuriating. However, when we can tolerate satiation, we become capable of compassionate mourning of the limits and losses in our lives (Klein, 1952).

How to eat with hunger

We need to help patients learn to find and experience hunger. This can be a long-term task. We need to ask them to imagine how hunger feels and where in the body it is felt. Often clients say, "I am a *little* hungry" or "I felt kind of empty." Sometimes these experiences indicate that physiological hunger is about to begin. But just as often, vague statements like these contain another meaning. Perhaps women are afraid of the need represented by hunger, as it means affirming our own needs. Perhaps some feel sad when they need something and others are triggered by dieting to want to sneak food without regard for hunger. We need to work on distinguishing stomach hunger from "mouth" hunger. On the other hand, as we eat what we want with real hunger, food can feel sensuous and taste better than it ever has because we have become subjects of our own desire, rather than objects of the desires of others. We are no longer imprisoned within the hungry, starving, vacant, airbrushed images of models pictured in advertising. Our work here is thoroughly embodied and goes to the heart of emotion.

Eating with hunger, as many eating problems specialists tell us today, is eating with mindfulness. That means paying attention to each bite in and of itself. For the most part, and especially as a client is developing this skill, eating mindfully means eating without the company of distractions such as the computer, without printed material, and without standing or walking at the same time. If you love to read when you eat, mindful eating suggests focusing on each bite before looking again at the printed material. When eating, it is important to empty the hands, because they have so many nerve endings that even holding the utensil while chewing and swallowing distracts the eater's ability to pay attention to the mouth, esophagus, and stomach. Clients are generally amazed by how powerful is the experience of focused, mindful eating. They consistently report that food has never tasted so delicious. Moreover, women consistently report feeling quite powerful when eating with full consciousness when they are hungry.

Yet, frequently women are frightened to eat with entitlement and consciousness because they feel dominated by the diet mentality, which says "watch out, you are going to get fat." Also, women report discomfort and guilt when paying attention to their own needs. The same patient will have times when eating is a pleasure and times when it provokes intense anxiety. As therapists, we need to inquire about and explore these different experiences of eating. This is not a short-term project; our patients need a relationship that holds them in their anxiety. Part of our work is helping patients to slow down, focus, and experience the right to eat what one is eating.

Eating "healthy" food is considered an individualistic moral issue rather than primarily a social-political-personal struggle. Patterns of food consumption intersect with social class, since "healthy" eating is a privileged aspect of being upper class. In general, food and body size have become so overloaded with a variety of meanings that it is very hard for us today to eat in peace. Therefore, more often than not, whatever relief women derive from taking in a bite of food, the eater self is soon derided and rejected by other parts of their psyches (i.e., the anti-libidinal ego or rejecting object as well as the culture's "internalized saboteur") (Gutwill, 1994). This kind of self-trashing is a regular part of the compulsive eating cycle. It is central to each kind of eating problem. Our clinical work is to offer the eater and the berater a chance to meet, with ourselves as witnesses to encourage these parts coming out of "the deep freeze" (Guntrip, 1969) of schizoid isolation and to tell us their stories, again and again. Our clients can then see and get to know their different self states or parts and bring them into the therapeutic relationship.

Clients take a while to learn to recognize and respond to hunger, which is the only way to feel the change in hunger, known as satiation. While we know the feeling of being "stuffed," that is quite different from actual satiation, the signal that one has eaten enough to satisfy the body's physiological hunger.

The experience of satiation is quite difficult to achieve for compulsive eaters, whether they are very large or just a bit larger than they wish to be, as well as for binge eaters and bulimics. Stopping at satiation, a hard-won capacity, represents learning to live with and grieve endings and disappointments. It challenges us to realize the reality of the depressive position in which we need to mourn how we have been hurt and how we have hurt others. Each small experience of an ending throughout life comes with sadness, as mourning one ending resonates with many other past experiences of loss and limits of our lives.

For example, when asked about what stopping with satiation would mean, one woman tearfully said:

P: If I stop eating I'll be abandoned. At least if I have food I won't starve as well.

T: So stuffing yourself seems to address how lonely and alone you felt for so much of your past, and sometimes even now?

P: Yes, I cling to it for dear life. Every time I leave people, as you know, I have to have food until I get calm again.

T: Separating from food feels the same as separating from all human connection. Eating promises that you won't have to feel fear, grief, or aloneness, but they really exist.

P: How will I survive if I feel my grief? I'll feel so scared, and I won't know what to do.

T: It will feel less overwhelming and terrifying than it always has if we work on it together and you allow yourself to feel those feelings with me" (Bloom et al., 1994, pp. 109–110).

It is also important to the way some clients are in a constant state of pseudo-separation as, for example, anorexics who bypass hunger and satiation completely and with them, any relationship to their real needs and desires. These patients are without hope for safe and useful attachment.

All people who have dieted for years, or *thought* that they should have been dieting, come to believe that they are unentitled to eat. This fear-filled diet mentality is hard to soothe and, as we have shown previously, leads to bingeing.

Merger and attachment issues are some of many conflicts that arise in the face of satiation. Staying with the difficulty that patients report when they are saying good-bye to food is what we do in our work. We need to stay with eating and body material by working with patients in a very detailed way to get to the material underlying the actual behavior with food and feelings about the body, to the meanings the behavior holds. My argument is that with eating and body image problems, following the experience with hunger, satiation, and food choice shines a metaphorical flashlight into the dark place of hidden schizoid experience.

The role of continual detailed inquiry

Patients with eating and body image suffering often bring in their "failures" with eating and insecurity in their bodies right at the start of the session if the therapist has made room for these thoughts and feelings to emerge. The work to help patients find their own internal natural environment, their hunger, satiation, and particular food desires is the basis for being able to do detailed inquiries about the many individual moments when they are unable to wait for hunger or stop at satiation as well as when they feel compelled to deny themselves the food they really want to eat. Once we honor the food and body experiences of each client, we can work with these eating and body hatred incidents, one at a time. We can then work to find the repressed or dissociated narratives underlying the symptoms. Our goal is to help patients translate their action symptoms from the language of food and body into the narrative of the self. We must maintain compassionate curiosity for the seemingly endless numbers of times that our patients cannot live in their own internal bodily or self-states because of the demands of the internalized parents, community, and socio-symbolic world.

This critical and central piece of our therapeutic work with eating and body hatred is carried out by what Harry Stack Sullivan, the father of interpersonal psychotherapy, called "detailed inquiries" (Sullivan, 1953). With respect to detailed inquiry, Sullivan meant that we "get into it" with patients; we explore their thoughts, behaviors, and feelings in detail. In general, most analysts do this beautifully, but in the "normative unconscious" world of fat and thin, paying close attention can be frightening or abhorrent, or it can seem like a waste of time or a defense against real depth work. It often seems repetitive and even occasionally feels boring. In addition, the material may stimulate shame in the female therapist about her own similar pain and self-criticism in this area. Men frequently cannot relate to the feelings involved. It is hard to stay present when patients are extremely anxious. These presentations regularly induce therapists into unproductive responses, one of which is especially typical, that is, the temptation to match the client's "action symptom" with our own impulse to "Do something now!" Thus, many analyses terminate with the patient's eating and body image problem intact and unrecognized.

We therapists must be able to join our clients again and again, as Bion (1967) suggests, without memory or desire, when they relate in a monotone or hysterical way, telling us they binged, threw up, or ate without hunger. It is especially challenging to listen to how a gaunt woman in front of us skipped her lunch salad because she had six mussels for Mother's Day dinner the night before. Often, patients cannot yet speak to us of their food restriction, so great is the manic defense. We need to dignify and investigate, in great detail, their many moments of hating their bodies, of shaming themselves because of their bodies. They might say, "I did it again. I hate myself. I am so fat. I feel disgusting." They may have eaten an entire pizza or a handful of grapes and a little bag of popcorn that was not on "their program."

These repetitive complaints may sound like whining, complaining without feeling entitled to the underlying pain. Therapists can intervene with questions such as the following:

- What happened just before you felt *so* fat, this time?
- How did that make you feel?
- Do you feel you are entitled to feel that way? No? Why not? How were your feelings (like angry, sad, frightened, needy) treated in your family, your marriage, your friendship group? How do you understand how these feelings are evaluated in our society?
- Where do you register these feelings in your body? Working with embodiment is critical to bringing our clients into their bodies, wherein all feelings reside.

My client, Marie, a beautiful young bulimic woman with a fat obsession, tried to appear very upbeat. She worked in a huge health care corporation near my office. She thought it was terrific that the company sponsored competitive weight-loss campaigns in order, as they said, to develop the competitive spirit of business among their workers. Even I was taken aback by that information.

Marie was endearing, creative, and socially able. But her brave face changed one day, when I asked her to report her last binge and purge in detail. As if in a dream, she told me that once inside her, food felt sickening. We then regularly stopped to inquire about the sickening feeling. As she felt increasingly safe in our relationship, Marie discovered that when full she saw an image of her stepfather grabbing her little girl self, putting her on his lap, and sexually fondling her. Even though we talked of her life all the time, until we could, together, follow the symptom, she did not remember the dissociated material of her actual abuse by her stepfather. She previously knew she didn't like him and he gave her "the creeps." She was upset about her mother's attachment to him. But this detailed inquiry about the purge gave her access to why she was so regularly anxious and in fact, a major reason why the constant dieting was necessary as a form of grounding her anxiety by focusing on calories and weight loss, which represented, as we have seen throughout this paper, personal safety. This vignette, of course, has the added dimension of clarity about the intrusiveness not only of consumer culture but also of her life in the corporate world, on our psyche-somas. Our work with her symptoms and teaching her to eat with her body's internal environmental signals gave her a feeling of far greater control over her life now than she had had as a child and young adult. Sometimes I do an exercise in which I ask clients to close their eyes, feel the couch, do a body scan, or I engage in a progressive relaxation exercise to help clients focus and enter the space of feeling in their bodies (Gendlin, 1996; Wooley, 1991). Or clients might be able to imagine shaping themselves into body sculptures that can help them visualize what the inner self looks or feels like. These methods, often taught to family and trauma therapists, are varied and personalized with respect to what the therapist knows about each client's history.

A great deal of time in therapy is spent bringing clients back to the feelings they experience when alone, but this time with the therapist in accompaniment as a caring witness. After intense focusing, I suggest that therapists ask, "So how do you feel now?" This question opens up the discussion to include transference responses, something we must welcome and track. Additionally it brings the therapy dyad back from a kind of dreamy state to the conscious narrative, thereby helping to integrate parts of self.

This process takes time and repeated detailed questions. I have been working with Carol for well over a year. She has a beautiful smile, which she wears a lot of the time. But for quite a long time, I felt she could not truly come forward and that the smile was part of her lovely outfit. Then she finally revealed that she could only feel safe if she was eating a diet-brand frozen food delivered to her house. I had known she was on a diet, but I did not realize how long it had gone on. Now, she was gaining weight and was both frightened and angry. She and her smile seemed so compliant, but in actuality she was evacuating what I had repeatedly suggested about finding her hunger and satiation, so powerful was her need *to lose weight*. This is not infrequent among clients who say, "I will try your way after I lose the weight." Recently, I asked if she could feel anything about what we talked about. She was frightened but relieved to admit that she could not. It was a relief to me as well. I decided to take a stronger stance given her pain and despair. I suggested that she couldn't, in my opinion, come to control her eating if she did not allow herself to try real food when she was physiologically hungry and eat until she came to be satiated

Next session she arrived without smiling and reported that she could not eat this way. She was adamant. I asked her for a specific memory of the most recent binge. It had followed a meal out with a friend with whom she admitted not feeling happy. This friend was rigid in advocating that Carol take up an alternative, which I thought was an orthorexic eating regime. She endlessly preached her program to Carol. Carol was furious with her friend's pushiness and contemptuous of her "eating solution." Examination of the details gave us a lot of material that she could finally *feel*, instead of the usual smiling compliance that represented her emotional absence from our sessions. In another session, she noticed that she was deeply anxious to come back from a visit to her childhood home, and she felt compelled to "settle herself in" with food. In our session previous to her trip, I had suggested that one way of reducing bingeing would be to allow the forbidden foods into her life so their "glitter" would be diminished. However, in this instance, she binged on the brownies she had purchased to practice reminding herself that brownies were just sweet food, some of which she might want as part of her meal. I had suggested that when beginning to eat with hunger, she think about what she wanted in that meal before she was satiated. She wanted a bit of a brownie at the end of the meal.

Not surprisingly, in the next session she told me quite firmly that she would not and could not use my ideas. Gone was her compliance! I thought about this new stance as an achievement. She insisted that she had to lose weight now! She had to throw me out, even though she had no alternative answers. We discussed how difficult it was to trust anyone, especially me. This led to an important period in our work in which we could honor her negative transference, a deep distrust of and anger at me, even as she experienced our work more deeply than she ever had. Carol felt that all food was illegal and dangerous, and in this sense she expressed the anorexic element co-existing with and intimately connected to her compulsive over-eating.

This experience led to an emotional discussion about how she had been adopted by her family, after living with a foster family for eight months. Her adoptive parents were very narcissistically wounded and tough on her and her brother. While her brother was beaten, her father was obsessed with Carol's fat and her mother was always mad at her, beat her, and complained about her. I knew the story, but could never feel it in as deep a way as I did in that session. This time we both felt it. Now we might be able to track her true grief.

With anorexics, the process is usually even rockier. Their defense is what Laura Kogel and Carol Munter (Bloom et al., 1994) call a *pan defense*, by which they mean that more of the patient's psyche-soma is locked up in ancillary ego-object structures away from their central ego/self. Here our work is less directive. It is, instead, educational, in this case focused more on their life story as we "hold" a space for growth of self-in-relationship.

The anorexic woman dramatizes the mandate that women should appear and not be. In her struggles for recognition through her symptomatology, the anorexic woman is trying to give shape and substance to her inner emptiness, believing (for good reason) that love, connection, and food only mean danger. Her energy is turned inward, her passionate ties are to her internal defense. Her anorexia is the logical extension of the exaggeration of some of the perverse demands of femininity on women (Bloom et al, 1994, pp. 61–62).

Psychoanalytic attitudes about eating and body image material

Most analysts have not been trained to engage this kind of eating and body image material consistently and in depth. They may believe that a thorough, good enough analysis will end the eating problem because the underlying issues will be sufficiently resolved. They may even believe that eating and body image material is an obsession that stands in the way of "the real underlying issues." For example, a prominent analyst presented a case in which her male patient had an obsession with perverse sexual fantasies. The presenter felt that she failed with this patient. She couldn't help him. She also told the audience that he was a serious compulsive eater. However, when I asked why she chose not to work with the eating problem, she said she didn't think it was useful to work in these pre-Oedipal issues around dependency. Such prejudices join with the lack of training in most analytic institutes on the subject of eating and body image suffering. Analysts are generally not trained in techniques for tracking food and body image material in a serious and analytic way.

In reality, most women leave an otherwise successful therapy with their eating problems intact, still hiding a schizoid, hopeless part of themselves. Countless women have come to our feminist psychoanalytic therapy practices because their otherwise fine analyses have left them with their eating behavior and body-hating selves untouched and unrecognized.

In addition, psychoanalysis is sometimes prone to a sort of elitism in which women and their eating problems are unconsciously seen as less significant than other important material. I believe this is because most of us accept the social denigration of women's everyday experiences and, furthermore, fear our own identification and devalued struggle with eating and body image symptoms. The data show us that female therapists rarely have had their own therapeutic experience with clinicians who were able do a "close reading" of eating experience and body image. Without a critical analysis, the social norm – hatred and fear of fat – remains an unconscious background set of assumptions that, as we have seen, good women are thin and fat women are disgusting. Therefore, among eating problems, anorexia and bulimarexia are more easily respected and sometimes even idealized: "I wish I had just a touch of anorexia," I commonly hear women laughingly say.

Eating disorder specialists' attitudes towards eating and body image material

On the other hand, non-analytically trained eating disorder specialists often come from working in various hospital settings where supervision was patchy at best. However, they have usually embraced the work of trauma therapists and are often more competent than untrained analysts, in working with those suffering with eating and body image. Historically, trauma therapists from the struggle of Freud with Ferenzci onward were not welcomed into psychoanalysis proper. Therefore, free of the paternalism of psychoanalysis, they were more able to see the suffering of women and children who were abused, soldiers returning from war, and boys abused in the church (Herman, 2009). Trauma therapists tend to stay close to the material of the moment-by-moment, year-to-year struggle of PTSD. They see symptoms as a way to tell a story, and they use cognitive-behavioral strategies and work deeply with the body. They make important client relationships and are quite dedicated to the field. However, despite their many skills and commitment, without analytic training therapists can more easily miss important opportunities to work with transference. They may miss the reality that transference feelings are inevitable, even when the therapist offers simple cognitive-behavioral information and suggestions. There are usually intense transference-countertransference reactions when somatic techniques and/or guided visualizations are used. Moreover, eating disorder therapists are not generally well trained in the relational aspect of termination experiences. They may not have experienced their own depth therapy that opens us to repressed and dissociated material within ourselves.

Working in the cultural countertransference: body co-motion

As depth psychoanalysts know, we need to follow the inevitable and challenging transference/counter-transference dance, which is foundational to a deep therapeutic experience. And we are also familiar with the notion that the relationship between patient and therapist creates what we call "the third" in relational and intersubjective psychotherapy (Ogden, 1994).

When working with eating and body image issues, we need to add an understanding of what I call "cultural counter-transference" to our repertoire. Because 80 percent of therapists are women, and 80 percent of their patients are women, the great majority of both are, by virtue of the social system they inhabit, not at peace with eating or their body image. As many of us have taken seriously the need to raise the subject of violent sexual abuse in treatment, we would also do well to create an appropriate treatment space by asking about any feelings either side of the dyad has about eating and body images. In other words, it is our responsibility to open the relationship to address whatever eating and body issues we all face. However, because these problems are both normative and denigrated, this is not always an easy task. The fear of fat is psycho-biologically and neurologically complex and it is part of the social unconscious. As I have said, uncritical therapists, like most people in our society, will want "to do something about it," and often will suggest addressing a symptom with an action (e.g., going on a diet), rather than taking a more reflexive stance.

For example, one day my client Sarit screamed at me that she was furious about her new knowledge that diets don't work. And because of me and "my ideas," she couldn't diet anymore and she was gaining weight. Although we had been working on eating with physiological hunger and stopping with the body's satiation for a few years, she couldn't put them to use in an effective way. At certain points in treatment, she saw me as the new "diet general" who victimized her. I instantly worried that I might have been too insistent with her. Had I expressed impatience? But I felt simultaneously angry at her blame and demand for me to see her as a victim. My awareness of my counter-transference blame, anger, and guilt opened me to curiosity about her transference, allowing us both to look at our interaction more deeply.

Upon further reflection, Sarit said she felt that I was like her actual demanding mother whom she could never satisfy. Mom had lived in a family in Poland where there had been many family suicides even before the Holocaust. Eventually, Mom was taken prisoner and sent to Auschwitz. There she was only saved from death because of her sexual attractiveness, which enabled her to be used sexually by the SS. Understandably, Sarit's mother was very restrictive with food, somewhat anorexic, and very anxious. But she was also deeply invasive during Sarit's childhood and given to violent temper tantrums directed at both Sarit's dad, who eventually left, and Sarit herself. Although her father remained close to she and her brother, mother's damage reigned. For example, Mom's terror of fat compelled her to control Sarit's portions at every meal. She screamed, hit, threatened, and criticized Sarit so much that she often ran to a telephone booth to call her father. She could not heal her mother, a victim whom she felt guilty about hating. This conflicted relationship became clearer as we explored the transference in which she experienced me as the new diet general.

The treatment of eating problems and body insecurity requires us to think about transference and counter-transference not only from the perspective of the client and therapist but also in the context of how both are affected by the society in which these problems are created. "Cultural counter-transference" is the name I give to the inevitable experience that requires women to compare their bodies and eating habits with each other. In this sense, sexist culture sets women against one another as we face the challenges of measuring up to an idealized image of women. Orbach (2009) has argued that because of our cultural surround and its transmission through the family, women do not have a stable sense of body safety. The social message is more powerful and assaults our sense of body knowledge and acceptability.

It is inevitable that in almost all treatments, female clients and their therapists share many feelings that are instantaneously and unconsciously transformed from feeling language into eating and body language (Bloom et al., 1994). The results create underlying "transference/counter-transference co-motions."[3] Therapist or client might compare herself to the other: "I wish I could be that disciplined . . . I wish I had that body . . . I suddenly can't stand this woman . . . I think she is judging my body . . . I am suddenly checking the size of my thighs and they are huge . . . Don't even talk about the rolls around my middle."

Clients are sometimes unable to look at their therapists' bodies. It can feel dangerous, as if it might overturn the client's idealization or positive regard for the therapist, a feature so central to developing the therapeutic relationship. At some point, though, it is necessary that the client be able to explore negative perceptions, judgments, and feelings towards the therapist.

One day a female colleague was treating a man afraid of intimacy with his girlfriend, and he called the therapist "round." The therapist asked, "What does 'round' mean to you?" He replied that round was fine, but he preferred his girlfriends to be slender. Upon exploration, they came to realize that when he had spoken about leaving this girlfriend, the therapist had asked if the client was afraid of being close to his girlfriend or to the therapist and what that feeling was like for him. After their exploration of this question, he realized he saw the therapist as fat because he was angry with her for challenging him to look at his own fears of being known. Until they realized this, my colleague, who is generally comfortable in her body, felt fat.

Often female therapists find they feel heavy or too small or weak in the middle of a session. They might sit taller in the chair to hide fat and rolls, shift this way or that to make their hips look smaller, feel their skin suddenly aging and lift their chin to hide its sag. These discomforts can be used clinically to wonder about what is being induced in the "body co-motion" of counter-transference. Indeed, it is an important ethic of our discipline that analysts have our own analysis and work in supervision and consult with others. A central reason for this ethic is that transference and counter-transference feelings are often manifestations of unconscious dynamics.

My client, Ann, who is also a therapist, told me that she felt so guilty about being thin that she tried to help women who were larger than she. Ann was a positively beautiful woman. Her patients did not know that she had become anorexic following a traumatic childhood in which she was abused by a famous movie star and his Mafia-connected group. Her empathy was, as is so often the case for women with a history like hers, exquisite. It hurt her that sometimes she even felt superior to and more virtuous than her clients. She knew that in fact she, in her thin body and beautiful face, had more power in society than they did. "I don't want to feel part of such a cruel and abusive social discourse. We are not the same," she argued, "yet there is something about my treatment with these women and about this method that falsely implies we are." Ann and her supervisor discussed these disturbing feelings and Ann's history, and their talk illuminated her experience in a number of ways. Above all, it was important to validate Ann's perception of social reality. Ann was not only very svelte, she was also extraordinarily beautiful. The supervisor hypothesized that Ann had carried her beauty as both gift and burden in her life.

For example, a colleague of Ann's had remarked on meeting her that she was so striking that he felt embarrassed. The therapist also empathized with the sting Ann felt at having been toppled from the arduously gained position of being on a pedestal when, in her late teens, she had gone from being anorexic to the point of hospitalization to gaining more than 100 pounds so that she looked quite heavy and was ostracized for being fat. We talked about Ann's beauty with all it complications. Ann knew and was honest about how her appearance was idealized, as well as the hatred, jealousy, and sadism that it aroused in those around her. To aggravate all this, Ann had survived severe, sadistic, and systematic sexual abuse and knew all too intimately the experience of being helpless in a power hierarchy. In these experiences her beauty had been both envied and abused as perpetrators had wanted to own her, to control the power she seemed to contain. She was aware that sometimes she could not help but identify with the aggressors and idealizers of her beauty. The superior/inferior schema about which Ann felt guilty, overtly based on beauty, encoded covert power systems that had touched her deeply in her experience of abuse and in the course of ordinary social life. Ann had been exposed to the worst in current social mores.

It was relieving and grounding for Ann to talk about all this in its fullest complexity, to analyze it, demystify it, and to be cared about in her upset and confusion. Ann's beauty was her own, not simply a dividend of social standards. In fact, as with many people who dissociate because of abuse, as a defensive measure she could read people very well. To survive, victims of abuse must develop a sixth sense. What was also so striking about her was an inner radiance and liveliness. Ann was a very attractive person, not for her appearance alone: She was powerful, deeply skilled, and committed to providing excellent care. Somewhere, somehow, her presence seemed to let people know that she truly was a survivor.

It is important to remember that Ann's svelte beauty and her clients' obesity are experienced in the context of a cultural ideal, which acts as a standard by which everyone's body is judged critically; no one escapes its sadistic and powerful scrutiny. This process is hidden, however, so the exchange between therapist and clients seems to be purely personal, when, in fact, it is *both* personal and social.

On the basis of this further discussion, Ann's supervisor advised her to encourage her clients to reveal, at appropriate times in the course of their work, how they felt about Ann's body and appearance. In pursuing this analysis, Ann saw how it would be possible to help her clients discover and name their experience with and relationship to her as well as to the social standard that affected their individual emotional experiences. The following questions might be helpful to these clients: What do they feel about Ann and about themselves in relationship to her? Do they distinguish their relationship to her appearance from the social ideal? Or do they conflate them? How do their experiences of her and of themselves reflect both their individual histories and their shared social history?

Towards social justice: psychoanalysis, feminism, and the 1 percent

In our culture, eating and body image suffering derives from the interaction of early and later psychic experience in the family, the school, and the neighborhood, all intersecting with the conditions of late consumer capitalism. The diet, beauty, style, and agribusiness corporations enter women's veins by what we see, hear, and embody hour by hour. Increasing numbers of men suffer now as well, in particular gay men and athletes (Wooldridge, 2016). Agribusiness, the diet and beauty industries, all support an ideological apparatus in which we are each meant to be individually responsible for our own personal well-being, which begins with "the look" of acceptability. In fact, recent estimates suggest that most Americans are exposed to around 4,000 to 10,000 advertisements each day (Marshall, 2015). Men are also insecure, fearful of eating, and seeking to establish self-respect through their muscled, slim bodies. Moreover, they want women who are "up to standard" in order to reflect that acceptability back onto them. Read the personals;

nary a man wants to date a woman his age. They want women who are much younger than themselves, "slim and in shape."

While we busy ourselves with achieving this impossible path to self-respect, we most often do not to see, much less hold responsible, the corporations and the governments that work for them. Instead, we are ideologically told to be personally able to "pull ourselves up by our own bootstraps." In Trumpland, neo-liberalism is moving towards authoritarianism, if not fascism, in front of our eyes. Social services such as education, welfare, medical services, senior services, and other similar social supports are being further slashed as injustice reigns in the judicial world. Deadly environmental destruction is intensified, and racism, xenophobia, sexism, and war-making are all on the rise.

In psychoanalytic theory, eating and body image problems, which are not primarily episodic as with young teens, but exist lifelong, are barely taken up. The most feminist, abstract relational and liberatory theory rarely comes down to the everyday lived experience of fear of food and body insecurity, even though these struggles kill at worst and always diminish and plague the majority of women across race, class, and gender identifications. When will it be honored as a serious issue of social injustice and deserving of analytic understanding and training?

Perhaps it is, as I have said, that the general denigration of women's embodied pain is central to patriarchy and profitable to capitalism. Historically, psychoanalysis has extruded social causes of psychological suffering in favor of reductionist individual psychodynamics (Russell, 1975). This paper has addressed eating and body image problems/disorders as an example of these larger issues, along with addressing clinical interventions that reunite individual pain and its social causes. It has been a fascinating field that for more than 30 years has held my interest because it allows me to bring together psychoanalytic theory, social theory, cognitive behavioral work, and embodiment, as well as to develop social action for preventing eating and body image problems.

Notes

1 I dedicate this chapter to my colleagues at the Women's Therapy Centre Institute with whom I have been lucky enough to find a home among socialist, feminist psychoanalysts and especially to those who have written with me: Carol Bloom, Andrea Gitter, Laura Kogel, and Lela Zaphiropoulous. I am grateful also to our whole organization, and to Luise Eichenbaum. Also, I want to thank Susie Orbach for her vision, hard work, and fine writings.
2 As is discussed throughout this chapter, I use the term *eating problems*, while most others in our field use the term *eating disorders*. I vary the two throughout the paper.
3 This phrase was created by Andrea Gitter, ADTR.

References

Aamodt, S. (2016). Why you can't lose weight on a diet. *The New York Times*. Retrieved from www.nytimes.com/2016/05/08/opinion/sunday/why-you-cant-lose-weight-on-a-diet.html?_r=0

Aron, L. (1992c). *The legacy of Sandor Ferenczi: Discovery and rediscovery*. Paper presented at the Twelfth Annual Spring Meeting of the American Psychological Association Division of Psychoanalysis (39) – Discovery and Rediscovery, April, Philadelphia. Available on tape through Audio Transcripts, Ltd., Alexandria, VA.

Bion, W. R. (1967). Notes on memory and desire. *Psycho-Analytic Forum*, *2*, 271–280.

Bloom, C., Gitter, A., Gutwill, S., Kogel, L., & Zaphiropoulos, L. (1994). *Eating problems, a feminist psychoanalytic treatment model*. New York: Basic Books.

Bollas, C. (1987). *The shadow of the object*. New York: Columbia University Press.

Bollas, C. (1989). *Forces of destiny: Psychoanalysis and human idiom*. London: Free Association Books.

Bromberg, P. (1998). *Standing in the spaces: Essays on clinical process, trauma & dissociation*. Hoboken, NJ: The Analytic Press.

Dinnerstein, D. (1976). *The mermaid and the minotaur: Sexual arrangements and human malaise*. New York: Harper and Row.

Eichenbaum, L., & Orbach, S. (1983b). *What do women want*? New York: Coward-McCann.

Elliott, A. (2002). *Psychoanalytic theory: An introduction*. Durham, NC: Duke University Press.

Engdahl, F. (2007). *Seeds of destruction: The hidden agenda of genetic manipulation*. Canada: Global Research.

Ewen, S. (1976). *Captains of consciousness: Advertising and the social roots of the consumer culture*. New York: McGraw-Hill.

Ewen, S. (1988). *All consuming images: The politics of style in contemporary culture*. New York: Basic Books.

Ewen, S., & Ewen, E. (1979). *Channels of desire: Mass images and the shaping of American consciousness*. New York: McGraw-Hill.

Fairbairn, W. D. (1952). *Psychoanalytic studies of the personality*. London: Tavistock Publications.

Gendlin, E. (1996). *Focusing-oriented psychotherapy: A manual of the experiential method*. New York: Guilford Press.

Guntrip, H. (1969). *Schizoid phenomena object-relations and the self*. New York: International Universities Press.

Guthman, J. (2011). *Weighing in: Obesity, food justice, and the limits of capitalism*. Berkeley, CA: University of California Press.

Gutwill, S. (1994). *Eating problems: A feminist psychoanalytic treatment model*. New York: Basic Books.

Herman, J. (2009). *Trauma and recovery: The aftermath of violence – from domestic abuse to political terror*. New York: Basic Books.

Klein, M. (1952). Some theoretical conclusions regarding the emotional life of the infant. In *Envy and gratitude and other works, 1946–1963* (pp. 61–93). New York: Delacorte.

Kovel, J. (1981). *The age of desire: Reflections of a radical psychoanalyst*. New York: Pantheon.

Layton, L. (2004). Relational no more: Defensive autonomy in middle class women, *Annals of Psychoanalysis*, *32*, 29–42.

Layton, L. (2006). *Attacks on linking: The unconscious pull to dissociate individuals from their social context*. Psychoanalysis, Class and Politics, Encounters in the Clinical Setting. London & New York: Routledge.

Marshall, R. (2015). *Red crow marketing.com by Ron Marshall entitled "how many ads do you see in one day?* Retrieved from www.redcrowmarketing.com/2015/09/10/many-ads-see-one-day/

Marx, K., & Engels, F. (1994). *The German ideology*. New York: Prometheus Books.
Mitchell, S. A. (1988). *Relational concepts in psychoanalysis – an integration*. Cambridge, MA: Harvard University Press.
Ogden, T. H. (1994). The analytic third: Working with intersubjective clinical facts. *International Journal of Psycho-Analysis*, *75*, 3–19.
Orbach, S. (1985). Accepting they symptom: A feminist psychoanalytic treatment of anorexia nervosa. In D. M. Garner & P. E. Garfinkel (Eds.), *Handbook of psychotherapy for anorexia nervosa and bulimia*. New York: Guilford Press.
Orbach, S. (1986). *Hunger strike*. New York: Norton.
Orbach, S. (2009). *Bodies*. New York: Picador.
Patel, R. (2007). *Stuffed and starved: The hidden battle for the world food system*. New York: Melville House.
Petrucelli, J., & Stuart, C. (Eds.) (2001). *Hungers and compulsions: The psychodynamic treatment of eating disorders & addictions*. New York: Jason Aronson, Inc.
Russell, J. (1975). *Social amnesia: A critique of contemporary psychology from Adler to Lang*. Boston: Beacon Press.
Sullivan, H. S. (1953). *The interpersonal theory of psychiatry*. New York: Norton.
Thompson, B. W. (1992). "A way outa no way": Eating problems among African-American, Latina and white women. *Gender and Society*, *6*(4), 546–561.
Winnicott, D. W. (1960). The theory of the parent-infant relationship. *International Journal of Psychoanalysis*, *41*, 585–595.
Winnicott, D. W. (1980). *The maturational processes and the facilitating environment*. Madison, CT: International Universities Press.
Wooldridge, T. (2016). *Understanding anorexia nervosa in males: An integrative approach*. New York: Routledge.
Wooley, S. C. (1991). Uses of countertransference in the treatment of eating disorders: A gender perspective. In C. L. Johnson (Ed.), *Psychodynamic treatment of anorexia nervosa and bulimia*. New York: Guilford Press.
Zaretsky, E. (1986). *Capitalism, the family, and personal life*. New York: Harper & Row.

15

ENDURING PERFECTIONISM

Seeing through eating disorder recovery and America's cultural complex

Kim L. Grynick

Introduction

Eating disorders could be considered a collective neurosis of Western modernity. America's alignment with values of progress and power create an arcane shadow that falls into the unconscious as an underworld side of the personality. The underworld in Greek mythology refers to the realm of Hades, which psychologically represents repressed, discarded, or disowned aspects of self that are held captive in the unconscious psyche through the chimera of positivistic, ego success, epitomized in eating disorder endeavors. Sigmund Freud and Carl Jung, the fathers of psychodynamic theory, suggest that which is repressed becomes a neurosis (Jung, 1966). Put another way, any one-sided pursuit inevitably erupts from the unconscious in a neurotic manner, such as culture's obsessive fascination with achieving a perfected body image. In the pursuit of idealized health and beauty, an enantiadromia, or pull toward the opposite occurs, that is, distortion, compulsion, sickness, and death. The resultant self-starvation or overindulgence can be imagined as a modern disguise for repression of instinct and paucity of soul, hidden within America's Puritan roots. Shadow aspects of self and culture are displaced upon the externalized eating disorder, or personified "Ed," as often referred to in the consulting room. I argue that treatment fails to reclaim instinctive, archetypal vitality, unconsciously striving toward the thread of perfectionism that is part of the genesis of the original condition, unwittingly contributing to the recalcitrant quality of eating disorders.

The modern medical paradigm and many well-intentioned clinicians conceptualize pathology through a diagnostic, problem-solving perspective. While the merit of evidenced-based practice is not to be dismissed, a solution-focused treatment plan can perpetuate perfectionism through unrelenting optimism, such as the fantasy of ideal weight, precision of cognitive-emotional control, heroic cessation of food rituals, fluidity of social skills, and model health. This forward, upward movement overlooks instinct and the natural order of life, such as aging, imperfection, decline, and death. Relapse may occur, in part, because the patient has not learned how to work with the shadow aspects of self, nor navigate developmental rites of passage. On the other hand, when one considers the fantasy of recovery one is working with, that is, the particular lens of perception of pathology and treatment, diverse possibilities for healing emerge. These findings suggest contemporary evidenced-based standards of care contribute to initial stability, yet full psychic, developmental, and physical health are attained and maintained through an integrative paradigm that includes depth psychological insights.

I situate my thesis in the field of psychodynamic psychology through the contributions of its successive founding fathers: Sigmund Freud, Carl Jung, and James Hillman. I include a brief introduction of feminist post-Jungians, whose work is of critical importance to the treatment of eating disorders and the rebalancing of patriarchy but beyond the scope of this chapter. Following the introduction of respective key concepts, I demonstrate how myth and metaphor open up understanding of essential depth psychological underpinnings in eating disorder recovery. This is further illustrated by a case study of a five-year course of treatment with a 12-year-old girl with anorexia. Finally, I explain eating disorders from the perspective of the cultural complex of Puritan perfectionism, planting seeds for further exploration.

Depth psychology

Sigmund Freud complemented the scientific paradigm of the nineteenth century through his psychosexual theory of the unconscious derived from the Oedipus Rex myth, generating what is known as psychoanalysis. Carl Jung, originally the intellectual heir to Freud's ideas, created analytical psychology based on the psychological process of individuation, which extended conscious and unconscious factors beyond Freud's singular focus on the sexual drive. While Jung's work has been scrutinized for being overly aligned with the numinous and questioned for a basis in his own childhood schizophrenia (Winnicott, 1964), Jung offers an example of working through the unconscious process, that is, the autonomous psyche, toward a teleological paradigm of wholeness. Robert Smith (1996) in *The Wounded Jung* presents Jung as "a wounded healer who, because he confronted throughout his life the divided parts of his own psyche, was able to become a healer of others" (p. 2). Parting from Freud, Jung descended into a confrontation of the unconscious, where he lived through his theories of archetypes and individuation. Jung meticulously documented his process in journals, which were later released as the controversial *Red Book* or *Liber Novus* (Jung, 2009).

James Hillman, the founder of archetypal psychology, was a post-Jungian who challenged that Jung's paradigm of individuation toward the self was bound in a limiting mother complex of growth. Hillman argued for a therapy of ideas, using myth and metaphor to open the imagination and explore polytheistic dynamics within the personality, in order to increase consciousness of what one is enacting. His idea is that there is a story behind every story, and "personal behavior is derived from something beyond the personal" (Hillman, 1960, p. 13). This paper works largely off of the premise of Hillman's vision.

Multiple post-Jungian feminist scholars have brought invaluable worth to the psychoanalytic field and specifically the treatment of eating disorders. Most notably is Woodman (1980, 1982, 1997, 2011; Woodman & Sharp, 1993), who initiated conscious femininity, which works to revive the feminine principle through body and soul. Maureen Murdock (1990), Polly Young-Eisendrath (1999), Helen Luke (1995), and Esther Harding (1971) are among other post-Jungians who have brought notable contributions to the field. While the important work of these bright and bold women is beyond the specific scope of this paper, their writings are an essential read.

Soul as an essential treatment consideration

What the soul wants is often in conflict with the ego's prerogative and the edict of society, which is one reason soul has become relegated to religion or pathology. The soul, or psyche, is a tireless archetypal idea whose language is metaphor and image. Jung (1968) claimed "image is psyche," which is a stepping-off point for Hillman (1960) who presses upon the importance of soul-making: "the stirring of an emotional and living factor of overwhelming importance for my well being now and for my death" (pp. 51–52). Soul is meaning making in everyday experiences, while holding the tension of a relationship with death, that is, soul often is present when something recedes, usually the ego. Western modernity is resistant to psyche's relationship with death, and thereby the natural condition of suffering the soul. James Hillman (1994) is not a proponent of healing, because he believes healing is a fiction that falls under the fantasy of transformation. I, as a psychotherapist, on the other hand, am concerned with healing, and argue that healing necessitates the capacity to form and understand narratives and metaphorical depictions of suffering. The hidden keys to healing lay in these creative realms.

How do we re-learn to suffer the soul? In therapy, it could be a recollection of a story, an image of what one has lost, or bearing the pain that lives in that picture. It is not only sitting with, but also relating to and even honoring, the indigestible emotions that clients with eating disorders repress through neurotic symptoms. Sometimes there is no move to make, but to be present with the symptoms and the soul, letting the fantasy of recovery fall apart so something new may emerge. Staying with the crumbling and dissolving image touches into the archetypal, inviting a deepening into soul-making. Hillman (1975) insists, "the restoration of images is the royal road to soul-making" (p. 23). Image is not only visual but also includes all senses: sound, smell, taste, and touch. This depth psychological sensibility invites therapist and client to feel into the myth they are caught up in. The enemy is the literal, a lack of creative vision.

Seeing through the fantasy of eating disorder recovery

In the post-Jungian psychoanalytic world and beyond, James Hillman (1975) was a spark in the grinding, a brilliant, bold thinker who stirred every complacent pot. He complained of a "poverty of ideas in academic and therapeutic psychology" (p. 123) and encouraged one to be psychological about psychology, that is, bringing consciousness to, or "seeing through," the fantasies of illness and healing. His therapy of ideas is compensation to personalized ego consciousness of Western modernity. Hillman's ideas embody life's archetypal questions and function as eyes of the soul. He believed a person's "expectation for nourishment, for help in psyche's struggle for awareness, is frustrated by psychology itself. The language of psychology insults the soul" (Hillman, 1960, p. 121).

When a client comes to an assessment for eating disorder treatment, what type of questions does the clinician ask? What language is used to shape the onset of the intervention? What image is held of the person as a being? Who is this eating disorder that has descended upon the family with such powerful authority over the individual? Can it be forced out? What method is called for in relating to this living creature: strategic, direct, passive, compassionate, educational, creative, religious, scientific? The way the patient is envisioned, including the image of the condition, treatment, and the self as therapist, is a response to a symbolic call from the personal and collective unconscious. Rather than seeking to cure a sick individual, cultivating imaginative possibilities, such as a sensibility toward the mythic, generates healing alternatives. This approach is not exclusive to the critical importance of medical monitoring and evidence-based practice but rather sees through the fantasy of the scientific paradigm as the only mode of healing. As Jung (1964) reminds us, "no matter what instruments he uses, at some point he reaches the edge of certainty beyond which conscious knowledge cannot pass" (p. 4).

The fantasy of eating disorder recovery suggests that Western culture operates upon fixed ideas of illness and wellness (*Diagnostic and Statistical Manual of Mental Disorders*; American Psychiatric Association, 2013), an invention that is based on successfully diagnosing, ordering, and adjusting behaviors, where the individual is responsible for the affliction and symptom change. Seeing through the fantasy is a move of curiosity, proposing limits to the construct of self-rule in eradicating an eating disorder. In psychological terms, the medical model is an Apollonian approach that indicates linear thinking of control and progress, situated in a hero myth around the superior will of ego. To question this modern fantasy is to ask if it is actually transmuted into a living and sustainable recovery. Or has recovery begun to resemble an audacious dogma? For example, eating disorder phone apps with names such as "Recovery Warrior," while effective in speaking to the young generation, champion the fantasy that heroic warrior efforts will overcome symptoms. The obstinate, uncompromising nature of eating disorders suggests differently. The fantasy of recovery is a compelling myth, but potentially malnourished with a restriction of ideas.

We live in a culture that makes clear delineations between good and bad, health and wellness. In so doing, psyche has become organized around pathology, which amputates our imaginative sensibilities for deeper soul messages that lay buried under neurotic conditions. "The border between madness and sanity, which created the field of psychopathology by placing some events here and others there, is a positivistic fiction and not an existential reality" (Hillman, 1975, p. 62). Pathology has been marginalized as a negative phenomenon, when perhaps it is the very condition the soul needs to grow. It is possible that the eating disorder is, in part, a necessary experience for the development of a personality, perhaps the only way a rite of passage can be navigated for that individual. While contentious, Hillman's view of pathology is to imagine suffering as necessary and its associated symptoms as patterns of value that are vital for a full-bodied existence. I suggest that creative and reflexive discernment in the service of restoring soul to the client is currently missing in most treatment paradigms. This may be best illustrated through narrative of a case example of a 12-year-old client and her mother, seeking treatment for anorexia nervosa.

The enchanted recovery of Anouk Birdee

Her beady eyes stared past steely curtains of stringy, stiff blond hair and far beyond me, off into a space and place where I was not welcome. Any question posed was met with stony silence, at most an inaudible mumble, a whisper of a voice smaller than a baby's coo. A secret murmur delivered from child into mother's tight, golden locks, transported a mysterious translation packaged with perceptible sarcasm and palpable exasperation that dispatched from mother to me like a demanding arrow, with only my clipboard for a shield. Daughter did not miss mother's sarcasm and flinched, but caught herself before anyone technically noticed, an imperceptible shudder like a little bird with ruffled feathers, she settled back into her untouchable position, curled up in her cold and lonely nest.

The intake continued in this manner, mother speaking for daughter, daughter odd and angry at obstacles in her steely path, especially me. Anouk remained gridlocked in her icy, obsessive, destination toward "perfection," simultaneously frail, fragile, and tremendously fearful. As the hour crawled along, daughter twitched and pulled at her hair, scratching bony arms and absent thighs, rolling hollow eyes to the ceiling, then back to track me. I wondered, as I'd mused countless times before, how I got into these tangles, interacting with the living dead, young maidens forsaken and forlorn at the adolescent crossover, snatched from the bright, flowery fields of childhood, down into Ed's (eating disorder) dark and merciless domain, cast under his cold-blooded spell, becoming more demon than daughter. Fatigued, wide-eyed, and cautious, parents search through me in hopes to have finally found a savior, a warrior, a wise woman, anyone who might possibly help. I respond with understanding nods, shoulders weary, but held high in confidence of having made the journey and survived. I offer expectant tales of recovery and myriad ideas for a treatment plan, crumbs of hope I sprinkle before them. Ravenously, parents gobble them up, while the child looks upon them with longing.

On one hand there is much to be done, a treatment team to set up, weigh-ins to be scheduled, meal plans, monitoring, and support systems to put in place. On the other hand, there is very little I can do but sit with the beast. Let him (Ed) know I am not afraid and will wait him out to find the girl under the fur and fangs. No one really wants to sit in Hades with all that is grave and diabolical. But parents' pay, and life demands me, to go down, down, down to the underworld to fetch their child from the clutches of midnight, to bring her home to the light. Rarely do they understand that she has already eaten the pomegranate seed (Boer, 2006), so I cannot retrieve the innocent one they wish for me to recover. I will bring back their young woman, if I can, but the child is gone, only clinging, like a ghost to the disorder. We are thick in a rite of passage that we may or may not survive. In time, the family will understand, but for now I must simply hold our ship steady for the voyage.

Personifying and pathologizing in conceptualizing treatment

James Hillman conceptualized the world as a psychological field of events, living experiences teeming with meaning beyond the personal. Complementary to the monotheistic certainty of the main, which functions around the singular existence of "I," Hillman (1975) invites a revival of the marginalized perspective of polytheistic multiplicity, suggesting inherent dissociability of the psyche. "We are each a field of internal personal relationships, an interior commune, a body politic" (p. 22). This body politic includes complexes, neurotic symptoms, and multiple parts of self that exert tremendous influence upon existence, including recovery from an eating disorder. Hillman illustrates psyche's multiplicity by reviving the gods and goddesses of mythic Greece, not as literal, but symbolic personification, which cultivates an image that opens up imagination. Personifying is a depth psychological way of seeing, where ego surrenders and homage is paid to the forces working upon us. The reader may resist the idea of a polytheistic psyche, specifically mention of gods and goddesses, but consider the intervention of sand tray, where imaginal figures depict stories that symbolize multiple aspects of self and other.

What does personification and a wider view of pathology mean for 12-year-old Anouk, her family, and myself as the therapist? What is going on in the tension of the therapy room? What myth or drama is being enacted behind the overt scenario of anorexia? A force has clearly taken hold of the family, the girl, and the clinician. What is the abnegation of food metaphorically communicating, the refusal of the most basic source of life? Sustenance on strike, vetoed, and exiled in protest, a vehement statement. Perhaps this is the mystery to be unearthed? The miniature, infantile mumble of Anouk's human voice has no relation to the savage, uncanny, relentlessness of Ed. It makes sense that this whispering child needs aggressive Ed to say something for her. But what?

The rituals of anorexia

Anouk needed Ed as a protector from a world of high academic and social expectations, plus the grim realities of a society that distressed her. Ed, her "God of Anorexia," sheltered her from entering worldly pressures, injustices, and brutalities. Anouk could worship Ed with complete devotion and thereby shut out a society that scared and threatened her with violation and death. In exchange, Ed would keep her body small and sexless, like a child, a sick baby who needed to be home under the care of mother. Safe.

Anouk's penance to Ed was to spin in endless, compulsive calorie counting, cutting carrots into minute molecules, eating only certain foods at precise times, to never cease movement of body, deny hunger, defy desire, and drop pounds like little pebbles on the long walk of death. The rituals that shaped Anouk's days and nights could be viewed as symbolic sacrifice for a society that no longer knows how to pay tribute to what is sacred. It is her very pathology that leads us to the healing questions: what in the soul of the world needs ritual and sacred attention? What in the world supports meaning and authentic beauty? Hillman's (1975) expanded view of pathologizing "liberates the parts of the soul trapped in the poverty of materialistic perspectives" (p. 161), in essence, revealing what society has forgotten and neglected.

Ritual is an essential underpinning of anorexia, securing a neurotic push toward lightness of spirit, a fierce striving for perfection in order to be free of the flesh and its entanglements, virginal, untouchable, saintly, to be like god. The spiritual and religious aspects of anorexia are further explored as rooted in the cultural complex of Puritan perfectionism. In lieu of sacred rituals that support the adolescent in crossing over to womanhood, she attempts to create her own rite of passage (Murdock, 1990) by separating herself with a special diet and binding her soul to repetitive rituals around eating, abstinence of pleasure, and isolation. To fully recover from an eating disorder, clinician and client are called to create personal and cultural rituals beyond restriction that support one through the spiral passages of life; soul hungers for ritual.

Anouk Birdee

All matter of attention was provided for stabilization of Anouk's physical health through a multi-disciplinary treatment team, while simultaneously attending to her tortured soul. Sessions in the first year were grueling, but when I surrendered to her stance of silence instead of resisting or attempting to overpower it, therapy became a peaceful time for both of us, a healing ritual. Anouk would accept a morsel from me in the form of a question about her heart, hopes, or dreams, which she would then draw inside a mandala circle. Toward the end of the hour she would whisper to me the secret stories of her soul that emerged from the sacred circle, which always included a flicker of the plight of girls becoming women in a chilling world. It was in the quiet tranquility of colored pencils and the ancient, palliative method of mandala, followed by furtive murmurs from Anouk's inner world, that the therapy and healing began.

Three years into our work together, still anxious and obsessive, but weight restored, Anouk and I sat in my new office with sand tray and a wall of mystical, magical figurines. Her first sand tray was a scene of Anouk and Ed depicted through a predatory, cutthroat monster that personified the eating disorder. Like the archetypal goddess Kali, Ed offered both destructive and constructive power, for he was killing her as he also protected her. Anouk picked a small, winsome purple elephant to represent herself, which she placed between the two back legs of the monster, as if he were guarding her. The remainder of the scene contained apples, cupcakes, books, mirrors, family members, and fear – the world around and within that Anouk did not know how to digest. By personifying the eating disorder, bringing an autonomous life and will to it, an imaginal doorway opened that allowed us to ask the monster questions: why was he here, what did he want or need, why was he so angry? The baby elephant of Anouk could also be accessed, a relationship formed with the silenced part of self. Even the apple and cupcakes on the table were animated and had opinions to contribute.

Eating disorder archetypes

For 20 years I have sat with girls, women, and eating disorders. Each soul who walks through my door feels familiar. There is a palpable knowingness of her story, like an old melody humming through my mind. This quality of recognition in the through-line of the eating disorder experience speaks to archetypes of the collective unconscious that show up repetitively in the therapy room, that is, core riddles to the mystery of an eating disorder. Archetypes are formative principles of instinctual power (Jung, 1960). They are dynamic patterns of behavior that animate and drive everyday thoughts and actions, "universal images that have existed since the remotest times" (Jung, 1969, p. 5), common psychic substrates of the personality. Archetypes rest upon the assumption of an unconscious in the individual and the collective of humanity, suggesting autonomous forces beyond will shape and inform our lives. This is critical to the conceptualization of the treatment I propose, which is qualitatively different from the scientific paradigm grounded in a bio-psychosocial model that does not include the unconscious as part of the ontology and maintenance of eating disorders.

Archetypes are a foreign vernacular within the modern dominant of science that heralds that which can be proven. There is no way to explain or encounter the exact nature of an archetype, but its numinous quality is experienced through dream, symbol, and myth. Jung (1972) emphasizes, "archetypes cannot be integrated simply by rational means, but require a dialectical procedure, a real coming to terms with them, often conducted with a patient in dialogue form" (p. 5).

Multiple instincts are repressed or played out in eating disorder behaviors, for example, desire, pleasure, sexuality, destruction, aestheticism, ritual, and rage. When the instinct behind an archetype is made conscious, it no longer binds the individual to base thoughts and behavior, such as eating disorder patterns and body objectification. Consciousness of instinct allows the spiritual side of the archetype to emerge and integrate into the personality, rather than remain split off in neurosis.

Jung (1969) identified primary archetypes one faces in the process of individuation: the ego, shadow, anima, animus, wise-old-man, child, and Self. Jung was a product of a patriarchal time, also wounded by his ambivalent relationship with his mother, and thus his theories contain limiting perspectives on women, but rather expansive ideas about the feminine that have been imagined forward to construct a positive feminine principle (Rowland, 2002). I mention this in that a girl may encounter her wise-old-woman on the path of individuation, rather than Jung's wise-old-man. The archetypes of individuation are not expanded here, but can be sourced throughout Jung's *Collected Works*. Apropos to eating disorder recovery are the archetypes of child, maiden, mother, and crone, which are integral to eating disorders, represented in the Greek myth of Persephone and her mother, Demeter, illustrating the rite of passage modern maidens must undertake.

The application of mythopoetic imagination in treatment

Applying myth to the enigma of an eating disorder fosters a complex understanding of the roots that feed the neurosis, and thus access to a more complete healing. Carl Jung (1970) teaches that myths "give expression to unconscious processes, and their retelling causes these processes to come alive again, and be re-collected, thereby re-establishing the connection between conscious and unconscious" (pp. 88–89). The narrative of myth brings one closer to the psychological core of any situation through the language of metaphor, which expresses archetypal truths under our habitual ways of living. Joseph Campbell (1988) advocates that myth opens the world to mystery, shows a shape of the universe beyond science, supports and validates a social order, and demonstrates how a human can live under any circumstances.

Mythopoetic imagination and archetypal psychology transcend monotheism, unlocking multivalent possibilities for living (and recovering), or as Hillman (1975) might say, a cornucopia of ideas, "myths do not tell us how. They simply give us the invisible background which starts us imaging, questioning, going deeper" (p. 158). Myth depicts the interrelatedness of gods and goddesses and the dual nature of their personality, meaning every god and goddess shows his or her light and dark aspect. Unlike the monotheistic tradition, all facets are incorporated into the whole. Considering Persephone, or the recovered individual, as containing both positive and negative poles of the personality, challenges the modern fantasy that recovery is a flight into the light of wellness. In other words, the odious cannot be expunged; it must be related to or it will re-emerge as ruthless relapse or some other unconscious factor, inducing havoc on the persona self.

Anouk Birdee

Over a course of five years, Anouk learned that Ed was not the god of light she had hoped for, but rather Hades, god of the underworld, who pulled her resistant self into the next phase of development. In the underworld journey, Anouk can be imagined as Persephone, forced to face her inner fragility and vulnerability to overwhelm in a culture that fails to support girls through the passage of adolescence into womanhood. Other than Anita Johnston's (1996) contribution *Eating by the Light of the Moon*, little has been written on the parallels between Persephone's plight and the perils of girls with anorexia. Facing grief and loss in the underworld, Anouk discovers an emerging inner strength, recognizing a young woman's voice, curious and expressive. While she continues to wrestle with society's objectification of the female form and feminine psyche, she now has complementary images of herself as fierce and tender, warrioress and lover, full of shadows and radiating light.

Persephone's rite of passage and mother-daughter attachment

The myth of Persephone, or her child-name Kore, meaning a girl of initiatory age, youth, or maiden, is the earliest story of attachment and the unique intimacies between mother and daughter. It is a coming-of-age journey that sorts through the dynamics of safety and fear, connection and separation, death and rebirth. Before the abduction, Persephone is enveloped in the protective folds of her devoted mother's wide skirts. Some have deemed their relationship a fused or enmeshed attachment (Hillman as cited in Downing, 1994), others a healthy bond. Consciously, Persephone is content to stay in the known security of her mother's care, yet the natural order of life calls the maiden to become her own woman, to cross over and integrate the skills of mothering and self-nurture.

Hades, a personified version of Ed, the eating disorder, abducts innocent Persephone from the fields of adolescence, pulling her into the darkness and restriction of his underworld kingdom. Hades promises riches in the form of beauty, power, and admiration if Persephone would simply submit to the new life. Persephone is bereft; she longs for her mother and the innocence she once knew. No matter her age, a girl or woman with an eating disorder is symbolically a maiden drawn into initiation. Culture provides scant means for psychic development, so child is pulled down unconsciously. The way through the transition is arduous. As Joseph Campbell (1988) acknowledges, "it is a terrifying experience to have your consciousness transformed" (p. 14). Persephone, Anouk, and all maidens with an eating disorder must find a new way of living.

Dara Marks (2006) declares that every Persephone needs a Demeter-mother to find her; the maiden cannot make it out of Hades alone. Persephone wants to return to her mother, yet there is a longing for something else. When mother and daughter finally reunite, they are joyful, but can no longer return to the idealized bubble of safety under mother's care. While in Hades, Persephone restricts food, "but secretly he slipped her a pomegranate seed, a sweet one, to eat" (Boer, 2006, p. 149). The pomegranate is a symbol of fertility and sexuality, abundant with seeds, deep fleshy red, and can be associated with a vaginal shape when split open. Eating the pomegranate seed is the symbolic act of Persephone accepting initiation and change of her psyche and physical body. Persephone eats of the seed and emerges into the upper world like a fresh shoot, sprung forth from the dormancy of winter.

For the girl who descends into anorexia and the underworld of Hades, separated from Mother, dancing with the dark god, refusing to eat, hollowed out in the lonely chamber as the untouchable queen, to re-emerge into the light, she now may think, "I want to take care of myself, be independent, think for myself, state my opinions, and act on my own behalf, but I don't want to upset my Mother. . . ". Hades serves as an intermediary, a structure to aid differentiation from mother. Demeter, too, has been initiated into a mode of relationship that can tolerate separation and her daughter's autonomy. Mother and daughter initiate each other and move into deepening complexity to discover separation and continuing love as compatible (Downing, 1994).

Persephone only emerges as goddess of spring through initiation and descent in the underworld. Similarly, a woman recovered from anorexia is healed specifically through the decent into the realm of Hades, that is, the eating disorder. In some ways she still lives there, always lives there, in that darkness. Our modern fantasy of recovery is to leave the cold, black land behind, to live forever, healthy, slender, and young in the sunshine-spirit of ego. Living through the ordeal transforms, yet we fail to recognize that it is the darkness, that is, pathology, which is the metamorphic force. As Hillman (1975) wisely proclaims, "we owe our symptoms an immense debt" (p. 71).

Eating disorders as cultural complex

Traditional thought views addiction, and thereby eating disorders, as an individual problem. Hillman (1995) disagrees, poetically stating, "since he and she are not the underlying cause of their suffering, neither can they be its cure" (p. 15). Hillman believes that our problems are lived inside our individual lives, but "our lives are lived inside fields of power" (p. 15). I propose that eating disorders, specifically anorexia nervosa, is a collective neurosis anchored in the power field of America's cultural complex of perfectionism.

Jung (1968) originated the idea of complexes, describing the personal complex as an "image of a certain psychic situation which is strongly accentuated emotionally and is, moreover, incompatible with the habitual attitude of consciousness"

(Paragraph 201). In other words, a complex resides in the unconscious, which means it possesses autonomy, exerting force upon the individual regardless of his/her conscious intent. Freud said that dreams were the royal road to the unconscious, whereas Jung asserts that complexes are the royal road to the unconscious. Complexes revolve around a core archetype, paralleling the idea of a split-off part of self (Winnicott, 1989). Complexes and their associated archetypes are the building blocks or blueprints of earliest human experience.

Complexes can also be cultural (Kimbles, 2000). An archetype, such as perfectionism, generates compelling agency among groups or entire cultures, exerting formidable influence on history and the shaping of memory. I present eating disorders, specifically America's cultural obsession with thinness and perfectionism, as a current cultural complex that has a profound effect on individuals who develop anorexia. Recovery is particularly challenged in a society where an enduring and commanding power in perfection is represented as the thin ideal.

Because eating is the source of life, humans' relationship with food has been complex since earliest time. Egyptian hieroglyphics depict purging as a health ritual. Romans were reported to use vomitoriums to expel food from feasting in order to continue gastro-festivities. China, Persia, and Africa also have a history of fasting-purging rituals. Fasting saints in the thirteenth century were known to waste and even die from self-starvation and other self-flagellations in the name of spiritual aestheticism. In 1689, physician Richard Morton wrote "A Treatise of Consumption," the first medical presentation of anorexia nervosa. In 1860, Lois Victor Marce suggested anorexia was not simply a medical condition but was psychiatric in origin. Freud believed anorexia was a repression of sexuality. Michelle Lelwica's (2009) book *The Religion of Thinness* explores spiritual hungers behind women's obsession with food and weight, with chapters on ritual, morality, and salvation, suggesting charged archetypal values associating restriction with godliness.

The cultural complex of thinness associated with anorexia holds awesome, reverent energy. Images of thin women arouse particularly strong emotions in all genders. At the core of the complex is the trajectory of sainthood and purity through the control of food and flesh. Thomas Kirsch (2004) points out that "cultural complexes contaminate people and their thinking" (p. 189). Thin has become associated with goodness as a complex "that dwells inside each of us and the groups we identify with and/or see as our rivals" (p. 186). It is critical to the well-being of our girls, women, and many boys and men, to see into the shadow side of this cultural complex, its shaping throughout history, and how memory has been aligned to retain images, accounts, and scientific proof to support the "truth" of "thin is good."

Kimbles (2000) asserts that "complexes express themselves in powerful moods and repetitive behaviors" (p. 159). This description is uncannily fitting for the culture of anorexia. Cultural complexes can be further understood as operating "through the group's expectations, its definition of itself, its destiny, and a sense of uniqueness . . . through the group's fears, enemies, and its attitudes towards other groups" (p. 159). Seized by an obsession with food and the penetrating fear of flesh, the individual with an eating disorder joins a special club, claiming identity in sickness or purity, and always the idealized pursuit of perfection. Its members are set apart from the madness of the world: "above it all" in anorexia, "privately raging through it" in bulimia, "buffered and numb" in binge eating. Underground communities such as pro-ana websites draw entranced members into a seductive web, solidifying a special and unique group identity.

Sadly, fierce in-group/out-group biases live within the eating disorder complex, generating and sustaining an ethical code of the culture as girls and women project their shadow upon one another (Kimbles, 2000). Individuals with anorexia secretly scorn those who struggle with bulimia or binge eating. Those with bulimia and binge eating feel gross, often "wishing to be anorexic," yet detesting their slim sisters with vicious jealousy. A callous hierarchy is formed, with anorexia as the ideal; bulimia, as a very distant underworld second; and binge eating, clearly at the bottom of acceptability. As Kimbles describes, "they involve rigidly polarized 'us/them' categories and are governed by stereotypes which harden into mutual negative projections" (p. 157). In the power-field of the cultural complex, competition becomes a way of life.

Unfortunately, this competitive field often extends into the professional community with a palpable tone of comparison or in-group out-group dynamics that can be observed at conferences. I suggest the eating disorder community may not be conscious of its shadow. The shadow is a neutral concept. It is always present; the importance is how we relate to it. Professionals promote recovery, but often inadvertently create structures of positioning and hierarchy, operating from a persona self. The persona pushes imperfection, instinct, and diversity underground. I echo Singer and Kimbles' (2004) advocacy for "enhanced capacity to see more objectively the shadow of the group in its cultural complexes" (p. 4).

Puritan perfectionism

I propose that the eating disorder complex is born from what Manisha Roy (2004) calls the Puritan ethic of perfectionism. European Puritans colonizing America believed they were the chosen ones doing God's holy work. Roy says, "Yahweh's righteousness and Christ's perfection created a God-image that demands perfection" (p. 73). The earliest roots of American history are buried in conquering land and native people, both aspects of the feminine principle, overpowered and objectified. In the Puritan religion, flesh was deemed sinful, while hard work, fasting, and suffering in the name of progress were revered under the eyes of God. These particular attitudes toward God evolve into attitudes toward power.

Puritan consciousness in America with "the heavy emphasis on self-negation" (Schenk, 2012, p. 54) and "the desire to extend power over the other" (p. 55), that is, the body, feminine, Earth, has far-reaching roots, dominating even the psyche of adolescent girls who quest for thinness in an effort to be saved from the fallen fate of the flesh, earning favor of The Father. American women with eating disorders have swallowed the Puritan edict whole, and hound it without mercy. Even as I come to the conclusion of this chapter, I hear the archetype of perfection harassing me to revise, improve, refine, and make my argument stronger, more perfect in order to compete in the world of academia and society at large. Having related to this inner shadow-demand, a force largely beyond conscious control, I cultivate new images of what it means to contribute to society and place my voice in the conversation of eating disorder treatment and recovery. Applying the lens of the Puritan narrative to individuals with eating disorders, including myself as a recovered clinician, is cathartic, like finally completing an unwieldy crossword puzzle.

Conclusion

I challenge a single practitioner to contest that eating disorders are indeed unwieldy. Science has offered immense gifts to aid understanding of genetic, biological, and neurological correlates in etiology and recovery. Evidenced-based practices provide therapists useful, effective tools. Still, a full and sustainable recovery is elusive. Primary researcher Walter Kaye (Adan & Kaye, 2011) asserts what many experience in practice, that "current treatments for eating disorder are inadequate" (p. 4).

I agree with Kaye's claim and, as outlined in this chapter, implore practitioners to see through the fantasies imbedded in our treatment paradigms. I call for a critical re-visioning of the indomitable constructs of eating disorder treatment, and in turn, a revival of the imagination and soul where the exacting questions of recovery become: how can humanity embrace its fragility? Will patriarchy surrender its one-sided power, so that daughters and sons are not compelled to unconsciously act out starvation of soul upon precious flesh? What is culture enacting in the pervasive prevalence of eating disorders? What are we recovering in the therapy room?

References

Adan, R., & Kaye, W. (Eds.) (2011). *Behavioral neurobiology of eating disorders*. New York: Springer.

American Psychiatric Association. (2013). *Diagnostic and statistical manual of mental disorders* (5th ed.). Washington, DC: Author.

Beck, A. (1976). *Cognitive therapy and the emotional disorders*. New York: Penguin Books.

Boer, C. (2006). *The Homeric hymns*. London & England: Asphodel Press.

Campbell, J. (1988). *The power of myth*. New York: Doubleday.

Downing, C. (1994). *The long journey home: Re-visioning the myth of Demeter and Persephone for our time*. Boston, MA: Shambhala.

Ellis, A. (1961). *A guide to rational living*. Englewood Cliffs, NJ: Prentice-Hall.

Harding, E. (1971). *Woman's mysteries ancient and modern*. New York: Harper Colophon Books.

Hayes, S., Strosahl, K., & Wilson, K. (2012). *Acceptance and commitment therapy: The process and practice of mindful change*. New York: Guilford Press.
Hillman, J. (1960). *The myth of analysis: Three essays in archetypal psychology*. Evanston, IL: Northwestern University Press.
Hillman, J. (1975). *Re-visioning psychology*. New York: Harper Perennial.
Hillman, J. (1994). *Healing fiction*. Putnam, CT: Spring Publications.
Hillman, J. (1995). *Kinds of power: A guide to its intelligent uses*. New York: Currency Doubleday.
Johnston, A. (1996). *Eating in the light of the moon: How women can let go of compulsive eating through metaphor and storytelling*. Secaucus, NJ: Carol Publishing Group.
Jung, C. G. (1960). On the nature of the psyche. In R. F. C. Hull (Trans.), *The collected works of C.G. Jung* (Vol. 8, p. 3). Princeton, NJ: Princeton University Press.
Jung, C. G. (1964). *Man and his symbols*. New York: Dell.
Jung, C. G. (1966). The practice of psychotherapy. In R. F. C. Hull (Trans.), *The collected works of C. G. Jung* (Vol. 16). Princeton, NJ: Princeton University Press.
Jung, C. G. (1968). Alchemical Studies. In R. F. C. Hull (Trans.), *The collected works of C. G. Jung* (Vol. 13). Princeton, NJ: Princeton University Press.
Jung, C. G. (1969). Archetypes of the collective unconscious. In R. F. C. Hull (Trans.), *The collected works of C. G. Jung* (Vol. 9, pp. 3–271). Princeton, NJ: Princeton University Press. (Original work published in 1934).
Jung, C. G. (1970). The spiritual problem of modern man. In R. F. C. Hull (Trans.), *The collected works of C. G. Jung* (Vol. 10). Princeton, NJ: Princeton University Press.
Jung, C. G. (1972). *Four archetypes: Mother/rebirth/spirit/trickster*. New York: Routledge. (Original work published in 1953).
Jung, C. G. (2009). *The red book: Liber novus*, ed. S. Shamdasani & (J. Peck & S. Shamdasani, Trans.). New York: Philemon Series & W.W. Norton & Co.
Kimbles, S. (2000). The cultural complex and the myth of invisibility. In T. Singer (Ed.), *The vision thing: Myth, political, and psyche in the world* (pp. 157–169). London, England: Routledge.
Kirsch, T. (2004). Cultural complexes in the history of Jung, Freud, and their followers. In T. Singer, T. & S. Kimbles (Eds.), *The cultural complex: Contemporary perspectives of psyche and society* (pp. 185–195). London, England: Routledge.
Lelwica, M. (2009). *The religion of thinness*. Carlsbad, CA: Gurze.
Linehan, M. (1993). *Cognitive behavioral treatment of borderline personality disorder*. New York: Guilford Press.
Lock, J., & LeGrange, D. (2013). *Treatment manual for anorexia nervosa: A family based approach*. New York: Guildford Press.
Luke, H. (1995). *The way of woman: Awakening the perennial feminine*. New York: Doubleday.
Marks, D. (2006). *Inside story: The power of the transformational arc*. Studio City, CA: Three Mountain Press.
Murdock, M. (1990). *The heroine's journey: Woman's quest for wholeness*. Boston, MA: Shambhala.
Rowland, S. (2002). *Jung: A feminist revision*. Cambridge: Polity Press.
Roy, M. (2004). When a religious archetype becomes a cultural complex: Puritanism in America. In T. Singer & S. Kimbles (Eds.), *The cultural complex: Contemporary Jungian perspectives on psyche and society* (pp. 64–77). New York: Routledge.
Schenk, R. (2012). *American soul: A cultural narrative*. New Orleans, LA: Spring.

Singer, T., & Kimbles, S. (Eds.) (2004). *The cultural complex: Contemporary Jungian perspectives on psyche and society*. New York: Routledge.
Smith, R. C. (1996). The wounded Jung: Effects of Jung's relationships on his life and work. Evanston, IL: Northwestern.
Winnicott, D. W. (1964). Memories, dreams, and reflection (Review of C.G. Jung, London: Collins and Routledge, 1963). *International Journal of Psychoanalysis*, *45*, 450.
Winnicott, D. W. (1989). *Playing and reality*. New York: Routledge.
Woodman, M. (1980). *The owl was a baker's daughter: Obesity, anorexia nervosa, and the repressed feminine*. Toronto, Canada: Inner City Books.
Woodman, M. (1982). *Addiction to perfection: The still unravished bride*. Toronto, Canada: Inner City Books.
Woodman, M. (1993). *Leaving my father's house: A journey to conscious femininity*. Boston, MA: Shambhala.
Woodman, M. (1997). *Dancing in the flames*. Boston, MA: Shambhala.
Woodman, M. (2011). *The crown of age: The rewards of conscious aging*. [Audio CD]. Louisville, CO: Sounds True Productions.
Woodman, M., & Sharp, D. (1993). *Conscious femininity: Interviews with Marion Woodman*. Toronto, Canada: Inner City Books.
Young-Eisendrath, P. (1999). *Women and desire: Beyond wanting to be wanted*. New York: Harmony Books.

INDEX

For Product Safety Concerns and Information please contact our EU
representative GPSR@taylorandfrancis.com
Taylor & Francis Verlag GmbH, Kaufingerstraße 24, 80331 München, Germany

www.ingramcontent.com/pod-product-compliance
Ingram Content Group UK Ltd.
Pitfield, Milton Keynes, MK11 3LW, UK
UKHW022219190926
475702UK00003B/438

* 9 7 8 1 1 3 8 7 0 2 0 1 1 *